ANNUAL EDITIONS

Criminal Justice

Thirty-second Edition

08/09

EDITORS

Joseph L. Victor
Mercy College, Dobbs Ferry

Joseph L. Victor is professor and chairman of the Department of Law, Criminal Justice, and Safety Administration at Mercy College. Professor Victor has extensive field experience in criminal justice agencies, counseling, and administering human service programs. He earned his B.A. and M.A. at Seton Hall University and his Doctorate of Education at Fairleigh Dickinson University.

Joanne Naughton
Mercy College, Dobbs Ferry

Joanne Naughton is assistant professor of Criminal Justice at Mercy College. Professor Naughton is a former member of the New York City Police Department, where she encountered most aspects of police work as a police officer, detective, sergeant, and lieutenant. She is also a former staff attorney with The Legal Aid Society. She received her B.A. and J.D. at Fordham University.

 **Higher Education**

Boston   Burr Ridge, IL   Dubuque, IA   New York   San Francisco   St. Louis
Bangkok   Bogotá   Caracas   Kuala Lumpur   Lisbon   London   Madrid   Mexico City
Milan   Montreal   New Delhi   Santiago   Seoul   Singapore   Sydney   Taipei   Toronto

ANNUAL EDITIONS: CRIMINAL JUSTICE, THIRTY-SECOND EDITION

1 2 3 4 5 6 7 8 9 0 QPD/QPD 0 9 8

ISBN 978–0–07–339772–6
MHID 0–07–339772–5
ISSN 0272–3816

Managing Editor: *Larry Loeppke*
Managing Editor: *Faye Schilling*
Developmental Editor: *Dave Welsh*
Editorial Assistant: *Nancy Meissner*
Production Service Assistant: *Rita Hingtgen*
Permissions Coordinator: *Shirley Lanners*
Senior Marketing Manager: *Julie Keck*
Marketing Communications Specialist: *Mary Klein*
Marketing Coordinator: *Alice Link*
Project Manager: *Jean Smith*
Senior Administrative Assistant: *DeAnna Dausener*
Senior Production Supervisor: *Laura Fuller*
Cover Graphics: *Tara McDermott*

Compositor: Laserwords Private Limited
Cover Images: Mikael Karlsson (008-3898)(foreground); Hisham F. Ibrahim/Getty Images (43244)(background).

Library in Congress Cataloging-in-Publication Data
Main entry under title: Annual Editions: Criminal Justice. 2008/2009.
 1. Criminal Justice—Periodicals. I. Victor, Joseph L., *comp*. II. Naughton, Joanne. Title: Criminal Justice.
658'.05

Editors/Advisory Board

Members of the Advisory Board are instrumental in the final selection of articles for each edition of ANNUAL EDITIONS. Their review of articles for content, level, currentness, and appropriateness provides critical direction to the editor and staff. We think that you will find their careful consideration well reflected in this volume.

Preface

In publishing ANNUAL EDITIONS we recognize the enormous role played by the magazines, newspapers, and journals of the public press in providing current, first-rate educational information in a broad spectrum of interest areas. Many of these articles are appropriate for students, researchers, and professionals seeking accurate, current material to help bridge the gap between principles and theories and the real world. These articles, however, become more useful for study when those of lasting value are carefully collected, organized, indexed, and reproduced in a low-cost format, which provides easy and permanent access when the material is needed. That is the role played by ANNUAL EDITIONS.

During the 1970s, Criminal Justice emerged as an appealing, vital and unique academic discipline. It emphasizes the professional development of students who plan careers in the field, and attracts those who want to know more about a complex social problem and how this country deals with it. Criminal Justice incorporates a vast range of knowledge from a number of specialties, including law, history, and the behavioral and social sciences. Each specialty contributes to our fuller understanding of criminal behavior and of society's attitudes toward deviance.

In view of the fact that the criminal justice system is in a constant state of flux, and because the study of criminal justice covers such a broad spectrum, today's students must be aware of a variety of subjects and topics. Standard textbooks and traditional anthologies cannot keep pace with the changes as quickly as they occur. In fact, many such sources are already out of date the day they are published. *Annual Editions: Criminal Justice 08/09* strives to maintain currency in matters of concern by providing up-to-date commentaries, articles, reports and statistics from the most recent literature in the criminal justice field.

This volume contains units concerning crime and justice in America, victimology, the police, the judicial system, juvenile justice, and punishment and corrections. The articles in these units were selected because they are informative as well as provocative. The selections are timely and useful in their treatment of ethics, punishment, juveniles, courts, and other related topics.

Included in this volume are a number of features designed to be useful to students, researchers and professionals in the criminal justice field. These include the table of contents, which summarizes each article, and features key concepts in bold italics; a *topic guide* for locating articles on specific subjects; a list of relevant *Internet References* sites; a comprehensive section on crime statistics; a *glossary*. In addition, each unit is preceded by an *overview* that provides a background for informed reading of the articles, emphasizes critical issues, and presents key points to consider.

We would like to know what you think of the selections contained in this edition of *Annual Editions: Criminal Justice.* Please fill out the postage-paid article rating form on the last page and let us know your opinions. We change or retain many of the articles based on the comments we receive from you, the reader. Help us to improve this anthology—annually.

Joseph L. Victor
Editor

Joanne Naughton
Editor

Contents

UNIT 1
Crime and Justice in America

The concepts in bold italics are developed in the article. For further expansion, please refer to the Topic Guide.

UNIT 2
Victimology

UNIT 3
The Police

The concepts in bold italics are developed in the article. For further expansion, please refer to the Topic Guide.

UNIT 4
The Judicial System

The concepts in bold italics are developed in the article. For further expansion, please refer to the Topic Guide.

UNIT 5
Juvenile Justice

The concepts in bold italics are developed in the article. For further expansion, please refer to the Topic Guide.

UNIT 6
Punishment and Corrections

The concepts in bold italics are developed in the article. For further expansion, please refer to the Topic Guide.

The concepts in bold italics are developed in the article. For further expansion, please refer to the Topic Guide.

Correlation Guide

The *Annual Editions* series provides students with convenient, inexpensive access to current, carefully selected articles from the public press. **Annual Editions: Criminal Justice 08/09** is an easy-to-use reader that presents articles on important topics such as the *justice system, victims, punishment, policing,* and many more. For more information on *Annual Editions* and other *McGraw-Hill Contemporary Learning Series* titles, visit www.mhcls.com.

This convenient guide matches the units in **Annual Editions: Criminal Justice 08/09** with the corresponding chapters in three of our best-selling McGraw-Hill Criminal Justice textbooks by Walker/Katz and Adler et al.

Annual Editions: Criminal Justice 08/09	The Police in America: An Introduction, 6/e by Walker/Katz	Criminology, 6/e by Adler et al.	Criminology and the Criminal Justice System, 6/e by Adler et al.
Unit 1: Crime and Justice in America	**Chapter 1:** Police and Society	**Chapter 1:** The Changing Boundaries of Criminology	**Chapter 1:** The Changing Boundaries of Criminology
	Chapter 2: The History of the American Police	**Chapter 2:** Counting Crime and Measuring Criminal Behavior	**Chapter 2:** Counting Crime and Measuring Criminal Behavior
	Chapter 3: The Contemporary Law Enforcement Industry	**Chapter 10:** Violent Crimes	**Chapter 10:** Violent Crimes
Unit 2: Victimology	**Chapter 2:** The History of the American Police	**Chapter 9:** Environmental Theory	**Chapter 9:** Environmental Theory
	Chapter 12: Police-Community Relations		
	Chapter 14: Accountability of the Police		
Unit 3: The Police	**All chapters**		**Chapter 16:** Enforcing the Law: Practice and Research
Unit 4: The Judicial System	**Chapter 2:** The History of the American Police		**Chapter 17:** The Nature and Functioning of Courts
	Chapter 14: Accountability of the Police		
Unit 5: Juvenile Justice	**Chapter 8:** Peacekeeping and Order Maintenance	**Chapter 2:** Counting Crime and Measuring Criminal Behavior	**Chapter 2:** Counting Crime and Measuring Criminal Behavior
			Chapter 15: Processes and Decisions
Unit 6: Punishment and Corrections	**Chapter 14:** Accountability of the Police		**Chapter 17:** The Nature and Functioning of Courts
			Chapter 18: A Research Focus on Corrections

Topic Guide

This topic guide suggests how the selections in this book relate to the subjects covered in your course. You may want to use the topics listed on these pages to search the Web more easily.

On the following pages a number of Web sites have been gathered specifically for this book. They are arranged to reflect the units of this *Annual Edition*. You can link to these sites by going to the student online support site at *http://www.mhcls.com/online/*.

ALL THE ARTICLES THAT RELATE TO EACH TOPIC ARE LISTED BELOW THE BOLD-FACED TERM.

Batterer programs
8. Do Batterer Intervention Programs Work?

Career
30. The 21st Century Juvenile Justice Work Force

Civilian complaint review board
19. Settling Disputes across a Table When Officer and Citizen Clash

Civil rights
3. Arraigning Terror
39. Private Prisons Expect a Boom

Colleges
12. Sexual Assault on Campus: What Colleges and Universities Are Doing About It

Constitution
42. Supermax Prisons

Corrections
30. The 21st Century Juvenile Justice Work Force
35. Felon Fallout
42. Supermax Prisons

Counter-terrorism
14. The NYPD's War On Terror

Courts
22. Looking Askance at Eyewitness Testimony
23. Why Do Hung Juries Hang?
25. Judges Turn Therapist in Problem-Solving Court
27. Justice & Antonin Scalia

Crime
1. What Is the Sequence of Events in the Criminal Justice System?
10. Violence and the Remaking of a Self
22. Looking Askance at Eyewitness Testimony

Crime statistics
9. Telling the Truth About Damned Lies and Statistics
33. Co-Offending and Patterns of Juvenile Crime

Criminal justice
1. What Is the Sequence of Events in the Criminal Justice System?
2. Preparing for the Future
6. Toward a Transvaluation of Criminal 'Justice': On Vengeance, Peacemaking, and Punishment
7. Trust and Confidence in Criminal Justice
16. Ethics and Criminal Justice: Some Observations on Police Misconduct

DARE program
29. DARE Program: Sacred Cow or Fatted Calf?

Death penalty
4. Of Crime and Punishment
26. When the Poor Go to Court
27. Justice & Antonin Scalia
29. DARE Program: Sacred Cow or Fatted Calf?
38. Do We Need the Death Penalty?
43. The Unique Brutality of Texas

Discretion
1. What Is the Sequence of Events in the Criminal Justice System?

Domestic spying
4. Of Crime and Punishment

Domestic violence
25. Judges Turn Therapist in Problem-Solving Court

Drug program
29. DARE Program: Sacred Cow or Fatted Calf?

Evidence
23. Why Do Hung Juries Hang?

Eyewitnesses
22. Looking Askance at Eyewitness Testimony

Excessive force
4. Of Crime and Punishment

Globalization
2. Preparing for the Future

Homelessness
25. Judges Turn Therapist in Problem-Solving Court

Illegal immigrants
39. Private Prisons Expect a Boom

International crime
14. The NYPD's War On Terror

Jail
26. When the Poor Go to Court

Judges
25. Judges Turn Therapist in Problem-Solving Court

Jury
20. Jury Consulting on Trial
21. Jury Duty: When History and Life Coincide
22. Looking Askance at Eyewitness Testimony
23. Why Do Hung Juries Hang?

Juveniles
28. Reforming Juvenile Justice
29. DARE Program: Sacred Cow or Fatted Calf?
30. The 21st Century Juvenile Justice Work Force
32. Jailed for Life After Crimes as Teenagers
33. Co-Offending and Patterns of Juvenile Crime

Law
6. Toward a Transvaluation of Criminal 'Justice': On Vengeance, Peacemaking, and Punishment

Law enforcement
17. Stress Management…and the Stress-proof Vest

Lawyers
26. When the Poor Go to Court

Internet References

The following Internet sites have been carefully researched and selected to support the articles found in this reader. The easiest way to access these selected sites is to go to our student online support site at *http://www.mhcls.com/online/*.

AE: Criminal Justice 08/09

The following sites were available at the time of publication. Visit our Web site—we update our student online support site regularly to reflect any changes.

General Sources

American Society of Criminology
http://www.bsos.umd.edu/asc/four.html

This is an excellent starting place for study of all aspects of criminology and criminal justice, with links to international criminal justice, juvenile justice, court information, police, governments, and so on.

Federal Bureau of Investigation
http://www.fbi.gov

The main page of the FBI Web site leads to lists of the most wanted criminals, uniform crime reports, FBI case reports, major investigations, and more.

National Archive of Criminal Justice Data
http://www.icpsr.umich.edu/NACJD/index.html

NACJD holds more than 500 data collections relating to criminal justice; this site provides browsing and downloading access to most of the data and documentation. NACJD's central mission is to facilitate and encourage research in the field of criminal justice.

Social Science Information Gateway
http://sosig.esrc.bris.ac.uk

This is an online catalog of thousands of Internet resources relevant to social science education and research. Every resource is selected and described by a librarian or subject specialist. Enter "criminal justice" under Search for an excellent annotated list of sources.

UNIT 1: Crime and Justice in America

Sourcebook of Criminal Justice Statistics Online
http://www.albany.edu/sourcebook/

Data about all aspects of criminal justice in the United States are available at this site, which includes more than 600 tables from dozens of sources. A search mechanism is available.

UNIT 2: Victimology

National Crime Victim's Research and Treatment Center (NCVC)
http://www.musc.edu/cvc/

At this site, find out about the work of the NCVC at the Medical University of South Carolina, and click on Related Resources for an excellent listing of additional Web sources.

Office for Victims of Crime (OVC)
http://www.ojp.usdoj.gov/ovc

Established by the 1984 Victims of Crime Act, the OVC oversees diverse programs that benefit the victims of crime. From this site you can download a great deal of pertinent information.

UNIT 3: The Police

ACLU Criminal Justice Home Page
http://www.aclu.org/CriminalJustice/CriminalJusticeMain.cfm

This "Criminal Justice" page of the American Civil Liberties Union Web site highlights recent events in criminal justice, addresses police issues, lists important resources, and contains a search mechanism.

Law Enforcement Guide to the World Wide Web
http://leolinks.com/

This page is dedicated to excellence in law enforcement. It contains links to every possible related category: community policing, computer crime, forensics, gangs, and wanted persons are just a few.

Violent Criminal Apprehension Program (VICAP)
http://www.state.ma.us/msp/unitpage/vicap.htm

VICAP's mission is to facilitate cooperation, communication, and coordination among law enforcement agencies and provide support in their efforts to investigate, identify, track, apprehend, and prosecute violent serial offenders. Access VICAP's data information center resources here.

UNIT 4: The Judicial System

Center for Rational Correctional Policy
http://www.correctionalpolicy.com

This is an excellent site on courts and sentencing, with many additional links to a variety of criminal justice sources.

Justice Information Center (JIC)
http://www.ncjrs.org

Provided by the National Criminal Justice Reference Service, this JIC site connects to information about corrections, courts, crime prevention, criminal justice, statistics, drugs and crime, law enforcement, and victims.

National Center for Policy Analysis (NCPA)
http://www.public-policy.org/~ncpa/pd/law/index3.html

Through the NCPA's "Idea House," you can click onto links to an array of topics that are of major interest in the study of the American judicial system.

U.S. Department of Justice (DOJ)

http://www.usdoj.gov

The DOJ represents the American people in enforcing the law in the public interest. Open its main page to find information about the U.S. judicial system. This site provides links to federal government Web servers, topics of interest related to the justice system, documents and resources, and a topical index.

UNIT 5: Juvenile Justice

Gang Land: The Jerry Capeci Page

http://www.ganglandnews.com

Although this site particularly addresses organized-crime gangs, its insights into gang lifestyle—including gang families and their influence—are useful for those interested in exploring issues related to juvenile justice.

Institute for Intergovernmental Research (IIR)

http://www.iir.com

The IIR is a research organization that specializes in law enforcement, juvenile justice, and criminal justice issues. Explore the projects, links, and search engines from this home page. Topics addressed include youth gangs and white collar crime.

National Criminal Justice Reference Service (NCJRS)

http://virlib.ncjrs.org/JuvenileJustice.asp

NCJRS, a federally sponsored information clearinghouse for people involved with research, policy, and practice related to criminal and juvenile justice and drug control, provides this site of links to full-text juvenile justice publications.

Partnership Against Violence Network

http://www.pavnet.org

The Partnership Against Violence Network is a virtual library of information about violence and youths at risk, representing data from seven different federal agencies—a one-stop searchable information resource.

UNIT 6: Punishment and Corrections

American Probation and Parole Association (APPA)

http://www.appa-net.org

Open this APPA site to find information and resources related to probation and parole issues, position papers, the APPA code of ethics, and research and training programs and opportunities.

The Corrections Connection

http://www.corrections.com

This site is an online network for corrections professionals.

Critical Criminology Division of the ASC

http://www.critcrim.org/

Here you will find basic criminology resources and related government resources, provided by the American Society of Criminology, as well as other useful links. The death penalty is also discussed.

David Willshire's Forensic Psychology & Psychiatry Links

http://members.optushome.com.au/dwillsh/index.html

This site offers an enormous number of links to professional journals and associations. It is a valuable resource for study into possible connections between violence and mental disorders. Topics include serial killers, sex offenders, and trauma.

Oregon Department of Corrections

http://egov.oregon.gov/DOC/TRANS/CC/cc_welcome.shtml

Open this site for resources in such areas as crime and law enforcement and for links to U.S. state corrections departments.

We highly recommend that you review our Web site for expanded information and our other product lines. We are continually updating and adding links to our Web site in order to offer you the most usable and useful information that will support and expand the value of your Annual Editions. You can reach us at: *http://www.mhcls.com/annualeditions/*.

UNIT 1

Crime and Justice in America

Unit Selections

Key Points to Consider

- Do you worry when paying bills and making purchases on-line that someone may be stealing your identity?

- Does the death penalty succeed in deterring others from committing heinous offenses?

- What steps do you think criminal justice should take to modernize and take advantage of available technology?

Student Web Site

www.mhcls.com/online

Internet References

Further information regarding these Web sites may be found in this book's preface or online.

Sourcebook of Criminal Justice Statistics Online
http://www.albany.edu/sourcebook/

Crime continues to be a major problem in the United States. Court dockets are full, our prisons are overcrowded, probation and parole caseloads are overwhelming, and our police are being urged to do more. The bulging prison population places a heavy strain on the economy of the country. Clearly, crime is a complex problem that defies simple explanations or solutions. While the more familiar crimes of murder, rape, assault and drug law violations are still with us, international terrorism has become a pressing worry. The debate also continues about how best to handle juvenile offenders, sex offenders, and those who commit acts of domestic violence. Crime committed using computers and the Internet also demands attention from the criminal justice system.

Annual Editions: Criminal Justice 08/09 focuses directly upon crime in America and the three traditional components of the criminal justice system: police, the courts, and corrections. It also gives special attention to crime victims in the victimology unit and to juveniles in the juvenile justice unit. The articles presented in this section are intended to serve as a foundation for the materials presented in subsequent sections.

The unit begins with "What Is the Sequence of Events in the Criminal Justice System?" an article that reveals that the response to crime is a complex process, involving citizens as well as many agencies, levels and branches of government. Then, in Nancy M. Ritter's article "Preparing for the Future: Criminal Justice in 2040", three criminal justice experts weigh in on changes they see occurring over the next thirty years. "Arraigning Terror" deals with the restructuring that took place after September 11 of the nation's intelligence-gathering institutions. In "Of Crime and Punishment," experts explore issues in the legal limelight. The FBI's computer crime crackdown efforts are discussed in "Global Co-op Feeds FBI's Botnet Fight."

In "Toward a Transvaluation of Criminal 'Justice': On Vengeance, Peacemaking and Punishment," Christopher R. Williams focuses on the anger, hate and violence that he says permeate the system of criminal justice.

Although law enforcement has made great progress regarding corruption, brutality and racism, Americans do not seem to have noticed, according to Lawrence Sherman in "Trust and Confidence in Criminal Justice."

What Is the Sequence of Events in the Criminal Justice System?

The Private Sector Initiates the Response to Crime

This first response may come from individuals, families, neighborhood associations, business, industry, agriculture, educational institutions, the news media, or any other private service to the public.

It involves crime prevention as well as participation in the criminal justice process once a crime has been committed. Private crime prevention is more than providing private security or burglar alarms or participating in neighborhood watch. It also includes a commitment to stop criminal behavior by not engaging in it or condoning it when it is committed by others.

Citizens take part directly in the criminal justice process by reporting crime to the police, by being a reliable participant (for example, a witness or a juror) in a criminal proceeding and by accepting the disposition of the system as just or reasonable. As voters and taxpayers, citizens also participate in criminal justice through the policymaking process that affects how the criminal justice process operates, the resources available to it, and its goals and objectives. At every stage of the process from the original formulation of objectives to the decision about where to locate jails and prisons to the reintegration of inmates into society, the private sector has a role to play. Without such involvement, the criminal justice process cannot serve the citizens it is intended to protect.

The Response to Crime and Public Safety Involves Many Agencies and Services

Many of the services needed to prevent crime and make neighborhoods safe are supplied by noncriminal justice agencies, including agencies with primary concern for public health, education, welfare, public works, and housing. Individual citizens as well as public and private sector organizations have joined with criminal justice agencies to prevent crime and make neighborhoods safe.

Criminal Cases are Brought by the Government Through the Criminal Justice System

We apprehend, try, and punish offenders by means of a loose confederation of agencies at all levels of government. Our American system of justice has evolved from the English common law into a complex series of procedures and decisions. Founded on the concept that crimes against an individual are crimes against the State, our justice system prosecutes individuals as though they victimized all of society. However, crime victims are involved throughout the process and many justice agencies have programs which focus on helping victims.

There is no single criminal justice system in this country. We have many similar systems that are individually unique. Criminal cases may be handled differently in different jurisdictions, but court decisions based on the due process guarantees of the U.S. Constitution require that specific steps be taken in the administration of criminal justice so that the individual will be protected from undue intervention from the State.

The description of the criminal and juvenile justice systems that follows portrays the most common sequence of events in response to serious criminal behavior.

Entry into the System

The justice system does not respond to most crime because so much crime is not discovered or reported to the police. Law enforcement agencies learn about crime from the reports of victims or other citizens, from discovery by a police officer in the field, from informants, or from investigative and intelligence work.

Once a law enforcement agency has established that a crime has been committed, a suspect must be identified and apprehended for the case to proceed through the system. Sometimes, a suspect is apprehended at the scene; however, identification of a suspect sometimes requires an extensive investigation. Often, no one is identified or apprehended. In some instances, a suspect is arrested and later the police determine that no crime was committed and the suspect is released.

Prosecution and Pretrial Services

After an arrest, law enforcement agencies present information about the case and about the accused to the prosecutor, who will decide if formal charges will be filed with the court. If no charges are filed, the accused must be released. The prosecutor can also drop charges after making efforts to prosecute (*nolle prosequi*).

A suspect charged with a crime must be taken before a judge or magistrate without unnecessary delay. At the initial appearance, the judge or magistrate informs the accused of the charges and decides whether there is probable cause to detain the accused person. If the offense is not very serious, the determination of guilt and assessment of a penalty may also occur at this stage.

Often, the defense counsel is also assigned at the initial appearance. All suspects prosecuted for serious crimes have a right to be represented by an attorney. If the court determines the suspect is indigent and cannot afford such representation, the court will assign counsel at the public's expense.

A pretrial-release decision may be made at the initial appearance, but may occur at other hearings or may be changed at another time during the process. Pretrial release and bail were traditionally intended to ensure appearance at trial. However, many jurisdictions permit pretrial detention of defendants accused of serious offenses and deemed to be dangerous to prevent them from committing crimes prior to trial.

The court often bases its pretrial decision on information about the defendant's drug use, as well as residence, employment, and family ties. The court may decide to release the accused on his/her own recognizance or into the custody of a third party after the posting of a financial bond or on the promise of satisfying certain conditions such as taking periodic drug tests to ensure drug abstinence.

In many jurisdictions, the initial appearance may be followed by a preliminary hearing. The main function of this hearing is to discover if there is probable cause to believe that the accused committed a known crime within the jurisdiction of the court. If the judge does not find probable cause, the case is dismissed; however, if the judge or magistrate finds probable cause for such a belief, or the accused waives his or her right to a preliminary hearing, the case may be bound over to a grand jury.

A grand jury hears evidence against the accused presented by the prosecutor and decides if there is sufficient evidence to cause the accused to be brought to trial. If the grand jury finds sufficient evidence, it submits to the court an indictment, a written statement of the essential facts of the offense charged against the accused.

Where the grand jury system is used, the grand jury may also investigate criminal activity generally and issue indictments called grand jury originals that initiate criminal cases. These investigations and indictments are often used in drug and conspiracy cases that involve complex organizations. After such an indictment, law enforcement tries to apprehend and arrest the suspects named in the indictment.

Misdemeanor cases and some felony cases proceed by the issuance of an information, a formal, written accusation submitted to the court by a prosecutor. In some jurisdictions, indictments may be required in felony cases. However, the accused may choose to waive a grand jury indictment and, instead, accept service of an information for the crime.

In some jurisdictions, defendants, often those without prior criminal records, may be eligible for diversion from prosecution subject to the completion of specific conditions such as drug treatment. Successful completion of the conditions may result in the dropping of charges or the expunging of the criminal record where the defendant is required to plead guilty prior to the diversion.

Adjudication

Once an indictment or information has been filed with the trial court, the accused is scheduled for arraignment. At the arraignment, the accused is informed of the charges, advised of the rights of criminal defendants, and asked to enter a plea to the charges. Sometimes, a plea of guilty is the result of negotiations between the prosecutor and the defendant.

If the accused pleads guilty or pleads *nolo contendere* (accepts penalty without admitting guilt), the judge may accept or reject the plea. If the plea is accepted, no trial is held and the offender is sentenced at this proceeding or at a later date. The plea may be rejected and proceed to trial if, for example, the judge believes that the accused may have been coerced.

If the accused pleads not guilty or not guilty by reason of insanity, a date is set for the trial. A person accused of a serious crime is guaranteed a trial by jury. However, the accused may ask for a bench trial where the judge, rather than a jury, serves as the finder of fact. In both instances the prosecution and defense present evidence by questioning witnesses while the judge decides on issues of law. The trial results in acquittal or conviction on the original charges or on lesser included offenses.

After the trial a defendant may request appellate review of the conviction or sentence. In some cases, appeals of convictions are a matter of right; all States with the death penalty provide for automatic appeal of cases involving a death sentence. Appeals may be subject to the discretion of the appellate court and may be granted only on acceptance of a defendant's petition for a *writ of certiorari*. Prisoners may also appeal their sentences through civil rights petitions and *writs of habeas corpus* where they claim unlawful detention.

Sentencing and Sanctions

After a conviction, sentence is imposed. In most cases the judge decides on the sentence, but in some jurisdictions the sentence is decided by the jury, particularly for capital offenses.

In arriving at an appropriate sentence, a sentencing hearing may be held at which evidence of aggravating or mitigating circumstances is considered. In assessing the circumstances surrounding a convicted person's criminal behavior, courts often rely on presentence investigations by probation agencies or other designated authorities. Courts may also consider victim impact statements.

The sentencing choices that may be available to judges and juries include one or more of the following:

- the death penalty
- incarceration in a prison, jail, or other confinement facility
- probation—allowing the convicted person to remain at liberty but subject to certain conditions and restrictions such as drug testing or drug restrictions such as drug testing or drug treatment

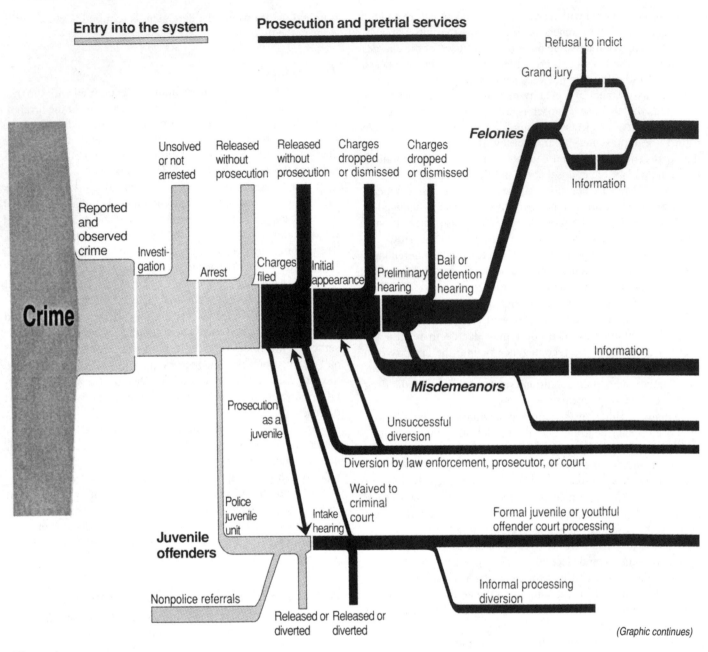

Figure 1

Note: This chart gives a simplified view of caseflow through the criminal justice system. Procedures vary among jurisdictions. The weights of the lines are not intended to show the actual size of caseloads.

- fines—primarily applied as penalties in minor offenses
- restitution—requiring the offender to pay compensation to the victim. In some jurisdictions, offenders may be sentenced to alternatives to incarceration that are considered more severe than straight probation but less severe than a prison term. Examples of such sanctions include boot camps, intense supervision often with drug treatment and testing, house arrest and electronic monitoring, denial of Federal benefits, and community service.

In many jurisdictions, the law mandates that persons convicted of certain types of offenses serve a prison term. Most jurisdictions permit the judge to set the sentence length within certain limits, but some have determinate sentencing laws that stipulate a specific sentence length that must be served and cannot be altered by a parole board.

Corrections

Offenders sentenced to incarceration usually serve time in a local jail or a State prison. Offenders sentenced to less than 1 year generally go to jail; those sentenced to more than 1 year go to prison. Persons admitted to the Federal system or a State prison system may be held in prison with varying levels of custody or in a community correctional facility.

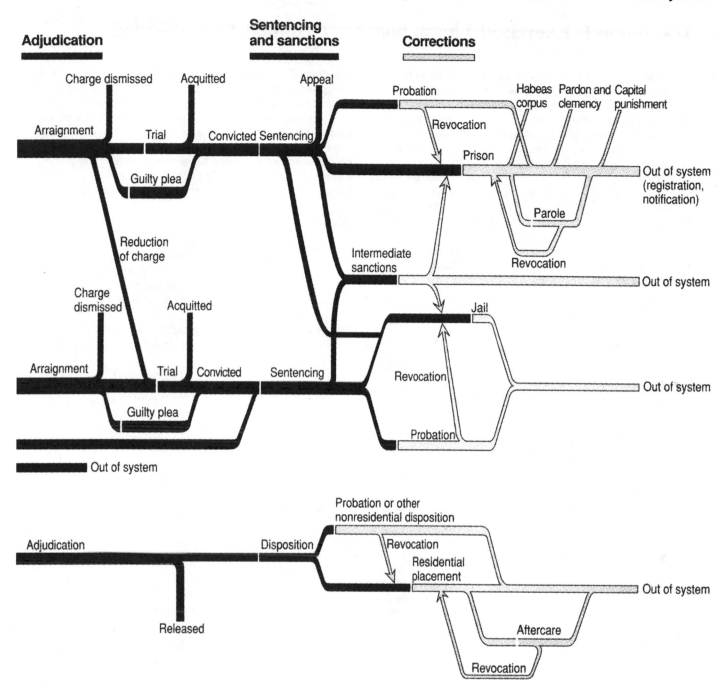

Figure 1 *(continued)*

Source: Adapted from *The challenge of crime in a free society*. President's Commission on Law Enforcement and Administration of Justice, 1967. This revision, a result of the Symposium on the 30th Anniversary of the President's Commission, was prepared by the Bureau of Justice Statistics in 1997.

A prisoner may become eligible for parole after serving a specific part of his or her sentence. Parole is the conditional release of a prisoner before the prisoner's full sentence has been served. The decision to grant parole is made by an authority such as a parole board, which has power to grant or revoke parole or to discharge a parolee altogether. The way parole decisions are made varies widely among jurisdictions.

Offenders may also be required to serve out their full sentences prior to release (expiration of term). Those sentenced under determinate sentencing laws can be released only after

they have served their full sentence (mandatory release) less any "goodtime" received while in prison. Inmates get goodtime credits against their sentences automatically or by earning them through participation in programs.

If released by a parole board decision or by mandatory release, the releasee will be under the supervision of a parole officer in the community for the balance of his or her unexpired sentence. This supervision is governed by specific conditions of release, and the releasee may be returned to prison for violations of such conditions.

Discretion Is Exercised Throughout the Criminal Justice System

Discretion is "an authority conferred by law to act in certain conditions or situations in accordance with an official's or an official agency's own considered judgment and conscience."[1] Discretion is exercised throughout the government. It is a part of decisionmaking in all government systems from mental health to education, as well as criminal justice. The limits of discretion vary from jurisdiction to jurisdiction.

Concerning crime and justice, legislative bodies have recognized that they cannot anticipate the range of circumstances surrounding each crime, anticipate local mores, and enact laws that clearly encompass all conduct that is criminal and all that is not.[2]

Therefore, persons charged with the day-to-day response to crime are expected to exercise their own judgment within limits set by law. Basically, they must decide—

- whether to take action
- where the situation fits in the scheme of law, rules, and precedent
- which official response is appropriate.[3]

To ensure that discretion is exercised responsibly, government authority is often delegated to professionals. Professionalism requires a minimum level of training and orientation, which guide officials in making decisions. The professionalism of policing is due largely to the desire to ensure the proper exercise of police discretion.

The limits of discretion vary from State to State and locality to locality. For example, some State judges have wide discretion in the type of sentence they may impose. In recent years, other states have sought to limit the judge's discretion in sentencing by passing mandatory sentencing laws that require prison sentences for certain offenses.

Notes

1. Roscoe Pound, "Discretion, dispensation and mitigation: The problem of the individual special case," *New York University Law Review* (1960) 35:925, 926.
2. Wayne R. LaFave, *Arrest: The decision to take a suspect into custody* (Boston: Little, Brown & Co., 1964), p. 63–184.
3. Memorandum of June 21, 1977, from Mark Moore to James Vorenberg, "Some abstract notes on the issue of discretion."

Bureau of Justice Statistics (www.ojp.usdoj.gov/bjs/). January 1998. NCJ 167894. To order: 1-800-732-3277.

Who Exercises Discretion?

These criminal justice officials . . .	must often decide whether or not or how to—
Police	Enforce specific laws
	Investigate specific crimes; Search people
Prosecutors	File charges or petitions for adjudication
	Seek indictments
	Drop cases
	Reduce charges
Judges or magistrates	Set bail or conditions for release
	Accept pleas
	Determine delinquency
	Dismiss charges
	Impose sentence
	Revoke probation
Correctional officials	Assign to type of correctional facility
	Award privileges
	Punish for disciplinary infractions
Paroling authorities	Determine date and conditions of parole
	Revoke parole

Recidivism

Once the suspects, defendants, or offenders are released from the jurisdiction of a criminal justice agency, they may be processed through the criminal justice system again for a new crime. Long term studies show that many suspects who are arrested have prior criminal histories and those with a greater number of prior arrests were more likely to be arrested again. As the courts take prior criminal history into account at sentencing, most prison inmates have a prior criminal history and many have been incarcerated before. Nationally, about half the inmates released from State prison will return to prison.

The Juvenile Justice System

Juvenile courts usually have jurisdiction over matters concerning children, including delinquency, neglect, and adoption. They also handle "status offenses" such as truancy and running away, which are not applicable to adults. State statutes define which persons are under the original jurisdiction of the juvenile court. The upper age of juvenile court jurisdiction in delinquency matters is 17 in most States.

The processing of juvenile offenders is not entirely dissimilar to adult criminal processing, but there are crucial differences. Many juveniles are referred to juvenile courts by law enforcement officers, but many others are referred by school officials, social services agencies, neighbors, and even parents, for behavior or conditions that are determined to require intervention by the formal system for social control.

At arrest, a decision is made either to send the matter further into the justice system or to divert the case out of the system, often to alternative programs. Examples of alternative programs include drug treatment, individual or group counseling, or referral to educational and recreational programs.

When juveniles are referred to the juvenile courts, the court's intake department or the prosecuting attorney determines whether sufficient grounds exist to warrant filing a petition that requests an adjudicatory hearing or a request to transfer jurisdiction to criminal court. At this point, many juveniles are released or diverted to alternative programs.

All States allow juveniles to be tried as adults in criminal court under certain circumstances. In many States, the legislature *statutorily excludes* certain (usually serious) offenses from the jurisdiction of the juvenile court regardless of the age of the accused. In some States and at the Federal level under certain circumstances, prosecutors have the *discretion* to either file criminal charges against juveniles directly in criminal courts or proceed through the juvenile justice process. The juvenile court's intake department or the prosecutor may petition the juvenile court to *waive* jurisdiction to criminal court. The juvenile court also may order *referral* to criminal court for trial as adults. In some jurisdictions, juveniles processed as adults may upon conviction be sentenced to either an adult or a juvenile facility.

In those cases where the juvenile court retains jurisdiction, the case may be handled formally by filing a delinquency petition or informally by diverting the juvenile to other agencies or programs in lieu of further court processing.

If a petition for an adjudicatory hearing is accepted, the juvenile may be brought before a court quite unlike the court with jurisdiction over adult offenders. Despite the considerable discretion associated with juvenile court proceedings, juveniles are afforded many of the due-process safeguards associated with adult criminal trials. Several States permit the use of juries in juvenile courts; however, in light of the U.S. Supreme Court holding that juries are not essential to juvenile hearings, most States do not make provisions for juries in juvenile courts.

In disposing of cases, juvenile courts usually have far more discretion that adult courts. In addition to such options as probation, commitment to a residential facility, restitution, or fines, State laws grant juvenile courts the power to order removal of children from their homes to foster homes or treatment facilities. Juvenile courts also may order participation in special programs aimed at shoplifting prevention, drug counseling, or driver education.

Once a juvenile is under juvenile court disposition, the court may retain jurisdiction until the juvenile legally becomes an adult (at age 21 in most States). In some jurisdictions, juvenile offenders may be classified as youthful offenders which can lead to extended sentences.

Following release from an institution, juveniles are often ordered to a period of aftercare which is similar to parole supervision for adult offenders. Juvenile offenders who violate the conditions of aftercare may have their aftercare revoked, resulting in being recommitted to a facility. Juveniles who are classified as youthful offenders and violate the conditions of aftercare may be subject to adult sanctions.

The Governmental Response to Crime is Founded in the Intergovernmental Structure of the United States

Under our form of government, each State and the Federal Government has its own criminal justice system. All systems must respect the rights of individuals set forth in court interpretation of the U.S. Constitution and defined in case law.

State constitutions and laws define the criminal justice system within each State and delegate the authority and responsibility for criminal justice to various jurisdictions, officials, and institutions. State laws also define criminal behavior and groups of children or acts under jurisdiction of the juvenile courts.

Municipalities and counties further define their criminal justice systems through local ordinances that proscribe the local agencies responsible for criminal justice processing that were not established by the State.

Congress has also established a criminal justice system at the Federal level to respond to Federal crimes such as bank robbery, kidnaping, and transporting stolen goods across State lines.

The Response to Crime is Mainly a State and Local Function

Very few crimes are under exclusive Federal jurisdiction. The responsibility to respond to most crime rests with State and local governments. Police protection is primarily a function of cities and towns. Corrections is primarily a function of State governments. Most justice personnel are employed at the local level.

From *Report to the Nation on Crime and Justice*, January 1998. Published by Office of Justice/U.S. Department of Justice.

Preparing for the Future
Criminal Justice in 2040

Nancy M. Ritter

What will criminal justice look like in 2040? There's no question that terrorism, the growth of multicultural populations, massive migration, upheavals in age-composition demographics, technological developments, and globalization over the next three or more decades will affect the world's criminal justice systems. But how? What forces will have the greatest influence?

Weighing in on these questions are three leading criminal justice experts:

- Bryan J. Vila, former chief of the Office of Justice Programs' National Institute of Justice's Crime Control and Prevention Research Division and now a professor at Washington State University, emphasizes the need to understand the evolution—or more accurately, the coevolution—of crime and crime fighting.
- Christopher E. Stone, Daniel and Florence Guggenheim Professor of the Practice of Criminal Justice at Harvard University's John F. Kennedy School of Government, believes that a new global, professional culture will influence the world's criminal justice systems in the decades to come.
- David Weisburd, professor of criminology at the University of Maryland and Jerusalem's Hebrew University Law School, says that how criminal justice looks in 2040 will largely depend on the research path we take: Will developments in policies and technologies be based on clinical experience or on evidence?

The Coevolution of Crime and Justice

Bryan Vila observes that criminals, like viruses, evolve over time and change as their potential victims take preventive measures. For example, Vila notes, as people install steering wheel locks or alarm systems to combat auto theft, thieves respond by using devices that neutralize such security systems.

Regardless of such coevolution across the wide range of crimes, *crime fighting,* Vila says, will continue to fall into three categories: reducing the opportunity for crime, changing the motivation of people who commit crimes, and altering people's fundamental values—including nurturing positive values in young children—to minimize the likelihood of future criminal behavior.

All this will have to be done within the context of changing demographics. As 2040 approaches, the proportion of males aged 15 to 29—traditionally, the most crime-prone group—will decline slightly, and the percentage of the over-30 population (and particularly those over 65) will increase substantially.

The impact? "There will be more people to be either victims or solutions," Vila observes. For example, he explains, an increase in the elderly population could result in greater victimization, but it could also lead to more elderly people using their discretionary time to report crime and guide children.

Technological advances will also have a great influence on crime fighting. Developments in surveillance, biometrics, DNA analysis, and radio frequency identification microchips will enhance crime prevention and crime solving. Increasingly sophisticated intelligence databases will likely be used not only by police officers and analysts, but by the general public—as is now common with sex offender registries.

The future will also bring improvements in interoperability systems that allow officials to talk electronically to one another, particularly during emergencies. And, Vila concludes, better connection among people and agencies will lead to a decrease in the attractiveness and vulnerability of crime targets.

Global Trends

Chris Stone predicts that global trends will play a significant role in how criminal justice is delivered throughout the world in 2040. Stone points to the dramatic growth in the number of foreign-born Americans and suggests that increasing diversity in populations will have a significant impact not only in the United States but worldwide.

Such growth has the potential for disharmony, Stone notes. In South Africa, for example, the court system now recognizes 11 official languages. As a result, lawyers may speak one language, the judge another, and the defendant, a third. Often, the only two people in the courtroom speaking the same language are the victim and defendant—with the judge, prosecutor, and defense lawyer relying on interpreters.

The lack of homogeneity extends beyond language to societal norms and expectations. What will foreign-born Americans expect of the U.S. justice system, given their experiences in their native countries? How will they regard the roles of the defense lawyer, prosecutor, and judge? Answers to these questions will shape the face of criminal justice in the decades to come.

Stone believes that a new professional culture is spreading through justice systems worldwide across five vectors:

Bilateral transfer of information between countries.

The bilateral transfer of information can lead to changes in a country's criminal justice system. For example, a delegation funded by the U.S. Agency for International Development travels to China to discuss prosecution systems. Thereafter, the Chinese host delegations from Germany and Australia. In the end, Stone observes, the Chinese are likely to mix and match, developing a hybrid system that is different from that of any other country—which, in turn, may influence others in Asia.

Multilateral innovation.

In the first case before the International Crime Court, for example, the chief prosecutor is a Korean American from New York City. Working with colleagues from Argentina, Belgium, France, and Germany, the team is creating new methods, norms, and ethics that Stone believes will influence practices in each member's own domestic systems.

Global dissemination of justice products.

The dissemination of justice products—such as court management computer systems, consulting services, and prison design—will also shape our criminal justice system in 2040. For example, Stone notes, a European-developed court management system has been successfully marketed in South Africa.

Hollywood.

With its tremendous influence on attitudes about justice, Hollywood also stands to influence the development of criminal justice systems throughout the world. The television program *Law and Order* is currently viewed in more than 40 countries, and *CSI* in more than 22. Although entertainment, such programs affect people's expectations of the justice system. For example, most countries do not try criminal cases in front of juries, yet American films and television create expectations that justice includes jury trials, perhaps lending support to the introduction of jury trials in Russia.

Empirical evidence.

Comparative evidence about what works, what doesn't, and why will play a major role in how the world's justice systems look in 2040. Stone offers some ideas for comparative research that could impact criminal justice in the future:

- *Civilian oversight of police.* An essential element of justice, comprehensive systems for civilian management are rapidly developing in many countries.
- *Prosecution.* More than a dozen countries in Latin America, for example, are exploring new roles for prosecutors, which could lead to a new relationship with victims and new systems for plea bargaining.
- *Indigent defense.* Pilot projects to improve public defense—which, Stone believes, is weak everywhere—are underway in Africa, Eastern Europe, and England, with alluring potential for comparative research.

Which Path to Take?

David Weisburd believes that the nature of criminal justice in 2040 will depend in large part on the primary research methodology. Is the criminal justice community better served by relying on the experiences and opinions of practitioners (the clinical experience model) or by research that tests programs and measures outcomes (the evidence-based model)?

Currently, the clinical experience model is the research path most frequently followed. Policies and technologies are based primarily on reports from practitioners about what they have found to work or not work. Sharing approaches and programs that seemed to work in one community with another community allows for quick application of successful ideas. The downside of this model is that a program may be widely adopted before scientific research demonstrates its efficacy in more than one place or application. For example, in one youth program aimed at reducing delinquency, counselors and parents believed that the treatments were effective, based on initial measures of success. However, subsequent evaluation revealed that participation in the program actually increased the risk of delinquency.

In the evidence-based model, a new program undergoes systematic research and evaluation before it is widely adopted. Now dominant in medicine—and becoming more popular in other areas such as education—the evidence-based model has been used successfully in criminal justice. For example, hot-spot policing (a policy adopted in the early 1990's that focuses police resources in high-crime areas) was preceded by studies that demonstrated its effectiveness.

But the evidence-based model also has shortcomings. Research requires a large investment of time and money, and many practitioners understandably would rather spend resources implementing an innovation than wait for confirming research. Time—always a precious commodity for policymakers and practitioners—can be a particularly frustrating component of the evidence-based model. Credible research requires time to adequately test an approach, often in more than one jurisdiction, before communities can adopt it on a large scale.

"Policymakers want to improve things while they have the power," Weisburd says. "They are under pressure to make an impact—so there is tension between the slowness of the evidence-based process and the pressure to move quickly."

Making the Evidence-Based Model Realistic

Weisburd proposes making the evidence-based model "more realistic." He believes this can be done by:

- Streamlining the process of developing evidence and conducting evaluations.
- Building an infrastructure to ensure that studies do not reinvent the wheel.
- Devising methods for getting studies off the ground faster, such as encouraging funders to help in the development of high-quality randomized experimental studies.
- Reinforcing a culture that emphasizes the exploration of which programs and practices do and do not work.

Weisburd also argues that Federal investment in the scientific evaluation of new practices and programs must be increased.

Researchers and practitioners must insist that "if you want us to make intelligent policy and not waste money by prematurely innovating in hundreds of departments, you must give us more money."

Global Alliances

All three experts emphasize the need to find new ways to work with professionals around the globe. For example, the Vera Institute in the United States has formed an alliance with academic and nonprofit organizations in other countries to conduct evaluations of the criminal justice process, from policing through sentencing.

Ultimately, Vila, Stone, and Weisburd agree, the world of 2040 will have a more shared culture due to such trends as globalization, mobility, and spreading diversity. Within this context, the priority over the next three and a half decades should be to develop policies and technologies that will help policymakers, decisionmakers, and citizens realize a criminal justice system that is fair, equitable, and respectful.

NANCY M. RITTER is a writer/editor at the National Institute of Justice.

From *National Institute of Justice Journal,* No. 255, November 2006. Published by Office of Justice/U.S. Department of Justice.

Arraigning Terror

ROGERS M. SMITH

After the September 11 attacks, the United States began a sweeping restructuring of the nation's intelligence-gathering and coercive institutions. The administration had two goals: first, to enhance information sharing and analysis among all U.S. military, intelligence, and law enforcement agencies. That task is necessary, though it poses dangers to civil liberties that the Bush administration has ignored. The second goal is to expand governmental powers to detain, prosecute, and convict persons suspected of terrorism without any meaningful procedural protections or oversight by the courts. This endeavor presents far more massive dangers, and the case for its necessity has not been made.

The Bush administration believes the United States is engaged in a wholly new kind of war in which, according to its National Security Strategy, it "must be prepared to stop rogue states and their terrorist clients before they are able to threaten or use weapons of mass destruction against the United States and our allies and friends." Knowing that this policy of preventive warfare is likely to be answered with violent assaults at home as well as abroad, the administration has begun to reconstitute all basic systems for exercising coercive force: the criminal justice system, conventional military operations, immigration control, and foreign intelligence gathering and special operations. It has also distanced itself from the developing system of international criminal law, notably by refusing assent to the International Criminal Court.

So far, the administration has taken five major steps to enhance the nation's ability to detect and deter terrorist threats by restructuring these coercive systems:

1. the passage of the USA Patriot Act on October 25, 2001;
2. the president's executive order issued November 13, 2001, authorizing detention and military trials for non-citizens suspected of terrorism;
3. the opening in January 11, 2002, of the Guantánamo, Cuba, naval base detention camp, where over 650 persons are still detained—the United States has declared them all to be "unlawful enemy combatants," not prisoners of war, without the individualized determinations of status required by the Third Geneva Convention of 1949;
4. the creation of a new Department of Homeland Security on Nov 25, 2002, which has absorbed many federal programs, including the Immigration and Naturalization Service and its anti-terrorist "Special Registration Initiative" targeted at Arabic and Muslim immigrants, which led to the questioning of roughly 130,000 male immigrants and alien visitors, the deportation of some 9,000 undocumented individuals, the arrest of over 800 criminal suspects, and the detention of 11 suspected terrorists (though on April 30, 2003, the administration announced that the Initiative was ending, so far only requirements for annual re-registration have been relaxed);
5. the creation by presidential order in May 2003 of the Terrorist Threat Integration Center (TTIC), an interagency body with participants drawn from the Department of Homeland Security, the State Department, the Defense Department, the FBI, the Department of Justice, and various intelligence bodies; it reports to the director of the Central Intelligence Agency.

The efforts to facilitate information sharing are warranted because investigators have now shown that, had there been sufficiently effective systems for data sharing and assessment in place, the September 11 attacks probably would never have happened. U.S. agencies actually had in hand solid information that could have been used to prevent the terrorists from entering the country or staying long enough to complete their plans. A number were on the terrorist "watch lists" of one or more intelligence agencies, but the officials issuing visas did not know this. Some of the terrorists were subsequently guilty of immigration violations, and some were also involved in minor legal infractions, providing grounds for deportation. But because their likely connections to terrorism had not been communicated, they were allowed to remain. If the different pieces of knowledge had been consolidated and analyzed, the plotters might well have been stopped long before they could act.

Still, innovations in data sharing inevitably pose new threats to civil liberties. Collectively these changes dramatically transform the American state, breaking down old barriers between foreign espionage operations and domestic law enforcement; the separation of immigration law enforcement from the criminal justice system; and divisions between national, state, and local police agencies.

Both the U.S.A. Patriot Act and the Homeland Security Act undermine the wall between foreign intelligence operations and domestic criminal law enforcement that was maintained throughout the cold war. Sections 203, 507, 508, 711, and 903 of the Patriot Act authorize extensive information sharing among all agencies, whether operating at home or abroad, whether federal, state, or local. Criminal records, educational records, and immigrant histories are all included, and so are the fruits of surveillance methods that would ordinarily be deemed to violate constitutional rights if employed by federal, state, or local criminal law officers in more routine investigations. Section 502 authorizes coordinated action among these heretofore generally distinct agencies. The act authorizing the new Department of Homeland Security goes further yet by not only mandating data sharing, but also placing many intelligence-gathering and immigration law enforcement functions under this single new agency. And despite the fact that immigration law violations are not crimes, immigrant data are now being entered into the National Criminal Information Center (NCIC), even if the data have not been checked to see if they are current and accurate. Instead, on March 24, 2003, the attorney general issued an order exempting the NCIC's Central Record System from national Privacy Act standards that require those records to be "accurate, timely, and reliable." And both the Departments of Homeland Security and Justice are seeking to involve state and local police in enforcement of immigration laws for the first time, the better to root out foreign terrorists. These information-sharing mandates are being pursued through a bewildering variety of new mechanisms, but the new Terrorist Threat Integration Center is intended to serve as the main integrating institution—though how it will do so remains unclear, and inadequate data sharing remains a major problem.

Many of these changes (and more) are needed, but it is also true that the old structures of law enforcement reflected important values that are now at risk. Because the courts have long held that U.S. governmental agents of all types can take actions overseas in regard to non-citizens, which would be unconstitutional if done to U.S. citizens, and certainly unconstitutional if done within the jurisdiction of the United States, many agencies of the U.S. government are in the habit of coercing witnesses, seizing evidence, and detaining suspects without any real procedural safeguards. When agencies long accustomed to acting without regard to constitutional restrictions abroad are allowed to join more fully in law enforcement efforts at home, there is clearly a danger that constitutional protections may be ignored here as well (especially when the administration is pressing to loosen those protections on a number of fronts). Even if intelligence-gathering agencies merely make data available that could not be legally obtained by a domestic agency, the practical result may be that U.S. law enforcement is freed of constitutional restrictions.

The increased intermingling of immigration and criminal law enforcement raises further worries. Some state and local police are concerned that as they get involved in immigration-law enforcement, they will receive less cooperation from immigrant communities, who will fear that any contact with any government agency might end in their deportation. Those fears are sustained, moreover, by the wealth of legal precedents holding that immigration officials can constitutionally take peremptory actions against non-citizens that other law enforcement officers cannot. If state and local police are simultaneously enforcing criminal laws and the more procedurally lax immigration laws, it becomes easier for them to act as though only the latter standards are binding on them. Thus, when we break down the walls between foreign and domestic enforcement efforts, and between immigration laws and criminal laws, we risk increasing the ways in which domestic criminal policing efforts may infringe constitutional rights, for citizens and non-citizens alike.

Those risks are vastly increased by the government's multi-pronged pursuit of its second goal—its efforts to detain, prosecute, and sometimes execute terrorists without regard for most of the procedural safeguards provided by the Constitution or international law. The president's order authorizing military tribunals, in particular, permits aliens suspected of knowing about or being directly involved in terrorist plots to be arrested without any showing of probable cause to a neutral magistrate and with no opportunity to communicate with an attorney. Suspects can then be detained indefinitely, or tried in closed military trials with the aid of military defense counsel, on the basis of any evidence that military officials deem to have "probative value," even if it is hearsay or illegally obtained. Accused persons can be denied the opportunity to see and hear all the evidence brought against them, convicted on a vote of two-thirds of a panel of military judges, without trial by jury, and sentenced to death without appeal to the civilian courts. The Defense Department has since added some additional procedural protections, such as the requirement that guilt be found "beyond a reasonable doubt," but the basic structure laid out in the president's original executive order still remains in effect. And even if persons are acquitted in such trials, the government can still incarcerate them indefinitely if it continues to believe they are national security risks.

Under section 412 of the Patriot Act and its general "war powers," moreover, the administration has claimed similarly broad powers to detain indefinitely *all* persons, citizens as well as aliens, who are suspected of being involved in terrorism or even of being "material witnesses" in terrorist investigations, without ever filing criminal charges against them or permitting access to an attorney. This is the way prisoners captured in Afghanistan and incarcerated at Guantánamo as "unlawful enemy combatants" are being treated.

Though the United States has justified these stringent measures as within the war powers bestowed by the Constitution, the United States has not formally declared war on terrorists, and it is hard to see how it could do so. Legally recognized wars are declared against rival states, not loose networks of organizations and individuals. As a result, the White House, Defense Department, and the Justice Department have defended their actions by using the heretofore obscure 1942 precedent of *Ex parte Quirin*. There the U.S. Supreme Court upheld secret military trials for Nazi saboteurs captured in Florida and on Long Island during the Second World War.

Though it has become common for both government officials and their critics to refer to this case as validating severe measures aimed at "enemy combatants" or "enemy aliens," those terms are not wholly accurate. *Quirin* does not focus on the powers of the U.S. government in relation to uniformed enemy combatants participating in legal international wars. It is instead the main source of the still ill-defined category of "unlawful" enemy combatants. Chief Justice Harlan Fiske Stone's opinion in *Quirin* stressed that lawful enemy combatants "are subject to capture and detention as prisoners of war by opposing military forces" according to international law. "Unlawful combatants are likewise subject to capture and detention, but in addition they are subject to trial and punishment by military tribunals for acts which render their belligerency unlawful." Such tribunals can, he made clear, be constitutionally conducted without the sorts of procedural safeguards, including Fifth and Sixth Amendment guarantees, ordinarily afforded to criminals, or the international law protections granted to lawful enemy combatants. And though most of the saboteurs tried in *Quirin* were enemy aliens, Stone affirmed that, if the U.S. government deems a person to be an unlawful enemy combatant, it makes no difference whether or not the person is a U.S. citizen. National security requires that such persons, too, be subjected to arrest, detention, and secret military trials if the executive branch deems such measures appropriate.

This precedent makes it entirely plausible for the administration to designate all those now involved in terrorism as "unlawful enemy combatants" or "belligerents." Terrorists clearly act "unlawfully," in violation of international laws of war as well as domestic and international criminal laws. But they are not conventional criminals, either in our eyes or their own—so what else can they be but "unlawful enemy combatants"? And if that is what they are, then *Quirin* also makes it plausible to argue that they can be arrested, detained, and secretly tried by military commissions without normal constitutional procedural protections, just as the Justice Department has been asserting, whether the suspects are aliens, dual nationals, naturalized citizens, birthright citizens, or anything else.

Yet plausible as those positions are, in the current context they have wide-ranging and worrisome implications. Because *everyone* even suspected of being involved in terrorism is by this definition an "unlawful enemy combatant" or "belligerent," then every investigation of possible terrorist activities can result in indefinite detentions and secret trials on the basis of any evidence that gives even minimal credibility to allegations of such involvement. Now consider what these legal powers mean in light of the new pooling of terrorist-related information among foreign and domestic security agencies; national, state, and local law enforcement bodies; and immigration officials that the United States is undertaking. The results of diverse forms of electronic surveillance, so-called "sneak and peek" searches for which warrants need not be shown in advance, questioning that occurs during indefinite detentions, and the mappings of the social networks of suspects, are all bound to produce data on the activities of citizens with whom foreign nationals or immigrants communicate, as well as on their non-American connections. When international and domestic security agencies; national,

state, and local police forces; and immigration officials are all entitled to share such information rapidly, even information that has not been checked for accuracy, everyone risks being subjected to coercive measures that would ordinarily be deemed unconstitutional, on the basis of evidence that could not survive customary procedural safeguards.

The application of these draconian measures to American citizens has already begun, most notably in the cases of Yaser Hamdi and José Padilla. Hamdi is a twenty-two-year-old Saudi who was born in the United States and therefore also possesses American citizenship, and who was allegedly fighting on behalf of the Taliban and al-Qaeda when captured on a battlefield in Afghanistan. He claims he was a noncombatant. Hamdi has been held for more than two years without formal charges in military prisons in Virginia and was denied access to lawyers until the Supreme Court agreed to examine his detention. Similarly, for well over a year the courts refused to offer any but the most limited judicial review of the confinement imposed on José Padilla, also known as Abdullah al-Muhajir, an American citizen and long-term resident arrested at O'Hare airport. He was detained incommunicado for some months as a "material witness" to terrorist activities, and though officials then accused Padilla of being an "unlawful enemy combatant" involved in a "dirty bomb" plot, he continues to be incarcerated in a military facility in South Carolina without formal charges. Over Justice Department objections, the Supreme Court has agreed to review his case as well, indicating that not even the Rehnquist Court accepts the Bush administration's claim that these actions can be taken entirely without judicial review. Whether that review will amount to more than a rubber stamp remains to be seen, however. American courts have rarely done well at protecting civil liberties in the face of what they perceived as novel national security threats.

What, then, can be done to provide procedural safeguards against abuse of the heightened information sharing that we must have? The Homeland Security Act did provide for the creation of a departmental officer for civil rights and civil liberties. In September 2003, the first such officer, Daniel F. Sutherland, published a "Strategic Plan," which was, however, little more than a promissory note; it did not specify how information sharing would be accompanied by civil liberties protections.

A variety of public and private agencies are providing more concrete suggestions. The congressionally created "Gilmore Commission," formally known as the "Advisory Panel to Assess Domestic Response Capabilities for Terrorism Involving Weapons of Mass Destruction," recommended in its fifth annual report that the president "establish an independent, bipartisan civil liberties oversight board to provide advice on any change to statutory or regulatory authority . . . that has or may have civil liberties implications (even from unintended consequences)." That seems a good idea, but it is doubtful that it could suffice. The advisory board would have no enforcement powers if its advice were ignored and civil liberties invaded.

The panel also repeated a previous recommendation for "a separate domestic intelligence agency" that would be distinct from the FBI's law enforcement activities "to avoid the impression that the U.S. is establishing a kind of 'secret police.' " The report argued that the " 'sanction' authority of law enforcement agencies—the threat of prosecution and incarceration—could prevent people who have important intelligence information from coming forward and speaking freely." This proposal is more promising, because this intelligence agency would have neither arrest powers nor immigrant incarceration or deportation powers. Its separation from those activities might help ensure that persons would not be subjected to coercion on the basis of unverified rumors alone. Still, if its information continued to be pooled without adequate checks for validity, the same dangers would exist.

The Gilmore Commission suggests this new domestic intelligence agency would operate under the requirements of the Federal Intelligence Surveillance Act and the Foreign Intelligence Surveillance Court (FISC) that it creates. That court holds closed sessions and can issue secret warrants for intelligence operations. Both Harvey Rishikof, former FBI legal counsel during the Clinton administration, and Thomas F. Powers, a law professor writing in the *Weekly Standard*, have endorsed the alternative idea of a new specialized "federal security court" or "terrorism court" (possibly incorporating the FISC). It would keep anti-terrorist intelligence operations secret while also trying cases with greater procedural protections for the accused than secret military trials afford. But those protections are so far undefined; and as long as this court acted secretly and provided a virtual blank check for all types of intelligence gathering, as FISC has done, it would not be much help in protecting civil liberties.

In December 2003, the Markle Foundation, chaired by Zoë Baird, issued its own task force report, entitled "Creating a Trusted Information Network for Homeland Security." This report focused on the need to enhance information gathering and sharing capacities while also protecting civil liberties and privacy. It argued that the new Terrorist Threat Integration Center must provide "appropriate institutional mechanisms" to achieve these ends. Though these mechanisms remained vague, the Markle task force did recommend the development of standards restricting the purposes to which data could be put, especially unchecked rumors; defining how long such data could be retained; providing for means of data authentication; and establishing regulations governing access to these data. It urged the president to issue an executive order providing such guidelines. While recognizing that "increased information sharing among law enforcement and intelligence entities is critical to the counterterrorism mission," the report expressed great concern that as 2004 began, "no clear government-wide direction has been established for appropriate handling of domestic information while protecting civil liberties."

So far, the administration has not responded to these suggestions or provided any such direction. It has only repeatedly disparaged one further alternative for protecting civil liberties—an option that has, however, never been truly discredited: the existing judicial system.

Though greater information sharing is surely required, why can't we, once we begin sharing data efficiently, combat terrorism while relying on domestic and international criminal justice systems? True, terrorists are not conventional criminals, but they are criminals nonetheless. The administration insists that it is too dangerous to delay detentions and prosecutions of terrorists until law enforcement agencies can constitutionally obtain sufficient evidence of criminal conspiracy to meet "probable cause" standards for arrest and "reasonable doubt" standards for conviction. The Justice Department also contends that covert intelligence operations would be seriously hindered if accused terrorists could see the evidence and witnesses against them. And Bush officials simply distrust international criminal justice institutions, believing that they will be used for political purposes against the United States.

But again, reports by congressional investigators and private news agencies indicate that the real problems preceding the September 11 attacks were not that we used only the criminal justice system to prosecute terrorists, nor that we did not have sufficient intelligence to identify likely terrorists. The main problems were failure to share and analyze data that we had. We also have ample precedents for conducting at least partly closed criminal trials, with the identities of undercover informants and the details of intelligence operations revealed to judges, but not to the defense attorneys and the accused, when necessary to protect ongoing investigations. Are those procedures too risky at present? There is no clear evidence to that effect, only speculation. And when we are undertaking capital cases, the burden of proof must fall on those arguing for abandoning the constitutional rights that have historically been the most effective, albeit still imperfect, bulwarks of American justice. There is no clear need to suspend those rights—and data sharing itself, with the rights in force, does not increase dangers to civil liberties nearly so much. Nor does the United States have the kind of negative experience with international criminal proceedings that justifies forgoing all efforts to see if they can work.

But if the United States continues to insist that ordinary criminal justice proceedings are inadequate to combat terrorism, and if it continues to restructure myriad institutions to promote information sharing and coordinated coercion, then the government cannot in good conscience ignore the need to make sure that civil liberties are protected in this brave new world of anti-terrorism. If the United States does not establish such safeguards, then many American citizens may increasingly come to feel that they are losing precious freedoms at home, even as Americans and innocent foreign civilians continue to lose their lives in wars that seek to establish freedom abroad.

ROGERS M. SMITH is the Christopher H. Browne Distinguished Professor of Political Science at the University of Pennsylvania and the author, most recently, of *Stories of Peoplehood: The Politics and Morals of Political Membership.*

Of Crime and Punishment

Experts Explore Issues in the Legal Limelight

Criminal Justice is one of the top fields of interest for today's college students. Perhaps this popularity is based on our intense interest in criminals and law and order. In the United States we grapple every day with the concept of justice, on the streets, in the courtrooms and even in the statehouse. *FDU Magazine* asked facility and alumni to tell us what they think of some of the most high-profile issues in criminal justice today. Their answers reveal the enormously complex considerations that can tip the scales of justice.

ROBERT VODDE ET AL.

The Death Penalty

The sentencing trial of admitted al Qaeda conspirator Zacarias Moussaoui raised many issues relating to the death penalty in the United States—from mitigating circumstances and mental condition to zero tolerance for terrorism. Robert Vodde, director of the University's School of Criminal Justice and former chief of police for Leonia, N.J., explores the most critical issues relating to the death penalty.

Debates surrounding the death penalty center on religious, ethical, political, legal and utilitarian issues. But perhaps the most argued in America is whether invoking the death penalty violates the U.S. Constitution, specifically the Eighth and 14th Amendments; i.e., is it cruel and unusual punishment? In 1972, the U.S. Supreme Court, in *Georgia v. Furman*, ruled that capital punishment was unconstitutional. Four years later, however, the court reversed itself in *Gregg v. Georgia* (1976). Since that decision, close to 7,000 criminals have been sent to death row, of which more than 1,000 have been executed.

The second issue of controversy addresses whether or not putting another human to death is morally and ethically right. As Cardinal Theodore McCarrick posited, can the death penalty "offer the tragic illusion that we can teach that killing is wrong by killing?"

The third issue calls into question the utility of the death penalty; i.e., is it pragmatic? Does it succeed in deterring others from committing heinous offenses such as murder? According to Katherine Beckett and Theodore Sasson in *The Politics of Injustice: Crime and Punishment in America*, there is a conspicuous absence of empirical data to suggest that there is any relationship between capital punishment and a reduction in crime. The authors point to states such as Texas and Florida, which have high execution rates and yet also have the highest homicide rates.

And lastly, does capital punishment discriminate against society's minorities and the disenfranchised, who lack the education, financial resources and influence to provide for a defense comparable to those more fortunate? Beckett and Sasson wrote that in 13 states with death penalty laws, "significant race-of-offender bias" had been documented. Furthermore, advances in DNA technology and forensic science have revealed that many defendants have been convicted based on wrong or tainted evidence or procedural anomalies.

Despite bans on capital punishment by the European Union and Latin America, it appears that most Americans favor the death penalty, although that number seems to be changing. While 75 to 80 percent of Americans polled by Gullup in 1989 favored the death penalty, a similar poll in October 2005 showed that number had dropped to 64 percent.

Putting aside whether the killing of another person is legally, constitutionally, religiously, morally, ethically or politically "right" or "wrong," the question remains: "What is society looking to achieve by taking the life of a fellow human and why?"

Domestic Spying

Americans were forced to weigh their right to privacy with the need to combat terrorism when U.S. President George Bush acknowledged that the government had sanctioned warrantless domestic eavesdropping on Americans. Paulette Laubsch, assistant professor of administrative sciences, and Ronald Calissi, director of FDU's School of Administrative Science, address whether it is sometimes necessary to carry out domestic eavesdropping, or domestic spying, inside the United States without judicial oversight.

September 11, 2001, changed how citizens of the United States view their freedom. As security measures were either imposed or strengthened, individuals were willing to give up some of the freedoms that they have held dear for centuries, if it was good for our security and safety. But as time passes, we start questioning why we cannot do certain things, or more appropriately, why government can restrict our freedoms.

In January 2006, the president acknowledged that he had authorized the National Security Agency (NSA) to intercept international communications from known terrorist agencies. The president has used as justification the Authorization for the Use of Military Force, the Foreign Intelligence Surveillance Act and the Fourth Amendment of the Constitution. Shortly after September 11, he also signed a secret order that allowed the NSA to eavesdrop on international communications that involved both U.S. citizens and residents.

U.S. Attorney General Alberto Gonzalez has determined that existing statutes and our Constitution give legal authority to the president to conduct domestic eavesdropping for the purpose of detecting and preventing another catastrophic attack on America. In the ongoing conflict with al Qaeda and its allies, the president has a primary duty under the Constitution to protect the American people, as well as the full authority necessary to carry out that solemn duty.

Citizens may generally agree that activities involving eavesdropping on terrorists abroad are necessary to ensure our safety and security; but, some of these individuals protest domestic eavesdropping, citing the limitation of our freedoms.

There have been times when so-called spying activities were acceptable. In World War II, the government had segments of the population under investigation, monitoring correspondence and activities. This example, of course, relates to a wartime situation of a different era.

As everyone knows, technology has sped up communication. Cellular phones have become mainstream, and individuals do not need a landline to discuss their concerns or plans. Computers have become a universal method of correspondence. These modalities, including personal digital assistants (PDAs), have made it possible to communicate from anywhere to anywhere at any time. This changes how crimes are planned and carried out. Crime fighting must also change.

Americans need to trust government to do what is necessary to keep the citizenry safe, and that can include warrantless domestic eavesdropping.

Police Profiling

But how does one know from whom we need to be protected? African-Americans in New Jersey have alleged that they have been unfairly targeted for police checks. More recently, Americans of Middle Eastern descent have felt the eye of the law has unfairly profiled them. Are there some cases where institutional or systematic profiles can be legally justifiable? James Kenny, associate professor of criminal justice and a retired supervisory treasury officer, offers his view.

When used properly, profiles are legitimate and effective law-enforcement tools. Most list various personality traits and behaviors associated with a group of persons who have committed crimes in the past. However, as human conduct is affected by many complex and ever-changing variables, these traits and behaviors cannot consistently predict the future behavior of specific individuals. Criminal conduct is more dependent on at-risk

individuals possessing the means, motive and ability to commit the offenses.

Profiles used to identify future criminal behaviors can cause great harm. Attempts to single out potentially violent individuals can stigmatize, traumatize and encourage already-troubled persons to act out, making profiling a self-fulfilling prophecy. And, profiling individuals is not very accurate at predicting extreme violence. At-risk individuals are unlikely to commit violence without various environmental, social and interpersonal factors interacting with each other and becoming more serious over time.

Despite the limitations of profiles, their use can alert authorities that an individual may need help and monitoring. The frequency, intensity and immediacy of the at-risk behaviors should dictate the type of intervention. In the less serious cases, the subject should not be viewed as potentially violent, but rather as an individual in need of assistance. At-risk individuals that are identified and helped promptly are unlikely to resort to violence.

Patriot Act

Soon after September 11, the House of Representatives and the Senate passed legislation granting new law-enforcement privileges through the USA Patriot Act. Are all of the privileges granted to the government by the act constitutional? FDU Magazine sought out Kimberly Scrio, BA'04 (T), a paralegal with Casey & Barnett, LLC, in New York City, to answer this question, which was the topic of her FDU honors thesis.

During times of national crisis the government is entrusted with the authority to implement any and all means necessary to secure the safety of the people. But at what point do the people begin to question the actions of government?

On October 26, 2001, both the U.S. House of Representatives and the Senate overwhelmingly passed the USA Patriot Act—343 pages of amendments and additions to previous laws designed to eliminate potential barriers in fighting terrorism.

According to the Department of Justice Web site, the Patriot Act "improves our counterterrorism efforts in several significant ways." It allows authorities to use tools already in use against organized crime and drug trafficking to investigate terrorist activities, facilitates information sharing among government agencies and updates existing law to reflect new technology and technological threats. In addition, the act imposes harsher penalties for those convicted of committing terrorist crimes.

The American Civil Liberties Union (ACLU) asserts that the Patriot Act tramples on the civil liberties of American citizens in several ways. The organization says the act violates the Fourth Amendment, which requires government to show probable cause before obtaining a search warrant. Second, the act violates the First Amendment by imposing a gag order on public employees required to provide government with their clients' personal information. The act also violates the First Amendment by effectively authorizing the FBI to investigate American citizens for, in part, exercising their freedom of speech. And, it eliminates the requirement for government to provide notice to individuals whose privacy has been compromised by a government investigation.

The act does intrude on an individual's right to privacy, but only in cases where the government suspects the individual is involved in terrorist-related activity. If the government is suspicious of an individual's activities, should it not have the ability to investigate that individual? Theoretically, law-abiding citizens will never have to worry about their right to privacy being violated because their activities will never be suspicious.

On the other hand, the Patriot Act does have the potential to trample on citizens' constitutional rights. The act relies on trusting investigators not to intrude upon these rights. Therefore, a strong argument can be made against the act, because, although government officials may not be currently abusing the act, the potential for abuse exists.

Thus the proverbial question once again arises. Should the people entrust the government with the authority granted by the USA Patriot Act in the name of national security, or should the people revolt against the Patriot Act for fear of potential government abuse? The fate of our national security may very well rest upon the answer.

Excessive Force

The use of force by the police has long been a contentious issue. Since the widely publicized Rodney King beating in Los Angeles, major efforts have been made to ensure such incidents do not take place. Patrick Reynolds, assistant director of the School of Criminal Justice, explains the measures taken to combat the use of excessive force.

Without a doubt, the most controversial issue in American policing is the use of force by police officers. On too many occasions, we have seen newspaper headlines reporting that an individual has been brutalized or, worse yet, killed by the police. The consequences of excessive and deadly force have been severe, affecting both police organizations and the communities they serve.

To reduce the occurrence of such incidents, better training and accountability mechanisms have been put in place. Police recruits are being taught that the level of force that they employ should only rise to the level of resistance being offered by a suspect.

Officers are trained to employ a continuum of force that ranges from the least amount, which would be the officer's mere presence, to the other extreme, the use of deadly force. Often the mere presence of a police officer will get most citizens to conform to the law. When an officer meets resistance from a suspect, that officer is legally authorized to escalate the level of force employed, depending on the resistance received from the suspect. The continuum of force ranges from an officer's presence to verbalization, command voice, firm grips, pain compliance, impact techniques and, finally, deadly force.

In addition, officers are taught to control their emotions in volatile confrontations and to utilize force only as needed. The most important issue regarding use of force is whether it was justified and consistent with the resistance being offered. The decision of whether or not to use force is an instantaneous one—and one of the most challenging situations a police officer may encounter. An incorrect decision by a police officer cannot be recalled.

In the vast majority of confrontations requiring the use of force, officers respond in a professional nature and utilize force that is justified. It is the few exceptions where officers overreact and use inappropriate force that seem to capture the media's attention.

Police organizations have gone to great lengths to minimize the number of instances where officers employ excessive force. The stringent hiring processes employed by police agencies exemplify this. Competitive testing, psychological screening and extensive background checks are being employed. Both recruit training and in-service training for seasoned officers focus on making good choices, maintaining professional standards and bridging the gap that has existed for many years between the community and the police.

Law enforcement and police behavior have come a long way in the past decade and will continue to improve, so long as there is full disclosure and analysis of police conduct—both positive and negative.

The War on Drugs

Has the War on Drugs been won or merely forgotten in favor of more dramatic issues? FDU Magazine *asked Richard Gray, assistant professor of criminal justice and a retired substance abuse treatment coordinator for the U.S. Probation Department in Brooklyn, "Are U.S. drug laws effectively reducing the impact of drug use and abuse on our society?"*

The best measurement of the effectiveness of the "War on Drugs" comes from the White House Office of National Drug Control Policy (ONDCP), which states, "The goals of the program are to reduce illicit drug use, manufacturing and trafficking, drug-related crime and violence, and drug-related health consequences."

If we focus on the most basic questions—"Is drug use down?" "Is crime down?" and "Are drugs less available?"—the answer to our larger question becomes apparent.

Drug use. According to National Household Survey on Drug Abuse (NHSDA) drug use by persons over age 12 has remained relatively stable since 1988 (the year the "Drug War" began). During this period, the number of persons who reported drug use in the previous month or the previous year has remained unchanged and the number of persons reporting any drug use has increased by about 7 million.

The organization Monitoring the Future examines access to drugs, drug use and attitudes toward drugs of the nation's junior and senior high school students. According to its 2005 study, there were minor declines in substance abuse by older teens, but previous declines in use among eighth graders had stopped. More importantly, the changes themselves were not statistically significant—they could be explained by chance alone. For all intents and purposes, there was no reduction in substance abuse among school children.

Drug-related crime. In general, crime is down in the United States. According to the Bureau of Justice Statistics, it has decreased significantly since 1993. However, since 1995, drug-related arrests have stayed relatively stable at approximately 1.5 million per year. Although reporting slightly lower arrest rates, the Bureau also reported that arrests for drug abuse violations increased steadily between 1991 and 1996 and remained stable from 1997 to 2005.

Drug availability. If supply is down, you cannot tell by the responses of high school students. The 2005 Monitoring the Future study found that marijuana was judged to be easy or very easy to get by 85 percent of 12th graders. LSD was perceived as less available; however, other hallucinogens have increased steadily in availability. On the brighter side, almost 8 percent fewer 12th graders than in the previous year perceived MDMA (ecstasy) to be fairly easy or easy to get. Despite this, cocaine, crack, hallucinogens, MDMA and amphetamines were rated as easily accessible by between 40 and 50 percent of students.

The government spends about $13 billion per year in its war against drugs. Have they been successful in stopping or significantly impacting substance abuse? Has the drug war decreased drug-related crime? Is the availability of illegal substances down? Insofar as the "War on Drugs" metaphor has failed us, we had best begin to think of a new strategy.

Global Co-op Feeds FBI's Botnet Fight

The FBI claims that fighting cybercrime is a top priority, right behind antiterrorism and counterintelligence, and it is seeing better results thanks to worldwide cooperation.

MATT HINES

Officials with the FBI claim that global law enforcement partnerships are playing a significant role in its ongoing efforts to stomp out botnets and other computer-borne crimes.

Security researchers have long maintained that one of the most significant obstacles to shutting down botnets is the distributed global nature of the individuals responsible for operating the networks of zombie PCs.

Botnets are banks of computers infected by virus programs that allow them to be secretly used to carry out many forms of electronic attacks.

The conventional wisdom has been that U.S. law enforcement officials have struggled to find the budget and manpower necessary to track down cyber-criminals operating on their own turf, let alone find a way to identify and arrest people distributing malware code or operating botnets who are based in foreign nations.

However, hot on the heels of its announcement of a round of arrests of U.S.-based botnet herders and the identification of over one million machines infected by the programs, FBI officials said that international cooperation is playing an increasingly important role in helping it stomp out cyber-crime.

"We've been successful in building relationships with foreign law enforcement officials and have agents in 60 countries around the globe working full time on cyber-crime along with police departments and other agencies," said Shawn Henry, deputy assistant director of the Cyber Division at the FBI. "We've seen some significant developments over the last few years in that area."

While Henry admitted that the very nature of cutting-edge botnet herders can make them hard to find as perpetrators move from one bank of infected machines to another quickly to avoid detection, he said that partnerships with foreign governments in the name of fighting cyber-crime are playing a vital role in aiding the agency's ability to thwart the attacks.

"This type of crime can be committed by someone with minimal resources, sometimes using publicly available tools, which makes it a challenge to identify who is responsible, but international cooperation has allowed us to pursue these efforts in many countries, and we are also helping other nations fight operators located in the U.S. as this is a problem that goes both ways," Henry said.

Rounded up by the agency in its most recent botnet hunt were Robert Alan Soloway of Seattle, who has been tabbed as one of the nation's leading sources of botnet-driven spam e-mail, along with James C. Brewer of Arlington, Texas, who is alleged to have infected several Chicago-area hospitals with botnet programs, and Jason Michael Downey of Covington, Kentucky, who is charged with running botnets that were used to carry out so-called denial-of-service attacks.

Taking such individuals offline has become a task secondary only to fighting terrorists and spies, according to Henry, who said that the FBI's current leadership is very much focused on expanding its ability to battle cyber-criminals.

Whereas the perception within the IT security community has been that computer-based attacks are further down the agency's pecking order and that its efforts to stop such crimes lack the same financial backing as its other pursuits, Henry said that the FBI is taking the problem more seriously than ever before.

"Cyber crime is our number three priority behind antiterrorism and counter-intelligence, we devote a lot of resources to it, and Director Mueller sees it as a significant criminal problem and is very supportive of our efforts," said Henry. "We also get ample support from the U.S. Department of Justice and have been successful with the legal tools that are being made available to us."

Despite making headway, Henry said that the battle against botnets and other forms of cyber-crime remains an "electronic cat and mouse game" as once law enforcement officials and the security community identify and block one technique being used by schemers, the perpetrators tend to move on to some newer modus operandi.

The FBI assistant director said that as part of the agency's effort to stop botnets and other attacks, it is hoping that businesses and consumers will become more vigilant and aggressive in lending a hand by keeping their computers protected with the latest anti-virus programs.

The agency is also advising potential victims of cyber-crime to pursue investigation of such activity by contacting their Internet service providers, and the FBI has said publicly that people should report any suspected illegal activity to such companies rather than communicating problems directly to itself or other law enforcement organizations.

Security industry experts lauded the FBI's work to identify and detain hackers as part of its Operation Bot Roast, which led to the arrests of Soloway, Brewer, and Downey, but at least one authority said that the agency may be creating false expectations of relief for businesses and consumers by telling them to fight crimes via their ISPs.

Web access providers, particularly those that cater to residential markets, have minimized help desk support to save overhead costs, and customers may find themselves with little recourse or being asked to pay for additional security services when they call their ISPs to complain, said Danny McPherson, chief research officer at security filtering specialists Arbor Networks. Arbor provides network behavior analysis tools to a number of well-known ISPs, including AT&T, British Telecom, EarthLink, and NTT.

In addition to leaving customers unsatisfied with their ability to respond to attacks, and potentially driving ISPs with minimal support budgets out of business, asking the service providers to become the de facto police for stopping botnet activity is impractical for a number of reasons, McPherson said.

"You tend to see a lot of people, not just law enforcement, calling for quarantines of suspected botnet infected IP addresses, but you can't just start blocking legitimate users who may not know they are involved, what if you stop someone from making a VoIP-based emergency services call?" McPherson questioned. "If someone gets blocked by their ISP, they're going to move to another provider; systems and solutions to automate the security defenses needed to address this problem are being developed, but it will take time, and most infrastructure out there won't natively support that sort of work today."

McPherson said that it is encouraging to see cooperation between U.S. law enforcement officials and foreign nations, but he believes that the botnet issue will remain a major problem nonetheless.

"It's good to see that there is more global information sharing going on, and that local governments are taking responsibility for cleaning up their own backyards, but with millions of bot hosts and more than 90 percent of those outside the U.S., I think they're still only putting a tiny dent in the problem at his point," said McPherson.

Other security industry experts agreed that it will take a lot more effort on the part of the international law enforcement community to have any noticeable impact on botnets and other cyber-criminals.

However, efforts such as Bot Roast will succeed in forcing botnet operators to increasingly worry that they may indeed be brought to justice for the crimes they commit, said Alan Paller, director of research for IT security training provider SANS Institute.

"At his point, the law enforcement community still can't get much done because so many of the perpetrators are located in so many places where there are no cooperative agreements," he said. "But what they are doing is increasing the risk and raising the cost of committing the crimes, which is just what law enforcement is good at; in the end they can't ever really stop people from trying to rob banks, but they can make it really dangerous and costly, just as they always have tried to."

Toward a Transvaluation of Criminal 'Justice': On Vengeance, Peacemaking, and Punishment

CHRISTOPHER R. WILLIAMS

Reflexive Statement

As both teacher and scholar of criminal "justice," I am continually reminded of a profound absence in popular and academic discourse on crime and justice. What seems conspicuous to me by its absence seems to others assumed and expected in its absence. The reactions I receive from students and colleagues at the very mention of attitudes and practices such as compassion, forgiveness, and mercy when mentioned in the context of criminal justice are surprising if not discouraging. I continue to be troubled by the degree to which resentment and retribution seem "natural" and expected to students, scholars, and practitioners of criminal justice. I am equally troubled by the degree to which prosocial, life-affirming values such as compassion and forgiveness are absent in the same discursive spheres. This essay reflects my continuing effort to understand the dynamics of anger, hatred, and violence that permeate not only the system of criminal justice, but human relations on all levels.

Introduction

> For *that man be delivered from revenge*, that is for me the bridge to the highest hope, and a rainbow after long storms.
>
> Nietzsche, *Thus Spoke Zarathustra*, II, 7

Human civilization displays a storied history of vengeance, cruelty, and other manifestations of the passion for justice (e.g., Jacoby, 1983; Solomon, 1989). The passion for justice, however, does not often beget justice. History is replete with suggestions that it has been and is far more likely to perpetuate vicious cycles of injustice, inhumanity, and regressing human welfare (e.g., Fuller, 1998). In place of extirpating such a cycle, "civilized" society has merely institutionalized and, consequently, legitimated this passion. The perpetuity of "wars" on crime and drugs, for example, can be regarded as indicative of a broader and deeper cultural ethos—one

characterized by anger, hatred, and a desire for vengeance and cathartic punishment of the identified "enemy." In manifest form, such sensibilities have contributed to increases in such criminal justice practices as mandatory minimum and determinate sentencing, justified or excused violations of human rights at the hands of police, court, and correctional officials, increased reliance on the death penalty, and a more general polarization of the rehabilitative sentiments prevalent in the 1950's and 1960's. As Bentham (1948) offered, such instances of institutionalized punitiveness are no less "evil" or violent than their non-legitimated counterparts; and, as Quinney (2000) reminds us, evil conceives only more and greater evil and violence conceives only more violence.

Understanding the problematic use of violence in the contemporary United States—particularly its appearance as an element of "justice"—requires acknowledging the permeation of the passion for vengeance at all levels of humanity and, further, the practice and perpetuation of such an ethos by the very institutions that are designed to remedy it. If criminal "justice" is to appear less as an instrument of cyclic maintenance and more as a means of promoting, affirming, and restoring social welfare, it should be conceptually reconstrued as and practically re-directed toward *overcoming* its historically impassioned underpinnings. In the interest of fostering nonviolent, cooperative, and healthy human relationships at every level of humanity—from intrapersonal through global—what is necessary is a transvaluation of criminal justice. A transvaluation entails an identification and reconsideration of the existing values that inform understandings, policies, and practices of criminal justice. More accurately, such a reconstitution entails recognition of the absence of affirmative values in the logic upon which practices of criminal justice are premised. Transvaluation implies that such a reconsideration occur, not only, but especially in the face of accepted morality and ethical practice. It requires an appeal to the "human" when current

21

practice, popular sensibilities and public desire demand the less-than-human.

A transvaluation of criminal justice, I will argue, requires acknowledging the primacy of *resentment* as the basis for much criminal justice policy and practice. Despite claims that the system of criminal justice operates in a reasoned, objective fashion, its underlying logic is the beneficiary of a tradition and culture that allows passion an integral role in the *concept* of justice itself. What becomes necessary is not mere embodiment of humanistic values in the agents of justice and the practices in which they engage but, rather, a corrective conceptualization of what criminal "justice" *is*.

Resentment is a multifaceted phenomenon, operating as a complex interplay of psychological (human emotion), cultural (social), and institutional (state policies and practices), which inform and are subsequently informed by human emotion and cultural reality. If resentment is acknowledged as a basis for harmful social attitudes and practices, what becomes more important is the displacement of such sentiments. Criminal "justice," in the interest of fostering a new ethos of affirmative social relations, requires a conceptual turn that overcomes resentment. As Jeffrie Murphy (1982) notes following Bishop Butler, overcoming resentment is, by definition, the basis of *forgiveness*. Forgiveness, in turn, serves as a psychological foundation for the institutional practice of *mercy*.

Forgiveness and mercy can be understood as keys to a reconstituted ideal of criminal "justice"—as humanistic alternatives to the institutionalization of anger and the desire for vengeance. Overcoming resentment, embodying forgiveness, and practicing mercy are certain to be met with staunch public disapproval. The tension existing on the political level is one of felt pressure from the public "to go to the upper limits of punishment" (Misner, 2000: 1306). Yet it is precisely when faced with such pressures and potential disapproval that the courage to do what is "just" is most necessary. In what follows, I offer a conceptual exploration of resentment, forgiveness, and mercy, attending in particular to distinctions necessary to insulate the latter from popular misconceptions as to their true character. While my primary focus is on criminal "justice," the importance of forgiveness and mercy should not be read as limited to that realm. Rather, overcoming resentment and a subsequent regard for forgiveness and mercy should be understood as essential concerns for the promotion of non-violent, compassionate, and benevolent relations in all spheres of human existence.

Resentment and the Passion for Justice

The relationship between resentment and criminal justice lies in the latter's use of vengeance as philosophically justified retribution. Though scholarly debate concerning the philosophy of punishment has attempted to distinguish between a retributive philosophy of punishment and punishment as vengeance (e.g., Primoratz, 1989), the latter inevitably

permeates our varied rationalizations of criminal punishment. Most forms of crime induce emotional reactions of anger and hatred in the experiencing and witnessing public. It is inevitable that public desire for emotional satisfaction or catharsis informs the political climate of the country (Misner, 2000: 1340). The logic applied in popular discourse concerning, for example, the death penalty and the desire for harsher punishment of criminal offenders is informed, not often by a rationally deduced logic of retribution, but by a "pre-philosophical intuition" (*ibid:* n139) or unreasoned desire to inflict harm upon those who have harmed "us."

To this degree, punishment is a political reality more than a philosophical one (e.g., Fairchild & Webb, 1985). The posture of the system of justice is in part a reflection of public desire and demand (e.g., Fuller, 1998). As a political reality, crime and justice cannot escape embodiment of popular sensibilities; and, in turn, as a social reality, popular sensibilities cannot escape embodiment of the political reality of crime and justice. As the social informs the political, so too does political rhetoric and corresponding institutional practice give force to the emotions, passions, and beliefs of the populous. Institutional practices effectively promote a broader cultural ethos that shapes not only public opinion, but human relationships on the level of community, family, and individual as well. The relationship between the social and the political with regard to "justice," then, is one of interdependence. As such, the relationship between resentment and criminal justice exists on several interrelated levels: anger as human emotion; the desire for vengeance as cultural ethos dictating appropriate experience and expression of such emotions; and cathartic retribution as an institutionalized characteristic of criminal "justice."

Resentment

"Resentment" refers to some negative feeling or feelings directed toward some person, persons, or organized collection of persons (e.g., social groups, cultures, institutions) that we perceive to have harmed us in some fashion. The negative feelings associated with resentment are often those of anger and hatred. What is significant is that the passion for vengeance is not equivalent to resentment; rather, the passion for vengeance is an incentive to action where resentment is the motivating psychological force. Aristotle suggested that what we think of as anger is doubly constituted: it entails both a belief that one has been wronged; as well as a subsequent belief that harming s/he or those responsible is desirable (i.e. wishing ill on the perpetrator) (Nussbaum, 1994: 90, 243). The two elements of what is commonly understood as anger are not one and the same. The initial experience of anger toward an offender and the subsequent desire to harm that offender in return (i.e. retaliation, vengeance) are distinct—though interrelated—aspects of the same psychological event. Anger does not necessarily entail a desire to retaliate, nor is anger sufficient to induce such a desire. To seek or wish harm upon an offending other requires either the absence of a moderating force of intervention, and/or the presence of an aggravating force of intervention.

Anger is often regarded as a problematic emotion in that it often involves a "desire to harm others . . . and so may lead to all sorts of problems for individuals, their community, and our society at large" (Lazarus and Lazarus, 1994: 13). Yet this desire occurs subsequent to the experience of anger. Anger itself may be a natural, human response to a *demeaning offense against me or mine*" (Lazarus & Lazarus, 1994: 20). The problematics of anger lie not in the emotional experience, but in the often corresponding retaliatory impulse. The desire for vengeance is not a visceral reaction; rather, anger is a visceral reaction and the desire for vengeance emerges only if the experience of anger is left unmoderated or unchecked. In such instances, anger—through desire—can find embodiment in individual and/or institutional behavior (i.e. decisions, policies, and practices). It is at this point where anger becomes troublesome—if not overtly harmful—to other persons, communities and society as a whole.

In addition to having an affective basis in individual psychology, resentment also entails a social psychological dynamic. The "me or mine" in the above quotation from Lazarus and Lazarus (1994) suggests that the harm arousing anger need not directly lead to our own suffering. It is reasonable to assume that when offended others are *not* perceived to be "like us" (i.e. as one of "mine"), the resentment felt and the desire for retaliatory action will not be similarly experienced. It is for this reason, perhaps, that many injustices or harms against other nations, races, ethnicities, species, etc. can be and are often trivialialized, while similar harms endured by those of our own nation, race, ethnicity, or species are magnified in terms of our emotional experience, the perceived degree of harm and suffering, and in our subsequent desire for action in the name of "justice." The most extreme scenario of this sort involves an offender who is "not like us" and a victim who is "like us." In this scenario, the experience of resentment and the passion for vengeance are likely experienced in excess. European-Americans, for example, have been shown to have more punitive attitudes toward criminals, especially when contrasted with attitudes of racial and ethnic minorities toward criminals. It has been suggested, for example, that such punitiveness reflects a broader prejudice harbored by European-Americans toward minorities more generally (Cohn, et al. 1991). European-Americans often understand or experience crime as a minority problem—i.e. a problem caused by minorities in that most criminals are perceived to be minorities (*ibid*). If crime can be understood as a problem caused by "them" which affects "us," it is likely that "we" will be less tolerant, understanding, forgiving and, consequently, more punitive. When such "us versus them" attitudes pervade a given culture, it is likely that resentment and the desire for vengeance against "them" will be an integral component of a generalized cultural ethos.

Culture and Resentment

In reference to Marongiu and Newman's (1987) exposition of the Sardinian Code of Vengeance, Solomon (1990: 247) suggests that, "the idea that vengeance is a primitive emotion or even an instinct neglects the enormous amount of cultural stimulation, support, and structure, as well as some semblance of legitimacy vengeance receives from particular social rules and expectations." Sardinian "justice" is centered around the core belief that retaliation is a personal or family matter—not one of institutionalized punishment. Though affective anger is often regarded as a universal human experience, culture invariably plays a role in how we experience and express it. The desire for vengeance and the expression of such desires appears subsequent to the initial affective experience and, unlike anger, cannot be regarded as universal nor purely natural. Culture both informs shapes, and provides a cognitive framework for assessing which offenses are appropriately responded to in anger, as well as informing and shaping the ways in which emotions are to be expressed and controlled (Lazarus & Lazarus, 1994).

As an expression of the desire for vengeance, violence and punishment as a form of violence are choices involving a cognitive dimension—the thought and belief that the offending other should be harmed. In this way, "punishment can no more be identified with revenge 'than love can be identified with lust' " (Misner, 2000: 1339). To exemplify this point, we can point to the historical character of the U.S. as one that has condoned aggression, violence and, more generally, "accomplishment of desired ends over a concern for legitimate and humane means" (Fuller, 1998: 164). Americans are taught that violence has been and is necessary as a means to achieve (or maintain) a desired state of affairs. Interestingly, Americans do not often acknowledge violence and aggression as a socially and morally desirable component of our value system. As Brown (1990) notes, violence has become part of our "underground" value system. While we are formally objectionable to the use of violence, we are quick to condone the use of violence if it is regarded as necessary in a given context. Not coincidentally the context within which violence has historically garnered the most support as a means to an end is that of war. It is popularly believed that violence is necessary in times of war. Should we be surprised, then, to find increasing levels of violence being condoned if not demanded by the public in the context of the ongoing "war" on crime? In short, violence appears as an inherent feature of the national character of the United States and has created a culture of violence wherein individual thoughts, feelings, and behaviors concerning violence are shaped in a manner consistent with cultural values. Though we are all prone to feel anger, the ways in which we experience and express our anger is shaped by culture. If vengeance and violence are culturally valued as "just" expressions of anger, we are likely to find aggression and violence at all levels of human relationships, from intra- and interpersonal through institutional and global.

The "War On Crime" as Institutionalized Resentment

Resentment becomes institutionalized to the extent that it finds embodiment in the rhetoric, policies and practices of our social institutions (e.g., the criminal justice system). Equally, if not more, problematic is the mutuality of the relationship between culture and institution. We should not consider the impact of human emotion on the system of justice without lending some attention to the impact of the system of justice on human emotion and desires based on those emotions. The system of justice not only expresses popular sentiment, but serves to define and shape popular sensibilities concerning crime and justice. The prevailing "war on crime" exemplifies this bilaterality with regard to affect and desire.

The "war" perspective on crime and justice has increasingly evidenced itself in various criminal justice practices as well as professional and popular sensibilities. Despite the fact that the ongoing "war" on social problems (e.g., crime, drugs, poverty) is merely a metaphorical war, it is one that has had a profound effect on the way we conceive of social problems and their solutions. The way we understand and experience crime, criminals, and justice becomes more consistent with the way we understand and experience war. The issue, however, is not how the "war on crime" has been used as an instrument of distortion but, rather, the *effect* that such an instrument has had on public perception and criminal justice practices.

Fuller (1998: 22) suggests that war rhetoric is intended to "mobilize the population to attack social problems." I would add that it is intended to impassion the population with a desire for vengeance by appealing to fears, vulnerabilities, and universal (negative) human emotions. While the anger we experience in relation to crime is not outside the realm of human nature, political rhetoric maintains the force necessary to define and mold such emotions and, further, to lend impetus to desires stemming from them. In particular, the "war" on crime engenders a belief that vengeance is an acceptable solution to human problems—not only should we experience resentment toward crime and criminals, but we should succumb to the passion to express that resentment by "fighting fire with fire."

Throughout this process, several effects become notable. First, the war on crime encourages the public to experience persons who violate criminal law and other social norms as "enemies," thus perpetuating the circulation of an "us and them" mentality and actuating a process of dehumanization. "Oftentime I have heard you speak of one who commits a wrong," in Gibran's (1923) words, "as though he were not one of you, but a stranger unto you and an intruder upon your world." To the degree that social reality is understood in terms of divisions of good and evil wherein "evil" is something other than ourselves, we lose our greater capacity to experience ourselves as part of the greater whole of humanity. In instances of criminal offense, any initial experience of compassion and understanding toward the suffering of the offender is easily negated by consideration for the suffering of the victim(s). The "us and them" mentality effectively establishes an ethic of sympathy for "us" at the expense of similar possibilities for "them." The latter sympathies, however, are essential to human welfare to the extent that they reflect an understanding of universal interconnectedness and a need for globalized compassion.

Failure to recognize and embody such a realization is demonstrably harmful on all levels. On a global level, for example, the "us versus them" mentality manifests as war between nations, races, religions, and even civil wars within nations, races, religions, etc. On a social level, it manifests as racism, ethnocentrism, and justifies exclusion, expulsion, and other forms of prejudice and overt discrimination. Most importantly, on the level of criminal justice, the "us versus them" mentality creates a social environment wherein policies of excess are practiced and condoned, if not demanded, by the public whose hypothetical "orderly community" is being threatened by "outsiders," "enemies," or simply "evil" people. As a result of the dissemination of these attitudes, we are further alienated from the experience of ourselves as part of the greater whole of humanity.

This has several significant consequences both within the criminal justice system and without. First, an "us and them" attitude toward others inhibits, if not destroys, our capacity to empathize and, thus, the possibility of compassion. Compassion is as much part of human nature as anger. As anger requires culture to shape its experience and expression, compassion requires culture to encourage its manifest existence as an integral component of human relationships. If our ability to identify with the "other" is destroyed, our ability to be compassionate toward the "other" is destroyed; if our capacity for compassion is destroyed, justice is destroyed. Secondly, the "us and them" mentality justifies treatment of persons who violate the criminal law as "enemies," "them," or something less-than-human. This, in turn, encourages or, at least, makes possible the condonation of excess in our treatment of such persons. Excess, in this context, manifests as ruthlessness, cruelty, and other injustices of the extreme. In addition, it encourages implementation of policies and practices that place less emphasis on fairness as opposed to desired ends (i.e. retribution). The last of these consequences implicates a problematic emphasis of the criminal justice system—namely, an emphasis on "doing" rather than "being." A transvaluation of criminal justice establishes the necessity of reversing this emphasis and, subsequently, a consideration of forgiveness and mercy as bases for the policies and practices of criminal justice.

Overcoming Resentment: Toward a Transvaluation of Criminal "Justice"

Within resentment is embedded a near inevitable propensity for the creation of further harm. Consequently, *overcoming* resentment is more and more a "humanitarian imperative," embodiment of which seems one of the few means of "recaptur[ing] a sense of humaneness" (Misner, 2000: 1306) on every level and in every sphere of human existence. In many ways, this means going beyond or rising above the passion for "justice." In the remainder of this essay, I focus on two interrelated "humanitarian imperatives:" forgiveness and mercy. Both are exercises in overcoming that offer means of going beyond the passion for justice. While reclaiming the attitude of forgiveness and practices of mercy are essential concerns at every level of human relating, they carry special significance at the institutional level. Forgiveness and mercy, like resentment, are contagious. As "educator" (e.g., Fromm, 1930), the State is positioned to effect both cultural and individual practices by way of example. To the degree that resentment and vengeance inform legal and penal responses to crime, forgiveness and mercy become imperative considerations as affirmative antitheses: forgiveness in our attitudes toward the offenses of others; and mercy in our treatment of the offenses of others.

Forgiveness and Attitudes Toward the Offenses of Others

I have suggested, following Aristotle, that responses to the offenses of others are not often merely affective, but also entail a cognitive component. The emotional experience of anger is not inexorably entwined to the belief or desire that another should be harmed as a consequence of her or his offense. The initial experience of anger following the experience or witness of wrongdoing may well be justified; yet the subsequent experience of resentment and consequent desire to harm s/he who is responsible for such sufferings is not inevitable. Rather, it is largely a learned *expression* of anger that is perpetuated and justified by broader cultural and institutional dynamics. As such, it becomes important to recognize alternative possibilities with regard to attitudes toward the offenses of others.

On the ethical spectrum, forgiveness lies opposite resentment. Forgiveness warrants special attention in that it is too often and too easily misinterpreted and subject to dismissal as a desirable attitude and practice. Forgiveness does not entail erasing some wrong nor erasing some wrong from the memory of either the offender or the victim. To forgive does not necessarily mean to forget. What forgiveness requires is that we "cease to hate" (Comte-Sponville, 2001: 119), or, cease to resent. The attitude of forgiveness carries no implication that one who has been wronged is in some way unjustified in *initial* feelings of anger. Instead, it asks that one *overcome* such contextually justified human emotions. It does not ask that we not *feel* anger nor that, consequent to being harmed, we never *have* desires for punishment and revenge. Forgiveness asks that, from the intrapersonal to the institutional and global spheres of human relating, we overcome that which is all too human in the emotional realm.

The value of forgiveness, then, lies in its role as a mediator between emotion and action. Unlike anger, forgiveness is not purely affective. Forgiveness stands alongside the cognitive component of anger—that which entails thoughts and beliefs related to the experience and expression of anger. In this regard, forgiveness is that which overcomes the experience of resentment and prohibits the realization in action of the desire for vengeance. In other words, forgiveness does not *replace* anger, but "checks" it. We may experience anger and be justified in our experience of anger, yet "not revengeful . . . [but] . . . inclined to be forgiving" (Aristotle, 1976: 161 [1126al-3]). Ignoring, overlooking, or forgetting an offense is indicative of an absence of anger. Yet anger may itself be regarded as desirable in that the *experience of anger is necessary for forgiveness*. What is problematic is the character of the experienced anger.

Aristotle suggested that anger be felt "in the right manner" and "for the right length of time." "The right manner" of anger is a core obstacle in both human relationships as well as justice. Resentment is often inappropriate in that it is directed toward wrongs or harms that are objectively trivial, but subjectively experienced as wicked, sinister, or evil. In other cases, though harms may not be trivial, there is considerable discord between subjective and objective assessments of the degree of harm. As Baumeister (1997) suggests, the anger experienced by a victim is rarely if ever in agreement with either the experience of the offender or even an objective assessment of the harm. There is a "magnitude gap" between victim and offender in terms of the experience of a harmful incident (*ibid*). Such differences in perception and emotional experience can often lead to excessive anger, hatred, and set the stage for excess in expression of anger.

Experiencing the offender as an "enemy" or, perhaps, "evil," "possessed," or a psychopath is the easiest means to dehumanize, distance oneself from the offender and, consequently, condone if not demand excessive treatment. Nussbaum (1994: 404) alludes to such a state of alienation from fellow human beings in quoting General Schwartzkopf on the Gulf War: "Look, these Iraqis are no better than animals. They are not up to our standards of civilization, they don't really belong to the same species. So it was good that we killed as many of them as we did, wasn't it? And it will be fine at any time to kill a lot more." Schwartzkopf's reference implicates, not only anger, but the manifestation of anger in action—it is illustrative of how easy it can be to "slip" from appropriate and justified anger to the excessive and unjustified (*ibid*: 403–04). Anger often becomes problematic in cases wherein some wrong was done and anger is a legitimate and justified response, yet the anger is not proportionate to the degree of harm.

A deficiency in our attitude toward the offenses of others, then, would entail ignoring or forgetting the offense(s). Deficiency is an important consideration in discourse on forgiveness in light of the popular belief that forgiveness amounts to overlooking or forgetting the offense. Forgiveness asks no such impossibility. As a "golden mean" (Aristotle, 1976) between the two undesirable extremes of deficiency and excess, forgiveness does not require us to be deficient in our attitudes toward the offenses of others, nor does it allow for excess in those same attitudes. Yet excess is arguably embedded in the attitudes currently prevalent in the criminal justice system and society at large. Resentment and desires for revenge (alternately, vengeance, retribution, or "justice") are characteristic attitudes of excess when applied to offenses of others. The "golden mean" in such cases is that of forgiveness, understood as justifiable anger, yet overcoming the hatred and desire for revenge that are all-too-common when understanding and forgiveness are absent. Forgiveness should not be understood as a natural and universal emotion, but as that which overcomes the natural human emotion of anger and checks the desire for vengeance. Because the embodiment of forgiveness in all spheres of human existence—from self to society—is an integral component of an affirmative, humanistic cultural ethos, it is essential that forgiveness find embodiment on the institutional level. Overcoming resentment at the institutional level is a question of policy and practice, however, not human psychology. In the former, embodiment of forgiveness manifests as the practice of mercy.

Mercy and Treatment of the Offenses of Others

Mercy can be understood as institutionalized forgiveness. Mercy is, by definition, "the virtue that triumphs over rancor, over justified hatred . . . over resentment, over the desire for revenge or punishment" (Comte-Sponville, 2001: 119). Mercy is that which offsets, balances, or "checks" the vice of vengeance already embedded in public consciousness and legal and penal policy and practice. For this reason, as Comte-Sponville suggests, mercy goes *beyond* justice. It asks more than justice insofar as that which it overcomes is that which is *justified*. Like forgiveness, however, it is important to understand what mercy is not. While mercy is a desirable and essential practice for human welfare, it is as much prone to misinterpretation as forgiveness.

Mercy is, first, not forgiveness. Mercy is better defined as treating others less harshly than we have the right to do by law, rule, tradition, etc. (Murphy, 1982). Unlike forgiveness, mercy involves the *expression* of our experienced emotions toward others who have offended. It is possible to forgive yet not express forgiveness and understanding through mercy. Likewise, it is possible—though not probable—to show mercy without having forgiven. Mercy implies or is preconditioned by the legal right to treat (i.e. punish) an offender in a way that is harsher or less forgiving than merciful treatment of the same offender. It is a decision to "check" both the passion for excess and the legal right to excess by tempering the type and/or extent of punishment with an air of understanding, compassion, and respect for the humanity of the offender. While forgiveness is the virtue that checks passion, keeping it within the bounds of justice, mercy is the expression in practice of that forgiveness and understanding. Without mercy—without discretion implied by mercy—justice can be "an intolerable engine of tyranny" (quoted in Misner, 2000: 1320).

Secondly, mercy is not clemency. Clemency can be understood as pardoning, excusing, or letting an offense pass without consequence and, in this regard, clemency is an occasional consideration for justice. Clemency, however, is fundamentally different from mercy. Comte-Sponville (2001: 119) defines clemency as the renunciation of punishment. To renounce punishment, for example, may entail an ethical opposition to punishment or one of its forms. One may stand opposed to capital punishment on ethical grounds, yet remain in hatred toward the offender who has taken innocent life. Thus, clemency is insufficient in that it does not negate the hatred that may follow the experience of harm. Such hatred is equally, if not more, problematic than punishment itself. It is, first and foremost, the hatred that forgiveness seeks to overcome and which allows for the possibility of mercy.

Further still, both forgiveness and mercy should not be confused with compassion or even the necessity of compassion in human attitude and action. While compassion is an essential—if not *the* essential—component of social justice, mercy pertains more specifically to criminal "justice." Compassion is understood as the experience of suffering at the sight, sound, or thought of another's suffering. The human capacity to empathize with others provides an emotional ground for the virtue of compassion. Yet compassion is one-dimensional in that it sympathizes with suffering only. The virtue of compassion requires us to identify with the past, present, or potential future suffering of others, putting ourselves "in another's shoes." Such empathic exercises are often limited to the degree that their effect varies in relation to the other's perceived likeness to oneself. In the example of the offender as "enemy," the monstrous murderer is turned into some*thing* less-than-human and, consequently, some*thing* different from oneself. Consequently, the capacity (or, perhaps, willingness) to empathize—even when great suffering is present—is limited if not altogether negated. In other cases, there may be no evidence of an offender's suffering at all or, if so, such evidence may be offset by the more pronounced and more readily understood suffering of the victim. A prime example of the latter is the introduction of victim impact evidence at the sentencing phase of criminal trials. Victim impact evidence relates, in written or spoken form, the suffering that the victim and/or victim's family has suffered as a consequence of the offender's actions. In such cases, juries and, perhaps, judges can more readily empathize with stories of victims suffering. Though offenders are offered opportunity to present evidence of their own suffering or other mitigating evidence, it is recognized that the weight of the latter may be little in light of evidence of victim suffering (e.g., Arrigo and Williams, 2004).

In many cases, then, compassion may not go far enough when confronted by criminal offenders. In cases involving no evidence of an offender's suffering or in which the offender's suffering seems insignificant in light of the victim's suffering, compassion may not be enough to allow us to overcome the anger, hatred, and desire for vengeance and punishment that is often experienced. For this reason, Comte-Sponville (2001: 120) suggests that mercy is the rarer and, certainly, more difficult virtue to embody. Faced with such difficulty, we must recognize that a virtue would not be a virtue if it were easy to embody. Mercy becomes all the more important when we consider that, if compassion is not available to open the door to forgiveness, then forgiveness may be necessary to open the door to compassion. Indeed, "it is easier to feel compassion once we have stopped hating" (*ibid*).

The difference between mercy and compassion is thus one of the subjects toward which one's emotions or actions are directed. Both mercy and compassion are other-directed in that they are both concerned with one's attitude toward others. The distinguishing feature lies in the characteristics of the other toward whom our attitudes are directed. Compassion entails a certain attitude toward the *suffering* of others, while mercy entails a certain attitude toward the *offenses* of others. As suggested, one and the same "other" may be both a subject of compassion and mercy. It is not uncommon that an offender has both harmed and suffered in some meaningful ways. Most offenders are or have been victimized, and many victims are or have been offenders. The abused spouse who's suffering has crossed the threshold of endurance and, in turn, harms the offending spouse exemplifies this point. The "victim" in such a case is the harmed spouse, the suffering of whose family and friends we are to empathize with. Yet most would agree that it is as easy—if not more so—to empathize with the suffering endured and currently experienced by the "offender." In such a case, the offending "victim" may be *both* a subject of compassion *and* a subject of our mercy.

As noted, however, other cases may provide no such suffering to empathize with. Such cases require movement beyond compassion and toward mercy. Much of the world's suffering may be perceived as innocent suffering and, thus, compassion is both a desirable response as well as a readily experienced response. What mercy offers is a virtuous and socially desirable response to situations in which we are confronted with wrongdoing—intentionally inflicted harm—wherein the offending party suffers in no significant or, at least, obvious way and, further, when the offending party may not be received as "like us" is any meaningful way. We may have less difficulty embodying mercy if we are able to identify with the offense(s) the subject has committed. It is easier to forgive the antisocial behaviors of rebellious juveniles—even in the absence of recognizable suffering—if we ourselves engaged in similar displays of antisocialism. Yet mercy offered because of an identification with the act committed still requires the process of identification. In this way it is only minimally different from mercy offered in light of compassion toward a suffering other. Embodiment of mercy requires that such virtuous attitudes and actions are offered, not only in easily forgivable cases or in cases that present the possibility of empathic identification, but even in—and especially in—the most disturbing of circumstances.

Criminal 'Justice' and Social Health: Toward an Affirmative Cultural Ethos

Durkheim (1965; see also Wolff, 1960) argued that retribution is necessary as social practice because of its contribution to social solidarity. Retribution is functional in that it is useful for the moral well-being of society as a whole. In anomic times, when moral erosion seems the hallmark of the collective character and traditional values and moral norms appear in a state of anarchy, law must be the tie that binds society. Retribution becomes *value-affirming* and restores a sense of moral orderliness in affirming the seemingly eroding normative structure of the community. While law can serve as educator and offer a restorative function to the whole of society, retribution as expression of the collective desire for vengeance is questionable as a desirable value to affirm. By embodying in forgiveness in attitude and mercy in practice, the system of justice has some capacity to promote values that are more conducive to social cohesion and solidarity than those of resentment. If eroding values are a product of individualism and diversity without unity, the values restoring a cultural ethos of community, unity, and general concern for the welfare of others are those of understanding, compassion, forgiveness, and mercy that instill a more general climate of nonviolence. In this case, it is the latter are affirmative of socially desirable and socially healthy humanitarian values. Punishment, in turn, has precisely the opposite effect.

Punishment, as Gilligan notes (2000: 746), "is the most powerful stimulus of violence that we have yet discovered." Whether criminal or noncriminal, the practice of responding to violence with violence, evil with evil, pain with pain is the most effective means of creating violence, evil, and pain (e.g., Gilligan, 1996). Punishment is counterproductive and its irony lies in the reality that punishment, as an effort to prevent or deter further harm, leads simply to more harm.

In part, this vicious cycle is reinforced precisely because teaching someone "a lesson" is, indeed, a lesson—one which latently functions to orchestrate the way we treat others. Both s/he who is punished, and we [who] are witnesses are implicated in its effect. As Justice Brandeis once noted, "Our government is the potent, the omnipresent teacher. For good or ill, it teaches the whole people by its example" (quoted in Gilligan, 2000).

Justice Brandeis was referring to the inevitability of criminal justice values finding embodiment in the attitudes and practices of our everyday lives. I have described, as well, how the attitudes and practices of the populous can, in turn, impact the values of criminal justice. This in itself is a vicious cycle that serves to justify and perpetuate punitive sensibilities on an intrapersonal, interpersonal, socio-cultural, and global level (e.g., Fuller, 1998; Braswell, Fuller, and Lozoff, 2001). It stands to reason, however, that such a cycle can be broken and the dawn of a new cycle is not beyond our social horizon.

Working toward such a dawn requires a transvaluation of criminal "justice." While not to suggest that a similar transvaluation is unnecessary on intra- and interpersonal levels, social institutions have the unique ability to article values that will be received—directly or indirectly—by vast numbers of people. In a society where the public looks to law, politics, and media for information about crime and justice, such institutions have an obligation to model practices that are conducive to social health. What would such a model entail? Certainly, our institutional attitude toward the offenses of others would not be one of resentment and hatred; our incentives to act toward the offenses of others would not be based on desires for vengeance that issue from resentment; and our practices or actual treatment of the offenses of others would not entail punishment as a fulfillment of the desire for vengeance. Resentment fuels the vice of vengeance, and punishment is an instrument of that vice.

As Quinney (2000: 28) points out, responses to crime that are motivated by hate are a form of violence themselves. Three thousand years of recorded Western civilization have shown that violence is the most effective means of creating more violence. Nonviolence, in turn, is the most effective means of fostering an air of nonviolence at all levels of human relationships (e.g., Quinney, 1991). As Tolstoy once replied to Lombroso, "all punishment is criminal" (Troyat, 1967: 579). Responding to crime with punishment, in turn, is inevitably criminogenic. As Fuller (1998) suggests, the means used predetermine the ends that can be attained. Means that promote health are those of nonviolence—actions issuing from compassion, forgiveness, and mercy at all level of human relationships. As the values intrinsic to vengeful means are pathogenic, the values intrinsic to positive means can be equally "ethogenic."

References

Aristotle (1976). *Nicomachean ethics.* J. Thomson (ed.). New York: Penguin.

Arrigo, B. & Williams, C. (forthcoming, 2003). Victim voices, victim vices, and restorative justice: Rethinking the use of victim impact evidence in capital sentencing. *Crime and Delinquency.*

Baumeister, R. (1997). *Evil: Inside human violence and cruelty.* New York: W.H. Freeman and Company.

Bentham, J. (1948). *An introduction to the principles of morals and legislation.* New York: Hafner.

Braswell, M., Fuller, J., & Lozoff, B. (2001). *Corrections, peacemaking, and restorative justice: Transforming individuals and institutions.* Cincinnati: Anderson.

Brown, R. (1990). Historical patterns in American violence. In N. Weiner, M. Zahn, and R. Sagi (eds.), Violence: *Patterns, causes, and public policy in San Diego*: Harcourt Brace Jovanovich.

Cohn, S., Barkan, S., & Aveni, A. (1991). Punitive attitudes toward criminals: Racial consensus or racial conflict? *Social Problems,* 38, 287–296.

Comte-Sponville, A. (2001). A small treatise on the great virtues. C. Temersor trld. New York: Metropolitan Books.

Dhammapada. (1994). T. Cleary (trld.). New York: Bantam Books.

Durkheim, E. (1965). *The rules of the sociological method.* S. Solovay & J. Mueller (trlds.). G. Catlin (ed.). New York: The Free Press.

Fairchild. E. & Webb, V. (1985). *The politics of crime and criminal justice.* Beverly Hills: Sage.

Fromm, E. (1930). The state as educator: On the psychology of criminal justice. In K. Anderson and R. Quinney (eds.), *Erich Fromm and critical criminology: Beyond the punitive society.* Urbana: University of Illinois Press.

Fuller, J. (1998). *Criminal justice: A peacemaking perspective.* Boston: Allyn and Bacon.

Gibran, K. (1923). *The prophet.*

Gilligan, J. (1996). *Violence: Reflections on a national epidemic.* New York: Vintage Books.

Gilligan, J. (2000). Punishment and violence: Is the criminal law based on one huge mistake? *Social Research,* Fall.

Jacoby, S. (1983). Wild justice. New York: Harper and Row.

Lazarus, R. & Lazarus, B. (1994). *Passion and emotion: Making sense of our emotions.* New York: Oxford University Press.

Marongiu, P. & Newman, G. (1987). *Vengeance.* Roman and Littlefield, Publishers, Inc.

Misner, R. (2000). A strategy for mercy. *William and Mary Law Review,* 41, 1303.

Murphy, J. (1982). Forgiveness and resentment. *Midwest Studies in Philosophy,* 7, 503–516.

Nietzsche, F. (1995). *Thus spoke Zarathustra.* W. Kauffman, trld. New York: The Modern Library.

Nietzsche, F. (1967). *The genealogy of morals and Ecce Homo.* W. Kauffman, trld. New York: Vintage Books.

Nussbaum, M. (1994). *The therapy of desire: Theory and practice in Hellenistic ethics.* Princeton, NJ: Princeton University Press.

Primoratz, I. (1989). *Justifying legal punishment.* New Jeresey: Humanities Press.

Quinney, R. (1991). The way of peace: On crime, suffering, and service. In R. Quinney & H. Pepinsky (eds.), *Criminology as peacemaking*. Bloomington: Indiana University Press.

Quinney, R. (2000). Socialist humanism and the problem of crime: Thinking about Erich Fromm in the development of critical/peacemaking criminology. In K. Anderson and R. Quinney (eds.), *Erich Fromm and critical criminology: Beyond the punitive society*. Urbana, IL: University of Illinois Press.

Solomon, R. & Murphy, M. (1990). *What is justice: Classic and contemporary readings*. New York: Oxford University Press.

Solomon, R. (1989). *The passion for justice: Emotions and the origins of the social contract*. Reading, MA: Addison Wesley Co, Inc.

Tachibana, S. (1926). *The ethics of Buddhism*. Oxford: Clarendon Press.

Troyat, H. (1967). *Tolstoy*. Garden City: Doubleday.

Wolff, K. (1960). Emile Durkheim et al., Writings on sociology and philosophy. New York: Harper and Row.

From *Humanity & Society,* Vol. 26, No. 2, May 2002, pp. 100–116. Copyright © 2002 by Association for Humanist Sociology. Reprinted by permission.

Trust and Confidence in Criminal Justice

LAWRENCE W. SHERMAN

C riminal justice in America today is a paradox of progress: While the fairness and effectiveness of criminal justice have improved, public trust and confidence apparently have not.

Criminal justice is far less corrupt, brutal, and racially unfair than it has been in the past. It is arguably more effective at preventing crime. It has far greater diversity in its staffing. Yet these objectively defined improvements seem to have had little impact on American attitudes toward criminal justice.

Understanding this paradox—better work but low marks—is central to improving public trust and confidence in the criminal justice system.

How Low Is Public Confidence?

Gallup polls over the last few years have consistently found that Americans have less confidence in the criminal justice system than in other institutions, such as banking, the medical system, public schools, television news, newspapers, big business, and organized labor.[1]

The most striking finding in the Gallup poll is the difference between the low evaluation of "criminal justice" and the high evaluation given to the police and the Supreme Court. Other sources of data show similar attitudes: Confidence in local courts and prisons is far lower than it is for the police.[2] These large differences suggest that Americans may not think of police in the same way as they do the criminal justice system.

The Racial Divide

A 1998 Gallup poll reports little overall demographic difference among the respondents saying they had confidence in the criminal justice system. But what is most clear is the difference in opinion between whites and blacks about the individual components of the criminal justice system and especially the police. Whites express considerably more confidence in the police, local court system, and State prison system than blacks (see Figure 1).

Race, Victimization, and Punishment. Racial differences also appear in rates of victimization and punishment: Blacks are 31 percent more likely to be victimized by personal crime than whites and twice as likely as whites to suffer a completed violent crime.[3]

The personal opinions of the survey respondents are consistent with a major theory about the declining public confidence in all government—not just criminal justice—in all modern nations, not just the United States. The concerns arise from the decline of hierarchy and the rise of equality in all walks of life. The rise in egalitarian culture increases the demand for government officials to show more respect to citizens.

Young black males are historically 10 times more likely to be murdered than white males.[4]

Arrest rates for robbery are five times higher for blacks than for whites; four times higher for murder and rape; and three times higher for drug violations and weapons possession.[5]

Blacks are eight times more likely to be in a State or Federal prison than non-Hispanic whites (and three times more likely than Hispanic whites). Almost 2 percent of the black population, or 1 of every 63 blacks, was in prison in 1996.[6]

Race and Neighborhood. What these data fail to show, however, is the extent to which the racial differences in attitudes, victimization, and punishment may be largely related to more blacks being the residents of a small number of high-crime, high-poverty areas concentrated in a small fraction of urban neighborhoods. This is the case even though Harvard University sociologist Orlando Patterson has estimated that

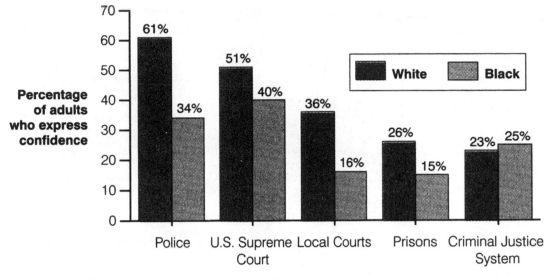

Figure 1 Confidence ratings for criminal justice system agencies, by race.

Source: The Gallup Organization, "Confidence In Institutions," Retrieved From The World Wide Web site HTTP://WWW.GALLUP.COM, October 10, 2000.

only 1 in every 30 black adults resides in these high-crime, high-poverty areas; the proportion is higher for children.

What we may understand as a problem of race in America may largely reflect conditions in those neighborhoods that are generalized by both blacks and whites to conditions of the larger society.

Due to limited national data, it is difficult to determine what precisely drives the lower levels of confidence in criminal justice among blacks, but insights from city-by-city analysis suggest two conclusions:

- **There is no race-based subculture of violence.** Blacks and whites who live in neighborhoods with similar conditions have similar views on the legitimacy of law. To the extent that race is associated with attitudes toward law, it may be a reflection of the greater likelihood that blacks reside in poverty areas.
- **There is no race-based hostility to police in high-crime areas.** High levels of dissatisfaction with police are endemic to high-crime areas. Whites residing in such areas express attitudes just as hostile as blacks toward police.[7] The distrust of police in high-crime areas may be related to the prevalence of crime rather than to police practice. If negative attitudes are driven by police practice, it may be because those practices fail to prevent crime rather than because police presence or behavior is excessive. Or it may be that the practice of policing in such areas offers less recognition and dignity to citizen consumers than is found in lower crime areas.

Strong Demands for Change

The findings and responses from a random digit-dialing telephone survey of 4,000 residents of 10 northeastern States in 1998 found that more than 80 percent—four out of five respondents—preferred the idea of "totally revamping the way the [criminal justice] system works" for violent crime; 75 percent said the same for all crime.[8] The responses varied little from State to State or from one demographic group to another. The majority of respondents believed that:

- Victims are not accorded sufficient rights in the criminal justice process.
- Victims are not informed enough about the status of their cases.
- Victims are not able to talk to prosecutors enough.
- Victims should be able to tell the court what impact the crime had on them, but most victims do not get that chance.
- Offenders, even if jailed, should reimburse victims for the cost of the crime.
- Offenders should acknowledge their responsibility for the crime.
- Victims should have the opportunity to meet with the offender to find out why the crime occurred and to learn whether the offender accepted responsibility.
- Ordinary citizens, not courts, should set penalties for non-violent crimes.
- Drug treatment should be used more widely for drug-using offenders.

The personal opinions of the survey respondents are consistent with a major theory about the declining public confidence in all government—not just criminal justice—in all modern nations, not just the United States. The concerns arise from the decline of hierarchy and the rise of equality in all walks of life. The rise in egalitarian culture increases the demand for government officials to show more respect to citizens.[9]

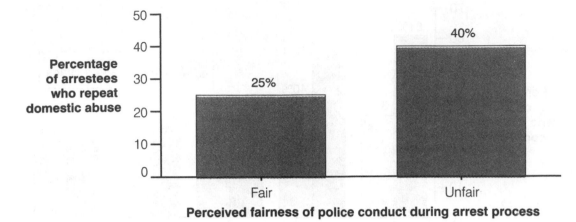

Figure 2 Repeat offending after arrest for domestic violence by perceived fairness of arrest process.

Source: Paternoster, R., R. Brame, R. Bachman, and L. W. Sherman, "Do Fair Procedures Matter? The Effect of Procedural Justice on Spousal Assault," *Law & Society Review*, 31(1997): 185.

Egalitarianism in Modern Culture: Raised Expectations, Reduced Trust

Americans' trust in government has declined sharply in the last quarter century.[10] A similar loss of trust has been found in 18 other democracies. Citizens now expect higher levels of recognition, respect, and status from the government. Criminal justice serves as a flash point for this change in citizen attitudes because so many Americans have contact with the criminal justice system and because the hierarchical design of criminal justice institutions juxtaposes so starkly with the egalitarian demands of the public.

As the spread of equality has combined with growing freedom from want, political culture has shifted away from Puritan views of a *hierarchical* communal democracy to Quaker views of a more *egalitarian* individualistic democracy. Indeed, the consistently greater support for police than for courts may result from a perception of police as egalitarian individualists (the new cultural ideal) while judges are seen as bossy conformists (the outdated ideal).

The massive three-decade decline of public trust in liberal democratic governments suggests a deeper paradox of success: As democracies become more materially successful and better educated, the perceived need for governance declines and expectations of government for appropriate conduct increase.[11] The crisis of government legitimacy has thus been prompted less by declining quality of government conduct than by increasing public dissatisfaction with institutions in general, driven by what Ronald F. Inglehart, Professor, University of Michigan, calls "postmaterialist values."[12]

Social changes taking place around the globe appear to be resulting in challenges to the legitimacy of virtually all forms of social hierarchy of authority (although not hierarchy of wealth)—of husbands over wives, doctors over patients, school-teachers over students and parents, parents over children, and government officials over citizens. This evolution may have led to widespread preference for the recognition of individual dignity over the recognition of communal authority.[13]

Thus, what Robert J. Sampson, Professor of Sociology, University of Chicago, and other scholars refer to as "legal cynicism"—the extent to which people feel that laws are not binding—is not the product of a criminal subculture.[14] It is a 400-year-old Christian political theology that has become globally accepted across people of all religions in a more egalitarian and individualistic modern culture.

In such a world, people are less likely to obey the law out of a sense of communal obligation, and more likely to obey laws they support through a personal sense of what is moral.

Consensus thus appears to be a much better fit to the new political culture. Standing up when judges enter a room and obeying orders barked out by police, for example, are procedural forms that may imply officials are more important than citizens. Such forms may do more to undermine legal trust than to build respect for the law.

Trust and Recognition

What changing culture may be creating is a world in which people trust *laws* but not *legal institutions*. This new world may be one in which trust in criminal justice is no longer automatic; it must be earned everyday, with each encounter between legal agents and citizens.

The research of Tom R. Tyler, Department of Psychology, New York University, shows that Americans—especially members of minority groups—are extremely sensitive to the respect they perceive and the procedures employed when they come into contact with criminal justice.[15] Tyler's evidence suggests that in building citizen trust in the legal system, it may matter less whether you receive the speeding ticket than whether the police officer addresses you politely or rudely during the traffic stop. Similarly, sentencing guidelines that punish possession of crack more harshly than possession of powdered cocaine may discriminate against blacks. But dissatisfaction may be greater with some police officers engaged in drug enforcement who treat suspects and arrestees like people who are enemies rather than like people who are equal fellow citizens.

Tyler concludes that the procedural justice perceived in treatment by legal officials affects the level of trust citizens have in government.[16] That level of trust, in turn, affects the pride we have in our government and the degree to which we feel we are respected by other members of our democracy—including the government.

Tyler further concludes that the odds of citizens reaching the conclusion that the law is morally right are much higher when citizens feel that the law has given each of them adequate recognition and respect.

Rather than creating a willingness to *defer* to the power of the law, Tyler suggests that respectful treatment creates a stronger *consensus* about what is moral and what the law must be. The consensus model assumes more equality than the deference model on which our legal institutions were designed.[17]

Consensus thus appears to be a much better fit to the new political culture. Standing up when judges enter a room and obeying orders barked out by police, for example, are procedural forms that may imply officials are more important than citizens. Such forms may do more to undermine legal trust than to build respect for the law.

Fitting Legal Institutions to the Culture: The Canberra Experiments

For all Americans, regardless of race, the central cause of declining trust may be the misfit of hierarchical legal institutions in an egalitarian culture. In many ways, citizens may experience the conduct of judges, prosecutors, and police as being overly "bossy" and unnecessarily authoritarian.

Results of experiments in Canberra, Australia, suggest that an egalitarian, consensual procedure of stakeholder citizens deciding the sentence for a crime creates more legitimacy in the eyes of both offenders and victims than the hierarchical, deferential process of sentencing by a judge.[18]

The experiments compared traditional court sentencing of youthful violent and property offenders to an alternative community justice conference making the same decisions.

Alternative Community Justice Conferences

In the Canberra experiments, the police invite victims, offenders, and their respective supporters to a meeting in which the offenders must not—for these purposes—dispute their guilt. At the meetings, everyone sits in a circle to discuss the harm the crime has caused, acknowledge the pain and emotional impact of that harm, and deliberate democratically as to how the offenders should repair that harm.

The egalitarian proceedings begin with the police officer moderating the proceedings, offering only questions, not answers. For example, what did the offender do? How did it hurt the victim? How does the victim feel about that hurt? How do the victim's friends and family feel? How do the offender's family and friends feel about what has been said? What would be the right way for the offender to repay the debt to the victim and to society? Does everyone agree? Is there anything the offender wants to say to the victim (sometimes the offender says "I'm sorry")? Is there anything the victim wants to say to the offender (possibly "I forgive you")?

One of the most important parts of the proceedings is that everyone is allowed to talk, just as in a Quaker meeting, but no one person dominates speech, as might happen in a Calvinist church or in an Anglo-American courtroom. Emotions can be intense at the conferences—unlike the restraint valued by Puritan cultures and Western courts.

No Lawyers. Lawyers are not allowed to attend the conferences as legal advocates for either an offender or the State, although they may attend as personal supporters. They are always on call, ready to act to protect anyone whose rights may seem abused. But as long as the victim-offender consensus is under discussion, everyone in the circle has equal authority, regardless of age or education.

Extra Time Required. A community justice conference takes, on average, about 70 minutes to resolve. A similar case in traditional court may take 10 minutes spread across several different appearances, which have no emotional significance for victim or offender, and thus leave citizens feeling like cogs in a wheel. A community justice conference is about the people present rather than the legal formalities. People come only once, prepared to stay until the case is resolved.

Trust in Justice. Research shows that sentences imposed in the community justice conferences and the traditional court process were fairly similar despite the major differences in the decision making procedures employed.[1] But the conferences produced far better results in terms of citizen respect for legal institutions.

[1]Sherman, L.W., H. Strang, and G.C. Barnes, "Stratification of Justice: Legitimacy of Hierarchical and Egalitarian Sentencing Procedures," unpublished manuscript, Fels Center of Government, University of Pennsylvania, 1999.

Offenders who were sent to conferences were far less likely than offenders who were sent to traditional court to say that they were pushed around; disadvantaged by their age, income, or education; treated as if they were untrustworthy; or not listened to. They also were more likely to report that their experience increased their respect for the justice system and the police, as well as their feeling that the crime they had committed was morally wrong.

Victims also were far more satisfied with community justice conferences than with court proceedings. Much of this difference may be because most victims of criminals sent to court were never informed of the offenders' court appearances, either before or after sentencing. The victims invited to community justice conferences with offenders, in sharp contrast, gained increased trust in police and justice, as well as decreased fear of and anger at the offender. (For more details, see "Alternative Community Justice Conferences.")

Building Trust One Case at a Time

The Canberra experiments suggest the highly personal nature of citizen trust in criminal justice. The *personal* legitimacy of legal agents may depend on a leveling of distinctions in rank between citizen and official.

As Albert J. Reiss, Jr., Professor Emeritus, Sociology Department, Yale University, observed, the legitimacy of police authority in the eyes of citizens varies widely from one situation to the next.[19] Thus, officials must earn the legitimacy of their authority one case at a time.

The most dramatic demonstration of this principle is the finding that *how* police make arrests for domestic violence affects the rate of repeat offending. Raymond Paternoster, Ph.D., University of Maryland, et al. demonstrated that offenders who were arrested for domestic violence and who perceived that the police officers' arresting procedures were fair were less likely to repeat the offense than offenders who perceived the arresting procedures as unfair.[20] Actions that constituted "procedural justice" included the police taking the time to listen to both the offender and the victim, not handcuffing the offender in front of the victim, and not using physical force.

As Figure 2 shows, the risk of repeat offending was 40 percent for offenders who had a low perception of police procedural fairness, but only 25 percent for those who perceived a high level of police fairness. The estimate of offending risk took prior levels of violence into account; hence the findings shown in Figure 2 increase our confidence that *how* the police make an arrest may affect the crime rate (much of which comes from repeat offending)—through trust and confidence in the criminal justice system.

Reducing Complaints Against Police. Other tests of the hypothesis that trust in criminal justice comes from egalitarian procedures can be seen in actions that have been shown to reduce complaints against police.

In sum, a growing body of theory and evidence suggests that it is not the fairness or effectiveness of decisions criminal justice officials make that determines the public's level of trust. Changes in modern culture have made the *procedures* and manners of criminal justice officials far more important to public trust and left officials out of step with modern culture.

In the 42nd and 44th precincts in The Bronx, complaints reached a 10-year high in 1996. But after the precinct commanders instituted a program to promote respectful policing and improve police relations with community residents, complaints dropped dramatically. Among the elements of the new program was vigorous training for officers on how to treat citizens respectfully, zealous monitoring of complaints, and follow through with consequences for officers who received complaints.

In addition, the simple elimination of the precinct's high desk and bar in front of the desk in the reception area helped the precinct present a less hierarchical face to the community. Research on the effects of the strategy, conducted by the Vera Institute of Justice, found that citizens began to perceive the police as responsive to community concerns.[21]

The second test of the procedural equality theory comes from a community with a population of almost one million; 55 percent of the population is African American.

Complaints dropped in this department of 1,400 officers when a new procedure for traffic stops was initiated in 1997–99. The procedure, called "Take Away Guns" (TAG), was one part of a larger strategy to reduce gun violence. One of the first steps the department took was to increase traffic enforcement—a 400-some percent increase—so that police had an opportunity to explain the program at each traffic stop and distribute a letter from the district police captain explaining the program. The letter contained the captain's phone number and invited citizens to call the captain with complaints or questions. Officers were trained to be very polite in explaining the program to drivers and then asking permission to search the car for guns.

The program not only received a high rate of compliance with the requests, but also received praise from the drivers stopped who approved of the efforts to get guns off the street. Over the first 2 years of the program, both gun violence and citizen complaints of excessive force by police dropped substantially.

In sum, a growing body of theory and evidence suggests that it is not the fairness or effectiveness of decisions criminal justice officials make that determines the public's level of trust. Changes in modern culture have made the *procedures* and manners of criminal justice officials far more important to public trust and left officials out of step with modern culture.

This explanation gains further support from scholarship on the effect of television and other communications media on the nature of authority and trust in government. For despite Tyler's focus on personal contacts with criminal justice, most citizens have little if any personal contact with legal officials. For this majority of Americans, the level of trust in criminal justice may depend on what they hear about criminal justice encounters with other citizens, a little-studied area. But it also may depend on how legal agencies are portrayed in entertainment and news media.

Authority and Media Celebrity

The future authority of the criminal justice system may well depend on how the system appears not just to those directly involved in the system, but to all citizens. That, in turn, may depend heavily on how criminal justice manages its image in the electronic media. Legal historian Lawrence Friedman notes that modern culture has changed the very nature of authority from *vertical* (where people look up to leaders in high position) to *horizontal* (where people look in to the center of society to find leaders who are celebrities, defined by the number of people who recognize their names and faces). "Leaders are no longer distant, awesome, and unknown; they are familiar figures on TV. . . . The horizontal society is [one in which] the men and women who get and hold power become celebrities" and the public come to know them, or think they know them, through the media. "By contrast," Friedman writes, "traditional authority was vertical, and the higher up the authority, the more stern, distant, and remote it was."[22]

A celebrity culture creates still another paradox: Americans now feel more personal connections with celebrities living far away than they do with legal officials in their own hometown. Just as many people felt more emotional loss at the death of Princess Diana than at the death of a neighbor, the celebrity culture makes us feel personal connections to people we do not know.

Thus, for all the programs designed to foster community policing or community prosecution with legal officials in the neighborhood, Americans still are more likely to form their impressions of criminal justice from vicarious contact through friends or through television shows than from personal experience with their own legal system. The evidence is clear: On a Wednesday night when police convene a neighborhood meeting in a church basement, more local residents are home watching television than attending the meeting.

We may well ask if there are any celebrities of American criminal justice, and if so, who they are—The Chief Justice of the Supreme Court? The director of the FBI? Probably not. These positions appear to fit Friedman's characteristics of traditional authority: stern, distant, and remote. Television's Judge Judy, on the other hand, is an internationally recognized celebrity, with far greater name-face recognition than the traditional authority figures.

Unfortunately, the entertainment values of the television business conflict with the core values of legal institutions. What sells TV audiences is conflict and putdowns, tools Judge Judy uses to portray a rude, in-your-face (but perhaps egalitarian), power-control image of the bench. Audiences find this fun to watch, although Judge Judy may confirm their worst fears, leaving them reluctant to have anything to do with the legal system.

The difficulty in using celebrity power to send messages about the trustworthiness of criminal justice is the clash of cultures between law and entertainment. The reticence of the legal culture conflicts with the chattiness of celebrity culture.

One can imagine a legal official appearing weekly on a talk show with a huge audience, saying things that could help shore up public faith in criminal justice as an egalitarian and fair system. One can equally imagine such a strategy being condemned by leaders of the American Bar Association, conservative journalists, and other defenders of traditional remoteness of authority.

The kind of public education programs that legal culture would approve of—such as tasteful PBS specials or public service announcements on radio and television—would seem unlikely to reach much of the public, let alone those citizens most distrustful of the system.

Portraying Values in the Media

The media often portray criminal justice through a morality play that explores themes of what Elijah Anderson, Charles and William L. Day Professor, Sociology Department, University of Pennsylvania, calls "street" and "decent" values. Based on years of field research in high-crime areas of Philadelphia, Anderson has observed people who exhibit "decent" values as patient, hopeful, respectful of authority, and with a belief in the predictability of punishment. Those who exhibit "street" values take on a bitter, impatient, antisystem outlook that is disrespectful of authority and demanding of deference.[23]

Television dramas that portray a hero's impatience with red tape may glorify the "street" enforcement of vengeance and personal respect. TV interviewers who ask officials provocative and insulting questions may reflect an effort to produce a "street" response.

The paradox of such media portrayals is that the more frequently legal officials are portrayed breaking the official rules out of distrust for "decent" government, the less reason the public has to believe the criminal justice system will treat citizens decently. By showing criminal justice agents pursuing street values, the media may create a self-fulfilling prophecy, defining conduct for legal officials and the public alike.

The research on respect for authority suggests that street sanctioning styles interact with different kinds of citizen personalities in ways that produce the following differences in repeat offending:

- Decent sanctioning of "decent" people produces the lowest repeat offending.
- Street sanctioning of "decent" people produces higher repeat offending.
- Decent sanctioning of "street" people may produce even higher repeat offending.
- Street sanctioning of "street" people produces the highest levels of repeat offending.[24]

The research on respect for authority consistently suggests that when people in positions of authority impose "street" attitudes or sanctions, the reaction is almost always negative. It is more productive for criminal justice officials to show more respect to, and take more time to listen to, citizens. To the extent that this message is portrayed in entertainment media and identified with celebrity authority, the criminal justice system might be able to increase its public trust and confidence. Yet to the extent that "decent" values are themselves communicated in an illegitimate way, it will be difficult to foster a more "decent" legal culture.

Half a century ago and half a world away, a French journalist observed during a 2-month tour of China in the early 1950's that police had become far more polite under Mao's early communism:

> In the olden days the Peking police were renowned for their brutality, and pedestrians frequently suffered at their hands, smacks in the face being the least form of violence offered them. Today they are formally forbidden to use any kind of force. Their instructions are to explain, to make people understand, to convince them.[25]

It may be easier to change official conduct in a dictatorship than in a democracy, but the power of electronic media may make the dynamics totally different today. Electronic communications comprise a highly democratized, free-market institution that cannot be manipulated easily for official purposes. But the media can be avenue in which celebrity power is built and put to use in fostering support for "decent" styles of criminal justice, both in the image and the reality of how criminal justice works.

The Domains of Public Trust

Three major domains appear to affect public trust and confidence in criminal justice:

- The conduct and practices of the criminal justice system.
- The changing values and expectations of the culture the system serves.
- The images of the system presented in electronic media.

Changes in each domain affect the others. Trust, as the product of all three combined, is likely to increase only when changes in all three domains can be aligned to create practices and values that are perceived to be fair, inclusive, and trustworthy.

Discovering how that can be made to happen is a daunting task. But the data suggest that fairness builds trust in criminal justice, and trust builds compliance with law. Thus what is fairer is more effective, and to be effective it is necessary to be fair.

Notes

1. Retrieved from the World Wide Web site http://www.gallup. com, October 10, 2000.

2. Maguire, K., and A. Pastore, eds., *Sourcebook of Criminal Justice Statistics, 1997*, Washington, DC: U.S. Department of Justice, Bureau of Justice Statistics, 1998 (NCJ 171147).

3. Maguire and Pastore, *Sourcebook*, 182, see note 2.

4. Reiss, A.J., Jr., and J. Roth, *Understanding and Preventing Violence*, Washington, DC: National Academy of Sciences, 1993: 64 (NCJ 140290).

5. Hacker, A., *Two Nations: Black and White, Separate, Hostile, and Unequal*, New York: Free Press, 1992: 181.

6. Maguire and Pastore, *Sourcebook*, 494, see note 2.

7. Sampson, R., and D. Bartusch, "Legal Cynicism and Subcultural Tolerance of Deviance: The Neighborhood Context of Racial Differences," *Law & Society Review*, 32 (4) (1999): 777–804.

8. Boyle, J.M., *Crime Issues in the Northeast: Statewide Surveys of the Public and Crime Victims in Connecticut, Delaware, Maine, Massachusetts, Vermont, New Hampshire, New Jersey, New York, and Rhode Island*, Silver Spring, MD: Schulman, Ronca, and Bucuvalas, Inc., 1999.

9. Fukuyama, F., *The End of History and the Last Man*, New York: Free Press, 1992.

10. Orren, G., "Fall From Grace: The Public's Loss of Faith in the Government," in *Why People Don't Trust Government*, eds. J.S. Nye, Jr., P.D. Zelikow, and D.C. King, Cambridge, MA: Harvard University Press, 1997: 83.

11. Fukuyama, *The End of History*, see note 9; Heclo, H., "The Sixties' False Dawn: Awakenings, Movements, and Postmodern Policymaking," *Journal of Policy History*, 8 (1996): 50–58; Balogh, B., "Introduction," *Journal of Policy History*, 8 (1996): 25.

12. Inglehart, R., "Postmaterialist Values and the Erosion of Institutional Authority," in *Why People Don't Trust Government*, eds. J.S. Nye, Jr., P.D. Zelikow, and D.C. King, Cambridge, MA: Harvard University Press, 1997.

13. Baltzell, E.D., *Puritan Boston and Quaker Philadelphia: Two Protestant Ethics and the Spirit of Class Authority and Leadership*, New York: Free Press, 1979.

14. Sampson and Bartusch, "Legal Cynicism and Subcultural Tolerance of Deviance," see note 7.

15. Tyler, T., *Why People Obey the Law*, New Haven, CT: Yale University Press, 1990; Tyler, T., "Trust and Democratic Governance," in *Trust and Governance*, eds. V. Braithwaite and M. Levi, New York: Russell Sage Foundation, 1998.

16. Tyler, "Trust and Democratic Governance," see note 15.

17. Baltzell, *Puritan Boston*, 369, see note 13.

18. See details of the Reintegrative Shaming Experiments project at http://www.aic.gov.au/rjustice/rise.

19. Reiss and Roth, *Understanding and Preventing Violence*, 2, 3, 59–65, see note 4.

20. Paternoster, R., R. Brame, R.Bachman, and L.W. Sherman, "Do Fair Procedures Matter? The Effect of Procedural Justice on Spouse Assault," *Law & Society Review*, 31 (1997): 185.

21. A more complete description of the Vera Institute of Justice study can be found in *NIJ Journal*, July 2000, p. 24, http://www.ncjrs.org/pdffiles1/jr000244f.pdf. The authors' presentation of findings also is available on videotape from NCJRS (NCJ 181106).

22. Friedman, L., *The Horizontal Society*, New Haven, CT: Yale University Press, 1999: 14–15.

23. Anderson, E., *Crime and Justice*, Chicago: Chicago University Press, 1999.

24. Just how much harmful impact "street" conduct by agents of criminal justice has been revealed by experimental and quasi-experimental research on diverse situations using different levels of analysis. See, for example, Nisbett, R.E., and D. Cohen, *Culture of Honor: The Psychology of Violence in the South*, Boulder, CO: Westview Press, 1996: 46–48; Raine, A., P. Brennan, and S.A. Mednick, "Birth Complications Combined With Early Maternal Rejection at Age 1 Year Predispose to Violent Crime at Age 18 Years," *Archives of General Psychiatry*, 51 (1994): 986; Greenberg, J., "Employee Theft as a Reaction to Underpayment Inequity: The Hidden Costs of Pay Cuts," *Journal of Applied Psychology*, 75 (1990): 561–568; Makkai, T., and J. Braithwaite, "Reintegrative Shaming and Compliance With Regulatory Standards," *Criminology*, 32 (1994): 361–385.

25. de Segonzac, A., *Visa for Peking*, London: Heinemann, 1956.

LAWRENCE W. SHERMAN is the Albert M. Greenfield Professor of Human Relations and Director of the Jerry Lee Center of Criminology at the University of Pennsylvania. Contact him at 3814 Walnut Street, Philadelphia, PA 19104, 215-898-9216, lws@pobox.upenn.edu

From *National Institute of Justice Journal*, Number 248, 2002, pp. 22–31. Published by Office of Justice/U.S. Department of Justice.

UNIT 2
Victimology

Unit Selections

Key Points to Consider

- What is needed in order to switch from calling oneself a "victim" of crime to a "survivor" of crime?

- Why do we need good statistics to talk sensibly about social problems?

- Do you think a violent adult can change after participating in a program?

Student Web Site
www.mhcls.com/online

Internet References
Further information regarding these Web sites may be found in this book's preface or online.

National Crime Victim's Research and Treatment Center (NCVC)
http://www.musc.edu/cvc/

Office for Victims of Crime (OVC)
http://www.ojp.usdoj.gov/ovc

For many years, crime victims were not considered an important topic for criminological study. Now, however, criminologists consider that focusing on victims and victimization is essential to understand the phenomenon of crime. The popularity of this area of study can be attributed to the early work of Hans Von Hentig and the later work of Stephen Schafer. These writers were the first to assert that crime victims play an integral role in the criminal event, that their actions may actually precipitate crime, and that unless the victim's role is considered, the study of crime is not complete.

In recent years, a growing number of criminologists have devoted increasing attention to the victim's role in the criminal justice process. Generally, areas of particular interest include establishing probabilities of victimization risks, studying victim precipitation of crime and culpability, and designing services expressly for victims of crime. As more criminologists focus their attention on the victim's role in the criminal process, victimology will take on even greater importance.

This unit provides a sharp focus on several key issues. The lead article, "Do Batterer Intervention Programs Work?" from the National Institute of Justice, looks at studies that have been conducted of the most common types of programs in New York and Florida. The need for good statistics in order to talk sensibly about social problems is the point of the next article, "Telling the Truth About Damned Lies and Statistics."

A rape victim's account of her traumatic experience follows next in "Violence and the Remaking of a Self." The perplexing response of some crime victims is explained by DeFabrique, Romano, Vecchi and Van Hasselt in "Understanding Stockholm Syndrome." "Sexual Assault on Campuses: What Colleges and Universities Are Doing About It," takes an in-depth look at the problem of sexual assaults on college and university campuses. Finally, "Ordering Restitution to the Crime Victim" provides an overview of state laws addressing the rights of victims to receive court-ordered restitution from offenders in criminal cases.

Do Batterer Intervention Programs Work?
Two Studies

For more than a decade, courts have been sending convicted batterers to intervention programs rather than to prison. But do these programs work? Two studies in Florida and New York tested the most common type of batterer intervention. Their findings raise serious questions about the effectiveness of these programs. However, problems conducting the research raise questions about the studies' findings.

JOHN ASHCROFT, DEBORAH J. DANIELS, AND SARAH V. HART

What DID the Researchers Find?

Batterer intervention programs do not change batterers' attitudes and may have only minor effects on behavior, according to these studies. The Florida study found no significant differences between those who had treatment and those who did not as to whether they battered again or their attitudes toward domestic violence. The study did find an apparent relationship between whether an offender was employed or owned a house and whether he reoffended: Those with the most to lose were the least likely to reoffend. In New York, batterers in a 26-week program were less likely to reoffend than those in an 8-week program, but neither group showed any change in attitudes toward women or domestic violence.

What Were the Studies' Limitations?

Researchers face serious problems in studying batterer intervention programs:

- Batterers drop out at high rates.
- Victims often relocate or become difficult to find.
- No measures have been designed to specifically assess batterers' attitudes.
- To protect victims, judges often override random assignment of batterers to a control group.

These research limitations can affect the quality of the collected data, which can, in turn, affect researchers' ability to draw verifiable conclusions. Although both studies tried to address these limitations, they could not avoid them entirely.

Batterer intervention programs have been proliferating in the United States for the past two decades. These programs give batterers an alternative to jail. They usually involve several months of attendance at group therapy sessions that attempt to stop the violence and change the batterers' attitudes toward women and battering.

Mounting evidence indicates that the programs might be ineffective.

Two recent evaluations, one in Broward County, Florida, and the other in Brooklyn, New York,[1] evaluated interventions based on the Duluth model, which is the most commonly used program in the Nation—many States mandate its use (see "Types of Batterer Interventions"). The Broward County study found that the batterer intervention program had little or no effect, and the Brooklyn study found only minor improvement in some subjects. Neither program changed subjects' attitudes toward domestic abuse.

However, limitations in the studies raise additional issues. Are the evaluations correct that these programs don't change batterers' behavior and attitudes, or do shortcomings in the evaluations cover up program effects? There is no adequate answer

Types of Batterer Interventions

The Broward County and Brooklyn batterer intervention programs were based on the Duluth model. The Duluth model's underlying theory is that batterers want to control their partners and that changing this dynamic is key to changing their behavior. Its curriculum uses a "power and control wheel" depicting tactics abusers use to control their partners. Themes counteracting these tactics are discussed in classes and group sessions that attempt to induce batterers to confront their attitudes and behavior.

There are several alternatives to the Duluth model. Cognitive-behavioral intervention views battering as a result of errors in thinking and focuses on skills training and anger management. Another model, group practice, works from the premise that battering has multiple causes and is best addressed through a combined approach that includes an individual needs assessment. Proponents of these programs believe that a more long-term approach than the Duluth model is necessary.*

Programs based on batterer typologies or profiles are gaining popularity. These interventions profile the batterer through a psychological assessment, then classify him by level of risk, substance abuse, and other factors that may influence which intervention is most likely to work for him. Programs based on this approach are still relatively new and not fully evaluated.

A controversial intervention is couples therapy, which views men and women as equally responsible for creating disturbances in the relationship. It is widely criticized for assigning the victim a share of the blame for the continuation of violence.

Notes

*Examples of these programs include Emerge and AMEND (Abusive Men Exploring New Directions). See Healey, K., C. Smith, and C. O'Sullivan, *Batterer Intervention: Program Approaches and Criminal Justice Strategies,* Issues and Practices, Washington, DC: U.S. Department of Justice, National Institute of Justice, 1998, NCJ 168638.

to this question. Both issues may need to be addressed in future programs and studies.

Broward County: Does Stake-In-Conformity Matter Most?

The Broward County study found no significant difference between the treatment and control groups in attitudes toward the role of women, whether wife beating should be a crime, or whether the State has the right to intervene in cases of domestic violence. It also found no significant difference between these groups in whether victims expected their partners to beat them again. Moreover, no significant difference was found in violations of probation or rearrests, except that men who were assigned to the program but did not attend all sessions were more likely to be rearrested than members of the control group.

Evaluators tried to determine what could account for differences in men's self-reports of physical violence. They considered whether the offender was assigned to treatment; the number of classes he attended; and such stake-in-conformity variables as marital status, residential stability, and employment. These last factors proved crucial.

Attending the program had no effect on the incidence of physical violence. Rather, offenders who were employed, married, and/or owned a home were less likely to batter again. Younger men and men with no stable residence (regardless of age) were more likely to abuse their partners. Older men who owned a home were less likely to do so.

Twenty-four percent of men in both the experimental and control groups were rearrested at least once during their year on probation. Again, attending the program had no effect. Rather, whether an offender was employed (a stake-in-conformity variable) seemed to have more influence on whether he was rearrested.

Brooklyn: Is Longer Treatment More Effective?

The Brooklyn study unintentionally had two experimental groups of offenders. After the study was underway, defense attorneys objected to the 26-week program's duration and cost and advised their clients not to participate. To preserve the study, offenders were offered an accelerated 8-week program, which created a second experimental sample.

Batterers assigned to 26 weeks of treatment were less likely than the control group and those assigned to 8-week classes to be arrested again for a crime against the same victim. Neither program changed batterers' attitudes toward domestic violence. There were significant differences in reoffending, however. Even though more offenders completed the shorter program, the 26-week group had fewer criminal complaints than either the control group or the 8-week group.

Men who attended the longer treatment committed fewer new violent acts than those who attended the shorter treatment or those who had no treatment. This may suggest that providing treatment for a longer period of time helped reduce battering during the term of treatment and for some time thereafter.

Program and Research Issues

Concerns about research methodology cloud most batterer intervention program evaluations, and these two studies were no exception. The major issues are—

- *Maintaining sample integrity.* Keeping assignments to batterer programs truly random is consistently a challenge.[2]
- *Low attendance, high attrition, difficulty following up.* High dropout and low response rates can lead to overly positive estimates of program effects.

- *Inadequate data sources.* Official records used to validate batterer and victim reports may be collected inconsistently across jurisdictions; also, they capture only those violations that reach the authorities. Evidence suggests that batterers often avoid rearrest by switching to psychological and verbal abuse.[3]

- *Difficulty measuring outcomes.* Evaluators lack good survey instruments to measure batterer behavior and attitudes. The revised Conflict Tactics Scale (CTS2) used in these studies was not designed for before and after measurements.[4] The Brooklyn study raised another issue common to batterer intervention program studies: Do evaluations examine the effects of the intervention or the effects of assignment to a treatment group?[5]

- *Who is defining success?* A final concern is broader in scope: Is a mere reduction in violence enough? These studies considered a reduction in violence to be a success based on the premise that it is unrealistic to expect batterers to abandon violent behavior after one intervention. But a "statistically significant reduction in violence" may mean little to a battered woman.[6]

A "statistically significant reduction in violence" may mean little to a battered woman.

New Directions for Protecting Victims

The bottom line is: What are the best ways to protect victims? Batterer intervention programs are one approach, although much remains to be learned about them—specifically, which program works best for which batterer under which circumstances.[7] But perhaps what is needed is a whole new approach.

Rethinking Intervention

The models that underlie batterer intervention programs may need improvement. New approaches based on research into the causes of battering and batterer profiles[8] may be more productive than a one-size-fits-all approach.[9] Researchers may also draw lessons from other disciplines, such as substance abuse interventions—for example, that length of treatment may influence the outcome.[10]

Improvements in how programs are put into practice may also be necessary, since variations in how programs are carried out may reduce their effectiveness. Researchers have noted greater effects in demonstration programs implemented by researchers than in practical programs implemented by juvenile or criminal justice agencies. Thus, the degree to which a program is faithful to the intervention model may determine how well it works. For example, some programs have few sanctions for dropping out, whereas others closely monitor attendance. This suggests the need to test the effectiveness of close monitoring and required attendance.

Although these studies focus on male batterers, women batter as well. The dynamics of battering appear to differ for men and women, which suggests a need for intervention programs designed specifically for female batterers. Currently, it appears that most women batterers are being placed in male-dominated batterer intervention programs.

Linking Batterer Programs to Other Programs and Responses

Batterer intervention programs may be effective only in the context of a broader criminal justice and community response to domestic violence that includes arrest, restraining orders, intensive monitoring of batterers,[11] and changes to social norms that inadvertently tolerate partner violence.

If monitoring is partly responsible for lower reoffense rates, as the Brooklyn experiment suggests, judicial monitoring may be a useful approach. The Judicial Oversight Demonstration initiative—a collaboration among the National Institute of Justice, the Office on Violence Against Women, and three local jurisdictions—is testing this idea.[12] Other innovations might include mandatory intervention (indeterminate probation) until the batterer no longer endangers his partner, an approach that has been used with sex offenders.[13]

Improving Evaluations

Although the quality of batterer intervention program evaluations has improved,[14] barriers remain. By collaborating, researchers, practitioners, and policymakers may be able to develop better strategies and improve the rigor of experimental evaluations.

For example, researchers need to find better ways to maintain contact with batterers and victims and better instruments than the revised CTS2.[15] They need to develop more reliable ways of validating batterer and victim reports than relying strictly on official records of rearrests and probation violations. Statistical tools can be applied to correct for nonrandom assignment and other problems.[16]

Since batterer intervention programs are a relatively new response to a critical social problem, it is too early to abandon the concept. More work needs to be done to determine the causes of battering and test new responses.

Notes

1. Davis, R.C., B.G. Taylor, and C.D. Maxwell, *Does Batterer Treatment Reduce Violence? A Randomized Experiment in Brooklyn,* final report to the National Institute of Justice, Washington, DC: National Institute of Justice, 2000, NCJ 180772; Feder, L., and D.R. Forde, *A Test of the Efficacy of Court-Mandated Counseling for Domestic Violence Offenders: The Broward Experiment,* final report to the National Institute of Justice, Washington, DC: National Institute of Justice, 2000, NCJ 184752.

2. Compromises in random assignment may have diluted the Brooklyn program's impact.

3. See Gondolf, E.W., "Patterns of Reassault in Batterer Programs," *Violence and Victims* 12(4)(1997): 373–87; and

Harrell, A.V., *Evaluation of Court-Ordered Treatment for Domestic Violence Offenders,* final report to the State Justice Institute, Washington, DC: The Urban Institute, 1991.

4. The revised CTS2 assesses offender reports of abuse. See Straus, M.A., S.L. Hamby, S. Boney-McCoy, and D.B. Sugarman, "The Revised Conflict Tactics Scale (CTS2): Development and Preliminary Psychometric Data," *Journal of Family Issues* 17(3)(1996): 283–316. Concerns about the types of batterers studied and the effects of mandating treatment are discussed in Davis, et al., *Does Batterer Treatment Reduce Violence?* 15–17.

5. The Broward study statistically tested for this possibility and found no treatment effect.

6. See Edleson, J.L., "Controversy and Change in Batterer's Programs," in *Future Interventions with Battered Women and Their Families,* ed. J.L. Edleson and Z.C. Eisikovitz, Thousand Oaks, CA: Sage Publications, 1996.

7. Gondolf, E.W., "Batterer Programs: What We Know and Need to Know," *Journal of Interpersonal Violence* 12(1)(1997): 83–98.

8. Holtzworth-Munroe, A., and G.L. Stuart, "Typologies of Male Batterers: Three Subtypes and the Differences Among Them," *Psychological Bulletin* 116(3)(1994): 476–97. Also see Wexler, D.B., "The Broken Mirror: A Self Psychological Treatment Perspective for Relationship Violence," *Journal of Psychotherapy, Practice, and Research* 8(2)(1999): 129–41.

9. Healey, K., C. Smith, and C. O'Sullivan, *Batterer Intervention: Program Approaches and Criminal Justice Strategies,* Issues and Practices, Washington, DC: U.S. Department of Justice, National Institute of Justice, 1998, NCJ 168638.

10. Taxman, F.S., "12 Steps to Improved Offender Outcomes: Developing Responsive Systems of Care for Substance-Abusing Offenders," *Corrections Today* 60(6)(1998): 114–117, 166. Also see Howard, K.I., K. Moras, and W. Lutz, "Evaluation of Psychotherapy: Efficacy, Effectiveness, and Patient Progress," *American Psychologist* 51(10)(1996): 1059–1064.

11. A. Klein, cited in Healey, et al., *Batterer Intervention: Program Approaches and Criminal Justice Strategies,* 10.

12. "Experiment Demonstrates How to Hold Batterers Accountable," *National Institute of Justice Journal* 244 (July 2000): 29.

13. Hafemeister, T.L., "Legal Aspects of the Treatment of Offenders With Mental Disorders," in R.M. Wettstein, ed., *Treatment of Offenders With Mental Disorders,* New York: Guilford Press, 1998: 44–125.

14. Davis, R.C., and B.G. Taylor, "Does Batterer Treatment Reduce Violence? A Synthesis of the Literature," *Women and Criminal Justice* 10(2)(1999): 69–93.

15. See Gondolf, E.W., "Batterer Programs: What We Know and Need to Know;" and Sullivan, C.M., M.H. Rumptz, R. Campbell, K.K. Eby, and W.S. Davidson, "Retaining Participants in Longitudinal Community Research: A Comprehensive Protocol," *Journal of Applied Behavioral Science* 32(3)(1996): 262–76.

16. See Jackson, S., et al., *Batterer Intervention Programs: Where Do We Go From Here?* NIJ Special Report, Washington, DC: U.S. Department of Justice, National Institute of Justice, June 2003, NCJ 195079: 26.

From *National Institute of Justice Report,* September 2003, pp. ii, 1–8. Published by the U.S. Department of Justice.

Telling the Truth about Damned Lies and Statistics

Joel Best

The dissertation prospectus began by quoting a statistic—a "grabber" meant to capture the reader's attention. The graduate student who wrote this prospectus undoubtedly wanted to seem scholarly to the professors who would read it; they would be supervising the proposed research. And what could be more scholarly than a nice, authoritative statistic, quoted from a professional journal in the student's field?

So the prospectus began with this (carefully footnoted) quotation: "Every year since 1950, the number of American children gunned down has doubled." I had been invited to serve on the student's dissertation committee. When I read the quotation, I assumed the student had made an error in copying it. I went to the library and looked up the article the student had cited. There, in the journal's 1995 volume, was exactly the same sentence: "Every year since 1950, the number of American children gunned down has doubled."

This quotation is my nomination for a dubious distinction: I think it may be the worst—that is, the most inaccurate—social statistic ever.

What makes this statistic so bad? Just for the sake of argument, let's assume that "the number of American children gunned down" in 1950 was one. If the number doubled each year, there must have been two children gunned down in 1951, four in 1952, eight in 1953, and so on. By 1960, the number would have been 1,024. By 1965, it would have been 32,768 (in 1965, the F.B.I. identified only 9,960 criminal homicides in the entire country, including adult as well as child victims). By 1970, the number would have passed one million; by 1980, one billion (more than four times the total U.S. population in that year). Only three years later, in 1983, the number of American children gunned down would have been 8.6 billion (nearly twice the earth's population at the time). Another milestone would have been passed in 1987, when the number of gunned-down American children (137 billion) would have surpassed the best estimates for the total human population throughout history (110 billion). By 1995, when the article was published, the annual number of victims would have been over 35 trillion—a really big number, of a magnitude you rarely encounter outside economics or astronomy.

Thus my nomination: estimating the number of American child gunshot victims in 1995 at 35 trillion must be as far off—as hilariously, wildly wrong—as a social statistic can be. (If anyone spots a more inaccurate social statistic, I'd love to hear about it.)

Where did the article's author get this statistic? I wrote the author, who responded that the statistic came from the Children's Defense Fund, a well-known advocacy group for children. The C.D.F.'s *The State of America's Children Yearbook 1994* does state: "The number of American children killed each year by guns has doubled since 1950." Note the difference in the wording—the C.D.F. claimed there were twice as many deaths in 1994 as in 1950; the article's author reworded that claim and created a very different meaning.

It is worth examining the history of this statistic. It began with the C.D.F. noting that child gunshot deaths had doubled from 1950 to 1994. This is not quite as dramatic an increase as it might seem. Remember that the U.S. population also rose throughout this period; in fact, it grew about 73 percent—or nearly double. Therefore, we might expect all sorts of things—including the number of child gunshot deaths—to increase, to nearly double, just because the population grew. Before we can decide whether twice as many deaths indicates that things are getting worse, we'd have to know more. The C.D.F. statistic raises other issues as well: Where did the statistic come from? Who counts child gunshot deaths, and how? What is meant by a "child" (some C.D.F. statistics about violence include everyone under age 25)? What is meant by "killed by guns" (gunshot-death statistics often include suicides and accidents, as well as homicides)? But people rarely ask questions of this sort when they encounter statistics. Most of the time, most people simply accept statistics without question.

Certainly, the article's author didn't ask many probing, critical questions about the C.D.F.'s claim. Impressed by the statistic, the author repeated it—well, meant to repeat it. Instead, by rewording the C.D.F.'s claim, the author created a mutant statistic, one garbled almost beyond recognition.

But people treat mutant statistics just as they do other statistics—that is, they usually accept even the most implausible claims without question. For example, the journal editor who accepted the author's article for publication did not bother to consider the implications of child victims doubling each year. And people repeat bad statistics: The graduate student copied the garbled statistic and inserted it into the dissertation prospectus. Who knows whether still other readers were impressed by the author's statistic and remembered it or repeated it? The article remains on the shelf in hundreds of libraries, available to anyone who needs a dramatic quote. The lesson should be clear: Bad statistics live on; they take on lives of their own.

Some statistics are born bad—they aren't much good from the start, because they are based on nothing more than guesses or dubious data. Other statistics mutate; they become bad after being mangled (as in the case of the author's creative rewording). Either way, bad statistics are potentially important: They can be used to stir up public outrage or fear; they can distort our understanding of our world; and they can lead us to make poor policy choices.

The notion that we need to watch out for bad statistics isn't new. We've all heard people say, "You can prove anything with statistics." The title of my book, *Damned Lies and Statistics*, comes from a famous aphorism (usually attributed to Mark Twain or Benjamin Disraeli): "There are three kinds of lies: lies, damned lies, and statistics." There is even a useful little book, still in print after more than 40 years, called *How to Lie With Statistics*.

We shouldn't ignore all statistics, or assume that every number is false. Some statistics are bad, but others are pretty good. And we need good statistics to talk sensibly about social problems.

Statistics, then, have a bad reputation. We suspect that statistics may be wrong, that people who use statistics may be "lying"—trying to manipulate us by using numbers to somehow distort the truth. Yet, at the same time, we need statistics; we depend upon them to summarize and clarify the nature of our complex society. This is particularly true when we talk about social problems. Debates about social problems routinely raise questions that demand statistical answers: Is the problem widespread? How many people—and which people—does it affect? Is it getting worse? What does it cost society? What will it cost to deal with it? Convincing answers to such questions demand evidence, and that usually means numbers, measurements, statistics.

But can't you prove anything with statistics? It depends on what "prove" means. If we want to know, say, how many children are "gunned down" each year, we can't simply guess—pluck a number from thin air: 100, 1,000, 10,000, 35 trillion, whatever. Obviously, there's no reason to consider an arbitrary guess "proof" of anything. However, it might be possible for someone—using records kept by police departments or hospital emergency rooms or coroners—to keep track of children who have been shot; compiling careful, complete records might give us a fairly accurate idea of the number of gunned-down children. If that number seems accurate enough, we might consider it very strong evidence—or proof.

The solution to the problem of bad statistics is not to ignore all statistics, or to assume that every number is false. Some statistics are bad, but others are pretty good, and we need statistics—good statistics—to talk sensibly about social problems. The solution, then, is not to give up on statistics, but to become better judges of the numbers we encounter. We need to think critically about statistics—at least critically enough to suspect that the number of children gunned down hasn't been doubling each year since 1950.

A few years ago, the mathematician John Allen Paulos wrote *Innumeracy*, a short, readable book about "mathematical illiteracy." Too few people, he argued, are comfortable with basic mathematical principles, and this makes them poor judges of the numbers they encounter. No doubt this is one reason we have so many bad statistics. But there are other reasons, as well.

Social statistics describe society, but they are also products of our social arrangements. The people who bring social statistics to our attention have reasons for doing so; they inevitably want something, just as reporters and the other media figures who repeat and publicize statistics have their own goals. Statistics are tools, used for particular purposes. Thinking critically about statistics requires understanding their place in society.

While we may be more suspicious of statistics presented by people with whom we disagree—people who favor different political parties or have different beliefs—bad statistics are used to promote all sorts of causes. Bad statistics come from conservatives on the political right and liberals on the left, from wealthy corporations and powerful government agencies, and from advocates of the poor and the powerless.

In order to interpret statistics, we need more than a checklist of common errors. We need a general approach, an orientation, a mind-set that we can use to think about new statistics that we encounter. We ought to approach statistics thoughtfully. This can be hard to do, precisely because so many people in our society treat statistics as fetishes. We might call this the mind-set of the Awestruck—the people who don't think critically, who act as though statistics have magical powers. The awestruck know they don't always understand the statistics they hear, but this doesn't bother them. After all, who can expect to understand magical numbers? The reverential fatalism of the awestruck is not thoughtful—it is a way of avoiding thought. We need a different approach.

One choice is to approach statistics critically. Being critical does not mean being negative or hostile—it is not cynicism. The critical approach statistics thoughtfully; they avoid the extremes of both naive acceptance and cynical rejection of the numbers they encounter. Instead, the critical attempt to evaluate numbers, to distinguish between good statistics and bad statistics.

The critical understand that, while some social statistics may be pretty good, they are never perfect. Every statistic is a way of summarizing complex information into relatively simple numbers. Inevitably, some information, some of the complexity, is lost whenever we use statistics. The critical recognize that this is an inevitable limitation of statistics. Moreover, they realize that every statistic is the product of choices—the choice between defining a category broadly or narrowly, the choice of one measurement over another, the choice of a sample.

People choose definitions, measurements, and samples for all sorts of reasons: Perhaps they want to emphasize some aspect of a problem; perhaps it is easier or cheaper to gather data in a particular way—many considerations can come into play. Every statistic is a compromise among choices. This means that every definition—and every measurement and every sample—probably has limitations and can be criticized.

Being critical means more than simply pointing to the flaws in a statistic. Again, every statistic has flaws. The issue is whether a particular statistic's flaws are severe enough to damage its usefulness. Is the definition so broad that it encompasses too many false positives (or so narrow that it excludes too many false negatives)? How would changing the definition alter the statistic? Similarly, how do the choices of measurements and samples affect the statistic? What would happen if different measures or samples were chosen? And how is the statistic used? Is it being interpreted appropriately, or has its meaning been mangled to create a mutant statistic? Are the comparisons that are being made appropriate, or are apples being confused with oranges? How do different choices produce the conflicting numbers found in stat wars? These are the sorts of questions the critical ask.

As a practical matter, it is virtually impossible for citizens in contemporary society to avoid statistics about social problems. Statistics arise in all sorts of ways, and in almost every case the people promoting statistics want to persuade us. Activists use statistics to convince us that social problems are serious and deserve our attention and concern. Charities use statistics to encourage donations. Politicians use statistics to persuade us that they understand society's problems and that they deserve our support. The media use statistics to make their reporting more dramatic, more convincing, more compelling. Corporations use statistics to promote and improve their products. Researchers use statistics to document their findings and support their conclusions. Those with whom we agree use statistics to reassure us that we're on the right side, while our opponents use statistics to try and convince us that we are wrong. Statistics are one of the standard types of evidence used by people in our society.

It is not possible simply to ignore statistics, to pretend they don't exist. That sort of head-in-the-sand approach would be too costly. Without statistics, we limit our ability to think thoughtfully about our society; without statistics, we have no accurate ways of judging how big a problem may be, whether it is getting worse, or how well the policies designed to address that problem actually work. And awestruck or naive attitudes toward statistics are no better than ignoring statistics; statistics have no magical properties, and it is foolish to assume that all statistics are equally valid. Nor is a cynical approach the answer; statistics are too widespread and too useful to be automatically discounted.

It would be nice to have a checklist, a set of items we could consider in evaluating any statistic. The list might detail potential problems with definitions, measurements, sampling, mutation, and so on. These are, in fact, common sorts of flaws found in many statistics, but they should not be considered a formal, complete checklist. It is probably impossible to produce a complete list of statistical flaws—no matter how long the list, there will be other possible problems that could affect statistics.

The goal is not to memorize a list, but to develop a thoughtful approach. Becoming critical about statistics requires being prepared to ask questions about numbers. When encountering a new statistic in, say, a news report, the critical try to assess it. What might be the sources for this number? How could one go about producing the figure? Who produced the number, and what interests might they have? What are the different ways key terms might have been defined, and which definitions have been chosen? How might the phenomena be measured, and which measurement choices have been made? What sort of sample was gathered, and how might that sample affect the result? Is the statistic being properly interpreted? Are comparisons being made, and if so, are the comparisons appropriate? Are there competing statistics? If so, what stakes do the opponents have in the issue, and how are those stakes likely to affect their use of statistics? And is it possible to figure out why the statistics seem to disagree, what the differences are in the ways the competing sides are using figures?

At first, this list of questions may seem overwhelming. How can an ordinary person—someone who reads a statistic in a magazine article or hears it on a news broadcast—determine the answers to such questions? Certainly news reports rarely give detailed information on the processes by which statistics are created. And few of us have time to drop everything and investigate the background of some new number we encounter. Being critical, it seems, involves an impossible amount of work.

In practice, however, the critical need not investigate the origin of every statistic. Rather, being critical means appreciating the inevitable limitations that affect all statistics, rather than being awestruck in the presence of numbers. It means not being too credulous, not accepting every statistic at face value. But it also means appreciating that statistics, while always imperfect, can be useful. Instead of automatically discounting every statistic, the critical reserve judgment. When confronted with an interesting number, they may try to learn more, to evaluate, to weigh the figure's strengths and weaknesses.

Of course, this critical approach need not—and should not—be limited to statistics. It ought to apply to all the evidence we encounter when we scan a news report, or listen to a speech—whenever we learn about social problems. Claims about social problems often feature dramatic, compelling examples; the critical might ask whether an example is likely to be a typical case or an extreme, exceptional instance. Claims about social problems often include quotations from different sources, and the critical might wonder why those sources have spoken and why they have been quoted: Do they have particular expertise? Do they stand to benefit if they influence others? Claims about social problems usually involve arguments about the problem's causes and potential solutions. The critical might ask whether these arguments are convincing. Are they logical? Does the proposed solution seem feasible and appropriate? And so on.

Being critical—adopting a skeptical, analytical stance when confronted with claims—is an approach that goes far beyond simply dealing with statistics.

Statistics are not magical. Nor are they always true—or always false. Nor need they be incomprehensible. Adopting a critical approach offers an effective way of responding to the numbers we are sure to encounter. Being critical requires more thought, but failing to adopt a critical mind-set makes us powerless to evaluate what others tell us. When we fail to think critically, the statistics we hear might just as well be magical.

JOEL BEST is a professor of sociology and criminal justice at the University of Delaware. This essay is excerpted from *Damned Lies and Statistics: Untangling Numbers From the Media, Politicians, and Activists,* published by the University of California Press and reprinted by permission. Copyright © 2001 by the Regents of the University of California.

From *Chronicle of Higher Education,* May 4, 2001, pp. B7–B9. Excerpted from *Damned Lies and Statistics: Untangling Numbers from the Media, Politicians, and Activists.* (University of California Press, 2001). Copyright © 2001 by Joel Best. Reprinted by permission of The Regents of the University of California via Rights link.

Violence and the Remaking of a Self

SUSAN J. BRISON

On July 4, 1990, at 10:30 in the morning, I went for a walk along a country road in a village outside Grenoble, France. It was a gorgeous day, and I didn't envy my husband, Tom, who had to stay inside and work on a manuscript with a French colleague. I sang to myself as I set out, stopping along the way to pet a goat and pick a few wild strawberries. About an hour and a half later, I was lying face down in a muddy creek bed at the bottom of a dark ravine, struggling to stay alive.

I had been grabbed from behind, pulled into the bushes, beaten, and sexually assaulted. Helpless and entirely at my assailant's mercy, I talked to him, trying to appeal to his humanity, and, when that failed, addressing myself to his self-interest. He called me a whore and told me to shut up. Although I had said I'd do whatever he wanted, as the sexual assault began I instinctively fought back, which so enraged my attacker that he strangled me until I lost consciousness.

When I came to, I was being dragged by my feet down into the ravine. I had often thought I was awake while dreaming, but now I was awake and convinced I was having a nightmare. But it was no dream. After ordering me to get on my hands and knees, the man strangled me again. This time I was sure I was dying. But I revived, just in time to see him lunging toward me with a rock. He smashed it into my forehead, knocking me out. Eventually, after another strangulation attempt, he left me for dead.

After I was rescued and taken to the Grenoble hospital, where I spent the next 11 days, I was told repeatedly how "lucky" I was to be alive, and for a short while I even believed this myself. At the time, I did not yet know how trauma not only haunts the conscious and unconscious mind but also remains in the body, in each of the senses, in the heart that races and the skin that crawls whenever something resurrects the buried terror. I didn't know that the worst—the unimaginably painful aftermath of violence—was yet to come.

For the first several months after my attack, I led a spectral existence, not quite sure whether I had died and the world was going on without me, or whether I was alive but in a totally alien world. The line between life and death, once so clear and sustaining, now seemed carelessly drawn and easily erased. I felt as though I'd outlived myself, as if I'd stayed on a train one stop past my destination.

> **After I was rescued and taken to the hospital, I was told repeatedly how 'lucky' I was to be alive. For a short while I even believed this myself.**

My sense of unreality was fed by the massive denial of those around me—a reaction that is an almost universal response to rape, I learned. Where the facts would appear to be incontrovertible, denial takes the shape of attempts to explain the assault in ways that leave the observers' worldview unscathed. Even those who are able to acknowledge the existence of violence try to protect themselves from the realization that the world in which it occurs is their world. They cannot allow themselves to imagine the victim's shattered life, or else their illusions about their own safety and control over their lives might begin to crumble.

The most well-meaning individuals, caught up in the myth of their own immunity, can inadvertently add to the victim's suffering by suggesting that the attack was avoidable or somehow her fault. One victims'-assistance coordinator, whom I had phoned for legal advice, stressed that she herself had never been a victim and said I would benefit from the experience by learning not to be so trusting of people and to take basic safety precautions, like not going out alone late at night. She didn't pause long enough for me to point out that I had been attacked suddenly, from behind, in broad daylight.

I was initially reluctant to tell people (other than medical and legal personnel) that I had been raped. I still wonder why I wanted the sexual aspect of the assault—so salient to me—kept secret. I was motivated in part by shame, I suppose, and I wanted to avoid being stereotyped as a victim. I did not want the academic work I had already done on pornography and violence against women to be dismissed as the ravings of a "hysterical rape victim." And I felt that I had very little control over the meaning of the word "rape." Using the term denied the particularity of what I had experienced and invoked in other people whatever rape scenario they had already constructed. I later identified myself publicly as a rape survivor, having decided that it was ethically and politically imperative for me to do so.

But my initial wariness about the use of the term was understandable and, at times, reinforced by others' responses—especially by the dismissive characterization of the rape by some in the criminal-justice system. Before my assailant's trial, I heard my lawyer conferring with another lawyer on the question of victim's compensation from the state (to cover legal expenses and unreimbursed medical bills). He said, without irony, that a certain amount was typically awarded for "*un viol gentil*" ("a nice rape") and somewhat more (which they would request on my behalf) for "*un viol méchant*" ("a nasty rape").

Not surprisingly, I felt that I was taken more seriously as a victim of a near-fatal murder attempt. But that description of the assault provided others with no explanation of what had happened. Later, when people asked why this man had tried to kill me, I revealed that the attack had begun as a sexual assault, and most people were satisfied with that as an explanation. It made some kind of sense to them. But it made no sense to me.

A few months after the assault, I sat down at my computer to write about it for the first time, and all I could come up with was a list of paradoxes. Just about everything had stopped making sense. I thought it was quite possible that I was brain-damaged as a result of the head injuries I had sustained. Or perhaps the heightened lucidity I had experienced during the assault remained, giving me a clearer, though profoundly disorienting, picture of the world. I turned to philosophy for meaning and consolation and could find neither. Had my reasoning broken down? Or was it the breakdown of Reason? I couldn't explain what had happened to me. I

was attacked for no reason. I had ventured outside the human community, landed beyond the moral universe, beyond the realm of predictable events and comprehensible actions, and I didn't know how to get back.

As a philosopher, I was used to taking something apparently obvious and familiar—the nature of time, say, or the relation between words and things—and making it into something quite puzzling. But now, when I was confronted with the utterly strange and paradoxical, philosophy was, at least initially, of no use in helping me to make sense of it. And it was hard for me, given my philosophical background, to accept that knowledge isn't always desirable, that the truth doesn't always set you free. Sometimes, it fills you with incapacitating terror, and then uncontrollable rage.

I was surprised, perhaps naively, to find that there was virtually nothing in the philosophical literature about sexual violence; obviously, it raised numerous philosophical issues. The disintegration of the self experienced by victims of violence challenges our notions of personal identity over time, a major preoccupation of metaphysics. A victim's seemingly justified skepticism about everyone and everything is pertinent to epistemology, especially if the goal of epistemology is, as Wilfrid Sellars put it, that of feeling at home in the world. In aesthetics, as well as in the philosophy of law, the discussion of sexual violence in—or as—art could use the illumination provided by a victim's perspective. Perhaps the most important questions that sexual violence poses are in social, political, and legal philosophy. Insight into those areas, as well, requires an understanding of what it's like to be a victim of such violence.

It occurred to me that the fact that rape has not been considered a properly philosophical subject—unlike war, for example—resulted not only from the paucity of women in the profession but also from the disciplinary biases against thinking about the "personal" or the particular, and against writing in the form of narrative. (Of course, the avowedly personal experiences of *men* have been neglected in philosophical analysis as well. The study of the ethics of war, for example, has dealt with questions of strategy and justice as viewed from the outside, not with the wartime experiences of soldiers or with the aftermath of their trauma.) But first-person narratives, especially ones written by those with perspectives previously excluded from the discipline, are essential to philosophy. They are necessary for exposing previously hidden biases in the discipline's subject matter and methodology, for facilitating understanding of (or empathy with) those different from ourselves, and for laying on the table our own biases as scholars.

When I resumed teaching at Dartmouth, the first student who came to my office told me that she had been raped. Since I had spoken out publicly several months earlier about my assault, I knew that I would be in contact with other survivors. I just didn't realize that there would be so many—not only students, but also female colleagues and friends, who had never before told me that they had been raped. I continued to teach my usual philosophy courses, but, in some ways philosophy struck me as a luxury when I knew, in a more visceral way than before, that people were being brutally attacked and killed—all the time. So I integrated my work on trauma with my academic interests by teaching a course on global violence against women. I was still somewhat afraid of what would happen if I wrote about my assault, but I was much more afraid of what would continue to happen if I, and others with similar experiences, didn't make them public.

It was one thing to have decided to speak and write about my rape, but another to find the voice with which to do it. Even after my fractured trachea had healed, I frequently had trouble speaking. I lost my voice, literally, when I lost my ability to continue my life's narrative, when things stopped making sense. I was never entirely mute, but I often had bouts of what a friend labeled "fractured speech," during which I stuttered and stammered, unable to string together a simple sentence without the words scattering like a broken necklace. During the assault itself, my heightened lucidity had seemed to be accompanied by an unusual linguistic fluency—in French, no less. But being able to speak quickly and (so it seemed to me) precisely in a foreign language when I felt I had to in order to survive was followed by episodes, spread over several years, when I couldn't, for the life of me, speak intelligibly even in my mother tongue.

The fact that rape has not been considered a properly philosophical subject results in part from disciplinary biases against thinking about the 'personal.'

For about a year after the assault, I rarely, if ever, spoke in smoothly flowing sentences. I could sing, though, after about six months, and, like aphasics who cannot say a word but can sing verse after verse, I never stumbled over the lyrics. I recall spending the hour's drive home from the weekly meetings of my support group of rape survivors singing every spiritual I'd ever heard. It was a comfort and a release. Mainly, it was something I could do, loudly, openly (by myself in a closed car), and easily, accompanied by unstoppable tears.

Even after I regained my ability to speak, more or less reliably, in English, I was unable to speak, without debilitating difficulty, in French. Before my ill-fated trip in the summer of 1990, I'd never have passed for a native speaker, but I'd visited France many times and spent several summers there. I came of age there, intellectually, immersing myself in the late 1970s in research on French feminism, which had led to my interviewing Simone de Beauvoir (in Rome) one summer. Now, more than 10 years after the assault, I still almost never speak French, even in Francophone company, in which I often find myself, given my husband's interests.

After regaining my voice, I sometimes lost it again— once for an entire week after my brother committed suicide on Christmas Eve, 1995. Although I'd managed to keep my speech impairment hidden from my colleagues and students for five and a half years, I found that I had to ask a colleague to take over a class I'd been scheduled to teach the day after the funeral. I feared that I'd suffer a linguistic breakdown in front of a lecture hall full of students.

I lost my voice again, intermittently, during my tenure review, about a year after my brother's death. And, although I could still write (and type) during this time, I can see now that my writing about violence had become increasingly hesitant and guarded, as I hid behind academic jargon and excessive citations of others' work. Not only had my brother's suicide caused me to doubt whether I, who had, after all, survived, was entitled to talk about the trauma I'd endured, but now I could not silence the internalized voices of those who had warned me not to publish my work on sexual violence before getting tenure. In spite of the warm reception my writing on the subject was receiving in the larger academic community—from feminist philosophers and legal theorists, people in women's studies, and scholars from various disciplines who were interested in trauma—I stopped writing in the personal voice and slipped back into the universal mode, thinking that only writing about trauma in general was important enough to justify the academic risks I was taking. And I took fewer and fewer risks.

After getting tenure, I was given sanctuary, for nearly two years, at the Institute for Advanced Study, in Princeton. There I gradually came to feel safe enough to write, once again, in my own voice, about what I considered to be philosophically important. It helped to be surrounded by a diverse group of scholars who, to my initial amazement and eternal gratitude, simply assumed that whatever

I was working on must be of sufficient intellectual interest to be worth bothering about.

My linguistic disability never resurfaced in my many conversations at the institute, although it returned later, after a particularly stressful incident at Dartmouth. That episode, more than eight and a half years after the assault, forced me to accept that I have what may well be a permanent neurological glitch resulting from my brain's having been stunned into unconsciousness four times during the attack. Although I had spoken out as a rape survivor at a Take Back the Night rally nine months after the event, it took me nearly nine years to acknowledge, even to myself, that the assault had left me neurologically disabled—very minimally, to be sure, in a way that I could easily compensate for, by avoiding extremely stressful situations, but disabled nonetheless.

People ask me if I'm recovered now, and I reply that it depends on what that means. If they mean, am I back to where I was before the attack? I have to say no, and I never will be. I am not the same person who set off, singing, on that sunny Fourth of July in the French countryside. I left her in a rocky creek bed at the bottom of a ravine. I had to in order to survive. The trauma has changed me forever, and if I insist too often that my friends and family acknowledge it, that's because I'm afraid they don't know who I am.

But if recovery means being able to incorporate this awful knowledge of trauma and its aftermath into my life and carry on, then, yes, I'm recovered. I don't wake each day with a start, thinking: "This can't have happened to me!" It happened. I have no guarantee that it won't happen again. I don't expect to be able to transcend or redeem the trauma, or to solve the dilemmas of survival. I think the goal of recovery is simply to endure. That is hard enough, especially when sometimes it seems as if the only way to regain control over one's life is to end it.

A few months after my assault, I drove by myself for several hours to visit my friend Margot. Though driving felt like a much safer mode of transportation than walking, I worried throughout the journey, not only about the trajectory of every oncoming vehicle but also about my car breaking down, leaving me at the mercy of potentially murderous passersby. I wished I'd had a gun so that I could shoot myself rather than be forced to live through another assault. Later in my recovery, as depression gave way to rage, such suicidal thoughts

were quickly quelled by a stubborn refusal to finish my assailant's job for him. I also learned, after martial-arts training, that I was capable, morally as well as physically, of killing in self-defense—an option that made the possibility of another life-threatening attack one I could live with.

Some rape survivors have remarked on the sense of moral loss they experienced when they realized that they could kill their assailants, but I think that this thought can be seen as a salutary character change in those whom society does not encourage to value their own lives enough. And, far from jeopardizing their connections with a community, this newfound ability to defend themselves—and to consider themselves worth fighting for—enables rape survivors to move once more among others, free of debilitating fears. It gave me the courage to bring a child into the world, in spite of the realization that doing so would, far from making me immortal, make me twice as mortal, doubling my chances of having my life destroyed by a speeding truck.

But many trauma survivors who endured much worse than I did, and for much longer, found, often years later, that it was impossible to go on. It is not a moral failing to leave a world that has become morally unacceptable. I wonder how some people can ask of battered women, Why didn't they leave? while saying of those driven to suicide by the brutal and inescapable aftermath of trauma, Why didn't they stay? Jean Améry wrote, "Whoever was tortured, stays tortured," and that may explain why he, Primo Levi, Paul Celan, and other Holocaust survivors took their own lives decades after their physical torture ended, as if such an explanation were needed.

Those who have survived trauma understand the pull of that solution to their daily Beckettian dilemma—"I can't go on, I must go on"—for on some days the conclusion "I'll go on" can be reached by neither faith nor reason. How does one go on with a shattered self, with no guarantee of recovery, believing that one will always stay tortured and never feel at home in the world? One hopes for a bearable future, in spite of all the inductive evidence to the contrary. After all, the loss of faith in induction following an unpredictable trauma has a reassuring side: Since inferences from the past can no longer be relied upon to predict the future, there's no more reason to think that tomorrow will bring agony than to think that it won't. So one makes a wager, in which nothing is certain and the odds change daily, and sets about willing to believe that life, for all its unfathomable horror, still holds some undiscovered pleasures. And one remakes oneself by finding meaning in a life of caring for and being sustained by others.

While I used to have to will myself out of bed each day, I now wake gladly to feed my son, whose birth gave me reason not to have died. Having him has forced me to rebuild my trust in the world, to try to believe that the world is a good enough place in which to raise him. He is so trusting that, before he learned to walk, he would stand with outstretched arms, wobbling, until he fell, stiff-limbed, forward, backward, certain the universe would catch him. So far it has, and when I tell myself it always will, the part of me that he's become believes it.

SUSAN J. BRISON is an associate professor of philosophy at Dartmouth College and a visiting associate professor of philosophy at Princeton University. She is the author of *Aftermath: Violence and the Remaking of a Self*, published by Princeton University Press.

Understanding Stockholm Syndrome

NATHALIE DE FABRIQUE, PSYD, STEPHEN J. ROMANO, MA, GREGORY M. VECCHI, PHD, AND VINCENT B. VAN HASSELT, PHD

Men, when they receive good from whence they expect evil, feel the more indebted to their benefactor.

—Niccolo Machiavelli

The world watched as Elizabeth Smart's family, both panicked and heartbroken, desperately cried out to news cameras and begged for their teenager's safe return. Viewers saw haunting images from a home movie that featured a beautiful young girl playing the harp like an angel. The terror of this 14-year-old snatched from her bed captivated the hearts and minds of millions.

So, when authorities rescued and safely returned her home, people questioned how, in 9 months, she could not escape or ask someone—anyone—for help. But, her abductors did not hold her captive, as initially believed. In fact, she walked in public, attended parties, and even refused to reveal her true identity when first approached by police. Perhaps, even more puzzling than her initial reluctance to escape was her apparent concern upon rescue about the fate of her captors. "What's going to happen to them? Are they in trouble?" she asked. When informed by officers that they likely would face punishment, she started to cry and sobbed the whole way to the station.[1]

This high-profile kidnapping generated a lot of scrutiny. In attempting to explain her reluctance to be rescued and her compassion toward the perpetrators, some mistakenly have suggested that Elizabeth Smart serves as yet another example of Stockholm syndrome and that her captors must have "brainwashed" her.[2] However, compassion alone does not define the condition, and this situation did not feature all elements necessary for development to truly occur. Instead, the case demonstrates the difficulty of gaining a true understanding of the phenomenon. Although scenarios resulting in the condition are rare, crisis negotiators must have a clear understanding of the psychological processes related to Stockholm syndrome to recognize and successfully address hostage and barricade-with-victim situations where it manifests.

Stockholm Syndrome Defined
Background

The term *Stockholm syndrome* was coined after the 1973 robbery of Kreditbanken in Stockholm, Sweden, in which two robbers held four bank employees hostage from August 23 to 28. During this time, the victims shared a vault and became very familiar with their captors—in fact, they wound up emotionally attached and even defended them after the ordeal. Today, people view Stockholm syndrome as a psychological response of a hostage or an individual in a similar situation in which the more dominant person has the power to put the victim's life in danger. Perpetrators occasionally use this advantage to get victims to comply with their demands.[3]

Disagreement exists over the identification of which factors characterize incidents that contribute to the development of Stockholm syndrome. Research has suggested that hostages may exhibit the condition in situations that feature captors who do not abuse the victim, a long duration before resolution, continued contact between the perpetrator and hostage, and a high level of emotion. In fact, experts have concluded that the intensity, not the length of the incident, combined with a lack of physical abuse more likely will create favorable conditions for me development of Stockholm syndrome. Apparently, a strong emotional bond develops between persons who share these life-threatening experiences.

The 1985 hijacking of TWA Flight 847 showcases these factors and demonstrates the variability among me hostages' responses. Shortly after takeoff from Athens, Greece, two terrorists armed with guns stormed the cockpit and demanded the diversion of me flight to Beirut, Lebanon. After capturing the plane, the perpetrators released the women and children. Two sailors and a group of wealthy American businessmen remained on the aircraft, and the captors held mem for 10 days. During the incident, the terrorists threatened the hostages with guns to their heads and in their mouths. They also beat one of the victims to death and dumped his body out of the tail section of the plane.

After the eventual rescue, reporters interviewed the captives as they disembarked. When asked to describe the captors, one hostage stated, "They weren't bad people; they let me eat, they let me sleep, they gave me my life."[4] However, while one victim did display feelings of compassion for the perpetrators, most of the hostages showed no evidence of Stockholm syndrome. On the contrary, because of the violent manner in which the terrorists treated nearly all of the victims, most of the captives expressed fear that their captors would kill them and understood that their greatest chance for survival lay in the audiorities' hands.

"Crisis negotiators . . . encourage its development because it improves the chances of hostage survival. . . . "

Characteristics

Stockholm syndrome is a paradoxical psychological phenomenon wherein a positive bond between hostage and captor occurs that appears irrational in light of the frightening ordeal endured by me victims. In essence, eventually, the hostage views the perpetrator as giving life by simply not taking it. Individuals involved in situations resulting in Stockholm syndrome display three characteristics, although these do not always exist together. Law enforcement officers must encourage and tolerate the first two components to, hopefully, induce the third, which preserves life.

1. Hostages have positive feelings for their captors.
2. Victims show fear, distrust, and anger toward the authorities.
3. Perpetrators display positive feelings toward captives as they begin to see them as human beings.

Frequency of the Phenomenon

According to the FBI's Hostage Barricade Database System, which contains data pertaining to over 4,700 reported federal, state, and local hostage/barricade incidents, 73 percent of captives show no evidence of Stockholm syndrome. And, while victims can display negative feelings toward law enforcement (usually out of frustration with the pace of negotiations), most do not develop the condition.[5]

One of the authors, a retired FBI expert, stated that in a career of over 30 years in law enforcement, he rarely witnessed behavior indicative of the development of Stockholm syndrome.[6] "I've seen the reluctance on the part of some hostages who refuse to come out without the hostage taker less than a handful of times." His explanation rests on the approximation that nearly 96 percent of hostage and barricade situations in the United States are domestic in nature; involve suicide, attempted suicide, and domestic violence; and include subjects with an existing relationship. He reports that for Stockholm syndrome

to occur, the incident must take place between strangers, and the hostage must come to fear and resent law enforcement as much as or more than the perpetrators.

The Psychological Process

Fully comprehending Stockholm syndrome requires an understanding of the process that leads to its development. Most important, this condition does not result from a conscious decision or a rational choice to befriend a captor. From a psychological perspective, the ego, described by Sigmund Freud as the "personality core," is responsible for providing people with defense mechanisms—ways for them to guard or distance themselves from and remain consciously unaware of unpleasant thoughts, feelings, and desires—and also helps individuals avoid hurt and disorganization.[7]

In hostage situations, the healthy ego seeks a means to achieve survival. In cases where Stockholm syndrome has occurred, the captive is in a situation where the captor has stripped nearly all forms of independence and gained control of the victim's life, as well as basic needs for survival. Some experts say that the hostage regresses to, perhaps, a state of infancy; the captive must cry for food, remain silent, and exist in an extreme state of dependence. In contrast, the perpetrator serves as a mother figure protecting her child from a threatening outside world, including law enforcement's deadly weapons. The victim then begins a struggle for survival, both relying on and identifying with the captor. Possibly, hostages' motivation to live outweighs their impulse to hate the person who created their dilemma.[8]

The Importance of Understanding

Crisis negotiators no longer consider the bonding that occurs between captive and captor in cases of Stockholm syndrome detrimental. They encourage its development because it improves the chances of hostage survival, despite the fact that it sometimes means authorities no longer can count on the cooperation of victims in working for their release or later prosecuting the perpetrators.[9] As such, individuals working as crisis negotiators must understand how the phenomenon unfolds, as well as ways to promote the psychological process, thus increasing the likelihood of a successful outcome.

Comprehending how Stockholm syndrome develops requires an understanding of the mind-set of the captive. Hostages have to concentrate on survival, requiring avoidance of direct, honest reactions to destructive treatment.[10] They must become highly attuned to the pleasure and displeasure reactions of their captors. As a result, victims seem more concerned about the perpetrator's feelings than their own. Hostages are encouraged to develop psychological characteristics pleasing to hostage takers, such as dependency; lack of initiative; and an inability to act, decide, or think. The captive actively devises strategies for staying alive, including denial, attentiveness to the captor's wants, fondness (and fear) of the perpetrator, apprehension toward interference by authorities, and adoption of the hostage taker's perspective. Victims are overwhelmingly grateful to captors for giving them life and focus on their acts of kindness, rather than their brutality.[11]

Law enforcement and psychology professionals have offered several opinions concerning the development of Stockholm syndrome. However, most agree on the conditions necessary for it to occur.

- A person held in captivity cannot escape and depends on the hostage taker for life. The captor becomes the person in control of the captive's basic needs for survival and the victim's life itself.

- The hostage endures isolation from other people and has only the captor's perspective available. Perpetrators routinely keep information about the outside world's response to their actions from captives to keep them totally dependent.

- The hostage taker threatens to kill the victim and gives the perception as having the capability to do so. The captive judges it safer to align with the perpetrator, endure the hardship of captivity, and comply with the captor than to resist and face murder.

- The captive sees the perpetrator as showing some degree of kindness. Kindness serves as the cornerstone of Stockholm syndrome; the condition will not develop unless the captor exhibits it in some form toward the hostage. However, captives often misinterpret a lack of abuse as kindness and may develop feelings of appreciation for this perceived benevolence. If the captor is purely evil and abusive, the hostage will respond with hatred. But, if perpetrators show some kindness, victims will submerge the anger they feel in response to the terror and concentrate on the captors' "good side" to protect themselves.[12]

Humanization of the Captive

While many experts consider encouraging the development of Stockholm syndrome to increase hostage survival difficult, crisis negotiators can attempt to humanize the captive in the mind of the perpetrator, thereby stimulating the emergence of the critical, third characteristic in the hostage taker—positive feelings toward the captive. To this end, determining the number of people involved, as well as their names, is paramount.

Another way negotiators can attempt to personalize the hostage is to ask the subject to pass on a personal message to the victim (e.g., "Tell Mark that his children love him very much and will be there to meet him when he comes out."). This type of dialogue reminds the perpetrator of the hostage's name and that the victim is a real person with a family. It also inserts a suggestibility statement ("when he comes out") that implies a peaceful resolution.

Trying to initiate Stockholm syndrome in the perpetrator involves a delicate blend of personalizing captives without overhauling them. "Most hostage takers want it to be all about them. If the negotiator asks too many questions about the hostages, he may begin to feel ignored and discounted. If you want to solve the hostage's problems, you need to solve the hostage taker's problems."[13] To strike the balance necessary for successful negotiations, asking about the welfare of the captor first, and the captive later, is key.

Using those simple strategies may assist in formulating a bond between the victim and perpetrator. That being said, law enforcement personnel must be aware that although they are attempting to maintain the "balancing act" of increasing rapport with the hostage taker and influencing the safety of the hostages, the ultimate goal is to peacefully resolve the crisis for all involved. If achieving that result involves manipulating hostage takers' belief that the focus remains on them, then negotiators must be willing to understand the rationale behind the maneuver and learn the skills necessary to employ it.

Conclusion

The subject of Stockholm syndrome, fueled, in part, by a number of high-profile cases, has generated a lot of discussion and opinions. Many people find the phenomenon as difficult to understand as it is fascinating.

> " . . . this condition does not result from a conscious decision or a rational choice to befriend a captor."

Although, at first, this psychological process may appear complex and uncontrollable, further exploration with those experienced in the area of crisis negotiation revealed that the condition and its effects can serve as a useful tool in successful outcomes. In understanding the basis behind the mental state and behavior of both the hostage taker and the captive, law enforcement agencies can place Stockholm syndrome in the appropriate perspective and see it as a catalyst in improving the training of hostage negotiators and encouraging peaceful resolutions.

Notes

1. Maggie Haberman and Jeane MacIntosh, *Held Captive: The Kidnapping and Rescue of Elizabeth Smart* (New York, NY: Avon Books, 2003).

2. Paul Wong, "Elizabeth Smart and Stockholm Syndrome"; retrieved from http://www.meaning,calarticles/stockholm_syndrome.htm.

3. http://en.wikipedia.org/wiki/Stockholm_syndrome

4. Pete Williams, "Twenty Years Later, Stethems Still Seek Justice"; retrieved from http://www.msnbc.msn.com/id/8219264.

5. G. Dwayne Fuselier, "Placing the Stockholm Syndrome in Perspective," *FBI Law Enforcement Bulletin,* July 1999, 22–25.

6. Stephen J. Romano served as chief of the Crisis Negotiation Unit of the Critical Incident Response Group at the FBI Academy.

7. Sigmund Freud, *The Ego and the Id: The Standard Edition* (New York, NY: W.W. Norton and Company, 1960).

8. Thomas Strentz, "Law Enforcement Policy and Ego Defenses of the Hostage," *FBI Law Enforcement Bulletin,* April 1979, 2–12.

9. Edna Rawlings, Dee Graham, and Roberta Rigsby, *Loving to Survive: Sexual Terror, Men's Violence, and Women's Lives* (New York, NY: New York University Press, 1994).

10. Ibid.

11. Anne Jones, "Post-Traumatic Stress Disorder, Rape Trauma Syndrome, and Battering"; retrieved from http://www.ojp.usdoj.gov/ovc/new/victempow/student/postram.htm.

12. Ibid.

13. Supra note 6.

Dr. de Fabrique is involved with clinical work in psychology and is an adjunct faculty member at Nova Southeastern University in Davie, Florida. **Mr. Romano,** a retired FBI special agent, operates a consulting/training firm in Greenville, South Carolina, servicing corporate and law enforcement clients. **Dr. Van Hasselt** is a professor of psychology at Nova Southeastern University in Davie, Florida, and a part-time officer with the Plantation Police Department. **Dr. Vecchi** serves as a special agent in the Behavioral Science Unit at the FBI Academy.

From *FBI Law Enforcement Bulletin,* July 2007, pp. 10-15, by Nathalie De Fabrique et al. Published by the FBI Academy/Department of Justice, Federal Bureau of Investigation.

Sexual Assault on Campus: What Colleges and Universities Are Doing about It

HEATHER M. KARJANE, BONNIE S. FISHER, AND FRANCIS T. CULLEN

C ampus crime in general and sexual assault in particular have been receiving more attention than in the past, and concern has been expressed at the highest levels of government. On the Federal level, Congress responded by enacting several laws requiring institutions of higher education to notify students about crime on campus, publicize their prevention and response policies, maintain open crime logs, and ensure sexual assault victims their basic rights.[1] The Clery Act, the most notable of these laws, mandates an annual security report from each Federally funded school (see "Recent Federal Laws on Campus Crime").

In 1999, Congress asked the National Institute of Justice to find out what policies and procedures schools use to prevent and respond to reports of sexual assault.[2] The resulting study revealed that schools are making strides in some areas but must continue efforts to increase student safety and accountability. After summarizing what is known about the nature and extent of sexual assault on campus, the researchers highlighted findings regarding response policies and procedures; reporting options; barriers and facilitators; reporter training and prevention programming; victim resources; and investigation, adjudication, and campus sanctions. The study's baseline information can be used to measure progress in how institutions of higher education respond to sexual assault.

The Scope of the Problem

Administrators want their campuses to be safe havens for students as they pursue their education and mature intellectually and socially. But institutions of higher education are by no means crime-free; women students face a high risk for sexual assault.

Just under 3 percent of all college women become victims of rape (either completed or attempted) in a given 9-month academic year. On first glance, the risk seems low, but the percentage translates into the disturbing figure of 35 such crimes for every 1,000 women students. For a campus with 10,000 women students, the number could reach 350. If the percentage is projected to a full calendar year, the proportion rises to nearly 5 percent of college women. When projected over a now-typical

---

Recent Federal Laws on Campus Crime

Starting in 1990, Congress acted to ensure that institutions of higher education have strategies to prevent and respond to sexual assault on campus and to provide students and their parents accurate information about campus crime. The major Federal laws pertaining to this study are:

Student Right-to-Know and Campus Security Act of 1990 (the "Clery Act"*) (20 U.S.C. § 1092). This law, Title II of Public Law 101–542, requires that schools annually disclose information about crime, including specific sexual crime categories, in and around campus.

Campus Sexual Assault Victims' Bill of Rights of 1992. This amendment to the 1990 act requires that schools develop prevention policies and provide certain assurances to victims. The law was amended again in 1998 to expand requirements, including the crime categories that must be reported.

*The act was renamed in 1998 the "Jeanne Clery Disclosure of Campus Security Policy and Campus Crime Statistics Act" in honor of a student who was sexually assaulted and murdered on her campus in 1986.

5-year college career, one in five young women experiences rape during college.[3]

Counter to widespread stranger-rape myths, in the vast majority of these crimes—between 80 and 90 percent—victim and assailant know each other.[4] In fact, the more intimate the relationship, the more likely it is for a rape to be completed rather than attempted.[5] Half of all student victims do not label the incident "rape."[6] This is particularly true when no weapon was used, no sign of physical injury is evident, and alcohol was involved—factors commonly associated with campus acquaintance rape.[7] Given the extent of non-stranger rape on campus, it is no surprise that the majority of victimized women do not define their experience as a rape.

These reasons help explain why campus sexual assault is not well reported. Less than 5 percent of completed and attempted rapes of college students are brought to the attention of campus authorities and/or law enforcement.[8] Failure to recognize and report the crime not only may result in underestimating the extent of the problem, but also may affect whether victims seek medical care and other professional help. Thus, a special concern of the study was what schools are doing to encourage victims to come forward.

Federal Law and the Schools' Response

Institutions of higher education vary widely in how well they comply with Clery Act mandates and respond to sexual victimization. Overall, a large proportion of the schools studied—close to 80 percent—submit the annual security report required by the Act to the U.S. Department of Education; more than two-thirds include their crime statistics in the report. Yet, according to a General Accounting Office study, schools find it difficult to consistently interpret and apply the Federal reporting requirements, such as deciding which incidents to cite in the annual report, classifying crimes, and the like.[9]

Definitions, even of such terms as "campus" and "student," are often a challenge and contribute to inconsistency in calculating the number of reported sexual assaults. Only 37 percent of the schools studied report their statistics in the required manner; for example, most schools failed to distinguish forcible and nonforcible sex offenses in their reports as required by the Clery Act.

The Issues and the Findings

Congress specified the issues to be investigated (see "Study Design"). Key areas of concern were whether schools have a written sexual assault response policy; whether and how they define sexual misconduct; who on campus is trained to respond to reports of sexual assault; how students can report sexual victimization; what resources are available to victims; and what investigation and adjudication procedures are followed once a report is made. Researchers also examined policies that encourage or discourage reporting and some promising practices (see "Promising Practices").

Definitions of Sexual Assault

Although the Clery Act instructs schools to use the FBI's Uniform Crime Report crime classification system as the basis for their annual statistics, schools may also define forms of "sexual misconduct" in their student code of conduct. Clear behavioral definitions—including definitions of consent and scenarios with nonstrangers—can help victims decide whether what happened to them should be reported to campus or law enforcement authorities. This strategy, used at schools with promising practices, directly challenges stranger-rape myths that disguise the problem and provide a false sense of safety.

Study Design[a]

In 1999, Congress mandated investigation of nine issues concerning how colleges and universities are responding to campus sexual assault. Most of these issues are discussed in this Research for Practice.[b]

To collect the mandated information, the researchers studied a random sample of schools in the United States and Puerto Rico that receive student financial aid from the Federal Government and therefore must comply with the Clery Act. Almost 2,500 schools were in the sample, including all Historically Black Colleges and Universities and all Tribal Colleges and Universities. Schools were classified using the U.S. Department of Education's classification system. Results were reported by school type. The policy analysis was derived from almost two-thirds of the dataset of results from 4-year and 2-year public institutions and 4-year private nonprofit schools.

The researchers used three methods to study how schools are complying:

- Content analysis of the written sexual assault policies of the schools.
- A survey of campus administrators that asked about the issues mandated for study.
- Using 29 criteria, onsite examination of 8 schools found to use promising practices in addressing sexual assault on campus.

The eight schools with promising practices were:

- Central Washington University, Ellensburg, Washington.
- Lafayette College, Easton, Pennsylvania.
- Lewis & Clark College, Portland, Oregon.
- Metropolitan Community College, Omaha, Nebraska.
- Oklahoma State University, Stillwater.
- University of California at Los Angeles.
- University of California at Santa Cruz.
- West Virginia State College, Institute, West Virginia.

Response rates varied by type of institution. Overall, 1,015 schools sent their policies, and 1,001 campus administrators participated in the survey.

Notes

a. A complete description of the study methodology is at Karjane, H.M., B.S. Fisher, and F.T. Cullen, *Campus Sexual Assault: How America's Institutions of Higher Education Respond,* final report to NIJ, Oct. 2002, NCJ 196676: chapter 2.
b. A list of the nine issues mandated for study can be found at ibid.: 12–13.

Congress asked about the prevalence and publication of school and State definitions of sexual assault. The researchers found:

- States have their own criminal codes; thus, definitions of acts that constitute sexual assault vary.
- Like State definitions, school definitions vary widely.
- A slight majority of the schools studied mentioned acquaintance rape in their sexual assault response policy.

Sexual Assault Response Policy

A formal policy that addresses sexual assault on campus is a statement of the school's commitment to recognizing and dealing with the problem. To meet the intent of the Federal laws, the policy should be widely and easily accessible to students.

Congress asked whether the schools have and disseminate a sexual assault response policy. The researchers found:

- Traditional 4-year public and private nonprofit schools—which educate the majority of students—are the most likely to have a written sexual assault response policy.
- About half the schools studied spell out specific policy goals; for example, not tolerating sexual offenses on campus or pursuing disciplinary action against perpetrators. This is more common in 4-year institutions and Historically Black Colleges and Universities (HBCUs).

Who Is Trained to Respond?

Students who are sexually assaulted are most likely to tell their friends first.[10] Research shows that social support from friends—and other "first responders"—can help the victim recognize what happened as a violation of the school's sexual misconduct policy and potentially a crime and encourage the victim to report it to the authorities.[11] For this reason it makes sense for schools to train students and staff in what to do if someone discloses that she or he has been sexually assaulted.

Congress wanted information about who is trained to respond to sexual assault and how much training is offered. The researchers found:

- Overall, only about 4 in 10 schools offer any sexual assault training. What training is available is usually for resident advisers and student security officers, not the general student population.
- Of the schools that provide training, about half train their faculty and staff in the school's response policies and procedures.
- Fewer than two in five schools train campus security personnel, even though formal complaints are likely to be reported to campus security. The majority of 4-year public institutions and HBCUs require this training.

How Do Students Report an Assault?

If students know what to do in the event of a sexual assault (for example, whom to notify) and what steps the school will take, they are more likely to feel reassured and report to authorities. The probability of reporting is also linked to concerns about confidentiality. Victims may be embarrassed or fear reprisal; and victims who may have been drinking before the assault might fear sanctions for violating campus policy on alcohol use. Confidential reporting can be essential in these instances. Some victims prefer anonymous reporting, which allows the crime to be "counted," while letting the victim decide whether to file an official report.

Congress asked what on- and off-campus reporting options are available to victims and what procedures the schools follow after an assault. The researchers found:

- Although 84 percent of the schools studied offer confidential reporting, only 46 percent offer anonymous reporting.
- Contact procedures are specified in the sexual assault response policies of almost three in four schools, with campus or local police the most frequently named contact.
- Even though almost half of schools with a contact procedure listed a phone number, less than half provide service after business hours.
- Information about filing criminal charges and campus reports is included in the policies of less than half the schools, although, following the pattern, the figures for 4-year institutions are higher.

Prevention Efforts and Resources for Victims

Services for victims are essential, but prevention is also key. Many 4-year colleges and universities offer a variety of educational programs geared to prevention, including rape awareness and self defense. Many schools also offer a combination of on- and off-campus services.

Congress asked what resources are available for victim safety, support, and health. The researchers found:

- About 6 in 10 schools offer safety-related educational programs. Of the programs offered by these schools, 6 in 10 address sexual assault.
- Of the schools that offer general educational programs, less than one-third include acquaintance rape prevention in the program. Even in 4-year public schools, less than half do so.
- Only about one-fourth of schools provide residence hall staff with safety training, have security staff on duty in the residences, or require overnight guests to register.
- For students who have been sexually assaulted, mental health crisis counseling is the most widely available service.

What Discourages Victims from Reporting?

The small proportion of sexual assault victims who report the offense to authorities attests to the existence of multiple reporting barriers.

When schools adopt sexual assault response policies, their goal is to protect victims and the general student population by holding the perpetrator accountable while also protecting the rights of the accused. But any policy that compromises or restricts the victim's ability to make informed choices about how to proceed may deter reporting. At the individual level, some victims do not initially recognize the assault as a crime, or they have concerns about their confidentiality. Others may not want to participate in adjudication because they want to avoid public disclosure; they are not certain they can prove a crime occurred or that the perpetrator will be punished. Nonstranger rapists are rarely convicted of their crimes.[12]

Congress asked what policies and practices may prevent reporting or obstruct justice. The researchers found:

- Campus policies on drug and alcohol use have been adopted at three-fourths of the schools studied. At more than half of these schools, administrators say these policies inhibit reporting.
- A majority of campus administrators believe that requiring victims to participate in adjudication discourages reporting; about one-third of schools still have such a policy.
- Campuses may unintentionally condone victim-blaming by overemphasizing the victim's responsibility to avoid sexual assault without balancing messages stressing the perpetrator's responsibility for committing a crime and strategies bystanders can use to intervene.
- A trauma response, which may involve high levels of psychological distress, some of it triggered by shame and self-blame, inhibits reporting.
- The desire to avoid the perceived—and real—stigma of having been victimized also inhibits reporting.

What Promotes Reporting?

Because barriers to reporting exist at many levels, a single policy or approach, such as allowing confidential reporting, is inadequate. The optimum approach to encourage reporting would be to combine a number of strategies, including making campus staff more responsive to reports of sexual assault and offering prevention education for the general student population as well as for specific groups.

Congress asked what policies aid in encouraging reporting. The researchers found:

- Services for victims, written law enforcement response protocols, coordination between campus and community, new student orientations, and campuswide

publicity about past crimes are seen by administrators as facilitating reporting.
- Administrators at almost 90 percent of the schools studied believe that prevention programs targeting athletes and students in the Greek system encourage reporting. Only about one in five schools offers such programs, however, although over half of 4-year public schools have them.
- As noted earlier, most administrators believe that a policy allowing confidential and anonymous reporting encourages both victims and other students to report assaults.
- Most administrators consider sexual assault peer educators to be conducive to reporting, but only about one in five schools offers this type of program. Again, 4-year public institutions and HBCUs are more likely to have such programs.

Although campus administrators believe these policies encourage reporting, few have adopted them.

Investigating and Punishing Victimizers

In responding to and adjudicating reports of sexual assault, schools need to balance the victim's need for justice with the rights of the accused. Bringing victimizers to justice is made more complex by the dual jurisdiction of campus administration and law enforcement. Sexual assault may be a violation of the school's sexual misconduct policy, with the accused brought before a disciplinary board or other body to determine his or her *responsibility* in violating the student code of conduct, but it is also a crime and therefore within the jurisdiction of the criminal justice system to determine *guilt*.

Congress asked what procedures schools have adopted for investigating sexual assault and disciplining and punishing perpetrators. The researchers found:

- Most reports of sexual assault on campus are dealt with through binding administrative actions, such as no-contact orders.
- An information-gathering or investigative process is used at only one-fourth of schools overall, only one-fourth of 4-year private nonprofit schools, and less than half of 4-year public schools.
- Due process for the accused is guaranteed in fewer than 40 percent of schools that have disciplinary procedures.
- In about 80 percent of schools, the body that decides whether the student code of conduct has been violated is the disciplinary board. In just over half the schools, this body also decides what sanction will be imposed.
- The most common penalty is expulsion, imposed by 84 percent of the schools. Many schools suspend offenders or place them on probation. Offenders may also be censured, required to make restitution, or lose privileges.

Promising Practices

The researchers identified promising practices at eight schools (see "Study Design") in the areas of prevention, sexual assault policy, reporting, investigation, adjudication, and victim support services. Some examples are included here.[a]

Prevention

A campus sexual assault education program should include comprehensive education about rape myths, common circumstances under which the crime occurs, rapist characteristics, prevention strategies, rape trauma responses and the healing process, and campus policies and support services. To reach the entire student body, these messages should be disseminated in many forms, i.e., through student orientation, curriculum infusion, resource center trainings, campus events, and public information materials. For example, Lafayette College's sexual misconduct policy is communicated to students where they live as well as where they learn, in a kind of "road show." Much larger University of California, Santa Cruz (UCSC), conducts a weekly saturation campaign of flier dissemination all over campus.

Several schools have peer educators and advocates who present programs that feature scenarios followed by facilitated discussion. Some campuses gear prevention and intervention programs to all-male groups, such as male athletes, fraternity members, and male members of ROTC. These prevention programs stress male culpability for committing the vast majority of sex crimes, men's individual and collective responsibility for helping to prevent these crimes, and the attitudes men may hold that foster the crimes. For example, UCSC supports a "Mentors in Violence Prevention" program that emphasizes the bystander's role in violence prevention, in part by using a "playbook" of strategies men can use to interrupt their peers when they believe they may be edging toward criminal behavior.[b]

Sexual Assault Policy

A school's sexual assault policy should be a reader-friendly, easily accessible, and widely distributed statement of the school's definitions and expectations regarding sexual conduct. The policy should:

- Clearly define all forms of sexual misconduct, including operational and behavioral definitions of what acts constitute consent and what acts constitute a sexual assault.
- Discuss the prevalence of nonstranger sexual assault.
- Describe circumstances in which sexual assault most commonly occurs.
- Advise what to do if the student or someone she/he knows is sexually assaulted.
- List resources available on campus and in the local community.
- Identify a specific person or office to contact when a sexual assault occurs (preferably available 24/7) and when and where to file a complaint.
- Strongly encourage victims to report the incident to

campus authorities and to the local criminal justice system.

- Provide for and list available reporting options, including a confidential option and preferably including an anonymous option.
- State the school's sanctions for violating the sexual misconduct policy.
- Provide an official statement prohibiting retaliation against individuals who report rape or sexual assault and specifying the school's disciplinary actions for retaliation attempts.
- Provide an official statement noting the separate actions available to the victim, i.e., reporting; investigating the report; informal administrative actions, such as issuing a no-contact order; formal adjudication on campus; and criminal prosecution.

Reporting

All eight schools allow anonymous, confidential, and third-party reporting. Highly recommended are reporting and response policies that allow the victim to participate in decisionmaking, to exert some control over the pace of the process, and to be in charge of making decisions as she/he moves through the campus adjudication and/or the local law enforcement system. Written response protocols ensure a coordinated, consistent, victim-centered response.[c]

For example, Oklahoma State University counsels student victims that reporting an incident, choosing to prosecute, adjudicating a complaint through the University, and filing a civil action are separate steps. Reporting the incident does not obligate the victim to prosecute, but does allow gathering of information. The student chooses whether to move to the next step in the process and is advised of the consequences of each action, what to expect, and how confidentiality will be maintained.

Investigation

Protocols to ensure confidentiality for the victim and the accused during the investigation are essential. Also important are protocols for shared collection and use of information to eliminate the need for the victim to retell the experience multiple times.

One of the most promising practices is providing victims access to a trained, certified Sexual Assault Nurse Examiner (SANE). SANE practitioners provide appropriate treatment and forensic examination. Their documentation of evidence can corroborate a victim's account.[d]

Adjudication

Many schools offer a range of adjudication options, from informal administrative actions that do not require a formal complaint to a formal adjudication board hearing. Proceedings should follow an established, documented, and consistent format that balances the rights of the complainant and the accused. Sexual misconduct adjudication boards are not criminal proceedings; their purpose is to establish

(Continued)

Promising Practices (*continued*)

whether the accused is responsible for violating the school's policy, not to determine the accused's guilt or innocence.[e]

Victim Support Services

The most promising practice in this area is the formation of partnerships between the school and the community to provide student victims access to a comprehensive, coordinated network of service providers—medical, psychological, advocacy, legal, and safety. More research is needed to help schools determine which practices are best for their campus and students.

Notes

a. A comprehensive review of promising practices is in Karjane, H., B. Fisher, and F.T. Cullen, *Campus Sexual Assault: How America's Institutions of Higher Education Respond,* final report to the National Institute of Justice, Oct. 2002, NCJ 196676.

b. See Katz, J., "Reconstructing Masculinity in the Locker Room: The Mentors in Violence Prevention Project," *Harvard Educational Review* 65(2)(1995): 163–174; also see Karjane et al., *Campus Sexual Assault:* 128.

c. See Karjane et al., *Campus Sexual Assault:* 133–134.

d. For more information about SANEs, see Littel, K., "Sexual Assault Nurse Examiner (SANE) Programs: Improving the Community Response to Sexual Assault Victims," *OVC Bulletin,* Washington, DC: U.S. Department of Justice, Office for Victims of Crime, 2001, available online at www.ojp.usdoj.gov/ovc/publications/bulletins/sane_4_2001/welcome.html. Also see Sommers, M.S., B.S. Fisher, and H.M. Karjane, "Using Colposcopy in the Rape Exam: Health Care, Forensic, and Criminal Justice Issues," *Journal of Forensic Nursing* 1(1)(2005): 28–34, 19.

a. For more about adjudication protocols and practices, see Karjane et al., *Campus Sexual Assault:* chapter 6 and 135–136.

- Only about half the schools keep the complainant apprised of the progress of the case; they are far more likely to notify the accused.
- Use of protocols for coordinating the responses of campus and local law enforcement agencies were found to be a promising practice, but only about one in four schools have them, most of these 4-year public institutions and HBCUs.

Do Schools Need to Do More?

The study confirmed that there is much confusion among schools about what the Clery Act requires. The fact that only 37 percent fully comply in reporting crime statistics indicates a need for guidance. The researchers recommend development of a policy that includes explicit and behavioral definitions of consent, sexual offenses, and other terminology and practices.

Many schools either do not have a sexual assault response policy or could not provide it for the study. The larger, 4-year institutions and HBCUs tend to have policies, often available on their Web sites, but these vary in clarity and thoroughness. This suggests a model policy could be useful to the schools as a template in developing their own.

More could be done to increase reporting. Practices that are perceived by college administrators to discourage or encourage reporting need to be examined empirically.

Because underreporting may be linked to the victim's inability to recognize sexual victimization as a violation of the school's student code of conduct and, further, as a crime, more research is needed into such issues as the perpetuation of stranger-rape myths, the relationship of the victim to the assailant, use of alcohol before the assault, and other contributory factors.

Notes

1. These laws affect all institutions of higher education that receive student financial aid from the Federal Government.

2. The study was mandated as part of the 1998 amendments to the Higher Education Act of 1965, Public Law 105–244.

3. Fisher et al., *The Sexual Victimization of College Women:* 10–11.

4. See ibid.: 17; also see Koss, M., C. Gidycz, and N. Wisniewski, "The Scope of Rape: Incidence and Prevalence of Sexual Aggression and Victimization in a National Sample of Higher Education Students," *Journal of Consulting and Clinical Psychology* 55(2)(1987): 162–170.

5. Fisher et al., "Extent and Nature of the Sexual Victimization of College Women": 89–90; 123–124.

6. Fisher, B.S., L.E. Daigle, F.T. Cullen, and M.G. Turner, "Acknowledging Sexual Victimization as Rape: Results From a National-Level Study," *Justice Quarterly* 20(3)(2000): 401–440. A study 13 years earlier reported that 3 in 4 women (73 percent) who had an experience that met Ohio penal code criteria for rape did not label the incident "rape." See Koss et al., "The Scope of Rape": 162–170.

7. See Bondurant, B., "University Women's Acknowledgment of Rape: Individual, Situational, and Social Factors," *Violence Against Women* 7(3)(2001): 294–314.

8. Fisher et al., *The Sexual Victimization of College Women:* 23.

9. *Campus Crime: Difficulties Meeting Federal Reporting Requirements,* Washington, DC: General Accounting Office, 1997.

10. Fisher, B.S., L.E. Daigle, F.T. Cullen, and M.G. Turner, "Reporting Sexual Victimization to the Police and Others: Results from a National-level Study of College Women," *Criminal Justice and Behavior: An International Journal* 30(1)(2003): 6–38.

11 Kahn, A., and V. Andreoli Mathie, "Understanding the Unacknowledged Rape Victim," in *Sexuality, Society and Feminism,* ed. C. Travis and J. White, Washington, DC: American Psychological Association, 2000: 337–403; Neville, H., and A. Pugh, "General and Culture-Specific Factors Influencing African American Women's Reporting Patterns and Perceived Social Support Following Sexual Assault," *Violence Against Women* 3(4)(1997): 361–381.

12. See Spohn, C., and D. Holleran, "Prosecuting Sexual Assault: A Comparison of Charging Decisions in Sexual Assault Cases Involving Strangers, Acquaintances, and Intimate Partners," *Justice Quarterly* 18(3)(2001): 651 688.

HEATHER M. KARJANE, PhD, is coordinator for gender issues at the Commonwealth of Massachusetts Administrative Office of the Trial Court. **BONNIE S. FISHER,** PhD, and **FRANCIS T. CULLEN,** PhD, are faculty in the Division of Criminal Justice at the University of Cincinnati. The Police Executive Research Forum conducted some of the field research.

From *National Institute of Justice Journal,* NCJ 205521, December 2005, pp. ii, 1–16. Published by the Office of Justice/U.S. Department of Justice.

Ordering Restitution to the Crime Victim

Introduction

Victims suffer staggering economic costs as a result of crime. The tangible cost of crime, including medical expenses, lost earnings, and public victim assistance costs, is an estimated $105 billion a year.[1] Crime victim compensation programs reimburse victims for part of this loss. During fiscal year 1998, state compensation programs paid close to $250 million to victims of violent crime.[2] However, most of the costs of crime are absorbed by the victims and victim service providers.

Restitution laws are designed to shift the burden. As one legislature noted, "It is the purpose of [restitution law] to encourage the compensation of victims by the person most responsible for the loss incurred by the victim, the offender."[3]

Status of the Law
Right to Restitution

Every state gives courts the statutory authority to order restitution. In addition, 18 of the 32 state crime victims' rights constitutional amendments give victims a right to restitution.[4]

In more than one-third of all states, courts are required by statute to order restitution unless there are compelling or extraordinary circumstances. Florida's law is typical, providing that "[i]n addition to any punishment, the court shall order the defendant to make restitution to the victim for: 1) Damage or loss caused directly or indirectly by the defendant's offense; and 2) Damage or loss related to the defendant's criminal episode, unless it finds clear and compelling reasons not to order such restitution."[5] In many states, the law requires restitution but allows broad exceptions to that rule. For instance, Connecticut and Nevada both require restitution "if restitution is appropriate."[6] Oregon provides that restitution shall be ordered "whenever possible."[7] Regardless of whether restitution is mandatory, about one-quarter of all states require courts to state on the record the reasons for failing to order restitution or for ordering only partial restitution.[8] This requirement is thought to further encourage courts to consider restitution to the victim when sentencing convicted offenders.

Where victims have a clear statutory right to restitution, the right has been found to apply to cases that result in a plea agreement. The California Court of Appeals recently ruled that restitution must be a part of every sentence, regardless of a plea agreement to the contrary: "The Legislature left no discretion or authority with the trial court or the prosecution to bargain away the victim's constitutional and statutory right to restitution. As such, it cannot properly be the subject of plea negotiations."[9] Oklahoma's statute expressly requires that restitution to the victim be part of every plea agreement.[10] Florida requires that an "order of restitution entered as part of a plea agreement is as definitive and binding as any other order of restitution, and a statement to such effect must be made part of the plea agreement."[11]

Although most restitution laws apply to crime victims in general, many states have enacted specific directives to order restitution to victims of particular offenses, such as crimes against the elderly, [12] domestic violence,[13] sexual assault,[14] hate crimes,[15] child abuse,[16] child sexual abuse,[17] drunk driving,[18] and identity fraud.[19]

Eligibility for Restitution

Generally, restitution laws provide for restitution to the direct victim(s) of a crime, including surviving family members of homicide victims. Many states also authorize an order of restitution to third parties, including insurers,[20] victim compensation programs,[21] government entities,[22] and victim service agencies.[23] Several states authorize restitution to any entity that has provided recovery to the victim as a collateral source.[24] Alaska authorizes a court to order restitution "to a public, private, or private nonprofit organization that has provided . . . counseling, medical, or shelter services to the victim or other person injured by the offense." [25] In a recent New York case, an appellate court ruled that a defendant could be required to make restitution to a victim's employer for the victim's sick leave.[26]

Restitution need not be limited to victims of crimes for which a defendant was convicted. When a defendant is charged with similar crimes against many individuals, as in the case of a serial rapist or a perpetrator of large-scale fraud, he or she may plead guilty to one or more counts in exchange for an agreement by the prosecutor to drop other charges. In such a case, as part of the plea agreement, the defendant may agree to pay restitution to all victims. Many states specifically allow this by statute.[27] For example, Idaho's restitution law states that the "court may, with the consent of the parties, order restitution to victims, and/or any other person or entity, for economic loss or injury for crimes which are not adjudicated or are not before the court."[28]

Losses for Which Restitution May Be Ordered

Restitution may be ordered to cover numerous crime-related expenses incurred by a victim. Typically, statutes specify that the following may be included in setting the restitution amount:

- Medical expenses.
- Lost wages.
- Counseling expenses.
- Lost or damaged property.
- Funeral expenses.
- Other direct out-of-pocket expenses.

Medical expenses are defined as medical services and devices (often including "nonmedical care and treatment rendered in accordance with a recognized method of healing"), physical therapy, and rehabilitation.[29]

Lost wages can include time lost from work because of participation in the court process.[30] Courts have even applied this to self-employed individuals who have had to close a business or forego employment while testifying.[31] California law specifies that parents can receive restitution for wages lost while caring for an injured minor victim.[32] Although Arizona's statute is not so specific, its Court of Appeals has interpreted that statute to reach the same conclusion: the "parents . . . stood in the shoes of the victim and were entitled to restitution for their lost wages incurred while taking [her] to medical appointments and juvenile court hearings on this case."[33]

Counseling expenses are generally recoverable. Many states extend restitution for counseling expenses to victims' family members. Some states limit family counseling expenses to cases of homicide,[34] whereas others allow such expenses whenever the counseling is related to the commission of the offense.[35]

In homicide cases, a family's funeral and travel expenses and the ordinary and reasonable attorney fees incurred in closing the victim's estate have been found to be proper restitution items.[36] Other funeral expenses that might be covered include a headstone, flowers, chapel music, minister's honorarium, and chapel fee.[37]

Restitution may also be ordered for other out-of-pocket expenses directly related to the crime. In cases of identity fraud, this may include expenses for correcting a victim's credit history and costs incurred in any civil or administrative proceeding needed to satisfy any debt or other obligation of the victim, including lost wages and attorney fees.[38]

Many states authorize courts to order defendants to pay interest on the restitution. For example, California's law provides that a restitution order shall include "interest, at the rate of 10 percent per annum, that accrues as of the date of sentencing or loss, as determined by the court."[39] In some states, attorney fees are also recoverable. In Oregon, attorney fees have been found by the courts to be recoverable as "special damages" if incurred to ensure indictment and criminal prosecution; the victim may later file a civil suit.[40] California's restitution statute provides for recovery of attorney fees and costs incurred for collecting restitution.[41]

In some states, future damages can be awarded. Iowa law specifically provides for future damages, stating that where the full extent of the loss is not known at the time of sentencing, the court is to issue a temporary order for a reasonable amount of restitution identified at that time. The court is authorized to issue a permanent supplemental order at a later date, setting out the full amount of restitution.[42] Arizona's Court of Appeals ruled that future damages were a permissible restitution element, reasoning that disallowing future expenses would defeat the legislative purpose of restitution, which is to make the victim whole.[43]

Meanwhile, Wyoming has a detailed statutory scheme for ordering restitution for long-term medical expenses. Under its law, the court is to consider and include as a special finding "each victim's reasonably foreseeable actual pecuniary damage that will result in the future as a result of the defendant's criminal activity."[44] Thus, a restitution order for long-term physical health care must be entered for any such damages.

Not every state allows restitution for future expenses, however. Indiana courts have stated that only actual costs incurred by the victim before sentencing may be considered for a restitution order.[45]

Considerations in Ordering Restitution

Restitution laws generally set out the elements the court is to consider before it rules on restitution. Alaska law provides that "[i]n determining the amount and method of payment of restitution, the court shall take into account the: 1) public policy that favors requiring criminals to compensate for damages and injury to their victims; and 2) financial burden placed on the victim and those who provide services to the victim and other persons injured by the offense as a result of the criminal conduct of the defendant."[46]

Most states also require the court to consider the current financial resources of the defendant, the defendant's future ability to pay, and, in some states, the burden restitution will place on the defendant and his or her dependents. States are beginning to move away from consideration of the defendant's ability to pay when setting the restitution amount. However, the defendant's assets and earning potential are taken into account in setting the payment schedule. Arizona's law states that the court "shall not consider the economic circumstances of the defendant in determining the amount of restitution,"[47] but the court is required to consider the economic circumstances of the defendant in specifying the manner of payment.[48] Similarly, in Florida, the court is charged only with considering the loss sustained by the victim in determining whether to order restitution and the amount of restitution. At the time the restitution order is enforced, the court is to consider the defendant's financial resources, the present and potential future financial needs and earning ability of the defendant and his or her dependents, and other appropriate factors.[49]

Current Issues
Conflicting Directives
Many states have conflicting restitution statutes. A state may have one statute that mandates restitution in every criminal case and another that expressly leaves the ordering of restitution to the court's discretion. States may give every victim the right to restitution "as provided by law" but fail to mandate that courts order restitution. In some states, a single statute contains conflicting provisions. For example, a Minnesota law states that every crime victim has the right to receive restitution as part of the disposition of a criminal charge or juvenile delinquency proceeding if the offender is convicted or found delinquent. The statute further provides that the court "shall grant or deny restitution or partial restitution and shall state on the record its reasons for its decision on restitution if information relating to restitution has been presented."[50] Other states have similar contradictions within their statutes. The Colorado Legislature addressed this issue in 1999 when it created a task force to develop a report on restitution and specifically charged the task force with identifying conflicting provisions in the law.[51]

Other Barriers to Restitution Orders
Despite progressively stronger restitution statutes, studies and anecdotal information suggest that crime victims are frequently not awarded restitution. In a 1996 study, less than half of the 1,300 crime victims surveyed reported that they were awarded restitution.[52]

As part of the same study, local criminal justice and victim service professionals were surveyed about their experiences with crime victims' rights and asked to identify why courts often failed to order restitution. The most common reasons were a victim's failure to request restitution, a victim's failure to demonstrate loss, the inability to calculate a victim's loss, the opinion that restitution was inappropriate in light of other penalties imposed (especially in cases where the defendant receives jail time), and a defendant's inability to pay.[53]

Most of these reasons can be addressed in whole or in part by statute.

A Victim's Failure to Request Restitution
One way to address a victim's failure to request restitution is to strengthen the laws that require a victim to be notified of the right to request restitution. Victims are commonly informed of the availability of restitution at the time they receive general information about crime victims' rights, either when the crime is reported or when the prosecutor files charges.[54] Early notification of a victim's right to request restitution gives the victim time to gather evidence to document losses. In some states, victims are informed of their right to request restitution again when they are notified of the sentencing hearing or asked to complete a victim impact statement.[55]

Other states simply place the burden of requesting restitution on the prosecutor.[56] Wisconsin law requires the court to prompt the prosecutor: "The court, before imposing sentence or ordering probation, shall inquire of the district attorney regarding the amount of restitution, if any, that the victim claims."[57] Finally, a few states have avoided the issue of victims failing to request restitution by eliminating the need for such a request. In Arizona, for example, restitution is mandatory in every criminal case:[58] "The fact that a victim does not request restitution does not change the court's obligation to order it."[59]

A Victim's Failure to Demonstrate and a Court's Inability to Calculate Loss
Unless they are given sufficient evidence regarding a victim's financial loss and the degree to which the victim was harmed, courts are reluctant to enter an order of restitution. As a result, many states have adopted statutory procedures to gather information about a victim's losses. Oregon requires the prosecutor to investigate and present evidence on the nature and amount of the victim's damages before or at the time of sentencing unless the presentence report contained such information.[60] Wisconsin, meanwhile, requires the prosecutor to request information about losses from the victim.[61]

Many states also require that detailed information about the victim's losses be included in the presentence report.[62] Georgia requires the victim impact statement to be attached to the file so that the judge or prosecutor can use it at any stage of the proceedings, including restitution consideration.[63] Delaware and Oklahoma require the victim to submit a particular form describing losses in detail.[64] Victims who seek restitution in South Carolina must submit an itemized list of all financial losses.[65] Several states provide assistance to the crime victim in preparing such documentation. Oklahoma law states that "[e]very crime victim receiving the restitution claim form shall be provided assistance and direction to properly complete the form."[66]

The Opinion That Restitution Was Inappropriate in Light of Other Penalties Imposed

Traditionally, laws provide for restitution as a condition of probation or suspended sentence. There was limited statutory authority to order both restitution and incarceration.[67] This may be why many judges believe it is inappropriate to order restitution in cases in which a defendant is imprisoned as well. New laws requiring courts to consider restitution in every case may be a response to this judicial reluctance to issue restitution orders.

A Defendant's Inability to Pay

One of the most common reasons for failing to order restitution has been a defendant's inability to pay. As noted earlier, many states have addressed this problem by providing that the defendant's financial circumstances are to be considered at the time the payment schedule is developed but not when the amount of restitution is set. The South Dakota statute states that even if the defendant is currently unable to pay restitution, a restitution plan must be presented that states the conditions under which the defendant will begin making restitution.[68] Similarly, Idaho's law states that the immediate inability of a defendant to pay is not a reason to not order restitution.[69]

Illinois courts have addressed this issue by ruling that restitution may be ordered regardless of the term of incarceration and a defendant's financial resources. "The fact that [restitution] may never be collectible is of no importance,"[70] according to one Illinois case. Meanwhile, proceedings in another Illinois case indicate that "[w]ith respect to defendants sentenced to lengthy prison terms, the fact of a term of imprisonment is simply one factor for a trial judge to consider when assessing a defendant's postincarceration ability to pay for purposes of fashioning terms of the restitution order."[71]

States have also acted to ensure that courts are presented with more complete information about a defendant's financial status. Oklahoma's law states that

> The court shall order the offender to submit . . . such information as the court may direct and finds necessary to be disclosed for the purpose of ascertaining the type and manner of restitution to be ordered. . . . The willful failure or refusal of the offender to provide all or part of the requisite information prior to the sentencing, unless disclosure is deferred by the court, shall not deprive the court of the authority to set restitution or set the schedule of payment. The willful failure or refusal . . . shall constitute a waiver of any grounds to appeal or seek future amendment or alteration of the restitution order predicated on the undisclosed information.[72]

Such failure or refusal is also an act of contempt.[73]

In California, the defendant is required to file a disclosure identifying all assets, income, and liabilities. Failure to disclose this information may be considered an aggravating circumstance in sentencing and "a factor indicating that the interests of justice would not be served by admitting the defendant to probation . . . conditionally sentencing the defendant . . . [or] imposing less than the maximum fine and sentence."[74]

New Mexico requires defendants to prepare a plan of restitution with the probation or parole officer, "and the court, before approving, disapproving or modifying the plan of restitution, shall consider the physical and mental health and condition of the defendant, his age, his education, his employment circumstances, his potential for employment and vocational training, his family circumstances, [and] his financial condition," among other factors.[75]

Providing information about a defendant's ability to pay restitution can give courts more confidence in ordering restitution. Perhaps more important, it helps to fashion a workable payment plan.

Conclusion

Restitution to crime victims is an important criminal law objective. The act of ordering restitution serves as an acknowledgment by the criminal justice system that the victim sustained harm. Payment of restitution can help rectify that harm. Legislatures nationwide are reexamining their statutes regarding this issue and continuing to refine and expand this area of the law. Not only are legislatures acting to encourage more restitution orders, the increasing attention paid to quantifying a victim's losses and investigating a defendant's assets before entering restitution orders will help improve the quality and workability of such orders. Victim service providers should continue to follow developments regarding this issue and be prepared to assist crime victims who seek restitution.

Notes

1. Miller, Ted, Mark Cohen, and Brian Wiersema (1996). *Victim Costs and Consequences: A New Look,* Washington, DC: National Institute of Justice, U.S. Department of Justice, p. 1.

2. National Association of Crime Victim Compensation Boards (1999). *Program Directory*, Alexandria, VA: National Association of Crime Victim Compensation Boards, p. 1.

3. ME. REV. STAT. ANN. tit. 17-A, § 1321 (West 2000).

4. ALASKA CONST. art. I, § 24; ARIZ. CONST. art. II, § 2.1; CAL. CONST. art. I, § 28; CONN. CONST. amend. 17(b); IDAHO CONST. art. I, § 22; ILL. CONST. art. I, § 8.1; LA. CONST. art. I, § 25; MICH. CONST. art. I, § 24; MO. CONST. art. I, § 32; N.M. CONST. art. II, § 24; N.C. art. I, § 37; OKLA. CONST. art. II, § 34; OR. CONST. art. I, § 42; R.I. CONST. art. I, § 23; S.C. CONST. art. I, § 24; TENN. CONST. art. I, § 35; TEX. CONST. art. I, § 30; WIS. CONST. art. I, § 9(m). Additionally, Montana recently adopted a

constitutional amendment broadening the principles on which laws for the punishment of crime are based to include restitution to crime victims. MONT. CONST. art. II, § 28.

5. FLA. STAT. ANN. § 775.089 (West 2000).

6. CONN. GEN. STAT. § 53a-28 (2000); NEV. REV. STAT. § 176.033 (2001).

7. OR. REV. STAT. § 137.106 (1999).

8. As examples, see IDAHO CODE § 19-5304 (Michie 2000); MD. ANN. Code art. 27, § 807 (2001); N.C. GEN. STAT. § 15A-1340.36 (2000).

9. *People v. Valdez*, 24 Cal. App. 4th 1194, 30 Cal. Rptr. 2d 4. (1994, 5th Dist.). See also *State v. Barrs*, 172 Ariz. 42, 43, 833 P.2d 713 (Ariz. Ct. App. 1992): "The right of restitution belongs to the victim. We know of no authority that would grant the state or the court the option of not pursuing a restitution order in the absence of a waiver by the victim." However, in an Indiana case, the court found that the trial court was prohibited from ordering restitution where restitution had not been part of the plea agreement. In that state, the ordering of restitution is not required but is in the court's discretion. Indiana law also clearly states that once the court accepts a plea agreement, it is bound by the terms of the agreement. *Sinn v. State*, 693 N.E.2d 78 (Ind. App. 1998).

10. OKLA. STAT. tit. 22, § 991f (2000).

11. FLA. STAT. ANN. § 775.089 (West 2000).

12. FLA. STAT. Ann. § 784.08 (West 2000).

13. MINN. STAT. § 518B.01 (2000); UTAH CODE ANN. § 77-36-5.1 (2000).

14. MONT. CODE ANN. § 45-5-503 (2000); TEX. CODE CRIM. PROC. ANN. art. 42.12 (Vernon 2000).

15. CAL. PENAL CODE § 422.95 (Deering 2001).

16. COLO. REV. STAT. § 18-6-401.4 (2000).

17. COLO. REV. STAT. § 18-3-414 (2000).

18. KAN. STAT. ANN. § 8-1019 (2000).

19. MASS. GEN. LAWS ch. 266, § 37E (2001).

20. 18 PA. CONS. STAT. § 1106 (2000).

21. *Id.*

22. MONT. CODE ANN. § 46-18-243 (2000).

23. IND. CODE ANN. § 35-50-5-3 (Michie 2000); MICH. STAT. ANN. § 27.3178(598.30) (Law. Co-op. 2000).

24. For example, ME. REV. STAT. ANN. tit. 17-A, § 1324 (West 2000); WIS. STAT. § 973.20 (2000).

25. ALASKA STAT. § 12.55.045 (Michie 2001). See also MICH. STAT. Ann. § 28.1073 (Law. Co-op. 2000).

26. *People v. McDaniel*, 219 A.D. 2d 861, 631 N.Y.S.2d 957 (4th Dept. 1995), *appeal denied*, 88 N.Y.2d 850, 644 N.Y.S.2d 697, 667 N.E.2d 347 (1996).

27. For example, see FLA. STAT. ANN. § 775.089 (West 2000); 730 ILL. COMP. STAT. 5/5-5, -6 (2001); WASH. REV. CODE § 9.94 A.140 (2001).

28. IDAHO Code § 19-5304 (Michie 2000).

29. FLA. STAT. ANN. § 775.089 (West 2000).

30. ALA. CODE § 15-18-66 (2001); *People v. Nguyen*, 23 Cal. App. 4th 32, 28 Cal. Rptr. 2d 140, *modified on other grounds, reh'g denied*, 23 Cal. App. 4th 1306e (6th Dist. 1994).

31. *State v. Russell*, 126 Idaho 38, 878 P.2d 212 (Ct. App. 1994).

32. CAL. PENAL CODE § 1202.4 (Deering 2001).

33. *In re Erika V.*, 983 P.2d 768; 297 Adv. Rep. 55 (1999).

34. N.H. REV. STAT. ANN. § 651:62 (2000).

35. MICH. STAT. ANN. § 28.1073 (Law. Co-op. 2000).

36. *State v. Spears*, 184 Ariz. 277, 292, 908 P.2d 1062 (1996).

37. *State v. Blanton*, 173 Ariz. 517, 520, 844 P.2d 1167 (Ct. App. 1993).

38. MASS. GEN. LAWS ch. 266, § 37E (2001).

39. CAL. PENAL CODE § 1202.4 (Deering 2001). See also IDAHO CODE § 19-5304 (Michie 2000); KY. REV. STAT. ANN. § 532.164 (Michie 2001); UTAH CODE ANN. § 76-3-201 (2000).

40. *State v. Mahoney*, 115 Or. App. 440, 838 P.2d 1100 (1992), Sup. Ct. *review denied, as modified by* 118 Or. App. 1, 846 P.2d 413 (1993).

41. CAL. PENAL CODE § 1202.4 (Deering 2001).

42. IOWA CODE § 910.3 (2001).

43. *State v. Howard*, 168 Ariz. 458, 459-60, 815 P.2d 5 (Ct. App. 1991).

44. WYO. STAT. ANN. § 7-9-103 (Michie 2001).

45. *Ault v. State*, 705 N.E.2d 1078 (Ind. App. 1999).

46. ALASKA STAT. § 12.55.045 (Michie 2001).

47. ARIZ. REV. STAT. § 13-804(C) (2000).

48. ARIZ. REV. STAT. § 13-804(E) (2000).

49. FLA. STAT. ANN. § 775.089(6) (West 2000). See also *Martinez v. State*, 974 P.2d 133 (Nev. 1999) (no requirement that court consider defendant's ability to pay in determining amount of restitution).

50. MINN. STAT. § 611A.04 (2000).

51. COLO. REV. STAT. § 16-11-101.5(6)(a) (2000).

52. Beatty, David, Susan Howley, and Dean Kilpatrick (1996). *Statutory and Constitutional Protections for Victims Rights*, Arlington, VA: National Center for Victims of Crime, table C-8, p. 39.

53. *Id.*, table D-28, p. 95.

54. For example, see ALA. CODE § 15-23-62 (2001); FLA. STAT. ANN. § 960.001 (West 2000); MISS. CODE ANN. § 99-43-7 (2001); OHIO REV. CODE ANN. § 109.42 (Anderson 2001).

55. MINN. STAT. § 611A.037; N.Y. CRIM. PROC. LAW § 390.30 (McKinney 2001).

56. For example, 725 ILL. COMP. STAT. 120/4.5 (2001).

57. WIS. STAT. § 973.20(13) (2000).

58. ARIZ. REV. STAT. § 13-603(c) (2000).

59. *State v. Steffy*, 173 Ariz. 90, 93, 839 P.2d 1135 (Ct. App. 1992).

60. OR. REV. STAT. § 137.106 (1999).

61. WIS. STAT. § 973.20(13) (2000).

62. For example, ALASKA STAT. § 12.55.025 (Michie 2001); KAN. STAT. ANN. § 21-4604 (2000); N.Y. CRIM. PROC. LAW § 390.30 (McKinney 2001).

63. GA. CODE ANN. § 17-10-1.1 (2000).

64. Del. Fam. Ct. R. Crim Proc 32; Okla. Stat. tit. 22, § 991f (2000).

65. S.C. Code Ann. § 16-3-1515 (Law. Co-op. 2000).

66. Okla. Stat. tit. 22, § 991f (2000). See also R.I. Gen. Laws § 12-28-9 (2001).

67. See Alan T. Harland, *Monetary Remedies for the Victims of Crime: Assessing the Role of the Criminal Courts*, 30 UCLA L. Rev. 52-128, at 75-76 (1982).

68. S.D. Codified Laws § 23A-28-3 (Michie 2001).

69. Idaho Code § 19-5304 (Michie 2000).

70. *People v. Mitchell*, 241 Ill. App. 3d 1094, 182 Ill. Dec. 925, 610 N.E.2d 794 (4th Dist. 1993), *appeal denied*, 152 Ill. 2d 572, 190 Ill. Dec. 903, 622 N.E.2d 1220 (1993).

71. *People v. Brooks*, 158 Ill. 2d 260, 198 Ill. Dec. 851, 633 N.E.2d 692 (1994).

72. Okla. Stat. tit. 22, § 991f (2000).

73. *Id.*

74. Cal. Penal Code § 1202.4 (Deering 2001).

75. N.M. Stat. Ann. § 31-17-1 (Michie 2000).

From *OVC Legal Series,* November 2002, pp. 1–7. Published by the Office for Victims of Crimes/U.S. Department of Justice.

UNIT 3
The Police

Unit Selections

Key Points to Consider

- Can racial profiling ever be a legitimate police tactic? Explain.

- Is police work the cause of suicides among officers, or does the availability of a gun just make it easier?

- Are civilian complaint review boards effective in combating police abuses?

Student Web Site
www.mhcls.com/online

Internet References
Further information regarding these Web sites may be found in this book's preface or online.

ACLU Criminal Justice Home Page
http://www.aclu.org/CriminalJustice/CriminalJusticeMain.cfm

Law Enforcement Guide to the World Wide Web
http://leolinks.com/

Violent Criminal Apprehension Program (VICAP)
http://www.state.ma.us/msp/unitpage/vicap.htm

Mikael Karlsson

Police officers are the guardians of our freedoms under the Constitution and the law, and as such they have an awesome task. They are asked to prevent crime, protect citizens, arrest wrongdoers, preserve the peace, aid the sick, control juveniles, control traffic, and provide emergency services on a moment's notice. They are also asked to be ready to lay down their lives, if necessary.

In recent years, the job of the police officer has become even more complex and dangerous. Illegal drug use and trafficking are still major problems; racial tensions are potentially explosive; and terrorism is now an alarming reality. As our population grows more numerous and diverse, the role of the police in America becomes ever more challenging, requiring skills that can only be obtained by greater training and professionalism.

In the lead article in the section, "The NYPD's War on Terror," Craig Horowitz describes the frustration with Washington's lack

of response to terrorism felt by NYPD's police commissioner, and the steps he has taken to try to make New York safe. The typical offender in violent crime categories is white, as pointed out by Tim Wise in "Racial Profiling and its Apologists."

The next article, "Ethics and Criminal Justice: Some Observations on Police Misconduct," deals with police misconduct in terms of ethical violations. In "Stress Management . . . and the Stress-proof Vest" the question of whether the police environment is responsible for the large number of police suicides is looked at by Robert Fox. In the next article, "Dealing with Employee Stress: How Managers Can Help—or Hinder—Their Personnel," the problem of how ineffective managers are creating a stressful work environment is explored. This section concludes with a report by Al Baker on how mediation is used to settle disputes between police and the public in New York City.

The NYPD's War on Terror

Frustrated by the lack of help from Washington, police commissioner Ray Kelly has created his own versions of the CIA and the FBI within the department. So how will we know if he has succeeded? If nothing happens.

CRAIG HOROWITZ

Buried deep in the heart of one of New York's outer boroughs, in an area inhabited by junkyards and auto-body shops, is an unmarked redbrick building that stands as an extraordinary symbol of police commissioner Ray Kelly's obsessive commitment to the fight against terrorism. Here, miles from Manhattan, is the headquarters of the NYPD's one-year-old counterterrorism bureau.

When you step through the plain metal door at the side of the building, it is like falling down the rabbit hole—you're transported from a mostly desolate, semi-industrial area in the shadow of an elevated highway into the new, high-tech, post-9/11 world of the New York City Police Department.

The place is so gleaming and futuristic—so unlike the average police precinct, with furniture and equipment circa 1950—that you half expect to see Q come charging out with his latest superweapon for 007. Headlines race across LED news tickers. There are electronic maps and international-time walls with digital readouts for cities such as Moscow, London, Tel Aviv, Riyadh, Islamabad, Manila, Sydney, Baghdad, and Tokyo.

In what is called the Global Intelligence Room, twelve large flat-screen TVs that hang from ceiling mounts broadcast Al-Jazeera and a variety of other foreign programming received via satellite. The Police Department's newly identified language specialists—who speak, among other tongues, Arabic, Pashto, Urdu, and Fujianese—sit with headphones on, monitoring the broadcasts.

There are racks of high-end audio equipment for listening, taping, and dubbing; computer access to a host of superdatabases; stacks of intelligence reports and briefing books on all the world's known terrorist organizations; and a big bulletin board featuring a grid with the names and phone numbers of key people in other police departments in this country and around the world.

The security area just inside the door is encased not only in bulletproof glass but in ballistic Sheetrock as well. The building has its own backup generator (everyone learned the importance of redundancy on September 11); and the center is staffed 24 hours a day, seven days a week.

Even the 125 cops in the bureau (hand-picked from nearly 900 applicants) look a little sharper. Some are in dark-navy polo shirts that bear the counterterrorism-bureau logo, and others are in suits that seem to be a cut above the usual discount-warehouse version of cop fashion.

Though the counterterrorism bureau is still in its infancy, law-enforcement officials from around the U.S. and overseas regularly come to see it and learn. And it was all put together practically overnight—it opened in February of last year, little more than a month after Ray Kelly was sworn in as police commissioner.

The bureau, along with the NYPD's totally revamped intelligence division, and the high-level hires from Washington—a lieutenant general from the Pentagon and a spymaster from the CIA—is part of Kelly's vision to remake the NYPD into a force that can effectively respond to the world's dangerous new realities.

There are now New York City police officers stationed in London working with New Scotland Yard; in Lyons at the headquarters of Interpol; and in Hamburg, Tel Aviv, and Toronto. There are also two cops on assignment at FBI headquarters in Washington, and New York detectives have traveled to Afghanistan, Egypt, Yemen, Pakistan, and the military's prison at Guantánamo Bay in Cuba to conduct interrogations. Members of the department's command staff have also attended sessions at the Naval War College in Newport, Rhode Island.

And there are the Hercules Teams, elite, heavily armed, Special Forces-type police units that pop up daily around the city. It can be at the Empire State Building, the Brooklyn Bridge, Times Square, or the stock exchange, wherever the day's intelligence reports suggest they could be needed. These small teams arrive in black Suburbans, sheathed in armor-plated vests and carrying 9-mm. submachine guns—sometimes with air or sea support. Their purpose is to intimidate and to very publicly mount a show of force. Kelly knows that terrorists do a lot of reconnaissance, and the Hercules Teams were designed to disrupt their planning. Like an ADT warning sign in front of a house, they're also intended to send a message that this is not an easy target.

The police commissioner now has what's called an STU (Secured Telephone Unit) on his desk. It is a phone line that enables him to talk to someone in the White House or the Pentagon without fear of being monitored. When a key on the phone is turned, the conversation is electronically encrypted.

"We are doing all these things," Kelly says over coffee in his fourteenth-floor office at police headquarters, "because New York is still the No. 1 target. We have been targeted four times, twice successfully, and the city remains the most symbolic, substantive target for the terrorists. These are cunning, patient, deliberate people who want to kill us and kill us in big numbers."

On a bright october day several weeks after September 11, Kelly and his wife, Veronica, were finally allowed to return to their Battery Park City apartment—not to move back in, but to pick up a few personal items. Before they left the building, one block from the World Trade Center, they went up to the roof. There, Kelly consoled his weeping wife as they looked in stunned disbelief at the devastation of their neighborhood.

Eight years earlier, back in 1993 when the Trade Center was attacked the first time, Kelly was police commissioner. Mayor David Dinkins was in Japan when the buildings were bombed, so Kelly essentially took charge. It was Kelly who went on television to calm the city, to let everyone know in his powerful Marine kind of way that everything was under control.

Now Kelly is staking his reputation and his legacy on the fight against terrorism. "Four months after 9/11, when Kelly was about to be sworn in, you just didn't get a sense of confidence at the federal, state, or local level that changes were being made," says former NYPD first deputy commissioner John Timoney, who was recently named police chief of Miami. "Ray could easily have said, 'What do I know about this stuff? It's the Feds' job.' It takes a lot of courage to do what he's doing. He's leaving himself open to be second-guessed and criticized if things don't go well. So he's making decisions that may benefit the city but be detrimental to him personally."

Kelly is familiar with being second-guessed and criticized. He served as NYPD commissioner during the final eighteen months of the Dinkins administration, in 1992 and '93. Though he was essentially finishing Commissioner Lee Brown's term, he did manage several significant accomplishments. He cleaned up and restructured Internal Affairs, which was a serious mess. And it was Kelly, not Bratton or Giuliani, who took care of the squeegee guys.

Not that anyone knows it. "When Bratton came in with his arrogance and swagger, he showed Ray up nine ways from Sunday," says a former high-level member of Bratton's own team. "Giuliani and Bratton lumped him in with Dinkins as one big ineffective management disaster."

"I knew we couldn't rely on the federal government. We're doing all the things we're doing because the federal government isn't doing them. It's not enough to say it's their job if the job isn't being done."

So Kelly has plenty of reasons to want to make his mark this time. Even so, isn't combating terrorism primarily a federal responsibility?

When I ask Kelly this question, he looks at me long and hard. He is a man who knows his way around Washington. In addition to his time in the mid-nineties as undersecretary of the Treasury, he was head of the Customs Service. He also worked for Interpol and was a special State Department envoy in Haiti where he was sent to establish and train a police force.

"I knew we couldn't rely on the federal government," Kelly says finally. "I know it from my own experience. We're doing all the things we're doing because the federal government isn't doing them. It's not enough to say it's their job if the job isn't being done. Since 9/11, the federal government hasn't taken any additional resources and put them here."

Has any kind of an increased federal presence been asked for? Soldiers? Fighter planes? More FBI agents? "Asked for?" he says, repeating my question incredulously. "Would you think it would have to be asked for? Look," he says, shifting in his chair and crossing his legs so the .38 in his ankle holster is visible. "It's a different world. We've redeployed. We've got 1,000 people on this. All seven subway tunnels under the river are covered, and it's the same with all the other sensitive locations. It's taken constant attention. It's extremely difficult. But make no mistake: It's something we have to do ourselves."

Every morning at eight, in the commissioner's conference room on the top floor of police headquarters (another NYPD venue where, by the way, you can watch Al-Jazeera), Kelly is briefed by his two key players in the counterterrorism battle: Lieutenant General Frank Libutti, who runs the department's counterterrorism bureau, and David Cohen, formerly No. 4 at the CIA, who is now in charge of the NYPD's intelligence division.

The two men couldn't play more to type if they were actors hired to fill these roles. Libutti, a fit, silver-haired 35-year veteran who was in charge of all Marine forces in the Pacific and the Persian Gulf, is, in a word, crisp. His navy pinstripe suit looks perfectly tailored, his shirt is starched, and he has an open, forthright manner. He is friendly in a lieutenant-general-determined-to-stay-on-message sort of way. He calls terrorists "the bad guys."

Cohen is a much grayer, more recessive presence. He has been described as "bookish," but that's not quite right. His look is much closer to that of, say, a software designer, someone who appears both geeky and cunning.

Cohen rarely gives interviews, and in the days following his appointment, he seemed to be amusing himself and perhaps trying to create a mysterious aura by playing with the reporters who questioned him. He was very sketchy on the details of his background. When asked his age, he'd respond only that he was "somewhere between 28 and 70." (For the record, he's 61.)

"I knew we had to do business differently," Kelly says of his marquee hires. "I thought we had to get some people with a fresh outlook and with federal experience to help us."

With Libutti, Kelly gets someone who has command presence, a man who has known pressure and conflict—he was injured three times in Vietnam. Libutti also has a record of accomplishment as someone who can, as they like to say in the military, organize and marshal forces and execute an objective. And in fact, he was able to "stand up" the counterterrorism bureau (Marine-speak for get it up and running) within weeks.

Job one for the new bureau is threat assessment on landmarks, public and private properties, and the city's infrastructure. The bureau has nine five-man teams, whose members were schooled at the federal law-enforcement training center in Georgia.

These teams could, for example, look at the Brooklyn Bridge, a Con Ed plant, or the offices of *New York* Magazine. Once an inspection is complete, the team produces a written report that includes detailed security suggestions. Though most of the sites are chosen by the bureau based on risk level, some are done by request. This process has helped the department establish closer ties to the business community.

The counterterrorism bureau also does independent intelligence analysis. The focus is on techniques. If two suicide bombers in a row in Israel are wearing Columbia ski jackets, for example, they'll identify the marker and issue an alert so cops here are aware of this.

Cohen's challenge, on the other hand, was to re-create and give new relevance to a division in the Police Department that already existed. "Our intelligence division was in essence an escort service," says Kelly. "They handled dignitaries and bigwigs when they came into town. It was an intelligence service in name only. We simply had to get better information. We didn't know what was going on in our own city, let alone the rest of the world."

On paper, Cohen is exactly what Kelly needed to execute his vision: a high-level guy from inside the intelligence community who has knowledge and access. Someone who can get the right people on the phone and find out what they know. Libutti is plugged in as well. Just before joining the NYPD, he was a special assistant to Homeland Security secretary Tom Ridge. He served as a liaison between Ridge and the Pentagon.

One morning in Libutti's ninth-floor office at police headquarters, he and Cohen talked about their roles. They are kind of like the Rumsfeld and Tenet of the Police Department. Cohen, who is fairly expansive considering his reputation, admits that when they signed on, their roles were not all that well defined.

"When we got here, there was no counterterrorism doctrine for a city like New York," he says in a faint Boston accent. "There was no playbook, no manual you could turn to and say, 'We should do two of these and a couple of the things in that chapter, and we have now built our counterterrorism program.' The process for us has been to write and implement the playbook simultaneously. And it's like trying to change the tires on a speeding car."

What comes through most clearly from the two men is that the lifeblood of their efforts is information. Cohen makes this point when he discusses the recent incident in London when authorities arrested three men suspected in a plot to unleash cyanide in the Underground: "When something like that happens, we need to know in real time everything we can find out about it. Obviously, the subway is a real hot spot for us given that three and a half million people a day use it. So we need to understand what kind of operation they tried to roll up, was it pre-surveillance-stage, was it pre-planning-stage, was it really cyanide, was the subway the real target? The more times things get rolled up overseas, the smarter we get. And the smarter we get, the stronger we get."

The flow of quality information is also critical in helping Kelly decide how to respond to threats. Most threats that come in, according to Cohen, don't name a place, so it is often difficult even to be sure New York is the target. "You have to understand the nuances of the threat," Cohen says. "Where it's coming from, how to define it, what it really means. Frank and I help interpret the information, and that enables the commissioner to make an informed decision about responding. This war is going to go on a long time, and you've got to calibrate your response. You don't want to burn everyone out."

What Kelly has done with Libutti and Cohen, essentially, is to create his own FBI and CIA within the New York City Police Department. "This is all about Ray Kelly's contempt for the Feds and how they blew it, over and over again," says a former member of the NYPD who knows the commissioner well.

"The Feds kept getting information they didn't act on," he continues. "So what Kelly's trying to do is say, 'Hey, just in case they don't fix all that stuff at the FBI and the CIA, we gotta find out the things they're finding out. And we gotta act on them.' Let's face it: A lot of this isn't rocket science. It's cultivating sources, talking to informants, running down leads, getting search warrants, and following up on every piece of information you get. In other words, it's good, solid investigative police work. The kind of thing New York cops do every day."

It's not every day, however, that a major figure in law enforcement like Kelly does something so contemptuous of the system. Yet there has been no outrage, no intramural rock-throwing over what he's done. Even the FBI, which has traditionally looked down on local cops, has barely raised an eyebrow over Kelly's moves.

One possible explanation for the FBI's passivity is that the agency has been under such relentless critical fire from Congress and the media that it is in no position to take on new battles. Another possibility is assistant FBI director Kevin Donovan, who was recently put in charge of the FBI's New York office. Donovan gets high marks for competence and as a team player. By all accounts, he is someone who looks to eliminate problems rather than create them.

But the most significant factor may be the most obvious. Given everything that has happened, the FBI may simply be happy to have the help. When I interviewed both Donovan and Joseph Billy, the agent in charge of counterterrorism in New York, they praised Kelly and his cops with alacrity.

"This is a very big city," says Donovan, "and we just don't have the resources to collect all the information. We don't have 40,000 eyes and ears on patrol like the NYPD. We have 1,100 agents in this office. And no one knows the streets here like the local officers. They know what to look for at two in the morning. They know what's out of place, what doesn't seem right. What Ray Kelly is doing makes perfect sense and is complementary to what we do. No city is better prepared right now than New York."

Tom Reppetto, who heads the Citizens Crime Commission and has written a history of the department called *NYPD: A City and Its Police*, more or less agrees with Donovan. In addition, he says, the FBI is not an immediate-response agency in any event. You wouldn't call the FBI, for example, if you found a bomb in Union Square Park.

"Remember, too, that the police can do a lot of the counterterrorism work as part of their regular duties," Reppetto says. "You'll notice there's been a surge in arrests of homeless people recently, and they seem to be getting arrested under bridges and in tunnels. Know why? Because police are spending a lot of time under bridges and in tunnels."

The relationship between the FBI and the NYPD has probably never been more critical than it is right now. The FBI-NYPD Joint Terrorism Task Force is one of the key instruments in the effort to protect the city. The task force was a relatively sleepy backwater run by the FBI but made up of both agents and detectives. One of Kelly's earliest moves was to pump up the number of detectives from 17 to 125, a huge commitment that the FBI matched. Kelly's intensity and his willingness to push the envelope were demonstrated early on when he tried to muscle control of the JTTF away from the FBI. According to sources, Kelly and Libutti sent a two-star police chief named Phil Pulaski over to the JTTF, which is housed at the FBI's New York headquarters.

Pulaski is generally viewed within the NYPD as brilliant—he designed and set up the police lab. However, as one cop put it to me, he also has a "Ph.D. in pissing people off." So he trooped over to the JTTF and told them, after the FBI had been in charge for over twenty years, that he was now the boss. Though you can imagine the reaction by the Feds, Donovan managed to maintain his cool and prevent a truly damaging explosion.

He simply told Libutti it was not going to work. "You can't send a guy to my house," the director reportedly said, "and have him say he's in charge. Especially without even calling me." Libutti said he was sorry and reeled Pulaski back in.

"Our intelligence service was in essence an escort service," says Commissioner Kelly. "They handled dignitaries and bigwigs when they came into town. We simply had to get better information."

But the response from the two sides when this episode is brought up is perhaps more revealing than the incident itself. "Pulaski had a job to do," says the FBI's Joseph Billy. "He had to integrate a large number of detectives into the task force, and he's a very results-oriented individual. There was some tension, but it all worked out. The FBI is still the lead agency for the JTTF."

Libutti is not quite as conciliatory: "Without criticizing their efforts, part of our responsibility is to reach out to the federal side and demand excellence in support of what we're doing. I got a guy over there—Pulaski—who's hard-charging. His job is to keep me posted, and he's going to press, press, press to turn over every rock to find out everything that's happening on the federal side. I think I know what's going on. What worries me is what I don't know."

Part of what Kelly learned during his first term as commissioner—and its aftermath—is the importance of perception. It may not be fair and it may not be right, but sometimes it is not enough just to do a good job.

Self-promotion is not Kelly's natural mode, but it seems he has learned a few things from watching eight years of Giuliani. Kelly has become the face of the NYPD in the same way that Giuliani was always the face of New York. If there's a bodega robbed in the Bronx on a Sunday afternoon, it is most likely Ray Kelly who will be on the six- and eleven-o'clock news.

He also must have recognized, coming back to the NYPD, that no matter what he did on the crime front, he would not get any credit. When the FBI crime stats were released last month, New York's numbers were terrific. That week, in an editorial celebrating the continuing crime decline, the New York *Post* congratulated Kelly this way: "The local crime rate continues to drop—even as crime nationwide is on the rise—because Kelly and Mayor Bloomberg continue to employ the previous administration's anti-crime tactics."

Terrorism, by contrast, is Kelly's fight. But for all of the risk and the additional headaches, Kelly may, ironically, end up getting very little credit on this front even if he succeeds. When you're battling street crime, success and failure are easy to measure. Murder goes up or goes down. Rapes increase or they decrease. But how do you measure the terrorist acts that didn't happen? The ones all the painstaking work may have prevented? In fact, some of the successes may never even be made public when they do occur.

In November, the *Times* ran a full-page story with the headline DEEPENING SHADOWS that stated in its lead, "Once again, it's not uncommon to feel a vague sense of dread when walking down a shadowy street." And "New Yorkers are more fearful these days."

"You don't want this kind of perception to fester," Kelly says with a hint of frustration in his voice. "I'm aware it's out there. But it is a little difficult to deal with when it's not based on some reality."

With the crime numbers way down from four years ago, why do average people say they feel less safe? What has changed for them? "The elephant in the corner of the room," Kelly says, "is 9/11. That's why people feel less safe."

So Kelly's job is to end the fear. Not the fear of conventional street crime, which continues to be under control, but fear of a menace that can be very hard to see. "Kelly's a very methodical guy who does things step-by-step, by the numbers," says Reppetto. "And he is clearly determined that if something does happen, nobody is going to be able to say they didn't do everything possible to stop it. There won't be some report issued afterward saying the NYPD fell short."

The most obvious tests of Kelly's new counterterrorism strategy are large public events. And two months ago, with several hundred thousand people gathered in Times Square for New Year's Eve, the pressure was really on the commissioner and the NYPD. They had executed what Kelly calls their "counterterrorism overlay package." Undercovers were everywhere. Intelligence officers mingled in the crowd. Sharpshooters were on the rooftops. Police boats were on the water, choppers were overhead, and Hercules Teams were ready to move.

Kelly also had the department's Archangel package in place, which includes ESU teams equipped to detect a chemical or biological attack and to respond if one does in fact occur.

Is New York less safe than it was? "You don't want this kind of perception to fester. I'm aware that it's out there. The elephant in the corner of the room is 9/11. That's why people feel less safe."

The five days leading up to the celebration had been especially difficult. There were intelligence reports detailing serious harbor threats, including information about a possible plan to stage eight separate diversionary acts culminating with a major terrorist attack. All the locations were covered. The water had an eerie, blacker-than-usual look to it because it was mostly empty. No pleasure boats were allowed out.

Police had also been looking for the five men who might have come across the border from Canada using illegal documents. Michael John Hamdani, the Pakistani document forger under arrest in Toronto, told the NYPD detective who interrogated him about the men. This prompted the FBI to instigate and then call off a nationwide manhunt. Hamdani, however, didn't say they were terrorists, just that they were trying to sneak into the U.S. For Kelly, this highlighted what he believes is an ongoing alien-smuggling problem. Cops hit various locations around the city during the day, and several arrests were made.

Kelly also had credible intelligence that something might happen between Christmas and New Year's Day at the stock exchange. All week, Hercules Teams had been flooding the financial district. And then, of course, there was the gathering in Times Square itself.

"We were covering a lot of bases," says Kelly. "But we were addressing all these things appropriately. We all felt we'd done everything we could've reasonably done to make the night a safe one. You can really see the force and the power of the Police Department manifestly displayed on a night like New Year's Eve."

Finally, at around 1:30 in the morning, when most of the crowd had drifted away, Kelly had a momentary flash of relief, and satisfaction. The night had been so well handled that there were only three arrests—for disorderly conduct—in a crowd of hundreds of thousands of people. But Kelly's pleasure was short-lived. "When you get past a particular event now, there's the next event you have to address. And we were concerned about New Year's Day."

Kelly has taken on this burden at an extraordinarily difficult moment for the Police Department. With the city facing its most serious deficits in 30 years, budget cuts have hit the department hard. By July, Kelly will be down 3,000 officers from the roughly 40,000-man force he took over last January. In addition, he has 1,000 cops assigned full-time to his fight against the terrorists.

In an attempt to fill in the gaps, Kelly has energetically tried to convince the federal government that the cost of protecting New York is no longer just a municipal responsibility. Though a half-billion dollars of need has been identified, Kelly and his staff have whittled it down to a $261 million list that includes money for training and equipment. Despite several trips to Washington, Kelly has so far made no progress.

He has also been a good soldier and not publicly fought with the mayor over budget issues. When the mayor was booed last week at the graduation ceremony for 2,108 new cops—largely because his budget-cutting included talk of police layoffs—Kelly enthusiastically came to his defense. However, the police commissioner was not always so sanguine about the cuts. When Bloomberg made his first statement last July calling for 7.5 percent cuts across all city departments, sources say, Kelly balked.

According to one source, Kelly initially told the mayor he couldn't play ball on the budget cuts. He was not going to be the police commissioner on whose watch crime began to go up because the department was underfunded and undermanned. Though everything was worked out amicably, Bloomberg's people actually contacted several former commissioners—including Bratton and Timoney—to see what they were up to. "The conversations were to put out friendly feelers that were one stop short of 'Are you still available?,'" says the source.

The potential downside for Kelly of this focus on counterterrorism is enormous. "I know there's a universe out there just waiting to say, 'Aha, I told you so,'" he says. "But let me tell you something. We're taking care of business. There is this notion that this administration cannot do it all, something's gotta give. Well, the city is safer than it's ever been in modern history."

Before September 11, the nightmare that haunted New York's police commissioners—and commissioners in other big cities as well—tended to revolve around police brutality and race—Amadou Diallo, say, or Rodney King. One commissioner who left his job not all that long ago while riding a wave of popularity in his city reportedly told a confidant that he believed he was "one 3 A.M. phone call away from having it all fall apart." Since 9/11, of course, "having it all fall apart" means something entirely different—and much scarier. "We don't know the time and we don't know the place," says Libutti, "but we do know the bad guys are coming back."

Sitting in his office one recent evening as a cold wind whipped across the plaza in front of police headquarters, Kelly showed no signs of the pressure he is under.

"I enjoy this job and I'm living in the moment," he said while eating a cookie. "The world has changed, but I believe I'm doing the right thing. We're the biggest, most important city in the world, and this is the biggest, most talented police force. And we have done everything we can reasonably do to prevent another attack."

Racial Profiling and Its Apologists

Racist law enforcement is rooted in deceptive statistics, slippery logic, and telling indifference.

TIM WISE

I t's just good police work." So comes the insistence by many—usually whites—that concentrating law enforcement efforts on blacks and Latinos is a perfectly legitimate idea. To listen to some folks tell it, the fact that people of color commit a disproportionate amount of crime (a claim that is true for some but not all offenses) is enough to warrant heightened suspicion of such persons. As for the humiliation experienced by those innocents unfairly singled out, stopped, and searched? Well, they should understand that such mistreatment is the price they'll have to pay, as long as others who look like them are heavily represented in various categories of criminal mischief.

Of course, the attempt to rationalize racism and discriminatory treatment has a long pedigree. Segregationists offer up many "rational" arguments for separation and even slave-owners found high-minded justifications for their control over persons of African descent. In the modern day, excuses for unequal treatment may be more nuanced and couched in calm, dispassionate, even academic jargon; but they remain fundamentally no more legitimate than the claims of racists past. From overt white supremacists to respected social scientists and political commentators, the soft-pedaling of racist law enforcement is a growing cottage industry: one rooted in deceptive statistics, slippery logic, and telling indifference to the victims of such practices.

As demonstrated convincingly in David Harris's new book *Profiles in Injustice: Why Racial Profiling Cannot Work* (New Press, 2002), racial profiling is neither ethically acceptable nor logical as a law enforcement tool. But try telling that to the practice's apologists.

According to racial separatist Jared Taylor of American Renaissance—a relatively highbrow white supremacist organization—black crime rates are so disproportionate relative to those of whites that it is perfectly acceptable for police to profile African Americans in the hopes of uncovering criminal activity. His group's report "The Color of Crime"—which has been touted by mainstream conservatives like Walter Williams—purports to demonstrate just how dangerous blacks are, what with murder, robbery, and assault rates that are considerably

higher than the rates for whites. That these higher crime rates are the result of economic conditions disproportionately faced by people of color Taylor does not dispute in the report. But he insists that the reasons for the disparities hardly matter. All that need be known is that one group is statistically more dangerous than the other and avoiding those persons or stopping them for searches is not evidence of racism, but rather the result of rational calculations by citizens and police.

Although in simple numerical terms, whites commit three times more violent crimes each year than blacks, and whites are five to six times more likely to be attacked by another white person than by a black person, to Taylor, this is irrelevant. As he has explained about these white criminals: "They may be boobs, but they're our boobs."

Likewise, Heather MacDonald of the conservative Manhattan Institute has written that racial profiling is a "myth." Police, according to MacDonald—whose treatment of the subject was trumpeted in a column by George Will last year—merely play the odds, knowing "from experience" that blacks are likely to be the ones carrying drugs.

Michael Levin, a professor of philosophy at the City College of New York, argues it is rational for whites to fear young black men since one in four are either in prison, on probation, or on parole on any given day. According to Levin, the assumption that one in four black males encountered are therefore likely to be dangerous is logical and hardly indicates racism. Levin has also said that blacks should be treated as adults earlier by the justice system because they mature faster and trials should be shorter for blacks because they have a "shorter time horizon."

Conservative commentator Dinesh D'Souza says that "rational discrimination against young black men can be fully eradicated only by getting rid of destructive conduct by the group that forms the basis for statistically valid group distinctions. It is difficult to compel people to admire groups many of whose members do not act admirably."

Even when the profiling turns deadly, conservatives show little concern. Writing about Amadou Diallo, recipient of 19 bullets (out of 41 fired) from the NYPD Street Crimes Unit, columnist Mona Charen explained that he died for the sins of his black brethren, whose criminal proclivities gave the officers good reason to suspect that he was up to no good.

Putting aside the obvious racial hostility that forms the core of many if not all of these statements, racial profiling cannot be justified on the basis of general crime rate data showing that blacks commit a disproportionate amount of certain crimes, relative to their numbers in the population. Before making this point clear, it is worth clarifying what is meant by racial profiling.

Racial profiling means one of two things. First, the over-application of an incident-specific criminal description in a way that results in the stopping, searching, and harassment of people based solely or mostly on skin color alone. An example would be the decision by police in one upstate New York college town a few years ago to question every black male in the local university after an elderly white woman claimed to have been raped by a black man (turns out he was white).

So while there is nothing wrong with stopping black men who are 6'2", 200 pounds, driving Ford Escorts, if the perp in a particular local crime is known to be 6'2", 200 pounds, and driving a Ford Escort, but when that description is used to randomly stop black men, even who aren't 6'2", aren't close to 200 pounds, and who are driving totally different cars, then that becomes a problem.

The second and more common form of racial profiling is the disproportionate stopping, searching, frisking, and harassment of people of color in the hopes of uncovering a crime, even when there is no crime already in evidence for which a particular description might be available. In other words: stopping black folks or Latinos and searching for drugs.

This is why general crime rates are irrelevant to the profiling issue. Police generally don't randomly stop and search people in the hopes of turning up last night's convenience store hold-up man. They tend to have more specific information to go on in those cases. As such, the fact that blacks commit a higher share of some crimes (robbery, murder, assault) than their population numbers is of no consequence to the issue of whether profiling them is legitimate. The "crime" for which people of color are being profiled mostly is drug possession. In that case, people of color are not a disproportionate number of violators and police do not find such contraband disproportionately on people of color.

All available evidence indicates that whites are equally or more likely to use (and thus possess at any given time) illegal narcotics. This is especially true for young adults and teenagers, in which categories whites are disproportionate among users.

Although black youth and young adults are more likely than white youth to have been approached by someone offering to give them or sell them drugs during the past month, they are less likely to have actually used drugs in the last 30 days. Among adults, data from California is instructive: although whites over the age of 30 are only 36 percent of the state's population, they comprise 60 percent of all heavy drug users in the state.

Although blacks and Latinos often control large drug sale networks, roughly eight in ten drug busts are not for dealing, but for possession. Drug busts for narcotics trafficking rarely stem from random searches of persons or vehicles—the kind of practice rightly labeled profiling—but rather, tend to take place after a carefully devised sting operation and intelligence gathering, leading to focused law enforcement efforts. As such, the usage numbers are the more pertinent when discussing the kinds of police stops and searches covered by the pejorative label of "profiling."

A Department of Justice study released in 2001 notes that although blacks are twice as likely as whites to have their cars stopped and searched, police are actually twice as likely to find evidence of illegal activity in cars driven by whites.

In New Jersey, for 2000, although blacks and Latinos were 78 percent of persons stopped and searched on the southern portion of the Jersey Turnpike, police were twice as likely to discover evidence of illegal activity in cars driven by whites, relative to blacks, and whites were five times more likely to be in possession of drugs, guns, or other illegal items relative to Latinos. In North Carolina, black drivers are two-thirds more likely than whites to be stopped and searched by the State Highway Patrol, but contraband is discovered in cars driven by whites 27 percent more often.

In New York City, even after controlling for the higher crime rates by blacks and Latinos and local demographics (after all, people of color will be the ones stopped and searched most often in communities where they make up most of the residents), police are still two to three times more likely to search them than whites. Yet, police hunches about who is in possession of drugs, guns, other illegal contraband, or who is wanted for commission of a violent crime turn out to be horribly inaccurate. Despite being stopped and searched more often, blacks and Latinos are less likely to be arrested because they are less likely to be found with evidence of criminal wrongdoing.

So much for MacDonald's "rational" police officers, operating from their personal experiences. Despite police claims that they only stop and search people of color more often because such folks engage in suspicious behavior more often, if the "hit rates" for such persons are no higher than, and even lower than the rates for whites, this calls into question the validity of the suspicious action criteria. If blacks seem suspicious more often, but are actually hiding something less often, then by definition the actions deemed suspicious should be reexamined, as they are not proving to be logical at all, let alone the result of good police work. Indeed, they appear to be proxies for racial stops and searches.

Nor can the disproportionate stopping of black vehicles be justified by differential driving behavior. Every study done on the subject has been clear: there are no significant differences between people of color and whites when it comes to the commission of moving or other violations. Police acknowledge that virtually every driver violates any number of minor laws every time they take to the road. But these violations are not enforced equally and that is the problem.

In one New Jersey study, for example, despite no observed differences in driving behavior, African Americans were 73 percent of all drivers stopped on the Jersey Turnpike, despite being less than 14 percent of the drivers on the road: a rate that is 27 times greater than what would be expected by random chance. Similar results were found in a study of stops in Maryland. On a particular stretch of Interstate 95 in Florida, known for being a drug trafficking route, blacks and Latinos comprise only 5 percent of drivers, but 70 percent of those stopped by members of the Highway Patrol. These stops were hardly justified, as only nine drivers, out of 1,100 stopped during the study, were ever ticketed for any violation, let alone arrested for possession of illegal contraband.

As for Levin's claim that whites should properly consider one in four black males encountered to be a threat to their personal safety, because of their involvement with the criminal justice system, it should be remembered that most of these have been arrested for non-violent offenses like drug possession. Blacks comprise 35 percent of all possession arrests and 75 percent of those sent to prison for a drug offense, despite being only 14 percent of users.

When it comes to truly dangerous violent crime, only a miniscule share of African Americans will commit such offenses in a given year and less than half of these will choose a white victim.

With about 1.5 million violent crimes committed by blacks each year (about 90 percent of these by males) and 70 percent of the crimes committed by just 7 percent of the offenders—a commonly accepted figure by criminologists—this means that less than 2 percent of blacks over age 12 (the cutoff for collecting crime data) and less than 3.5 percent of black males over 12 could even theoretically be considered dangerous. Less than 1.5 percent of black males will attack a white person in a given year, hardly lending credence to Levin's claim about the rationality of white panic.

T he fact remains that the typical offender in violent crime categories is white. So even if black rates are disproportionate to their population percentages, any "profile" that tends to involve a black or Latino face is likely to be wrong more than half the time. Whites commit roughly 60 percent of violent crimes, for example. So if 6 in 10 violent criminals are white, how logical could it be to deploy a profile—either for purposes of law enforcement or merely personal purposes of avoiding certain people—that is only going to be correct 40 percent of the time? So too with drugs, where any profile that involves a person of color will be wrong three out of four times?

Additionally, the apologists for profiling are typically selective in terms of the kinds of profiling they support. Although whites are a disproportionate percentage of all drunk drivers, for example, and although drunk driving contributes to the deaths of more than 10,000 people each year, none of the defenders of anti-black or brown profiling suggests that drunk driving roadblocks be set up in white suburbs where the "hit rates" for catching violators would be highest.

Likewise, though white college students are considerably more likely to binge drink (often underage) and use narcotics than college students of color, no one suggests that police or campus cops should regularly stage raids on white fraternity houses or dorm rooms occupied by whites, even though the raw data would suggest such actions might be statistically justified.

Whites are also nearly twice as likely to engage in child sexual molestation, relative to blacks. Yet how would the Heather MacDonalds and Dinesh D'Souzas of the world react to an announcement that adoption agencies were going to begin screening out white couples seeking to adopt, or subjecting them to extra scrutiny, as a result of such factual information?

Similarly, those seeking to now justify intensified profiling of Arabs or Muslims since September 11 were hardly clamoring for the same treatment of white males in the wake of Oklahoma City. Even now, in the wake of anthrax incidents that the FBI says have almost certainly been domestic, possibly white supremacist in origin, no one is calling for heightened suspicion of whites as a result.

The absurdity of anti-Arab profiling is particularly obvious in the case of trying to catch members of al-Qaeda. The group, after all, operates in 64 countries, many of them non-Arab, and from which group members would not look anything like the image of a terrorist currently locked in the minds of so many. Likewise, Richard Reid, the would-be shoe bomber recently captured was able to get on the plane he sought to bring down precisely because he had a "proper English name," likely spoke with a proper English accent, and thus, didn't fit the description.

The bottom line is that racial profiling doesn't happen because data justifies the practice, but rather because those with power are able to get away with it, and find it functional to do so as a mechanism of social control over those who are less powerful. By typifying certain "others" as dangerous or undesirable, those seeking to maintain divisions between people whose economic and social interests are actually quite similar can successfully maintain those cleavages.

No conspiracy here, mind you: just the system working as intended, keeping people afraid of one another and committed to the maintenance of the system, by convincing us that certain folks are a danger to our well-being, which then must be safeguarded by a growing prison-industrial complex and draconian legal sanctions; or in the case of terrorist "profiles," by the imposition of unconstitutional detentions, beefed-up military and intelligence spending, and the creation of a paranoiac wartime footing.

Until and unless the stereotypes that underlie racial profiling are attacked and exposed as a fraud, the practice will likely continue: not because it makes good sense, but because racist assumptions about danger—reinforced by media and politicians looking for votes—lead us to think that it does.

TIM WISE is a Nashville-based writer, lecturer and antiracist activist. Footnotes for this article can be obtained at tjwise@mindspring.com.

Ethics and Criminal Justice: Some Observations on Police Misconduct

BRYAN BYERS
Ball State University

One need not look far to see evidence of the societal importance placed on ethics in criminal justice. Ethics has been a hot topic in the 1990s and promises to be equally important as we venture into the new millennium. Often, the issue of ethics in criminal justice is considered synonymous with police ethics. However, ethics touches all of the main branches of criminal justice practice as well as the academic realm. Due to the high profile nature of policing in our society, however, ethics is commonly connected with policing. Therefore, particular focus is given to this dimension in the following discussion. Within this essay the topic of ethics is addressed by first examining a general understanding of this concept. Second, a brief discussion of our societal concern over ethics and criminal justice practice is examined. Third, the discussion centers on selected scholarship in criminal justice ethics. Finally, some concluding remarks are offered.

Ethics and Ethical Issues: A Primer

According to the Merriam-Webster Dictionary, "ethics" is defined as (1) "a discipline dealing with good and evil and with moral duty" or (2) "moral principles or practice." The first definition suggests that ethics is a discipline or area of study. This certainly has been the case when we examine the academic field of Philosophy. Criminal justice is, admittedly, a hybrid discipline drawing from many academic fields—one being Philosophy. Interestingly, a good portion of the published academic scholarship in criminal justice ethics is philosophical in nature and can be found in the journal *Criminal Justice Ethics*. The other part of the definition suggests that ethics is a combination of cognition ('moral principles') and behavior ('practice'). Therefore, we might conclude that ethics is the study of the principle and practice of good, evil, and moral duty.

As we consider the nature of criminal justice, and in particular policing, within contemporary society, the behavior of law enforcement officers is continually the target of ethical evaluation. The field of law enforcement has been under scrutiny during various historical epochs for behavior that has been called into question on ethical grounds. Whether it be search and seizure "fishing expeditions" prior to *Mapp v. Ohio*,

the fallout from the Knapp Commission report (*à la Serpico*) or the latest instance of police misconduct to flood the media, essentially the concern is over conduct or behavior. Cognitive processes and the socialization that reinforces unprofessional and unethical conduct influence the onset and proliferation of undesirable behavior. Thus, while one must be concerned with psychological and sociological forces that help to produce police unprofessionalism and unethical behavior, we should not lose sight of the role choice has in police misconduct.

One would be hard pressed to produce credible evidence to suggest that policing has not become more professional over the past several decades. It seems equally unreasonable to suggest that the entire field of policing is corrupt and permeated with graft. However, and as most readers will know, such an explanation has been offered. The venerable "rotten barrel theory"[1] of police corruption suggests such permeation within a police department. As most readers know, the rotten barrel theory of police corruption suggests that unethical and illegal behavior not only occurs at the individual officer level but is pervasive enough within a police department that unethical conduct may be traced to top administrative officials.

Another interpretation of police corruption is the "rotten apple theory."[2] This approach does not suggest that corruption and unethical conduct is so pervasive that it spreads to the highest ranks and throughout the organization. This approach, rather, suggests that there are a few "rotten apples" in a police department and inappropriate behavior is isolated to a few individuals. Police administrators have been keen on this explanation in the wake of police corruption because it avoids suggestion of wholesale departmental corruption, allows for a tidy response (e.g., fire the offending officer), and does not necessarily have to result in a tarnished image of an entire department.

An additional form of police misconduct has also been identified. In addition to the rotten apple and the rotten barrel, there may also be a "rotten group theory" of police corruption. According to a 1998 report by the General Accounting Office on police corruption in the United States, "The most commonly identified pattern of drug-related police corruption involved small groups of officers who protected and assisted each other in criminal activities, rather than the traditional patterns of non-drug-related police corruption that involved just a few isolated individuals or systemic corruption pervading an entire police department or precinct."[3]

Whether unethical behavior is systematic, small group, or individual, one cannot deny the importance placed on the intellectual process that allows for such conduct to take place. One might still be left wondering what it is about policing that produces opportunities to engage in unethical behavior. That is, what is it about the policing profession that affords officers the opportunity to engage in unethical conduct? The answer might be found in the concepts of "authority" and "power." Police wield a tremendous amount of power and authority within society. The powers to arrest, question and detain are entrusted with the police. The authority given to the police to protect our belongings and persons is unmatched by any other profession. Unethical or illegal behavior results when a law enforcement officer makes a conscious decision to abuse authority or wield power that is not appropriate to the situation. What is fundamental to unethical behavior by police is the conscious decision to abuse authority or power and circumstances, peer pressure, socialization, loyalty, and individual psychology are secondary in their ability to explain the behavior.

It might be best to interpret the role played by factors such as circumstances, peer pressure, socialization, loyalty, and individual psychology as a means of excusing or justifying the unethical or illegal act committed by an officer. That is, while the individual officer makes a decision to violate the public's trust and engage in unethical behavior, one might suggest that the officer's loyalty to his peers was a justification for the conduct. Let us examine this dynamic by way of an ethical dilemma. Assume that Officer X has just pulled over a drunk driver and realizes that the suspect is a fellow officer and friend. In fact, the driver has helped Officer X out of a few "tight spots" over the years. Instead of placing the colleague through a field sobriety test, Officer X helps his buddy park the car and then drives him home with the understanding from his friend that he will "sleep it off." What was the ethical dilemma? The choice between doing what was appropriate (the field sobriety test and subsequent arrest if appropriate) and being loyal to his friend. This situation, at the very least, describes a scenario ripe for abuse of discretion. Since discretion is a power that police have, it can be abused. Thus, many might examine this situation and suggest that the officer abused his discretionary authority. The officer made a decision to abuse his power but did so out of loyalty to the friend that is promoted through socialization behind the "blue curtain."

Concern Over Ethics: Can We Call It a Trend?

Media reports of police misconduct pepper us whenever there is an incident of alleged misbehavior or corruption. It might be the nightly newscaster reporting on the Rodney King incident at the start of the 1990s. It could be the recent case of the Philadelphia Police Department officers viewed on tape kicking a downed felony crime suspect at the birth of the twenty-first century. Whatever the instance, the topic of ethics and ethical behavior within the criminal justice profession grabs headlines. The

media likes to report on such "ethical misadventures" because it sells. Some of the public, and powerful leaders, use such instances to legitimize their negative attitudes toward police. The police loathe the "bad press" in the wake of their self-perception of "doing good" for the community.

The media might be the only winner in the wake of police misconduct. However, the public loses and so do the fields of policing and criminal justice, in general. Even the academic field of criminal justice loses because policing is so closely linked in the public mind to it. I am reminded of this reality when recalling my flight back from the 1991 Academy of Criminal Justice Sciences meeting in Nashville. As plane passengers do, I began a conversation with the person seated next to me. We engaged in the typical small talk of "where are you from" and "where are you going." When my fellow passenger heard that I was returning from a "criminal justice" meeting, his response was immediate and unequivocal. He said, "why are cops such jerks?" The conversation occurred in the wake of the Rodney King incident and he was referring to the behavior of the L.A. police officers captured on tape. Admittedly taken aback, I was speechless. Part of the reason was personal, given my experiences in the field as a practitioner and those of close family members and friends. The other part of my speechlessness was professional and social scientific in nature, given how astounding it was to me to find a person willing to generalize so broadly from one highly celebrated incident. This seemingly innocuous exchange had an indelible impression on me. It made me think about the impact the field of criminal justice might have in the topic of ethics.

There is little doubt that real world events and their impact on the collective conscience influence the academic field. In fact, one could reasonably argue that societal events drive research agendas and define, to some degree, what is popular to investigate criminologically and what is not. Ethics may be no exception. For instance, the Rodney King incident, one might argue, had a tremendous impact not only on the practical dimensions of policing and police-community relations but also on the academic field of criminal justice. For instance, the book jacket for *Above the Law: Police and the Excessive Use of Force* by Jerome Skolnick and James Fyfe has a frame from the Rodney King video just below the title. The impact goes beyond one book, however.

Using 1991 as a pivotal year, given that the Rodney King beating occurred then, the author decided to conduct a computer search for articles on ethics in criminal justice. The findings, albeit not scientific, are interesting nonetheless. Using Periodical Abstracts, an on-line search method at my institution and offered through the university library, a search was conducted for "criminal justice" + "ethics" comparing the years 1986–1990 to 1991–1999. What I wanted to find out is this: were there more publications in criminal justice ethics prior to Rodney King or after? Since the incident occurred relatively early in 1991, that year was placed in the "post-Rodney King" group of years. From 1986 (the first year the index covers) through 1990, there were 28 "hits" or publications on criminal justice ethics. From 1991 through 1999 there were 152 publications. Admittedly, the "post" period encompassed nine years and the "pre" period only contained five years. However, it is still rather telling that such a difference exists.

Only time will tell if the aforementioned suggests a trend for the discipline. However, there is certainly every indication that criminal justice scholarship and practice will continue with an emphasis on ethics. A key reason why ethics promises to have a strong future presence has less to do with the lasting impact of Rodney King and more to do with constant reminders that ethical misadventures keep occurring. For example, during the past ten years, the cities of New Orleans, Chicago, New York, Miami, and Los Angeles, to name a few, have all reeled in the aftermath of ethical transgressions among their sworn law enforcement officers.

Ethics and Criminal Justice Practice

In addition to the Rodney King case, there have been many other instances in which law enforcement officers have been found in ethically compromising or illegal positions. Every major city police force in the United States has experienced some form of unethical or illegal behavior within its ranks. Some of the situations in recent history have involved drugs and drug units. A few examples are listed below:

- A 1998 report by the General Accounting Office cites examples of publicly disclosed drug-related police corruption in the following cities: Atlanta, Chicago, Cleveland, Detroit, Los Angeles, Miami, New Orleans, New York, Philadelphia, Savannah, and Washington, DC.[4]
- On average, half of all police officers convicted as a result of FBI-led corruption cases between 1993 and 1997 were convicted for drug-related offenses.[5]
- A 1998 report by the General Accounting Office notes, ". . . several studies and investigations of drug-related police corruption found on-duty police officers engaged in serious criminal activities, such as (1) conducting unconstitutional searches and seizures; (2) stealing money and/or drugs from drug dealers; (3) selling stolen drugs; (4) protecting drug operations; (5) providing false testimony; and (6) submitting false crime reports."[6]
- A 1998 report by the General Accounting Office notes, "Although profit was found to be a motive common to traditional and drug-related police corruption, New York City's Mollen Commission identified power and vigilante justice as two additional motives for drug-related police corruption."[7]
- As an example of police corruption, the GAO cites Philadelphia, where "Since 1995, 10 police officers from Philadelphia's 39th District have been charged with planting drugs on suspects, shaking down drug dealers for hundreds of thousands of dollars, and breaking into homes to steal drugs and cash."[8]
- In New Orleans, 11 police officers were convicted of accepting nearly $100,000 from undercover agents to protect a cocaine supply warehouse containing 286 pounds of cocaine. The undercover portion of the investigation was terminated when a witness was killed under orders from a New Orleans police officer.[9]

Part of the fallout from a major finding of unethical or illegal behavior within a police department is a call to "clean up" the agency. As a result, departments in the aftermath of such an embarrassing situation might become more open to citizen review panels, pledge to re-examine their internal affairs division, require officers to participate in "ethics training," or reinforce the importance of "ethics codes."

The concept of citizen review panels has been in existence for several decades; the first panel may have been formed in Philadelphia around 1958. Citizen review panels, sometimes also called civilian review boards, are in place in some jurisdictions for the purpose of assisting with the investigation of citizen complaints that police officers within the jurisdiction engaged in the unfair treatment of civilians. Review panels can help to build or repair strained police-community relations. However, officers sometimes respond to such efforts with a defensive posture and resentment over "civilians trying to tell them how to do their job."

A department might also pledge to examine its own internal affairs division, the policy and procedure for investigating complaints and cases against officers, and typical responses to officers who have violated departmental policy and/or who have violated the law. It is important to note from the onset that a police department internal affairs division runs the risk of being considered "suspect" from officers and a community's citizenry alike. Officers can view internal affair or "I.A." as the "enemy" and a division that is bent on punishing officers who are risking their lives on the streets every day. From the community, there might be the perception that the police department cannot possibly take on the task of investigating itself. At the very least, this cannot be done "ethically." Thus, I.A. can find itself in a no-win situation. Whether a division in a large department or an officer charged with this responsibility in a smaller department, the I.A. role is critical. However, internal remedies are effective only if they are meted out in a fair and just fashion. I.A. recommendations that are carried out by police administration must bolster the respect of line officers. If perceptions exist that an officer has been treated unfairly, the department will lose any deterrent effect I.A. recommendations might produce.

Yet another response is the concept of "ethics training" for police officers and recruits. The notion of "ethics *training*" (with an emphasis on 'training') is an interesting one given that the concept of 'training' assumes that what a person is being "trained in" can be taught. In this case, the term 'ethics training' suggests, either correctly or incorrectly, that ethics can somehow be taught to people. I prefer the term "Ethics Awareness Training" in lieu of the aforementioned. Why? The reason is rather elementary. Is it possible to teach someone to be ethical as "ethics training" might suggest? This seems far-fetched, at best. If a department has an officer who has a propensity toward unethical behavior, and this person was not weeded out during the hiring process, the best one might hope for is a heightened awareness and sensitivity for ethical issues and dilemmas.

Emphasizing codes of ethics, common today in most disciplines and professions,[10] is another avenue for police departments in the wake of ethical scandal. However, if a code of ethics[11] is printed in the departmental policy and procedure manual, never to be referred to again, it will have very little impact. A code of ethics for any department or organization must be a "living document" that is referenced often and held in high esteem. The code should be a document that officers have pride in and believe to be relevant to their lives as law enforcement officers. Otherwise, the code will have little, if any, impact on officer decision making and conduct.

The Scholars Weigh In

As mentioned above, a large portion of the academic scholarship in criminal justice ethics is philosophical in nature. However, a few academicians have attempted to examine ethics in criminal justice empirically and quantitatively. When discussing scholarship in criminal justice ethics, a few names immediately come to mind, including James Fyfe, Herman Goldstein, Victor Keppeler, Carl Klockars, Joycelyn Pollock, Lawrence Sherman, Jerome Skolnick and Sam Souryal. This is certainly not an exhaustive list, and we cannot possibly survey all of the literature in this field here. However, I would like to spend a few moments discussing two major studies funded by NIJ. The studies are *The Measurement of Police Integrity* by Klockars, Ivkovitch, Harver, and Haberfeld[12] and *Police Attitudes Toward Abuse of Authority: Findings from a National Study* by Weisburd and Greenspan.[13] Both studies were published in May of 2000. While the two studies do not represent the entire literature on police ethics, both studies are national in scope, recent and empirical.

The Klockars et al. study used 3,235 police officer respondents from 30 police agencies within the United States. The respondents were given 11 vignettes describing various types of possible police misconduct. In response to each vignette, officers were asked to answer six questions intended to measure ". . . the normative inclination of police to resist temptations to abuse the rights and privileges of their occupation." While the results indicate vast differences from agency to agency regarding the "environment of integrity," one finding is consistent with the protections afforded members of the police subculture. The survey revealed that most officers would not report a fellow officer who was engaged in "less serious" types of misconduct (e.g., running a security business on the side, receiving free meals and gifts, or even leaving a minor traffic accident while under the influence). What this suggests, even though the survey revealed little tolerance for what was defined as "serious" police misconduct, is that there is a culture of acceptance within police ranks for some forms of misconduct. While such conduct is typically referred to as "grass eating" (less serious forms of police misconduct) as opposed to "meat eating" (more serious forms of police misconduct), many members of society would find the behavior unacceptable. James W. Birch in *Reflections on Police Corruption*[14] makes an interesting observation regarding such behavior. He states that the public creates an environment for "grass eating" that makes it difficult to not accept the "discount" or the free meal. It would appear that there may be a different definition of what constitutes "misconduct" depending on whether a person is a member of the police subculture or an outsider looking in.

The second NIJ study, by Weisburd and Greenspan, entitled *"Police Attitudes Toward Abuse of Authority: Findings From a National Study"* is the result of the Police Foundation's national telephone survey of over 900 officers from various agencies across the country and addresses police attitudes concerning excessive force. The results indicate that the majority of respondents believed it was not acceptable to use more force than was legally permissible to effect control over a person who had assaulted an officer. However, respondents reported that "... it is not unusual for officers to ignore improper conduct by their fellow officers." Other findings suggest that the majority of officers/respondents believed that serious instances of abuse were rare and that their department maintained a 'tough stand' on police abuse of citizenry. What about possible solutions to the problem of police abuse? Officers report two fruitful avenues for addressing police abuse. First, it was reported police administrators could have an impact on the occurrence of police abuse by "taking a stand" against abuse and through better supervision. Second, officers believed that training in ethics, interpersonal skills and cultural diversity would be effective in preventing abuse. What about turning fellow officers in for abuse? This was perceived as risky. While the majority of officers maintained that the "code of silence" was not essential to good policing, the majority also maintained that whistle blowing was not worth the consequences within the police subculture.

Toward a Conclusion

It is difficult to conclude this discussion because there is so much more to say about the topic of ethics in criminal justice. However, I will attempt to make a few concluding observations to make closure on this discussion. First, ethics is an important area within criminal justice practice and scholarship since criminal justice practitioners, especially the police, are continually under scrutiny. Therefore, the discipline has an obligation to remain interested in this topic and to promote the study of ethics. Second, scholars can be of assistance to practitioners by studying the sociological and psychological forces that impact ethical and unethical behavior. There is much the academy can offer criminal justice agencies in the form of research within organizations and training pertinent to ethics. Third, unethical behavior is the result of a conscious decision-making process to abuse one's authority while in a position of public trust. However, one must still take into account social forces that help to perpetuate, excuse, and justify unethical behavior. Fourth, there has been a proliferation of ethics scholarship in criminal justice since the Rodney King case but there is a need for more research of an empirical nature much like the two studies profiled in this essay. While qualitative and philosophical literature is important to our understanding of ethics in criminal justice there is a need for additional research of a quantitative nature. With more study of ethics and ethical dilemmas faced by police, we might better understand the dynamics that propel officers into the dark side of policing and the factors that serve to justify misbehavior.

Notes

1. Police Deviance and Ethics. http://faculty.ncwc.edu/toconnor/205/205lec11.htm.

2. Knapp Commission Report. (1973). New York: George Braziller.

3. Government Accounting Office. Report to the Honorable Charles B. Rangel, House of Representatives, Law Enforcement: Information on Drug-Related Police Corruption. Washington, DC: USGPO (1998 May), p. 3.

4. Ibid. p. 36–37.

5. Ibid. p. 35.

6. Ibid. p. 8.

7. Ibid. p. 3.

8. Ibid. p. 37.

9. Ibid. p. 36.

10. The Academy of Criminal Justice Sciences (ACJS) recently adopted a code of ethics modeled after the American Sociological Association's (ASA) code.

11. The International Association of Chiefs of Police (IACP) has a model code of ethics and also publishes a training key on ethics and policing.

12. Klockars, C.B., S.K. Ivkovich, W.E. Harver, and M.R. Haberfeld. (2000, May). "The Measurement of Police Integrity." National Institute of Justice, Research in Brief. U.S. Government Printing Office: Washington, DC.

13. Weisburd, D. and R. Greenspan. (2000, May). "Police Attitudes Toward Abuse of Authority: Findings from a National Study." National Institute of Justice, Research in Brief. U.S. Government Printing Office: Washington, DC.

14. Birch, James W. (1983). "Reflections on Police Corruption." *Criminal Justice Ethics*, Volume 2.

Stress Management . . . and the Stress-proof Vest

ROBERT FOX

Police commit suicide at up to three times the national average and are eight times more likely to kill themselves than to become a victim of a homicide. They divorce at double the national average, and up to 25% have alcohol abuse problems. By profession, police officers are at high risk for stress disorders.

It would be convenient to dismiss this data by saying that high-risk individuals select law enforcement as a career, but research suggests otherwise. Most data indicates that the personality profiles of police officers entering the academy differ little from those of the population as a whole.

A survey of more than 10,000 law enforcement officers revealed that more than 90% said their major reason for becoming a cop was "to make a difference." This suggests a desire to help rather than to engage in risky scenarios. So what is wrong with the law enforcement environment?

The answer, in short, is loss of identity. The police officer is a standardized uniform with hat and a stern visage. How many of us really see the face of the officer who has vowed to protect our homes and families? Cops know that they are often dehumanized by the citizenry. They know they are expected to put their lives on the line if necessary. This kind of pressure requires strong support, yet many police officers voice the fear that the department might not back them up if they get into trouble.

While law enforcement spends millions of dollars on body armor, nothing protects the officer from two internal bullets-loss of identity and cynicism. Against these lethal weapons, cops need a "stress vest."

A Paradigm for Stress

Stress is a force that necessitates change. Neither good nor bad, it is simply the energy that presses upon us as we struggle to survive. How we use this energy determines the quality of our lives.

Such energy, used productively, is called eustress, or "good stress;" energy used destructively is termed distress or "bad stress." Burning the midnight oil to study for exams is an example of eustress; staying out all night drinking and partying when you have to get up and go to work the next day is distress. Whether we are happy or unhappy depends on the kinds of stress in our lives, and whether the level of that stress is within our comfort zones.

Eustress meets basic human needs and contributes to wellness, while distress jeopardizes human welfare. When you think of stress, think about the energy we use to enjoy and fulfill ourselves instead of the distress of fear and worry. A productive life is based on a positive outlook, good self-esteem, and discipline, where time and energy are invested in eustress to meet one's personal basic human needs.

The undisciplined person, characterized by low self-esteem and a negative outlook, is prone to gratification that often denies one's basic human needs. A life dominated by distress often leads to cynicism, loss of hope, and an attitude that whatever can go wrong, will.

It's all about outlook and attitude. One can focus on stress as a positive force, as the energy for accomplishment and the enjoyment of all life has to offer, or as a negative force, as the energy needed to combat fear and cynicism, where the only goal seems to be surviving another day. Understanding and fulfilling basic needs is the key. When one uses stress energy in the pursuit of becoming all that one can be, then life is good and fulfilling, and basic needs are met. But when one's needs are thwarted and go unfulfilled, that stress energy may become a destructive force.

Human Beings, Basic Needs and Stress

Every human being has personal, social, occupational and spiritual needs. While healthy human development requires a certain level of satisfaction in each of these areas, the level will differ from person to person. Some people are more social and family-oriented; some are more spiritual; some need greater career satisfaction. In a similar vein, the amount of stress that allows one to function best is highly individual. Let's look at these areas of basic human needs a little more closely.

Personal Wellness: Physical and psychological wellness-safety, security, self-esteem and identity. A healthy person eats right, exercises, gets proper rest, recreates, looks good, feels good, and is vital in every way.

Social Wellness: Family and friends-relationships, communication and intimacy. A socially healthy person is connected to other people and has satisfying relationships.

Occupational Wellness: Purpose and work-love what you do, and do what you love. An occupationally healthy person is capable of giving his best and receives the appreciation and satisfaction that is deserved.

Spiritual Wellness: Meaning of life beyond our understanding and control. A spiritually healthy person has a comfortable understanding of the greater meaning of life and his place in the world. This person lives according to that understanding.

Identity and Cynicism

Police officers rarely get to follow a case from start to finish, so they often feel disconnected and thwarted in terms of satisfaction. Shift work and arbitrary deployment, which are common in police work, further marginalize the individual. Marginalization is common in paramilitary organizations, highly structured, vertical bureaucracies in which orders become more impersonal as they drop from higher levels.

Most veteran police officers agree that it is hard to maintain an individual identity in a profession where one has to wear a uniform and be recognized more in terms of the profession than as an individual. Over time, the powerful "cop culture" tends to obliterate one's civilian identity, and many police officers find themselves becoming alienated from society.

As they lose their sense of identity and control, many become cynical, feeling that no one than other police officers can understand them; this creates an "us against them" mentality. In short, they have become police officers who happen to be human beings rather than human beings who happen to be police officers.

When this occurs, communication with one's spouse, family, and friends outside law enforcement becomes difficult. While the police officer still has personal, social, and spiritual needs as any human, these may be ignored or rationalized in favor of the police identity.

Social and esteem needs, including praise and acceptance, may now be sought from police management and colleagues instead of from family and friends. Cynicism may obliterate spiritual needs. For many, personal wellness may be ignored or even undercut by socially accepted—but often destructive—behaviors within the "cop culture," such as drinking together after hours.

Police officers with strong personalities can be hard to control. But police officers are not soldiers, even though law enforcement was largely based and modeled on military culture. Each police officer, after his shift, is expected to go back into that very community as one of its functioning members. And this is where identity conflicts will often occur.

How, then, can the job help people develop and maintain stronger personal identities? How can law enforcement managers encourage police officers to take care of their personal, social and spiritual wellness, as well as their careers? And what can management do to attenuate the forces within the paramilitary structure that erode personal identity, but without compromising the mission of policing?

From Industrial to Humanistic Management

Fifty years ago, most people considered themselves lucky to have a job, and autocratic management styles with little flexibility or sensitivity for the individual were commonly accepted. Households and businesses, schools and police departments were usually vertical hierarchies with little tolerance for diversity.

But times have changed, and many of today's enlightened leaders recognize that economic and social forces have necessitated accompanying changes in management styles. The ideas of psychologist Abraham Maslow and management guru Peter Drucker, for example, promote the importance of communication and good relations between management and workers for high morale and maximum performance.

In many organizations, autocratic leadership has given way to more sophisticated styles that work with instead of over workers. In sports, legendary, iron-fisted coaches like Woody Hayes, Vince Lombardi and Adolph Rupp have been replaced by those who relate more positively to their players. And it wasn't long ago that Sam Walton, the founder of Wal-Mart, revolutionized the business world by focusing on the needs of his employees—or associates, as he called them—instead of on the needs of his stockholders, thus pioneering a new concept of retail management.

Of course, not all institutions have thrived in this evolution of enlightenment. Some have still not learned the importance of employee morale and so continue to struggle with a high incidence of employee suicide, alcoholism, drug abuse, absenteeism, domestic violence, and divorce.

There are signs that many within law enforcement are seeking change. They are becoming aware that healthy, well-balanced people make the best police officers and that higher morale and less stress will improve the quality of law enforcement. But changing a culture is very difficult and takes time.

The complexity of this wellness challenge is not lost on former IACP President Joseph G Estey, chief of the Hartford, VT Police Department. In a recent interview, Estey said law enforcement had come a long way in integrating the importance of individual officer wellness into management's priorities. But he was quick to add, "Change in large organizations is slow, and more needs to be done—and will be done, as these new ideas become more accepted."

Estey maintained that most chiefs are aware of and concerned with the stress that individual officers endure because police work is more complex today than ever before. But whether the job-related stresses are an outgrowth of increased scrutiny by the media and the public or ramped-up internal pressures, certain basic assumptions will be helpful in determining better policies.

Assumption 1: Higher morale and reduced stress will improve the quality of law enforcement. Low morale hinders law enforcement effectiveness and is detrimental to the personal lives of police officers. Assumption 2: The healthiest person makes the best police officer. Healthy police officers should see themselves as humans who happen to be police officers, not police officers who happen to be humans.

Outfitting Police Officers with a "Stress Vest"

Unlike standard issue Kevlar body wear, the "stress vest" comes in two distinct layers: the personal and the institutional. The personal "stress vest" is what every individual police officer must learn to acquire. Just like a healthy diet contains a variety of foods, a healthy identity requires personal, social, and spiritual wellness, as well as occupational wellness.

Every officer must 1) learn to wake up each morning with "an attitude of gratitude." Gratitude for life, family, friends, and the freedoms and opportunities we have. Feeling grateful is an important part of taking control of one's life and maintaining a positive identity. It combats cynicism, the emotional cancer that destroys hope. Every officer must 2) take care of his personal needs: exercise regularly, eat a balanced diet, and maintain good body composition; enjoy private time for hobbies and special interests; and get sufficient rest and relaxation.

Further, each officer must 3) have meaningful relationships outside of law enforcement. Good communication with family and friends is critical to a healthy identity and a happy life. And all the officers must 4) recognize that there is something in this world that is bigger than we are as individuals. Connect with your purpose and meaning in life and be honored and grateful that you have the opportunity to fulfill that higher purpose.

The Institutional "Stress Vest"

Help for police officers must come from the top. Not long ago, at the end of a course I taught on stress management in law enforcement, one student—a retired police officer—contributed to the class discussion with this lament: "The NYPD had my body for 25 years and made me feel insignificant when they could have had my mind for nothing and made me feel important." Perhaps this man's superiors would have been more helpful had they understood a point articulated by William James, the great American psychologist, who said: "The deepest principle in human nature is the craving to be appreciated." Indeed, one can imagine appreciation as one of the raw materials used

to create the aforementioned "stress vest." How can law enforcement managers raise their consciousness and provide the help and appreciation needed by their officers?

Every police manager must 1) recognize and embrace the notion that individual police officers are suffering from stress-related problems exacerbated by the work environment. A chief must be a role model not only as a law enforcement officer but as a well-balanced human being who exemplifies personal, social, and spiritual wellness, and 2) be educated and trained in modern management theory that will equip him with more effective organizational, personnel and communication skills.

Further, 3) police academy training curricula should have a stress-management component, and should invite a spouse or significant other to participate in exercises that focus on communication skills and sensitivity to the demands of the job, 4) departments should develop opportunities for officers to exercise and recreate together by creating fitness centers and gymnasiums for law enforcement personnel, and 5) in-service sensitivity training should be required for all police officers.

Also 6) workplace activities such as picnics and holiday parties should include and celebrate officers' families and 7) police officers must be recognized as people who have needs outside law enforcement. They should be given more individual recognition on the job, their professional opinions should be solicited and considered, and more consideration should be exercised for personal and family obligations such as children's birthdays and graduations.

In summary, the keys to the two-layer "stress vest" are simple. Each police officer must take personal responsibility to develop and maintain a balanced identity that begins with an "attitude out of gratitude," and where occupational wellness is only one part. And management, realizing that police officers are humans first, must create policies designed to show appreciation for individual accomplishments and positive contributions.

DR. ROBERT A. FOX is a professor at the John Jay College of Criminal Justice in New York City. Teaching at John Jay College for the past 10 years, he developed a course in stress management in law enforcement. He can be reached at rfox@jjay.cuny.edu.

Dealing with Employee Stress
How Managers Can Help—or Hinder—Their Personnel

JAMES D. SEWELL, PhD

Stress is a critical issue within contemporary organizations and society. For law enforcement agencies, it can arise from a variety of sources. For example, stress may stem from circumstances or incidents that occurred as a result of the unique nature of an officer's job or personal life issues. Or, problems that develop similar to those in any workplace may cause it.

Unfortunately, some management practices also create stress in the life of the individual employee. While contemporary leadership and supervisory courses foster effective management techniques, some managers, often trained in traditional policies or management practices or, perhaps, more interested in their own advancement, forget that their actions can create a stressful work environment and impact the success and well-being of a work unit or organization. How are these less than effective managers creating such stress?

> **"Effective law enforcement now . . . requires managers who adopt a reasoned, flexible approach to the changing demands. . . . "**

What Are They Doing?
Ineffectively Dealing with Assignments

Especially in law enforcement, many assignments and responsibilities must carry a sense of urgency because they are important and necessary and have a strict deadline. Yet, not every action is or needs to be portrayed as a crisis, particularly on the administrative side of an agency. Stress results when managers treat all assignments as the crisis du jour and pressure employees to labor under unnecessary deadlines and stressful conditions for normal tasks. Others fail to understand the magnitude of the tasks they assign or do not appreciate the time, detail, and effort necessary to bring a project to fruition. Unrealistic expectations and deadlines often make staff feel unnecessarily burdened and frustrated by their assignments.

Furthermore, managers who attempt to exert and maintain control over employees and their work by assigning it in a piecemeal fashion cause stressful environments. In these instances, employees continually must return to their supervisors for additional information before they can successfully complete any assignment.

A clear distinction exists between knowing what is going on within an organization and among employees and trying to perform or dictate staff members' jobs. Supervisors who micromanage place too much emphasis on structuring and controlling subordinates' work-days and dictating the only acceptable response to assigned tasks. They tend to focus too little on developing employees' knowledge, skills, and abilities that will help them work independently and achieve their own success.

Communication is, of course, a critical element in effective agency management. Some managers may find interpersonal communication difficult, and they may avoid interaction with employees, choosing to communicate only via written memoranda or e-mail. Others might limit face-to-face contact with their subordinates, preferring to stay in their own offices. In all of these cases, effective communication is less likely to occur, and employees frequently fume with frustration.

Difficulties in Evaluating Performance

Law enforcement personnel recognize that discipline and performance evaluations are necessary parts of the job. They expect, however, that managers will administer both fairly and consistently. Organizational stress arises when managers show favoritism to certain subordinates, invoke discipline for no apparent reason, or evaluate staff against ill-defined or arbitrary standards.

In most agencies, while the majority of employees appropriately respond to community or organizational expectations for their performance, some fail to meet these standards or display the professional values exhibited by their peers. In such cases, employees expect managers to deal with problem personnel. When managers ignore non-performance or provide excuses for these subordinates without addressing the actual problem, they undermine morale and add to the stress and frustration of those who simply seek to do right and expect bosses to do the same.

Supervisors who appreciate employees' accomplishments and comprehend the volume and intensity of their workloads remain key to positive emotional health of personnel. Yet, in spite of this accepted fact of management, some still fail to acknowledge the impact of multiple assignments and the demands required of professional performance. These managers who have yet to learn to say thank you cause stress for their employees and fail to reach their own expected leadership potential.

Inappropriate Responses

Effective law enforcement now, perhaps more than ever, requires managers who adopt a reasoned, flexible approach to the changing demands placed upon them and their resources. Community concerns, internal politics, and external political realities frequently have generated inflexible, knee-jerk managerial responses to the immediate issue. Such ill-timed and poorly planned reactions lack adequate consideration about anticipated or unintended consequences and place the most significant stress upon the individuals who carry out the decisions and most directly live with the results.

Perhaps, employees feel most frustrated when managers refuse to give or share credit for a team's success or decline to accept responsibility for failure. People desire appreciation and acknowledgment of their contributions to a group's accomplishments. At the same time, they respect managers who acknowledge their own failures and recognize that many frustrations within an organizational unit should not rest solely on an individual employee.

". . . some management practices also create stress in the life of the individual employee."

What Steps Can Managers Take to Reduce Employee Stress?

How can managers reduce the stress they cause employees and improve their own effectiveness? In addition to understanding the impact of their actions on subordinates

and continuing to learn and apply productive leadership and management skills, managers can take several other specific steps.

Communicating with Others

In many organizations, a collapse of communication causes the breakdown in relations between labor and management. Within smaller units, when managers fail to communicate with their employees or do not encourage reciprocal communication, negative results ensue. Effective leadership within an agency and management of human resources require effective and ongoing communication at all levels. To ensure such communication, everyone within the organization must view managers as fair, open, and honest. Trust between managers and subordinates is required for the most successful operations. From the beginning, employees should understand managers' expectations, particularly in regard to how they want personnel to approach their jobs and how they plan to conduct discipline and performance evaluations.

The aura of crisis some managers attach to work efforts and communicate to their employees too frequently results from their failure to adequately plan. Devoting time to planning for their organization's operations and even for their own day will reduce the stress that they cause for their subordinates.

Times of great stress are, of course, dramatic ones for law enforcement employees. One of the important roles managers play during such periods is a safety valve, an emotional outlet through which employees appropriately can vent their anger, fear, frustration, and concerns. At the same time, managers must successfully buffer subordinates from the stress produced by those higher in the chain of command, including elected and appointed officials outside the agency.

Personnel appreciate managers who communicate a direct interest in their performance and are involved in the activities of the organization. In law enforcement agencies, employees respect leaders who remember their roots, spend time on the street in spite of administrative demands, and support subordinates as they do their jobs. By its nature, contemporary law enforcement is a stressful profession, and that stress permeates the department. However, effective leadership practices can increase communication and reduce the tension attributed to the organization and its hierarchy. "Law enforcement leaders wanting to reduce the psychological stress caused by poor supervision and apathetic attitudes toward employees must be committed to making the workplace a 'worthplace'—where people care about people and where employee needs are emphasized and by developing a healthy environment that is perceived by the employees as a good place to work."[1]

"Personnel appreciate managers who communicate a direct interest in their performance. . . . "

In addition, knowing and focusing on employees—their strengths, weaknesses, career aspirations, and families—can lead to effective workplace communication. Armed with that knowledge, managers can appropriately assign tasks and responsibilities and ensure that employees perceive their work as meaningful and valuable.

Sending Positive Messages

The law enforcement profession is, by its nature, a challenging experience. Officers and support personnel deal with people in their worst times of crisis, pain, and raw emotions. Managers must realize the importance of their support of subordinates, especially when the crisis impacts those personnel. Such a role, akin to that of a cheerleader, becomes particularly necessary when the negative issues occur within the organization itself, rather than as a byproduct of the work, and managers have to maintain the morale of the agency. Managers must maintain an outwardly positive attitude, especially in the presence of their subordinates—for the health and mission of the organization, they cannot afford to be viewed as negative or against the administration.

Further, employees can frequently become pawns between battling managers. In the context of effectively dealing with employee stress, managers should have two primary considerations. First, within proper legal and ethical boundaries, they have an obligation to maintain loyalty to the organization and the people for whom they work. Second, they have a responsibility to keep their own counsel. Employees do not need to hear their own bosses' emotional outbursts toward the organization, its hierarchy, or their own peers.

It is, of course, important to acknowledge the seriousness of contemporary law enforcement and its critical social mission. At the same time, managers should recognize that such an intense environment still needs humor and personality. This profession requires that its personnel, for their own mental health, should search for the positive side, accepting that the seriousness of job tasks can be alleviated. Managers who take their jobs and themselves too seriously risk damaging the emotional well-being of their personnel, as well as themselves.

Part of the maturation process for organizational leaders requires them to realize they must accept responsibility for their subordinates' actions, which are not always under the manager's direct control, as well as for their own. Absent criminal or ethical violations, it may be more appropriate

---

Reducing Employee Stress
12 Tips for Managers

1. Ensure effective two-way communication with employees.
2. Be fair and honest in communications with personnel and confirm that they understand your expectations.
3. Act as a safety valve to allow employees to vent and protect them from stress from others higher in the chain of command.
4. Be involved in employee assignments and available for guidance.
5. Project a positive attitude.
6. Lighten up.
7. Accept the responsibility of both leadership and management.
8. Learn to balance home, office, and personal stress.
9. Foster a healthy working environment.
10. Learn to build and encourage employees' self-esteem.
11. Plan effectively.
12. Display organizational loyalty and maintain your own counsel.

---

for managers to accept some of the responsibility when subordinates fail to reach the desired accomplishment and then use the situation as a learning experience for all.

Focusing on the Employee

Effective job performance requires a balance of professional demands, family responsibilities, and personal issues. Failure to acknowledge and accept the relationship between each frequently can result in conflict, frustration, and anger that spill over all parts of a person's life. Performing effectively on the job entails simply learning to balance employment demands with life's other elements. For managers, this also means that they not only learn to apply such balance in their own lives but also accept it as a necessity for the healthy work and personal lives of their employees.

Managers also should work to develop those who serve in their organizations, helping them do their jobs more effectively and with fewer distractions through programs in stress and time management and personal finance, for instance. Such development results in an investment in the future of the agency through its people.

Conclusion

By the very nature of their chosen profession, with its high demands and heavy personal toll, law enforcement officers will continue to experience stress throughout their careers. The various methods managers use to administer assignments, evaluate performance, and handle responsibility can directly impact the amount of employee stress.

However, managers can effectively mitigate some of these stressors frequently caused by organizational issues, poor leadership, and ineffective management. Managers who communicate with their personnel by acting as a safety valve, taking a direct interest in their performance, and focusing on their strengths and weaknesses can help eliminate tension. It is critical, then, that leaders and managers in law enforcement agencies recognize how they contribute to the stress of their employees and take aggressive steps to reduce their stress-causing practices.

Note

1. Richard M. Ayres, *Preventing Law Enforcement Stress: The Organization's Role* (Alexandria, VA: National Sheriffs' Association, 1990), 33–35.

From *FBI Law Enforcement Bulletin,* July 2006, pp. 1–6, by James D. Sewell. Published by the FBI Academy/Department of Justice, Federal Bureau of Investigation.

Settling Disputes Across a Table When Officer and Citizen Clash

AL BAKER

In 1993, at a time when New York City was racked with police scandals, a new city law created the Civilian Complaint Review Board so that accusations against police officers could be handled by an independent agency. Cases would be investigated and then sent to the full board, which would recommend punishment when wrongdoing was found.

Buried deep in the law was an unusual option for the accused and the accusers. It called for mediation, a clearing of the air in which both parties would meet face-to-face in a room with a mediator but without lawyers, to explain themselves and, sometimes, vent their anger. If mediation worked, the case would be closed, the allegation erased.

At first, this option was rarely used—just 14 cases were mediated in 1998, for example—but it has become considerably more common in recent years, especially since Police Commissioner Raymond W. Kelly clarified some departmental controls on the process in 2004, making it far more palatable to officers.

Mediated cases jumped to a high of 113 in 2004, and this year they are on track to go even higher. Through the end of August, 92 of the 5,144 complaints received had been mediated. The percentage is small, but mediated cases take about half as long to send to the board (115 days, on average) as investigated cases (223 days), officials said.

Mediation sessions are closed and the discussions are confidential, but board and police officials recently allowed *The New York Times* to talk with the participants after a mediation session. What emerged was a glimpse of an unfiltered approach to resolving seemingly intractable disagreements that is not nearly as touchy-feely as it sounds. Sometimes, assumptions and anger can drop away quickly when accuser meets the accused.

Since it is the accused and not the accuser who is wearing a blue police uniform, the approach can seem almost upside down. Some experts call mediation a bad deal for officers, and although many officers are certainly skeptical or dismissive of the process, some who participated said they were surprised by how much they got from it. The officers said they relished the opportunity to explain why they do their jobs the way they do. At the same time, their accusers said that although mediation failed to wipe away their anger completely, it certainly gave them new insights.

"I told them even if it was the White House, we would have done the same thing, so they understand we are doing our job and they wanted to be heard," Officer Jack Ng, accused of waving his weapon while subduing a suspect, said of the two men who filed a complaint against him and his partner. "So we understood them and they understood us."

Mediation is not available for the most serious allegations of abuse. In fact, Christopher Dunn, of the New York Civil Liberties Union, said that "because mediation stops the investigation and guarantees there will be no discipline, it should be used in only the narrowest of circumstances involving the most minor of offenses."

In cases that do come to mediation, the two sides sit across a table in a private space to talk about what led to the complaint. It is a no-holds-barred encounter that can turn emotional; participants scream, curse or cry. Mediators are neutral, not judges, and both sides are protected: An apology from an officer cannot be used in a lawsuit, and an admission by a civilian is not grounds for arrest.

The program is voluntary for both sides. Complaints against officers are not automatically withdrawn if an officer goes to mediation. If either side is unhappy with mediation, then the case could go back to a traditional investigation or end as "mediation attempted." That happens very rarely, officials said. Instead, the case is usually listed as mediated and both sides sign a "resolution agreement."

Officer Ng's experience was cited by both sides as an example of a successful mediation.

He and his partner, Leon Guzman, got a radio call on Oct. 3, 2005: a man with a gun on Grand and Allen Streets. They happened to be on that corner, and they saw two men fitting the description. They left their patrol car, and drew their guns; the men separated, the officers chased them, stopped them, frisked them and eventually let them go.

Mark Gerse and Sam Orlando watched the episode, and their account differed from the officers'. Mr. Gerse and Mr. Orlando were at work in the Lower East Side Harm Reduction Center, a needle exchange office at 25 Allen Street, and to them the officers appeared overzealous.

"These guys came in like it was the Wild West," said Mr. Gerse, the center's deputy executive director. "They came in with guns drawn, ready to shoot it up. Anything could have happened; guns could have gone off. That was our basic complaint."

Mr. Gerse and Mr. Orlando, the center's health care coordinator, filed their complaint 44 minutes after the episode. Later, the two sides agreed to mediate. They did so on May 16. It took roughly an hour.

It was the first civilian complaint for Officers Ng and Guzman, who work in Transit District 4. Officer Ng, 30, feared that the men would demand an apology. Officer Guzman, 37, said he thought the mediation would end in disagreement. "I thought there might be a little hollering," he said.

Mr. Gerse and Mr. Orlando were also nervous.

"I thought it was going to turn into a shouting match," said Mr. Orlando, 46. Mr. Gerse, 50, said, "I was uncomfortable." He added: "It's very uncomfortable to be with cops."

But the perceptions of all four were different afterward.

"I really got to look at police officers in a total new light of respect and where they are coming from," Mr. Orlando said. "Obviously, these are two highly trained police officers who knew what they were doing and are capable of handling their weapons."

Officer Guzman said, "We got to say our side of the story, and they seemed to understand. We did everything positively."

Interestingly, neither side was swayed in its account of what happened. Mr. Gerse and Mr. Orlando say both officers entered their needle exchange office, but the officers said it was only Officer Ng who went inside. Mr. Gerse and Mr. Orlando say the officers had their guns drawn, which could have threatened clients who believe they are in a safe place and might be discouraged from coming back.

The officers say that Officer Ng entered to chase a suspect, and that Officer Guzman stayed outside on the street with the second suspect.

"My perspective was that they went too quick, they jumped too quickly," Mr. Gerse said. "The bottom line is they just said they would do better and we said we would do better, and we both agreed that our resolve to work together in the future is a good thing."

When asked, Officer Guzman said he had not discussed his mediation experience with his colleagues. Interviews with other officers indicated a deeper skepticism. Just because they go along with mediation, several said, it doesn't mean they believe in it.

"They'll give it a try," a veteran officer said of his colleagues. "The path of least resistance is what a lot of guys will take. They don't want to get in trouble; they don't want to have a bad record. They're probably intimidated by the system and feel they won't get a fair shake. So this is a way out."

As one police supervisor put it, "The feeling is, it's the least of all evils."

"In the ideal situation, both parties can understand their actions and reactions," said Charles M. Greinsky, a former member of the Civilian Complaint Review Board who helped start the program.

"They can march back into their respective worlds with a better understanding of the other's perspective."

That is not so when cases are investigated, when the two sides cannot exchange information, "so a misunderstanding may remain," said Florence L. Finkle, the board's executive director.

The confidentiality agreement that both sides sign shields mediators and participants from being called to testify in any legal proceedings that may come of the dispute. No tape recording is made; any notes are destroyed; lawyers must wait outside the mediation room at the board's headquarters at 40 Rector Street.

Mr. Dunn, of the civil liberties group, said the case involving Officers Ng and Guzman should never have made it to mediation. "For the safety of the public and the integrity of the C.C.R.B., these kinds of cases must be fully investigated," he said.

And Maria Haberfeld, the chairwoman of the department of law and police science at John Jay College of Criminal Justice, said she believed mediation could only hurt police officers, especially if their actions were within departmental guidelines.

Much of what occurs in police work is outside the view of most civilians, she said, so the public sees a slice of a situation and often makes inaccurate judgments. The sides are inherently unbalanced: one has power to use force in society, the other does not.

By entering mediation, officers are surrendering some authority; the process itself can be the punishment, Dr. Haberfeld said. "The connotation is, you have already indicted the officer," she said. "You are already coming from the perspective of the officer doing something wrong."

The board has 30 to 40 mediators available. Half are lawyers and the rest come from fields like human resources and social work. Mediators are required to complete a 40-hour state training course in mediation theory, as well as follow-up practical training by the state. Before joining the board program, they must have two or three years' experience mediating, and undergo two one-day training courses, one at the board and the other at the Police Department, said Andrew Case, a spokesman for the board. He said refresher training courses are also given.

Ms. Finkle said it is decided that a complaint case may best be resolved with mediation rather than investigation, roughly 75 percent of city officers accept it, though more than half of the civilians reject it.

Governments in other states, and other nations, are calling to ask questions about how to adapt the program. Officials from Oregon and Michigan, for instance, as well as from London, Bolivia, Uzbekistan and Russia have expressed interest.

Commissioner Kelly said he hoped the trend toward more mediation continued.

"I like the concept of mediation," he said. "I think it's win-win for both the public and for police officers who receive complaints. It gives everyone an opportunity to express their position."

UNIT 4

The Judicial System

Unit Selections

Key Points to Consider

- Are experts truly unbiased, or do they shade their testimony to favor the side that is paying them?

- Does a poor person get treated fairly by the criminal justice system?

- Do you think prosecutors should receive some sort of discipline when they cause an innocent person to be convicted of a crime?

Student Web Site

www.mhcls.com/online

Internet References

Further information regarding these Web sites may be found in this book's preface or online.

Center for Rational Correctional Policy
http://www.correctionalpolicy.com

Justice Information Center (JIC)
http://www.ncjrs.org

National Center for Policy Analysis (NCPA)
http://www.public-policy.org/~ncpa/pd/law/index3.html

U.S. Department of Justice (DOJ)
http://www.usdoj.gov

The courts are an equal partner in the American justice system. Just as the police have the responsibility of guarding our liberties by enforcing the law, the courts play an important role in defending these liberties by applying and interpreting the law. The courts are the battlegrounds where civilized 'wars' are fought without bloodshed to protect individual rights and to settle disputes.

The articles in this unit discuss several issues concerning the judicial process. Ours is an adversary system of justice, and the protagonists—the state and the defendant—are usually represented by counsel.

In the opening article in this section, "Jury Consulting on Trial," D. W. Miller discusses the notion of "scientific jury selection." Following is "Jury Duty: When History and Life Coincide" in which a jury's gender and racial politics are discussed by a former juror.

In "Looking Askance at Eyewitness Testimony," the problem of unreliable eyewitness evidence is examined by D. W. Miller. Some suggestions for reducing the number of "hung" juries are presented by the National Institute of Justice article, "Why Do Hung Juries Hang?"

Next, Robert Worth looks at new laws in towns and counties across the country that banish anyone convicted of a sex crime against a minor. Following that is an article, "Judges Turn Therapist in Problem Solving Court," which asks whether defendants need jail, or just new meds. "When the Poor Go to Court" shows how being poor can affect the treatment one receives in court. This unit concludes with "Justice & Antonin Scalia," where the author sketches a picture of provocative Supreme Court Justice Antonin Scalia.

Jury Consulting on Trial

Scholars doubt claims that jurors' votes can be predicted.

D.W. MILLER

"Beware of the Lutherans, especially the Scandinavians; they are almost always sure to convict," Clarence Darrow advised fellow defense lawyers in a 1936 *Esquire* article called "How to Pick a Jury." By contrast, the "religious emotions" of Methodists "can be transmuted into love and charity." Irishmen, he added, are "emotional, kindly, and sympathetic." But the Presbyterian juror "believes in John Calvin and eternal punishment. Get rid of him with the fewest possible words before he contaminates the others."

Judges instruct jurors to render verdicts based on evidence and law, not prejudice and sympathy. But few lawyers believe that fallible humans simply leave their backgrounds, opinions, and attitudes outside the courtroom. So they still aspire to predict how jurors' biases will affect their deliberations.

Of course, in assembling a jury or shaping an argument, lawyers no longer credit the quaint stereotypes expressed—perhaps tongue in cheek—by Darrow. Many lawyers are content to rely on experience and intuition to identify people unfriendly to their side and strike them from a jury. Those who can afford it, however, are turning to trial consultants to conduct mock trials, design community surveys, and probe the attitudes and experiences of potential jurors.

Many of the nearly 400 members of the American Society of Trial Consultants are trained social scientists. But scholars question how much trial consultants have really improved upon Darrow.

"The plausibility of being able to predict is very low," says Shari Seidman Diamond, a professor of law at Northwestern University and a leading researcher of jury behavior. "Who makes the decision is less important than how the evidence is presented," says Saul Kassin, a professor of psychology at Williams College.

"The best conclusion is that there are cases where jury-selection consultants can make a difference but that such cases are few and far between," write Neil J. Kressel and Dorit F. Kressel in *Stack and Sway: The New Science of Jury Consulting* (just out from Westview Press). "Like the fanciful stereotypes about jurors that lawyers trusted in the past, scientific jury selection can help attorneys manage their stress far more often than it helps them capture a verdict."

No Crystal Ball

The notion of "scientific jury selection" took hold in the early 1970s, when the late Jay Schulman, a sociologist at Columbia University, and a team of colleagues helped defend antiwar activists accused of plotting to kidnap Henry Kissinger. After conducting surveys and interviewing a cross section of the community, the defense used its peremptory challenges to eliminate members of the jury pool considered likely to vote for conviction. The jury ultimately hung, on a 10–2 vote for acquittal.

Since then, however, scholars have found little evidence that social science makes a big difference in jury selection. "For most cases, most of the time, people decide on the basis of evidence," says Mr. Kressel, a psychologist at William Paterson University. "We know from mock-jury research that personality variables don't matter that much."

In a study of 461 mock jurors in Ohio, Michael Saks, a professor of law and psychology at Arizona State University, measured 27 attitudes and background characteristics and then asked the jurors to render a verdict in a fictitious burglary case. The best predictor of their decisions was their answer to the question "Do you believe crime is mainly the product of 'bad people' or 'bad social conditions'?" But that explained only 9 percent of the variation among verdicts. Together, those personal attributes accounted for very little.

It's an Art

Steven D. Penrod, a psychologist at the University of Nebraska at Lincoln, got similar results in a study of Massachusetts jurors. He tested the salience of 21 personal characteristics in four kinds of cases. He found that the single best predictor of an inclination to vote guilty in a rape case was whether jurors agreed that evidence of physical resistance was necessary to convict. But that predictor alone explained only 7 percent of the variation in outcomes, and the best predictors in each case were not helpful in any others.

Mr. Kressel and his wife, a lawyer, concluded that scientific jury selection matters mainly when a case is very public, the facts are inflammatory, and the evidence favors neither side.

That scholars' insight into juries is hazy should not be surprising. Courts hardly ever allow researchers to watch deliberations firsthand, so they have to rely on cruder methods to divine how personality affects jury deliberations: post-trial interviews, case studies, and mock juries among them. Furthermore, scholars have found that observations rarely apply in all situations.

"Who makes the decisions is less important than how the evidence is presented."

"It's not really a science—it's more of an art," says Neil Vidmar, a professor of psychology and law at Duke University who has himself been a consultant on pre-trial publicity. "Almost every case is unique. It's got different facts, it's got a different context." Even so, the data that the nation's trial consultants collect in hundreds of cases each year might still be valuable to scholars—except that the information is all proprietary and closely held.

In their book, the Kressels argue that the value of scientific jury selection rests on a chain of unproven assumptions: that potential jurors give honest answers to personal questions, that jurors' pretrial verdict preferences will determine their final votes, and that jurors stricken from a jury pool will be replaced by ones that lawyers find more favorable. But that hasn't deterred scholars like Linda Foley.

A trial consultant and professor of psychology at the University of North Florida, Ms. Foley also conducts academic research on decision making by jurors that may prove useful in court. She has studied, for instance, why some jurors are less sympathetic than others to rape victims who sue their assailants. She found that college-age men are much less likely to sympathize with victims the same age than with those who are older. She speculates that young men can imagine themselves being falsely accused of rape by a peer, and so defensively attribute a plaintiff's fate to her own behavior.

In theory, lawyers armed with such insights could refine their efforts to choose favorable jurors and craft effective arguments. Since the 1970s, for example, researchers have believed that people who score high on a scale of "authoritarian" attitudes seem to be more likely to convict. Even that trait, however, has counterintuitive implications. Authoritarian types, says Ms. Foley, tend to make snap judgments, but they also tend to conform to the majority. In general, researchers have failed to connect attitudes with verdicts in predictable ways.

Ms. Foley's experiments this semester exemplify both the promise and perils of efforts to put jurors' motivations under a microscope. Several times a week, she assembles a new group of North Florida students in Jacksonville to play jury in a fictitious medical-malpractice lawsuit.

On a recent Wednesday morning, seven women and three men filed into a conference room near Ms. Foley's office, in the psychology department. First they filled out a lengthy questionnaire exploring their personality traits. Then they watched a videotape of dueling experts.

"Martin Madison," a 53-year-old accountant, had died of a brain aneurysm after complaining of headaches and dizziness. Were the hospital and its emergency-room doctor negligent? In that day's version of the experiment, the expert hired by Mr. Madison's widow boasted of his years of clinical experience, while the defense expert brandished his tenured professorship at the Johns Hopkins University and a long list of publications on aneurysms.

As usual, a handful of jurors dominated the discussion that followed. The forewoman, a ponytailed student in a sweatshirt and baseball cap who said she had worked in a hospital, criticized "Dr. Hector" for failing

Flies on the Wall of the Jury Room

Harry Kalven Jr and Hans Zeisel, who pioneered academic research on juries in the 1950s, were among the first American scholars to observe real jurors deliberating. For decades, it seemed they would also be the last.

When they revealed that they had taped the deliberations of five civil juries in a federal court in Wichita, Kan., without the jurors' consent, they were unprepared for the uproar that followed. The U.S. attorney general censured the project, Congress held hearings, and dozens of jurisdictions moved to ban "jury-tapping." With few exceptions, outsiders have been unwelcome in the jury room ever since—until now.

Not So Passive

Shari Seidman Diamond, a law professor at Northwestern University, and Neil Vidmar, a professor of law and psychology at Duke University, noticed in the mid-1990s that courts in Arizona had begun experimenting with giving jurors more latitude to participate in court, such as taking notes, asking questions of witnesses, and discussing testimony before the lawyers had rested their cases. To investigate the effects of such reforms, they won permission from courts, juries, and litigants to videotape 50 civil cases.

In many ways, the American legal system treats jurors like empty repositories for information, holding their opinions and experiences in check.

The first findings from their Arizona Jury Project, in a paper to be published soon in the *Virginia Law Review,* seem to confirm that jurors often confound the courts' expectations of their passive role. In many ways, the American legal system treats jurors like empty repositories for information, holding their opinions and experiences in check until a judge dispatches them to the jury room. That is the premise

for the legal practice of "blindfolding"—excluding certain facts, such as defendants' past criminal acts, that might unfairly influence jury verdicts.

In their paper, Ms. Diamond and Mr. Vidmar investigate two such matters thought to influence jurors' decisions in lawsuits: whether defendants and plaintiffs are covered by insurance, and how much the parties will owe in lawyers' fees. They found some evidence that those factors might affect juries' verdicts on defendants' liability, and even more evidence that they count when juries consider damages: At that stage, the researchers found, juries frequently overlook or misunderstand judges' instructions not to speculate about those issues, and take into account testimony about insurance revealed inadvertently or through an exception to courtroom rules.

Of the 40 cases in which insurance was relevant, the scholars found that jurors raised the issue in 34. Comments like the following were typical:

"His insurance paid all his bills, so he's not really out anything."

"This is what we have insurance for . . . . [O]ne of the plaintiff's doctor's said she sent the claims to plaintiff's insurers so the plaintiff is probably not paying for most of this."

"Insurance usually covers chiropractic care. Why should we give her above and beyond what she is probably going to get on her insurance?"

In 16 of those cases, or 40 percent, the authors write, "the discussion was substantial enough that an effect [on the verdict] could not be ruled out." In three cases, "a juror's verdict preference can be directly linked" to the juror's expressed beliefs about a litigant's insurance coverage.

In 24 of 33 applicable cases, juries discussed lawyers' fees in their deliberations. In four cases, the fees actually affected their decisions on damages: Three juries raised their damages award to cover their estimate of the plaintiff's legal bill, and the fourth reduced its award because jurors thought the plaintiff's lawyers did not deserve the full one-third contingency that they were likely to charge.

Ms. Diamond and Mr. Vidmar believe that the problem is exacerbated by judges who respond to juries' queries about taboo subjects with terse

Flies on the Wall of the Jury Room (*continued*)

answers. "The traditional approach of merely for-bidding evidence on certain topics is of limited value when jurors draw on life experiences and peek through blindfolds," they conclude. So the authors recommend that courts confront the problem squarely. A more comprehensive instruction to juries, they write, would acknowledge their tempta-tion to consider forbidden topics, explain why the courts have deemed them irrelevant, and remind them that any such speculation would have [to] rely on guesswork. In mock-trial studies, they say, that approach has worked.

—D.W.M.

to order timely tests once he had diagnosed the aneu-rysm. "People die, that's all I gotta say," said Juror 105, a young man with a brush cut, but he went along with the majority, which laid most of the blame for the patient's death on the doctor.

Courts hardly ever allow researchers to watch deliberations firsthand, so scholars have to rely on cruder methods to divine how personality affects jury deliberations.

Only Juror 98, a woman in khaki pants and a jean jacket, remained dubious. "How do we know it would have made a difference?" she said. "The aneurysm was so big, he might have died on the MRI table."

Later, Juror 98 stood alone in her reluctance to com-pensate the Madison family beyond lost income. Despite her misgivings, the group awarded hefty damages and apportioned fault between the doctor and the hospital in a ratio of 70:30. Before leaving, the jurors filled out another survey, to assess how influential they had found each of their peers.

After observing 32 of those mock juries, Ms. Foley will investigate whether jurors in such cases are more easily persuaded by expert witnesses with impressive credentials or by those with more clinical experience. But she also hopes to learn more about the effects of personality on juries' decisions: Do jurors' views of guilt and liability in particular cases correspond predictably to measurable attitudes and personality traits, such as a belief in a just world, a predilection for manipulating others, or a ten-dency to see issues in absolute terms? And does a juror's influence during deliberations correspond predictably to measurable leadership traits and an ease with public speaking?

Muddy Waters

That kind of experiment has limits. For one thing, the psy-chology students she relies on are hardly representative of eligible jurors in Jacksonville, much less the nation. Furthermore, with such a small pool to draw from, some of the subjects are bound to be acquainted, a fact that may muddy her analysis of how members of the group influence one another. Jurors 100 and 101 had walked in holding hands, while Jurors 103 and 104 appeared to be identical twin sisters.

As a check on those flaws, Ms. Foley is collaborat-ing with a trial consultant in Pompano Beach who will eventually conduct similar experiments with a cross section of "real people." But that research is at least a year away.

Even if research offered lawyers a wealth of predictive information, they would often have trouble using it. For instance, they don't have utter discretion over the number and kind of questions asked during jury selection. Research-ers have established, for instance, that people who support capital punishment are generally more likely to vote to con-vict. But lawyers aren't allowed to probe jurors' attitudes toward the death penalty unless they are trying a capital case. "Depending on the judge, the lawyers don't have a lot of leeway about what kinds of questions they can ask," says Ms. Foley. "So they try to get at the essence in one or two questions."

Those caveats hardly mean that trial consultants have no influence. Even the Kressels agree that consultants appear to be effective at post-selection tasks, such as helping lawyers hone their arguments and understand how ordinary people will see the issues. "In most instances, it's the techniques and practices of social science that are helpful, rather than any particular body of knowledge," says Duke's Mr. Vidmar.

"This is an opportunity to test the clarity and plausibility of an argument in a more systematic way," says Northwestern's Ms. Diamond. "That's a valuable thing, because there's nothing sadder than seeing an unnecessarilyunintelligible presentation of evidence. That makes it harder to make a decision based on the evidence."

Jury Duty: When History and Life Coincide

ELISABETH I. PERRY

Not long ago, I served on a jury for the first time. Most people groan when a jury summons arrives, but I was thrilled. I hadn't received one since 1964, and I had avoided serving then on grounds that I only later realized were discriminatory.

When the first summons came, I was a history graduate student in Southern California, busy teaching sections of "Western Civilization" and preparing for a trip to France for my dissertation research. I panicked. I didn't have time for jury duty! I read the summons through, hoping for a way to escape its imperative. At last I got down to the list of exempted categories. Surely "student" or "teacher" would be on it. No, but "woman" was.

I had no idea why. My graduate-student friends were equally ignorant. One suggested that it was because women menstruate. "You know how they get emotionally unstable every month," he said. I had never suffered from such instability, but getting out of jury duty on any grounds looked good to me. With barely a moment's hesitation, I checked the "woman" box.

Years later, I regretted that act of youthful insouciance. In the mid-1970s, I began to do research in a field new to me, American women's history. I wanted to write a biography of my paternal grandmother, Belle Moskowitz, the social reformer and suffragist who served as New York Gov. Alfred E. Smith's political strategist in the 1920s. After the book came out in 1987, I started a new, still continuing, project that, to myself, I call "From Belle to Bella," on the New York Women active in politics from Moskowitz to Bella Abzug, the colorful New York congresswoman of the 1970s.

Early on in the project, I learned why I had been able to get out of jury duty. When women's suffrage was ratified in 1920, more than half the states had not yet legalized woman jurors. Over the next two decades, a number changed their laws to allow women to serve—but only on an elective basis.

In New York, opposition to women on juries rested on two widely held stereotypes. The first was that women were not "fit" to serve: They were incapable of rational judgment and too "delicate" to tolerate the gory details of criminal behavior. The second was that their domestic roles—watching over children and preparing meals—made it hard for them to be away from home. It is interesting that the strongest opposition came from rural women, who argued that jury service would place an extraordinary burden on their already difficult lives.

We think too little about the role that gender and race play in the jury room.

By 1937, several national and local developments—including the U.S. Department of Justice's approving women as jurors for all federal courts, and a case in which an all-male jury convicted a woman of infanticide—finally persuaded New York legislators to allow women on juries. With a bow to the state's rural women, they made service nonmandatory.

Convinced that women would always be treated as second-class citizens unless they had an equal obligation to civic duties like jury service, a small cadre of New York women persisted in a campaign for mandatory service. Although they made little progress, and gave up their campaign in the 1950s, their cause was making its way through the federal judicial system. In 1975, the U.S. Supreme Court ruled in *Taylor v. Louisiana* that all juries must represent a "fair cross section" of the community. The issue of voluntary versus mandatory service was henceforth moot.

As I reported for jury service, I was thus pleased to have the opportunity. Friends warned me that I might have a long and boring wait before being called. "Take a lunch and a book," they advised. They also predicted that I probably wouldn't make it onto a jury. "Attorneys never pick women academics," they said. Not true. By that afternoon, I was empaneled on a jury for a murder trial and told to count on being there all week.

In his memoir of jury duty last year, *A Trial by Jury*, the historian D. Graham Burnett notes that we expect much, but think too little, about what happens in the jury room. That, I found, is also true about the role gender plays on a jury.

The case before us was complicated. Late one night, two armed men in their 20s, members of the same gang, confronted a third man at the front door of his home. By their own admission, they intended to "get back at him" for an insult. When the man saw their guns, he fled upstairs, out a back porch, and jumped to the alley below. The two would-be assailants followed. A few moments later, the man who fled lay dead in a cellar stairwell. He had seven bullets in his body.

His pursuers had been seen. Knowing that, they threw their shirts into a dumpster and ran. The police found the shirts and picked up one man quickly. He denied having been the shooter, plea-bargained on the lesser charge of burglary (armed breaking and entering), and had begun serving five years. The police did not find his partner for six months. A bruiser of a man, that was our defendant. He had been called in only as "backup," he said, and denied shooting the fatal bullets. Neither man's weapon was ever found.

The testimony was confusingly presented and strikingly incomplete. The prosecutor seemed ill prepared. The public defender was brand-new at her job. The jailed assailant testified, but was so terrified by the presence of the defendant's buddies in the courtroom that he was barely audible. We did, however, grasp his central point: His partner had fired the fatal shots. There was much "expert" testimony about DNA tests on the discarded shirts and the locations of spent shells and bullets; there were photographs of the crime scene and the deceased's body, which we passed among us. We noted that his genitals had been pierced by a bullet. No one flinched, but it was a gruesome sight.

The defendant testified, with his lawyer concentrating more on establishing his good character—despite prior convictions on drug and weapons charges, he was about to be married and to become a father—rather than his innocence, which she could not prove.

The testimony took a day and a half to be heard. None of it illuminated the key question in the case. Someone had fired seven bullets into an unarmed man fleeing for his life. Which assailant had been the shooter?

Had the one person I failed to convince dug in his heels because he wasn't willing to accept a woman's suggestion?

We, the jury, retired to deliberate. It turned out that we all agreed that the evidence had been poorly presented, but we were nowhere near unanimity. Two jurors favored a finding of first-degree murder. Eight favored second-degree, and two were undecided. We read and reread the judge's instructions about being sure "beyond a reasonable doubt." Endlessly, we rehearsed the definitions of "murder in the first" (planned), "murder in the second" (unplanned), "manslaughter" (recklessly endangering another's life), and "burglary," with which our defendant was also charged. But no matter how many hours we talked and recast our votes, we could reach unanimity only on "burglary." At 5 P.M. on a Friday evening, the judge declared

a mistrial on the murder charge. We never found out if the state would try the case again.

Months have passed since my jury service, and I still think about what happened, both in the courtroom and the jury room, to bring about such an unsatisfactory ending. In part, the answer has to do with the way the rules that regulate juries hindered our ability to make well-informed judgments. In our court (although not, I have since learned, in all courts), we were not allowed to take notes. When an elderly juror snoozed, well, that was just too bad. Nor could we question witnesses or lawyers; in our system, the lawyers are in control of presenting the evidence.

Further, our judge refused to let us see the transcript. After the trial was over, she came to the jury room to answer questions. Her tone was consoling. Mistrials are common in murder trials, she said, because the burden of proof is so high. "Why couldn't we consult the transcript?" I asked. Because, she answered, you might focus too closely on one part of the testimony. "We want you to weigh all of the evidence, and we trust that 12 jurors from different walks of life will remember enough correctly to make a sound judgment."

Although probably based on experience, her position disturbed me. Why deny jurors the chance to refresh their memories? Until we had begun to deliberate, we had no idea which part of the testimony was going to be crucial. By the time we knew, it was too late.

More than the limitations on what jurors could see, ask, or hear, however, the gender and racial politics of the jury's deliberations—and the way gender and race overlapped with each other—proved determinative to the trial's outcome. And that is where my scholarship and experience came together for me.

Gender issues were only indirectly at stake in the trial, but it still made a difference that four of us on the jury were women. And it mattered that only *four* of us were. The two jurors who initially wanted first degree murder were both men. During a break, one of them, a middle-aged white man, made hostile remarks about the judge. She's "me-e-e-an," he drawled. He liked "my women" to be "ladylike," "on a pedestal."

The other man, a retired African-American, had a deep bass voice. When he kept raising its volume to assert his points, I had to ask him to stop shouting. Later, a soft-spoken young African-American woman, who must have found the man intimidating, took me aside and thanked me.

Five of the jurors were white, and seven were African-American, as were all the major players in the trial except the judge and the public defender. Our deliberations reached a climax when, on Friday, the soft-spoken young woman, undecided until then, suddenly blurted out that nothing had convinced her that the bullets in the dead man's body came from a gun our defendant had carried. With intense feeling, she warned that, should we convict the man, we would be "lynching him just because he was a big black nigger."

A shocked silence fell over the room. Her language threw us. What's more, many of us felt guilty. Maybe we had rushed to judgment because our defendant was "big" and "black." By then, the two men who originally voted for a first-degree verdict had already "come down" to second degree. But the young woman remained unconvinced that the evidence was persuasive enough for even that.

We took a short break. When we sat down again, I suggested that, perhaps we should consider manslaughter. No matter which assailant was lying, I argued, we knew "beyond a reasonable doubt" that our defendant had arrived on the scene armed, and that his "reckless" behavior had endangered the victim's life. At the very least, our defendant was partially responsible for the death.

We took a new vote. This time, everyone, including the young woman, agreed on manslaughter—except for the deep-voiced, African-American man. He had already compromised enough by accepting second-degree murder, he said.

It took us barely a minute to agree on the burglary charge. We all sensed that the defendant, despite his lawyer's efforts to convince us otherwise, was dangerous. On the other charges, we were "hung."

Clearly, the interplay of race and gender were complex. The young African-American woman's reference to "lynching," and her use of the inflammatory "N" word, was the group's only overt reference to race. Two of the men had originally voted for the harshest sentence; yet one of them, surely the most "sexist" of the men on the jury, had allowed himself to be swayed by a woman's impassioned plea. All but one man had accepted my proposal for manslaughter. Had the one person I failed to convince dug in his heels because I had asked him to compromise? Was he unwilling to accept a suggestion from a woman? Was he just a stubborn person? I'll never know.

Perhaps that's the point. As the historian Linda K. Kerber showed in her 1998 book *No Constitutional Right to Be Ladies: Women and the Obligations of Citizenship*, until quite recently our laws—because of either ban or exemption—often meant that no women served on juries. And the lack of diversity had an impact, in different ways in different cases.

My experience was undeniably frustrating. I cannot pin down just how race and gender affected each of us on my panel. Indeed, the influence of diversity on a jury cannot be foretold along stereotypical lines—just as it cannot be foretold in the classroom or in society at large. Disqualifying jurors along racial or ethnic or gender grounds is a strategy that cannot have predictable results.

Defending diversity on college campuses, in the work force, or in society, is not a matter of saying that X, or Y, or Z will happen if you include more women, more members of minority or ethnic groups. But my experience showed me that my feminist forebears did make a difference by working so hard to include women on juries. The interplay among factors on a jury will always be complex, messy, and unpredictable. To deny any group participation would skew our system of justice. To allow, indeed to require, women to serve on juries is crucial to creating a true panel of peers. It is crucial to keeping our system of justice as fair and as honest as we can make it.

ELISABETH I. PERRY is a professor of history at Saint Louis University. Her books include *Belle Moskowitz: Feminine Politics and the Exercise of Power in the Age of Alfred E. Smith* (Oxford University Press, 1987; reprinted by Northeastern University Press, 2000). Her article "Culture, Strategy, and Politics in the New York Campaign for Women's Jury Service, 1917–1975" appeared in *New York History (Winter, 2001).*

Looking Askance at Eyewitness Testimony

Psychologists, showing how errors reach the courts, offer advice on handling such evidence.

D. W. MILLER

Ronnie Bullock was sentenced to 60 years in jail for kidnapping and raping a young Illinois girl. Edward Honaker spent a decade in a Virginia prison for sexually assaulting a woman at gunpoint. Kirk Bloodsworth was shipped off to Maryland's death row for raping and strangling a 9-year-old girl.

All three of those men were convicted in part because eyewitnesses or victims firmly placed them at the scene of the crime. But not one of them was guilty. They were among the first convicts to be exonerated by DNA tests proving that someone else was responsible.

Some psychologists believe that such mistakes happen in thousands of courtrooms every year. But most crimes leave no DNA traces to rule out the innocent. For more than two decades, psychological researchers have asked, How could so many witnesses be wrong, and what can be done about it? Only recently have they seen their findings influence the way the criminal-justice system handles eyewitness testimony.

Psychologists have conducted hundreds of studies on errors in eyewitness identification. In some cases, of course, witnesses simply lie. But research has shown that flawed police procedures and the vagaries of memory often lead witnesses to identify the wrong person, and that credulous jurors too easily credit their testimony.

To those familiar with the mountain of evidence about the way the human mind works, that comes as no surprise. "Why should people make good eyewitnesses?" asks Gary L. Wells, a psychologist at Iowa State University who is widely considered the dean of eyewitness research. In the presence of danger, he says, "we're wired for fight or flight. What helped for survival was not a quick recall of details."

The findings of Mr. Wells and his colleagues are finally gaining currency in the halls of criminal justice. In part that is due to the gradual acceptance of expert testimony on eyewitness identification.

Far more crucial, however, is the growing roster of convicts cleared by DNA evidence. In 1996, the U.S. Department of Justice released a report on the first 28 known cases of DNA exoneration. After studying those and 12 subsequent cases, Mr. Wells discovered that mistaken eyewitness testimony had played a part in about 90 percent of the convictions.

Missing the Key Details

Concerned about the high rate of eyewitness error in the DNA cases, U.S. Attorney General Janet Reno invited him to a meeting in early 1997. As a result of their conversation, the department's National Institute of Justice asked Mr. Wells and five fellow scholars to join a panel of law-enforcement officials, criminal-defense lawyers, and prosecutors created to write guidelines for handling eyewitness testimony.

The guide, published in October, gave scholars the opportunity to show that human memory is not a highly reliable tool for determining guilt in the courtroom. For example, contrary to popular belief, people under stress remember events no better than, and often less well than, they do under ordinary circumstances. Witnesses also perceive time as moving more slowly during traumatic events. That, in turn, leads them to overestimate how much time they had to notice details, a key factor of their credibility in court. And studies have found that witnesses to a crime are so distracted by the presence of a weapon—a phenomenon called "weapon focus"—that they remember little else with accuracy.

Researchers cannot ethically recreate the trauma of real crimes. But plenty of field research suggests that witnesses are apt to misidentify people.

Gary L. Wells: "Why should people make good eyewitnesses?" In times of danger, "we're wired for fight or flight. What helped for survival was not a quick recall of details."

For example, many studies have tested the ability of convenience-store clerks and bank tellers to recall customers they encountered in non-stressful situations. Around a third of the time, the employees wrongly identified faces from "lineups" that did not include the person they had actually met.

The Deterioration of Memory

In addition, all sorts of factors inhibit our ability to recognize and recall facial detail. For instance, psychologists have established that most of us have more difficulty recognizing people of a different race. And memory deteriorates very quickly over time.

Elizabeth F. Loftus, a psychologist at the University of Washington and a pioneer in research on false memory, has discovered that it's remarkably easy to alter one's recollection without realizing it. Human beings are highly susceptible to incorporating "post-event information"—newspaper articles, comments by police, conversations with other witnesses—into their recollections.

Witnesses also have been known to identify as criminals people they recognized from some other encounter, a process called "transference." In one bizarre example, an Australian psychologist and memory researcher named Donald Thomson was himself once identified by a rape victim as her attacker. Not only was his alibi airtight—he was being interviewed on live television at the time—but she had mistaken him for the rapist because she had seen his face on her television screen during the assault.

Improving Police Procedures

Of course, policymakers can't do much to improve the flaws in our memories. So scholars like Mr. Wells, who wanted to reduce eyewitness mistakes, began to focus on things that the justice system can control—particularly police procedures.

One of the biggest problems with eyewitness identification, researchers have found, is that uncertain witnesses are often prompted to finger the person whom police have detained, even when the suspect is not the same person they spotted at the scene. Witnesses viewing a lineup tend to assume that police have caught the person they saw. So they think their job is to find the face that most resembles the description they gave to police.

The police sometimes exacerbate that tendency by designing lineups poorly. Imagine a witness to a liquor-store robbery who says the robber was white, stocky, and bearded. Based on that description, the police identify a suspect and ask the witness to look at a lineup of live individuals or at a spread of photos (known as a "six-pack").

Too often, say researchers, the "distractor" faces used by police do not closely match the witness's description, or the suspect's photo looks different from the others. If the suspect stands out in any way—if his is the only color photo in the six-pack, for instance—the witness is far more likely to say, "That's the guy."

Lineups are also fraught with the possibility of mistaken identity, researchers report, because of our tendency to overlook differences in facial appearance among people not of our race. Not only are white witnesses, say, more likely to mistake one black suspect for another (and vice versa), but police officers may overestimate the degree to which the distractors they choose match the suspect's description.

Recently, Mr. Wells has raised the alarm about the way a witness's confidence can be manipulated. Witnesses are easily influenced during and after the lineup—by talking with other witnesses or police interviewers—to be more certain of their choice than their recall warrants. Police investigators, for example, may praise a witness for "picking the right guy" out of the lineup.

That taint frequently makes its way to the jury box. Understandably, jurors put a lot of stock in a witness who can point to the defendant and say, "He's the one. I'll never forget his face." But scholars have learned that the degree of confidence during trial is a poor predictor of a witness's accuracy. And, they warn, jurors ought to be particularly skeptical if they learn that a witness professed more confidence on the witness stand than in the squad room. Recall, they say, doesn't improve over time.

Asking the Right Questions

Until recently, the criminal-justice system made little use of those findings. Defense lawyers, of course, have embraced and exploited them at least since the 1980's. But according to Brian L. Cutler, a psychologist at Florida International University, they have rarely been able to use the research to cross-examine eyewitnesses or police.

"Defense lawyers have no special training—they don't know what questions to ask," says Mr. Cutler. "If they do ask the right questions, how well-equipped are jurors to evaluate the questions?" Unfortunately, jurors cling to a belief that "the way memory works is a matter of common sense," he says. "It just isn't so."

"People expect it's like videotape, that we attend equally well to everything out there," says Roy S. Malpass, a psychologist at the University of Texas at El Paso who served on the Justice Department panel. In fact, he says, "we're highly selective."

No one knows how often eyewitness error leads to false convictions, but some scholars have taken a stab at the question. In their book *Mistaken Identification: The Eyewitness, Psychology, and the Law* (Cambridge University Press, 1995), Mr. Cutler and Steven D. Penrod, of the University of Nebraska at Lincoln, do some courtroom calculations: If just 0.5 percent of America's yearly 1.5 million convictions for serious crimes are erroneous—a rate suggested by some studies—then other research allows the authors to infer that well over half of those defendants, or around 4,500 innocent people, are convicted on false eyewitness testimony.

All that may change now that the nation's top law-enforcement officials have created new guidelines for police conduct. The Justice Department report, "Eyewitness Evidence: A Guide for Law Enforcement," reads like a primer on eyewitness research. Among other things, it instructs investigators who assemble a lineup to:

* Select "distractors" that match the witness's description, even simulating tattoos or other unusual features if necessary.

As Expert Witnesses, Psychologists Have an Impact—But Only a Case at a Time

Until a few years ago, when the U.S. Department of Justice invited six psychologists to help reshape police procedures for eyewitness identification, scholars had only one way to influence criminal justice: one defendant at a time. Many have themselves testified to educate juries about the pitfalls of witness memory.

Like a lot of his colleagues, Gary L. Wells, a psychologist at Iowa State University who testifies four or five times a year, got into that line of research in part to save innocent defendants from false imprisonment, and to force police to improve methods for interviewing witnesses and identifying suspects. "There was a time 20 years ago when I was so naive as to think that all I had to do was document the problem and the police would change their procedures," he says. But eventually he decided that "the courtroom was never the place to have that kind of impact."

"Judges are reluctant to tell police how to do their jobs," he says. And judges tend to hew to the established view that juries are the arbiters of witness credibility.

That has been changing slowly. In 1993, the U.S. Supreme court ruled in *Daubert* v. *Merrell Dow Pharmaceuticals, Inc.* that new federal rules of evidence permitted a broader standard for allowing expert psychological testimony. Since then, says Solomon Fulero, a psychologist at Sinclair Community College, in Dayton, Ohio, several convictions have been overturned because the trial judge had not allowed such experts to testify.

Still, there's a limit to the broad change that scholars can effect by testifying. According to Mr. Wells, there just aren't that many experts: About 50 to 75 psychologists testify in court regularly, and only about 25 of them actually do original research in the field.

Furthermore, their services can be pricey. While rates vary widely, the psychologists themselves report fees of up to $3,500 a case, although most will take some clients *pro bono.*

Witness Credibility

In general, the experts try to avoid challenging the credibility of individual witnesses or the conduct of the police officers who worked with them. "The goal of the defense is to cast doubt on the credibility of a particular witness. But that's not my job," says Mr. Fulero, who was invited to join the Justice Department's eyewitness-testimony panel because of his courtroom experience, not his scholarly *vitae.* What he can testify to, he explains, is that "eyewitnesses are not as accurate, over all, as the jurors believe them to be."

Unfortunately for defendants, that means the research doesn't always help their cause.

"The deep problem," says James M. Doyle, a Boston defense lawyer who served on the panel, "is that the research is all statistical and probabilistic, but the trial process is clinical and diagnostic." In other words, a jury expects the experts to say whether a witness is right or wrong, when all an expert can really do is explain how to assess the odds.

Mr. Wells echoes many of his colleagues when he says that he's not really in it for the money. He was among the half-dozen scholars who helped to fashion the new Justice Department guidelines for handling eyewitness testimony. If they are widely adopted, he says, "we have no business in the courtroom on this issue. My purpose is to make expert testimony unnecessary."

He may get his wish. According to participants, prosecutors on the Justice Department panel were concerned that quick-witted defense lawyers would use the new guidelines to impeach eyewitness testimony.

Mr. Doyle, who has co-written a lawyer's guide to the research, *Eyewitness Testimony,* calls that a reasonable fear. In the past, his colleagues have had difficulty incorporating the science into their cross-examination techniques, because they haven't taken the trouble to understand the research methods, he says. Now they won't have to.

On the other hand, he doubts that's a bad thing. "One thing police and defense lawyers share is that we don't really want to deal with innocent people. It's not necessarily easier or better for me to represent innocent people. I would just as soon the police did their jobs."

—D. W. Miller

- Remind the witness that the suspect they saw may not even be in the lineup, and that the lineup is intended to clear the innocent as much as it is to identify the guilty.
- Avoid any comments that might influence the witness's selection.
- Ask for and record the witness's degree of certainty immediately.
- Photograph or film lineups to make the police more accountable to the defense.

Before they can take their new influence for granted, psychologists say, there is more to be done. For one thing, police officers and prosecutors need to be educated about the guidelines, which do not have the force of law. But Mr. Wells and others believe that both groups will embrace them once defense lawyers in the courtroom begin to hold the guidelines up as the gold standard of diligent police work.

No Double-Blind Lineups

The social scientists didn't win every battle. Despite their urgings, law-enforcement officials on the Justice Department panel batted down two key suggestions for improving police lineups. Research suggests that lineups are more accurate when they are double-blind—in other words, when the investigator in charge doesn't know which person is the suspect—and sequential—when the witness sees faces one at a time.

According to participants, police representatives nixed the former idea, because logistically it would be difficult to round up investigators who didn't know who the suspect was. More important, they said, it would be a tough sell to their fellow cops, because it smacks of mistrust and requires them to cede control of an investigation to someone else.

After scholars lost the battle to include double-blind procedures, participants say, they gave up on demanding sequential lineups. Without the first precaution, they explained, sequential lineups might be even more vulnerable to manipulation than simultaneous lineups are.

John Turtle, a panel member and a psychologist at the Ryerson Polytechnic Institute, in Toronto, believes that he has a high-tech solution to all those concerns. He has developed computer software that purports to take the bias out of the photospread lineups, which constitute about 80 percent of those in the United States and virtually all of those in Canada.

All a police investigator would need to do is scan a photo of the suspect into a computer and sit the witness down in front of the screen. The machine would then automatically choose photos of others who match the witness's description from a large database, and offer standardized, neutral instructions that wouldn't nudge the witness toward a particular response.

Psychologists deny they are imputing bad faith to police investigators. It's human nature, they say, to want your results to match your expectations. The scholars are simply urging police officers to treat their procedures for handling witnesses with all the care of scientific experiments. "Human memory is a form of trace evidence, like blood or semen or hair, except the trace exists inside the witness's head," says Mr. Wells. "How you go about collecting that evidence and preserving it and analyzing it is absolutely vital."

Why Do Hung Juries Hang?

PAULA HANNAFORD-AGOR, ET AL.

A criminal trial can be very expensive. It is even more costly when it has to be redone—and that's just the monetary cost. Retrials also take an emotional toll on victims and witnesses.

With these facts in mind, the National Center for State Courts examined deadlocked, or "hung," juries to see what characteristics they share and how they might be avoided. As one part of the study, surveys of jurors, judges, and attorneys were conducted in four jurisdictions. The Central Division, Criminal, of the Los Angeles County (California) Superior Court and the Superior Court of the District of Columbia were selected because of reported concerns about hung jury rates in those jurisdictions. The Maricopa County (Arizona) Superior Court was chosen because of an innovative procedure there that permits judges to allow further evidence and arguments when a jury reports it is deadlocked. The Bronx County (New York) Supreme Court was included because, like the other sites, it had a high volume of felony jury trials (allowing for quick collection of data) and had court personnel willing to cooperate in the study. A total of 382 cases were included in the analysis.

A second part of the study took a closer look at 46 of the cases, trying to determine the primary and peripheral causes of deadlock. This subgroup, while too small to provide statistically significant numbers, nonetheless offers some interesting insight into the factors leading to a hung jury.

Quantity of evidence and length of trial did not appear to affect the likelihood of a hung jury. However, the quality of the evidence was a very important factor.

What Is a Hung Jury?

The definition of a "hung jury" varies, and this led to differences in the reporting of hung juries across jurisdictions. Some counted a jury as "hung" if it failed to reach a verdict on any charge or on any defendant. Some only counted a hung jury if the jury failed to reach a verdict on all counts or on all defendants.

To control for these disparate definitions, the research team's analysis included several categories of jury deadlock. Juries that hung on all counts occurred least frequently (8 percent of cases studied). Juries hung on the first count of the indictment (generally the most serious charge) in 10 percent of cases and on at least one count charged in 13 percent of cases. The number of defendants tried was related to the likelihood of the jury deadlocking. In 12 percent of single-defendant cases, the jury hung on at least one count, but that figure increased to 27 percent when multiple defendants were tried.

Effect of Multiple Counts

As predicted by the researchers, the number of counts affected the likelihood of a hung jury. As the number of counts increases, so does the opportunity for disagreement. So, the more counts, the more likely that a jury will hang on at least one of them. On the other hand, more counts also means more opportunity for jurors to agree. Accordingly, juries that hang on all charges generally had fewer counts to consider.

The type of crime charged also made a difference in the jurisdictions studied. Drug cases constituted 28 percent of the total sample, but only 12 percent of the hung juries. In contrast, juries in murder cases were more likely than was expected to hang on at least some counts given their proportion of the total caseload— 13 percent of the sample, but 24 percent of the hung juries.

Effect of Complex Evidence

Cases with complex evidence or complex legal instructions may make it more difficult for jurors to reach agreement. When asked to rate how easy the trial was for them and their fellow jurors to understand, members of hung juries were more likely to describe the trial as complex and difficult. Interestingly, judges and attorneys did not share the jurors' perceptions; they rated the complexity of the evidence and law as comparable in hung and verdict cases.

Case complexity rarely appeared as the primary cause of jury deadlock in the second part of the study. However, it did play a peripheral role for some of the hung juries.

Effect of Quality of the Evidence

Quantity of evidence and length of trial did not appear to affect the likelihood of a hung jury. However, the quality of the evidence was a very important factor. By far, the most frequently

Reason	Site			
	Los Angeles	Maricopa	Bronx	Washington, DC
Weak Case	12	5	—	10
Police Credibility	2	—	2	3
Juror Concerns About Fairness	1	1	—	5
Case Complexity	—	—	—	2
Dysfunctional Deliberation Process	—	—	—	—
Unknown	—	1	1	1
Total Number of Cases	15	7	3	21
Total			46*	

*These in-depth case studies were a subsample of the 382 cases studied.

Figure 1 Primary reasons for hung jury, by site.

perceived primary cause of hung juries in the second part of the study was weak evidence (see Figure 1). When asked to rate the strength of the prosecution's case, members of hung juries displayed much more disagreement in their ratings then did members of verdict juries. Another effect was seen when jurors were asked to rate the ambiguity of the evidence. When a jury's average rating of evidence "closeness" was high (that is, the jurors did not view the evidence as clearly in favor of the prosecution or the defense), that jury was significantly more likely to have been unable to reach a verdict on at least one charge (see Figure 2).

Sentiments about Fairness of the Law

Another factor leading to hung juries was the degree to which jurors believed that the law they were instructed to apply was fair and would lead to the legally correct outcome. The concern seemed to be not one of sympathy for the individual defendant, but rather dissatisfaction with the fairness of the law in principle or its application in that particular trial.

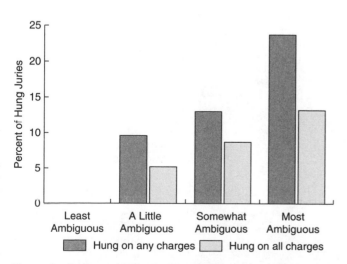
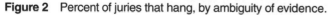

Figure 2 Percent of juries that hang, by ambiguity of evidence.

Recommendations for Decreasing the Number of Hung Juries

What can policymakers do in jurisdictions with unacceptably high hung jury rates? One popular proposal is to eliminate the requirement of a unanimous verdict in felony trials, adopting a supermajority rule (for example, 11–1 or 10–2) instead. There is no question that this approach would substantially reduce the number of hung juries in most jurisdictions. Proponents of this approach point out that it eliminates the "veto power" of individual jurors who unreasonably or illegitimately seek to thwart a consensus.

But such an approach may address the symptoms of disagreement among jurors without addressing the causes. Moreover, a nonunanimous verdict rule might affect a jury's deliberations in unintended ways, such as cutting off minority viewpoints before jurors have had an opportunity to consider them thoughtfully.

Other solutions, based on other theories of juror deadlock, may prove to be more effective. Some approaches being tried are:

- Better preparation of evidence by prosecutors and defense attorneys.
- Better tools to help jurors understand the evidence and the law, such as permitting jurors to take notes, allowing jurors to question witnesses, and providing written copies of instructions.
- Better guidance for jurors on how to engage in productive deliberations.

Effect of the Deliberation Process

Several aspects of the jury deliberation process appeared to affect the final trial result in the jurisdictions studied. These included:

- Members of hung juries reported taking their first vote earlier than the members of verdict juries—on average, within the first 10 minutes of deliberation.
- Where jurors ultimately could not reach a verdict, there was less likely to be a large majority in the first vote favoring either conviction or acquittal.
- Compared to verdict jurors, members of hung juries were more likely to categorize fellow jurors as "unreasonable people" and were more likely to feel that one or more jurors "dominated" the deliberations.

The deliberation process was never reported as a primary reason for a hung jury, but it did contribute to jury deadlock at a secondary level in over one-fourth of the trials.

Presumptions Proven Wrong

A number of presumptions about the causes of hung juries have been expressed in recent years. Many observers have asserted that the primary cause of jury deadlock is individual jurors holding out for illegitimate reasons. Some also view the problem as racial or ethnic bias or conflict. Others see jury nullification—the refusal of some jurors to base their verdict on the evidence and the law—as the main cause. A variety of proposals based on these presumptions have been offered to deal with the problem of hung juries. (See "Recommendations for Decreasing the Number of Hung Juries.")

However, prior to this research project, only a handful of studies gave more than superficial consideration to the dynamics of hung juries. On this slim basis, it was difficult for policymakers to reach informed judgments about the probable effect of various reform proposals.

This research—which combined a limited survey of hung jury rates, a jurisdictional study of felony jury trials, and case studies of the 46 hung juries documented in the sample—provides a clearer picture of the reasons for hung juries and should help those who are searching for ways to decrease the number of cases requiring retrial because of jury deadlock.

For more information contact **PAULA HANNAFORD-AGOR** at the National Center for State Courts, Center for Jury Studies, 300 Newport Avenue, Williamsburg, VA 23185, 757–259–1556, phannaford@ncsc.dni.us.

From *National Institute of Justice Journal,* Issue no. 251, July 2004, pp. 25–27. Published by Office of Justice/U.S. Department of Justice.

Exiling Sex Offenders from Town

Robert F. Worth

In Hillsborough County, Fla., local officials voted unanimously in June to ban convicted sex offenders from public hurricane shelters. In Ohio, prosecutors have begun moving to evict sex offenders who live too close to a school. And in towns and counties across the country, including Binghamton, N.Y., and Brick, N.J., local officials have passed laws in recent months that effectively banish anyone convicted of a sex crime against a minor.

The new crackdown comes after several horrific and well-publicized cases, including two involving young girls, Jessica Lunsford, 9, and Sarah Lunde, 13, who were abducted and murdered this year in Florida by registered sex offenders. Although state lawmakers across the country have introduced similar proposals aimed at sex offenders, some local elected officials say they have received so many anxious calls from constituents that they cannot afford to wait.

"These measures are a cry for help," said Richard A. Bucci, the mayor of Binghamton, where a law barring sex offenders, passed in May, has been suspended until a court challenge is resolved. "There is a broad concern that the system in place is not working, and that these individuals are prone to repeat their crimes."

The new laws typically bar offenders from living, working, or in some cases even being within 2,500 feet of a school, day care center, park, or school bus stop. In some cases, that means offenders cannot live or work within the town at all. Mr. Bucci and other local officials who have drafted the laws say the intention is simple: to keep sex offenders as far away from children as possible.

But many forensic psychiatrists, victim advocates and law enforcement officials say the effort to zone out sex offenders is unlikely to make towns and cities safer, and could even be harmful. They say other solutions, including longer sentences, are more effective, though they may be more costly.

The restrictions could create a false sense of security, since many convicted sex offenders did not live or work near their victims, said Ernie Allen, the president of the National Center for Missing and Exploited Children. The laws could also end up bouncing sex offenders from one community to the next, setting off a competitive spiral of ever-tougher "not in my backyard" ordinances.

Worse, some experts say, the laws could drive some sex offenders out of sight and away from the sources of stability in their lives, perhaps putting them at greater risk of committing more crimes.

"When you push offenders out of the more populated areas, they can lose access to jobs and treatment, and it makes them harder to track," said Jill S. Levenson, a researcher on sexual violence at Lynn University in Boca Raton, Fla., who published a study of sex offender zoning laws this year.

The new zoning initiatives come as many states are making efforts to strengthen federal mandates like Megan's Law, the landmark 1996 measure named for a child victim in New Jersey that orders law enforcement officials to notify communities about sex offenders in their midst. There are now more than 500,000 registered sex offenders. The public debate has grown more heated since the child murders in Florida. In May, the revelation that some sex offenders were receiving taxpayer-financed Viagra through Medicaid prompted a national uproar, and Congress quickly passed a provision barring offenders from receiving the drugs.

One common concern has been flaws in public registries and notification policies. In New York, where some offenders are scheduled by law to drop off the registry starting next year, Gov. George E. Pataki has proposed to keep them on for life. Pending federal legislation would create a national registry to fill in the gaps in state lists and help track offenders who move across the country.

But some proposals go much further. In Alabama, the State Assembly voted unanimously in July to require surgical castration for some offenders. (The State Senate did not support the measure.) In Florida, Gov. Jeb Bush signed a new law in May that will increase penalties for those who molest children younger than 12, and force them to wear satellite-based G.P.S. tracking devices for life after they leave prison.

Other states, including New York and New Jersey, are weighing stricter supervision of offenders, through G.P.S. tracking, more frequent visits from parole officers, and limits on where offenders can work and live, like the so-called distance-marker laws being passed by towns and counties.

"These predators seem to orbit around these areas—wherever there are children they want to get close," said State Senator Leonard T. Connors Jr. of New Jersey, a Republican from Forked River who is the primary sponsor of a bill that would forbid convicted sex offenders from living within 500 feet of any New Jersey school, day care center or playground. "They can't help themselves. So it's our duty to protect the children and see that the sex offenders are separated."

Many of the new laws appear to be driven by the perception that sex offenders in general are bound to repeat their crimes, and only the most drastic measures can stop them.

In fact, a number of studies have found that pedophiles—the group of sex offenders that has provoked the most public fear—have recidivism rates of more than 50 percent, and do not tend to respond to treatment. But many other criminal groups have higher recidivism rates than these "high-risk" sex offenders, said Dr. Karl Hanson, a Canadian researcher and leading authority in the field.

And outside of the high-risk cases, sex offenders are unlikely to repeat their crimes, studies suggest. Sex offenders over all are less likely to be rearrested than drunk drivers, drug offenders, and domestic violence offenders, Dr. Hanson said. Violent repeat offenders like those who committed the child murders in Florida earlier this year are extremely rare.

The first distance-marker laws appeared almost a decade ago, and 14 states have now passed versions of them. Some states, though, have expressed doubts about the laws' effectiveness. Minnesota and Colorado considered passing versions of the law, and decided against it after commissioning studies. Minnesota's study, published by the State Department of Corrections in 2003, showed no relationship between offenders' proximity to schools and their risk of committing new crimes. It concluded that new restrictions would make it harder to track offenders and would "not enhance community safety."

The laws have been challenged in court on the grounds that they violate the Constitution by subjecting sex offenders to an additional punishment after their release from prison. But state and federal appeals courts in Iowa rejected that argument earlier this year, ruling that the laws were administrative measures justified by the state's interest in preserving public safety.

The local distance-marker laws, which began to proliferate earlier this year after the child murders in Florida, may not fare as well in court. Unlike their state counterparts, they often bar sex offenders from working or even being in the restricted areas—a modern-day sentence of exile. They are therefore vulnerable to the argument that they violate the Eighth Amendment's ban on cruel and unusual punishment, said Robert A. Perry, the legislative director of the New York Civil Liberties

Union, which has filed a supporting brief for the plaintiff in a suit filed against the new law in Binghamton. The local laws could also be challenged on the grounds that they conflict with the state's authority to legislate such matters.

"Distance-marker laws are a Band-Aid," said Laura A. Ahearn, the director of Parents for Megan's Law, a national organization based in New York. A better answer, she said, is longer prison sentences and some form of supervision for life. Those approaches, she added, are expensive, and have been less popular with legislators for that reason.

Another option now under consideration in New York and other states is civil commitment, in which the most dangerous offenders can be transferred indefinitely to secure psychiatric institutions after their prison terms. Housing offenders this way is far more expensive than prison, and has generated criticism on constitutional grounds.

Distance-marker laws are cheaper. But they can blur the difference between dangerous sexual predators—who are not likely to be deterred by them—and moderate or low-risk offenders, who are more amenable to treatment and far less likely to commit more crimes, said Dr. Richard Hamill, a forensic psychologist who runs a treatment center in Albany.

Refining those distinctions would better serve the public, Dr. Hamill said. New York State now classifies offenders using an outdated system that often mistakenly identifies a high-risk offender as lower-risk, and vice-versa. That inaccuracy, Dr. Hamill said, can result in dangerous offenders' being released into communities without sufficient warnings, and relatively harmless ones' being treated as pariahs.

Even some of the elected officials who have passed distance-marker laws acknowledge that they may not be the best defense against sex offenders, and are vulnerable to legal challenges.

"I think all the towns will get involved, and it'll be one-upmanship, and then the courts will probably get involved," said Joseph C. Scarpelli, the mayor of Brick, N.J., which passed a law last month that bars sex offenders from living or working within 2,500 feet of a school, park, playground, day care center, or school bus stop.

But Mr. Scarpelli defended the intent of the law, which drew applause from dozens of residents who had come to the Town Council's meeting to witness the vote.

"I think it sends a loud and clear message: we don't want anybody moving to town that is of that persuasion," he said.

Judges Turn Therapist in Problem-Solving Court
Do Defendants Need Jail, or Just New Medication?

Leslie Eaton and Leslie Kaufman

The traditional role of a judge is a stark one: to decide who wins and who loses, who is innocent and who is guilty, who goes to prison and who goes free.

Starting about 15 years ago, however, some judges began experimenting with a more active approach, intervening in the lives of drug addicts to get them into treatment and keep them out of overcrowded jails and overburdened courtrooms. Now, in drug treatment courts, judges are cheerleaders and social workers as much as jurists.

New York State is pushing this approach to new frontiers, creating a homelessness court, domestic violence courts and mental health courts. Backed by the state's chief judge, and bolstered by the court system's own research, these new courts are, among other things, trying to cut down on the number of people who appear in courtrooms over and over again.

Judges—who in law school may have mastered the rules of procedure or the penal code—are now meant to know about the science of addiction, the pathology of wife batterers, the bureaucracy of welfare programs.

In this small but rapidly growing world, then, you can find Judge Jaya K. Madhavan in the Bronx, trying to help a pregnant woman facing eviction clear up her housing crisis. You can find Justice Matthew J. D'Emic in mental health court, dealing with murder, kidnapping—and whether or not an arsonist needs to change his psychiatric medicines.

And you can find Judge Miriam Cyrulnik giving a young man in her Brooklyn domestic violence court the choice between jail and anger-management classes.

For the most part, these innovations have been greeted with enthusiasm.

"It's a very important new revolution" in the way courts work, said Bruce J. Winick, a former city health official who is now an academic expert on what he calls "therapeutic jurisprudence."

And while New York and California are at the forefront of this movement, there are now hundreds of such courts nationwide, from Hartford to Honolulu, addressing problems like drug abuse and drunken driving; Anchorage opened a court last year dedicated to dealing with the problems of veterans.

But as the number of these courts has exploded—there are now 188 in New York State and 84 in the works—so has criticism.

In the past, when judges have been given so much discretion in the way they handle cases, the results have been uneven, so uneven that they led to the imposition of strict sentencing guidelines in some courts as a way to restore consistency.

And some legal scholars have raised concerns about judges—who are mostly middle class and often politically connected—imposing some of their personal values on people from very different backgrounds.

Lawyers who represent poor clients say that these courts, whatever their good intentions, have left judges intimately—and uncomfortably—involved in the everyday lives of an increasing number of people.

"At what point do you say, 'O.K., we have enough poor people under court control?'" asked Robin G. Steinberg, executive director of the Bronx Defenders.

And some critics have trouble not so much with the theory but with the way these courts operate. Because while these courts may seem kind, even lenient, critics say, in practice they are unduly harsh, assuming that defendants are guilty from the outset and making it hard for them to defend themselves.

"We are sliding backward, without even realizing it, toward an inquisitorial system of justice," James A. Yates, a State Supreme Court justice in Manhattan, told an audience of criminal defense lawyers last month.

Times Square Came First

The interventionist approach—known in New York as problem-solving courts—dates to 1989, when a judge in Miami decided to try to order treatment for drug addicts. Soon after, New York developed the Midtown Community Court to deal with quality-of-life crimes in Times Square. At that court, prostitutes, for example, are ordered to perform community service and can receive training for a new career.

In recent years, the problem-solving idea has spread across the country, according to studies done for the Department of

Justice, which has spent tens of millions of dollars on these experimental programs. New York alone has received almost $17 million since 2000, and the state's chief judge, Judith S. Kaye, says the efforts are worth it—for the people accused and for the court system, which handles 4 million cases a year.

"We're seeing the same people again and again and again," Judge Kaye said, because of factors like substance abuse and family dysfunction. With problem-solving courts, she added, "we can use the time that person is before us more constructively, for recovery and rehabilitation."

To an outsider, a "problem-solving court" might not look very different from a traditional one. These courts exist, for the most part, in regular courthouses, and there are judges in robes and court officers in uniform.

But there are significant differences. The judges often have an unusual amount of information about the people who appear before them. These people, who are often called clients, rather than defendants, can talk directly to the judges, rather than communicating through lawyers.

And the judges monitor these defendants for months, even years, using a system of rewards and punishments, which can include jail time. Judges also receive training in their court's specialty and may have a psychologist on the staff.

Drug courts generally have a positive track record. A 2003 study of six New York drug courts found that participants were almost a third less likely to be rearrested than similar defendants in the regular criminal courts.

But the results for newer courts are unclear. For example, a specialized court in Harlem for nonviolent parolees is supposed to help them by providing treatment programs and services like job training.

But a 2003 study found that participants in the court program still too often wound up back in jail.

On a recent morning in the mental health court in Brooklyn, the caseload included two women charged with trying to kidnap babies, another woman who stalked a junior high school classmate who she believes is her husband, and a young man who started a fire that shuttered a small public housing complex.

Such cases, where the defendant is accused of a serious crime yet is seriously mentally ill, are the bane of courtrooms across the country. In many of those cases, no one thinks imprisonment is a smart punishment. Yet in a regular court, a judge would possess few other options.

Mental health court, where the goal is to match defendants with appropriate therapy, has been in existence for about two years and it is widely applauded by prosecutors and defense lawyers.

Justice D'Emic presides over the court as a father figure, usually genial but sometimes stern. The relationships are almost intimate. The judge may note a change in a defendant's appearance or comment on a particularly fetching piece of clothing, and often talks to the defendant directly instead of through a lawyer. Many defendants who have passed through the court say Justice D'Emic has turned their lives around.

Alternative Courts

Courts in which judges can play an active role in litigants' lives are becoming more common in New York State. Since the first court of this type in the state, Midtown Community Court, opened in Manhattan in 1993, their number has grown to 188, with 84 more planned

Court Type	Currently Operating	Planned	First Year of Operation	Description
Drug Treatment	138	56	1995	Mandate and actively monitor drug treatment, rather than incarceration, for nonviolent addicted offenders.
Domestic Violence	19	8	1996	Provide services like anger management and strengthen the monitoring of defendants.
Integrated Domestic Violence	18	11	2001	Allow a single judge to hear many different kinds of cases—criminal domestic violence, family and matrimonial.
Community*	6	1	1993	Focus on high-crime areas and combine punishment with aid, like job training or counseling, for offenders.
Mental Health	5	5	2002	Send mentally-ill offenders to community-based treatment instead of jail, if possible.
Homelessness	1	0	2005	Attempt to address underlying problems, like mental illness and low job skills, of tenants facing eviction.
Sex Offender Management	0	3	—	Will focus on strengthing the monitoring of convicted sex offenders and ensuring that probation is enforced.
Bronx Community Solutions	1	0	2005	Pilot program that applies the community court approach, on a larger scale, to criminal cases in the Bronx.

*Includes subcourts, including the parole re-entry court in Harlem.
Sources: Office of Court Administration, Center for Court Innovation

Take, for example, the man who started the fire, an immigrant from Barbados who is now 25. When he arrived in Justice D'Emic's courtroom at the beginning of 2003, he had been hospitalized nine times in five years; in his delusional state he believes he is the son of God.

Call Me Anytime

Justice D'Emic decided that he could safely return to live with his mother if he stayed on his medications. It was the judge who later warned him to change his medicine when he started skipping appointments, complaining of stomach cramps.

But the judge did not insist on prison. He did, however, give the man his personal cellphone number and told him to call if he was in a jam again. The man says he used it only once, to ask the judge for advice about a girl to whom he was considering proposing.

In this instance, as in many of the cases that come before mental health court, the insistence on therapy appears to have benefits. The man has signed up for city-sponsored job training (despite telling the judge he preferred to become a rapper). If all continues to go well, he will "graduate" from court with only a misdemeanor on his record.

His lawyers credit the court for his progress. "He would have been in jail without it, there is no doubt," said Mary Elizabeth Anderson, a lawyer with the Legal Aid Society.

Of all the problem-solving experiments, courts that specialize in domestic violence are probably the most controversial. Advocates for victims tend to think they are too lenient, saying that batterers deserve jail time, not anger-management treatment.

But public defenders have darkly dubbed these courts "victims' courts," contending that they are meant to protect the person—usually a woman—bringing charges rather than determining the guilt or innocence of the person being charged with the crime.

That is certainly how it appeared to 19-year-old Jewell P., who asked that his last name be withheld to protect his privacy. He turned up in domestic violence court hoping to clear his name, only to be tempted to settle the case and accept treatment.

His troubles began last October, Jewell said, when his girlfriend gave birth to their child and they began to quarrel over the extent of his child support. After one particularly heated fight, court records show, the girlfriend complained to the police that he had pulled out some of her hair and punched her in the ribs.

Jewell insists he never touched her. A high school graduate with no criminal record, Jewell was arrested, charged with assault in the third degree, and sent to Rikers Island until he posted bail. He was eventually ordered to stay away from his girlfriend and daughter for a year.

But in the misdemeanor domestic violence court, the prosecution made an offer that was hard to resist: If Jewell completed 12 weeks of anger-management courses, the assault charge would be wiped from his record and maybe the court would limit the order of protection.

Outside, in the hallway, Steven E. Kliman, his Legal Aid Society lawyer that day, explained that it was probably the best deal he could get. Although he was tempted, Jewell ultimately rejected the plea because of its terms: if he was late to anger-management class even by five minutes, he would be locked out of the program, and if he failed the program, the full assault charge would be reinstated.

Mr. Kliman said that Jewell, who is awaiting trial, was lucky to have choices. Too many of his clients, irrespective of their guilt, take the plea—either because they cannot make bail or because the orders of protection would rob them of the only place they have to live.

A One-ZIP-Code Court

Judge Madhavan's courtroom in the Bronx is the home of New York's newest problem-solving court. It does not handle criminal matters; it deals with landlords and tenants and aims to reduce homelessness in one Bronx ZIP code, 10451.

In a $3 million pilot project financed by the United Way, the court employs teams of lawyers and social workers, available right in the courthouse, to consult with tenants facing eviction—almost none of whom have lawyers.

Unlike a regular housing court, its goal is not merely to deal with the crisis of the moment, but also to deal with underlying problems—mental illness, language difficulties, low job skills—that lead to homelessness.

It is labor intensive for Judge Madhavan and his staff, though it appears to be a labor of love on the part of the judge, a 35-year-old former Legal Aid lawyer who has been on the bench less than a year. He may hear as many as 100 cases a day, most of them negotiated agreements between landlords' lawyers and the tenants who are behind on their rent.

The tenants are not merely asked if they understand the agreements, as they would be in a regular court; they are also questioned about where they are going to get the money they owe, which is usually two or three thousand dollars. If the answers are not satisfactory, the judge sends the tenants down the hall to the welfare office or, if they are eligible, to the homelessness-prevention program. Not that he can order them, exactly, but his "Take this piece of paper next door and tell them I sent you" carries a lot of authority.

Landlords get scrutiny too, as the judge tries to ensure that the deals also provide for repairs requested by the tenants.

And the judge is also on the alert for problems like elder abuse or domestic violence. Judge Madhavan describes himself as an impartial fact-finder. But he is also "part social worker, part therapist, part lawyer," he said. "I wear many hats." (Including, reluctantly, the green eyeshade of an accountant while poring over tangled rent records.)

To take on so many roles requires many hours. The judge arrives at his chambers at 7:30 A.M., although the courtroom doors do not open until 9:30. He works after the doors have closed, too, looking over cases at night.

It is a sacrifice that Judge Madhavan, who spent his early childhood about two blocks from the courthouse, seems to think is worth it; he said happily that since the program began, he has not seen a single eviction in the ZIP code.

But asking every judge in the system to take on all those roles—and all that work—seems like a stretch. Fern A. Fisher, the administrative judge whose brainchild the homelessness program is, said that all the Civil Court judges have the legal knowledge to do it.

But, she noted delicately, "Some people are more equipped to problem-solve than others."

When the Poor Go to Court

Across the nation, many indigents wind up being sentenced to jail time without ever seeing a lawyer.

KIT R. ROANE

L ast July, a homeless man named Hubert Lindsey was stopped by police officers in Gulfport, Miss., for riding his bicycle without a light. The police soon discovered that Lindsey was a wanted man. Gulfport records showed he owed $4,780 in old fines. So, off to jail he went.

Legal activists now suing the city in federal court say it was pretty obvious that Lindsey couldn't pay the fines. According to their complaint, he lived in a tent, was unemployed, and appeared permanently disabled by an unseeing eye and a mangled arm. But without a lawyer to plead his case, the question of whether Lindsey was a scofflaw or just plain poor never came up. Nor did the question of whether the fines were really owed, or if it was constitutional to jail him for debts he couldn't pay. Nobody, the activists say, even bothered to mention alternatives like community service. The judge ordered Lindsey to "sit out" the fine in jail. That took nearly two months.

Lindsey isn't the only poor American to face a judge on dubious charges without adequate legal representation. Far from it. More than 40 years after the Supreme Court ruled that competent counsel was a fundamental right of all Americans accused of crimes, the American Bar Association says thousands of indigent defendants still navigate the court system each year without a lawyer, or with one who doesn't have the time, resources, or interest to provide effective representation. Whether they face serious felony charges or misdemeanors, the poor often find themselves alone in a sometimes-Kafkaesque system where they have little, if any, voice.

Without advocates, some poor defendants serve jail time longer than the law requires or plead guilty to crimes they didn't commit just to get out of jail. A few, as has been documented, receive the death penalty or life in prison because their court-appointed lawyers were incompetent, lazy, or both. Most shocking, says Norman Lefstein, who chaired the American Bar Association's Indigent Defense Advisory Group, "is the lack of overall real success, the lack of progress" given the overwhelming evidence that inadequate counsel often leads to wrongful conviction. The many cases we know about "likely are only the tip of the iceberg," he says. "This is an enormous problem."

Kicking and screaming. It's also quite a complicated one. The federal government has been slow to the game, both in providing funds or setting rules. That means that each state, and often each county, is left to its own devices on deciding how to fund and institute indigent-defense programs. Funding is a perpetual problem. In New York alone, there are more than 95 different systems. Sometimes, representation is determined by whichever lawyer bills taxpayers the least, no matter that the lawyer could have a full load of other pending cases.

It's not hard to see why the bottom line has such pull. Most states have a hard time coming up with the necessary dollars for indigent-defense programs, and only 27 attempt to provide full funding. That leaves already-strapped cities and counties on the hook for most of the costs—costs that must be weighed against local needs, from new roads to sewer upgrades and firehouses.

Shortfalls in some places are acute. In Alabama, pay cuts have caused lawyers representing indigent death penalty clients to flee the system. In New Mexico, a lack of funds to hire lawyers for indigent defendants caused the court of appeals there to place an ad for lawyers willing to work free.

While several states have enacted some reforms in recent years, most have been dragged kicking and screaming to the table, often on the heels of civil rights lawsuits, court orders, or striking examples of injustice made public. And while such reforms are welcome, critics say the jury is still out on how well they are implemented. In Georgia, for instance, new public defenders are required to contact their clients within 72 hours of their arrest, but there is no requirement that they do much else until a defendant has his day in court. In one case, a public defender representing a severely mentally ill woman facing a parole violation had contacted his client only once after her arrest and was not scheduled to see her again until a bond hearing set for nearly two months later. John Cole Vodicka, director of the Prison and Jail Project, a watchdog group active in southern Georgia, says the public defender didn't even meet with the woman personally on the first occasion; he sent her a form letter. Cole Vodicka left several messages for the lawyer, saying that he knew the woman from his church and that he could help get in touch with character witnesses with knowledge of her troubles and her mental illness. The lawyer failed to call him back, Cole Vodicka says. The woman's case is pending. Asked about the case, Samuel Merritt, the head of the public defender's office in that circuit, said his office should have fought more aggressively to schedule the woman's bond hearing for an earlier date, but he says the new system is generally working very well.

At least Georgia is trying. In many cities and states, advocates say, it appears officials have just ignored the law. The New York Civil Liberties Union has threatened to file suit against New York State. While New York City, which has a well-funded legal-aid office, is in many ways a model for other locales, the rural counties upstate are another story. In Schuyler County, lawyers for the National Association for the Advancement of Colored People's legal defense fund say an investigation they conducted revealed a system where indigent defendants routinely sat in jail for weeks or months without seeing a lawyer. Often they went through the entire court process, from arrest, to arraignment, on through bail hearings and even through plea bargains, without ever consulting an attorney. One public defender, they say, deliberately kept his phone off the hook.

Then there's Gulfport, the second largest city in Mississippi, which, up until Hurricane Katrina hit, was beating the pavement looking for those who owed fines for things like public profanity—at $222 a pop. The result of Gulfport's fine-reclamation project was that while it collected modest sums of money, it also packed the county jail with hundreds of people who couldn't pay. The Southern Center for Human Rights filed a federal civil rights lawsuit against Gulfport last July. Attorney Sarah Geraghty says that before bringing the case against the city, she witnessed hundreds of court adjudications involving Gulfport's poor in which no defense attorney was present or even offered. Many defendants, Geraghty said, were obviously indigent, mentally ill, or physically disabled, like Hubert Lindsey; some had been jailed for fines they had already paid. One mentally ill woman attempted suicide by jumping from an elevated cell in the county jail after she was picked up for having failed to pay several city fines; the lawsuit alleges that police then grabbed her again on the same charge a few months later, causing her to miss the surgery scheduled to fix the broken bones in her feet.

The city says it is still reviewing the lawsuit, but there is talk of a settlement. And Geraghty, who recently sat in on the court's proceedings again, says judges are now advising indigent defendants of their rights. But it never should have taken a lawsuit, adds Geraghty, noting that the problem with the city's actions was clear: "It's illegal. Period."

Justice & Antonin Scalia

The Supreme Court's Most Strident Catholic

JULIA VITULLO-MARTIN

After being nominated as a Supreme Court Justice by President Ronald Reagan in 1986, Antonin Scalia faced down the Democratic-controlled Senate Judiciary Committee by refusing to discuss his views on any question likely to come before him as a sitting justice. Yet his confirmation hearings became a virtual lovefest. Scalia handled his interrogation so engagingly that the Senate voted ninety-eight to zero to confirm him. Reagan was said to have danced around the Oval Office, singing "Scalia/I've just picked a judge named Scalia," to the tune of *West Side Story's* "Maria."

Reagan knew what he was getting. Scalia would soon establish himself as one of the most brilliant and belligerent conservatives ever to sit on the high court. The late Justice William Brennan's reputation as the most influential Supreme Court justice of his generation would shortly pass to Scalia, asserted Michael Greve, cofounder of the libertarian Center for Individual Rights, a public-interest law firm in Washington, D.C.

From today's perspective, in which Scalia has emerged as a reliable proponent of hard-right views on issues from property rights to the death penalty, his confirmation hearings seem to have happened in a parallel universe. Some senators even called Scalia by his nickname, Nino. It became clear that Nino was a man of many parts—Nino, the tennis player, opera singer, pianist, poker player, raconteur, man about town, father of nine. Potential enemies were declawed by his accomplishments and affability. Howard Metzenbaum, for example, an outspokenly liberal Ohio Democrat, announced that Scalia's conservatism was irrelevant and that all that mattered was his "fitness." Senator Edward Kennedy worried that Scalia might be "insensitive" on women's rights, but concluded that one could hardly "maintain that Judge Scalia is outside the mainstream."

His immigrant saga—the only child of a Sicilian father and a first-generation Italian-American mother—was lavishly praised. Born in 1936, he spent his early childhood in Trenton, New Jersey, before the family moved to New York, when his father became a professor of Romance languages at Brooklyn College. He graduated first in his class from Saint Francis Xavier, a Jesuit high school in Manhattan, first in his class from Georgetown University, and cum laude from Harvard Law School. He went on to practice law from 1961 to 1967 with Cleveland's most prestigious firm, Jones, Day, Cockley, and Reavis—named after

the city's first family of Virginia, became general counsel to the White House Office Telecommunications Policy, chaired the Administrative Conference of the United States, and became assistant attorney general in the U.S. Department of Justice's Office of Legal Counsel. In 1977, he joined the law faculty at the University of Chicago, from which he was appointed in 1982 to the nation's second most important court, the U.S. Court of Appeals for the D.C. Circuit.

Even the legal press was effusive about Scalia's Supreme Court confirmation. Tony Mauro in the *Legal Times* predicted that Scalia would become the court's "intellectual lodestar."

How, then, did this exemplar of charm and learning become what he is today—the scourge of the country's liberal establishment? FindLaw columnist Edward Lazarus, for example, recently questioned Scalia's integrity, arguing that his reputation as "a rigorous and thoroughly principled jurist" has always seemed to him "largely a myth." (Lazarus's own moral claim to fame: he betrayed the ethics of his Supreme Court clerkship by publishing the first and only insider account of the workings of the Court. But that's another story.) Ex-prosecutor and best-selling legal commentator Vincent Bugliosi's inflammatory charge is that "having Justice Antonin Scalia speak on ethics is like having a prostitute speak on sexual abstinence." Peter Laarman, minister at New York's Judson Memorial Church, gave a sermon naming Justices Scalia and Clarence Thomas as members of the "scary lunatic fringe occupying most of the seats of power."

Scoffing at the idea that our "maturing" society's "evolving standards of decency" might in and of themselves make the death penalty unconstitutional, Scalia said that the Constitution he interprets and applies is not living but dead.

But the pièce de résistance of liberal loathing can be found in a July 8, 2002, OpEd in the *New York Times* by Princeton professor Sean Wilentz. Wilentz attacked a speech Scalia had given at the University of Chicago Divinity School (and reworked for the conservative journal, *First Things*), arguing that the Eighth Amendment's prohibition of cruel and unusual punishment does not proscribe the death penalty. Scalia's remarks, wrote Wilentz, "show bitterness against democracy, strong dislike for the Constitution's approach to religion, and eager advocacy for the submission of the individual to the state. It is a chilling mixture for an American."

More important for Wilentz and his political allies, this is a chilling mixture for a chief justice—a job Scalia is rumored to want and that President George W. Bush is rumored to want him to have. While the chief is only first among equals, he has the crucial task of assigning opinions in which he is in the majority. A powerful, congenial chief such as Chief Justice Earl Warren—or William Rehnquist, for that matter—can mold the court in his image through persuasive deliberations and adept assignments. Scalia puts little effort into winning over those who disagree with him. Harvard Professor Lawrence Tribe once pointed out that Scalia's "vigor and occasional viciousness" in his written opinions may "alienate people who might be his allies in moving the Court to the right. I therefore hope he will keep it up." There's little reason to think that as chief Scalia wouldn't keep it up. After all, he recently attacked all his colleagues, asserting that the justices on the Court were no better qualified to rule on the right to die than nine people selected at random from a Kansas City phone book. He also took them on individually. He ridiculed Justice Stephen Breyer, for example, for writing a decision so vague that it gave trial courts "not a clue" as to how to carry it out. He mocked Justice David Souter for resorting "to that last hope of lost interpretive causes, that Saint Jude of the hagiography of statutory construction, legislative history."

Scalia can be particularly provocative, even shocking, on race. In a majority opinion on racially based jury selection, he attacked Justice Thurgood Marshall, saying that his dissent "rolls out the ultimate weapon, the accusation of insensitivity to racial discrimination—which will lose its intimidating effect if it continues to be fired so randomly." Given that Marshall knew far better than Scalia the reality of racial discrimination when he saw it—he was surely the only justice in the history of the Supreme Court to have once been dragged to a river by a lynch mob—even years later Scalia's words seem intemperate and misplaced.

He can also be combative on issues that usually call for compassion. He says that the death penalty, for example, is not a "difficult, soul-wrenching question." Scoffing at the idea that our "maturing" society's "evolving standards of decency" might in and of themselves make the death penalty unconstitutional, Scalia said that the Constitution he interprets and applies is not living but dead. Or, as he prefers to put it, "enduring." It means today not what current society (much less the Court) thinks it ought to mean, but what it meant when it was adopted. Scalia has even affronted his conservative Catholic supporters. He's argued (correctly) that the pope's opposition to the death penalty expressed in *Evangelium vitae* is not "binding teaching" requiring adherence by all Catholics—though they must give it

thoughtful and respectful consideration. When Cardinal Avery Dulles said he agreed with the pope's position, Scalia answered that this was "just the phenomenon of the clerical bureaucracy saying, 'Yes, boss.'"

What the pope has to say is irrelevant to him as a judge, says Scalia, since his own views on the morality of the death penalty have nothing to do with how he votes judicially. However, one's moral views do govern whether or not one can or should be a judge at all. "When I sit on a Court that reviews and affirms capital convictions," said Scalia, "I am part of 'the machinery of death.'" The Supreme Court's ruling is often the last step that permits an execution to proceed. Any judge who believes the death penalty immoral should resign, he says, rather than "simply ignoring duly enacted, constitutional laws and sabotaging death-penalty cases."

How, then, can Scalia continue to serve as a judge in a court that has repeatedly upheld abortion, which he regards as immoral? Capital cases, argues Scalia, are different from the other life-and-death issues the Court might hear, like abortion or legalized suicide. In these instances, it is not the state that is decreeing death, but private individuals whom the state has decided not to restrain. One may argue (as many do) that society has a moral obligation to interfere. That moral obligation may weigh heavily upon the voter, and upon the legislator who enacts the laws, Scalia argues, but a judge "bears no moral guilt for the laws society has failed to enact."

Ironically, despite Scalia's carefully drawn, if dubious, distinctions, Scalia's antagonist Wilentz accuses him of believing that Catholics, as citizens, would be unable to uphold views that contradict church doctrine. A shocked Wilentz says that Scalia "sees submission as desirable." This, Wilentz continues, is "exactly the stereotype of Catholicism as papist mind-control that Catholics have struggled against, and that John F. Kennedy did so much to overcome."

O bedience, for good or ill, is indeed an ongoing Scalia theme. He has joked more than once that the keys to being a good Catholic and a good jurist are the same: being strong enough to obey the relevant law. Still, he has not urged submission on American Catholic citizens.

Wilentz also writes that despite calling himself a strict constructionist—actually, he doesn't—Scalia wants to impose "a religious sense that is directly counter to the abundantly expressed wishes of the men who wrote the Constitution." This is not strict constructionism, says Wilentz. It "is opportunism, and it threatens democracy."

Is Wilentz right? Is Scalia an opportunist who threatens the very democracy whose Constitution he has sworn to uphold? Or is he a brace originalist, seeking to return to the principles of the American Founding Fathers that the Court discarded in the last fifty years?

The answer is not yet clear. Part of the anger Scalia arouses is a result of how successful he has been in restoring respect for the Constitution's actual words. Calling his approach textualism, Scalia argues that primacy must be given to the text, structure, and history of any document—Constitution or statute—being interpreted. Judges, he says, are to eschew their own "intellectual, moral, and personal perceptions." Scalia says he takes the Constitution as it is, not as he wants it to be.

In effect, of course, this is an attack on much of twentieth-century jurisprudence, which has created a host of new constitutional rights by embracing such Holmesian ideas as the "balancing of competing interests" and Justice William Brennan's "living Constitution." This expanded vision of the Constitution gave judges enormous power to assert that their individual policy preferences and social goals—however unpopular—were also the law. As Scalia wrote in his solo, and prescient, dissent in the case recognizing the constitutionality of the now notorious Office of the Special Prosecutor: "Evidently, the governing standard is to be what might be called the unfettered wisdom of a majority of this Court, revealed to an obedient people in a case-by-case basis. This is not only not the government of laws that the Constitution established, it is not a government of laws at all."

Larry Kramer, a law professor at New York University, calls Scalia's belief that judges should renounce their own desires when interpreting the law "judicial asceticism." He argues that Scalia's "formalism, textualism, and originalism are only means: denial and self-control are the reasons."

If Scalia's first sin in the eyes of doctrinaire liberals is his textualism, make no mistake about the fact that his second sin is that he is a practicing Catholic—or, as commentators repeatedly mention, a "devout" Catholic. (How the devotion is known is not clear.) Of course, the sins of textualism and Catholicism are not unrelated—both reflect respect for the written word, an ordered universe, and an attachment to tradition. And both have a long contentious relationship with liberalism. Wilentz probably put his finger on something important when he wrote, "One senses that Mr. Scalia's true priority is to get secular humanists off the federal bench."

Certainly, there is something admirable in Scalia's allegiance to tradition and his stubborn refusal to pander on moral issues—both of which predictably incite his critics to excess. Harvard Law Professor Alan Dershowitz, for example, calls Scalia the "voice of Spanish clerical conservatism." The liberal *American Prospect* magazine scathingly refers to Scalia's "Jesuitical" logic. The editor of Salon.com wrote that defenders of the Bush v. Gore decision, in which Scalia played such a large role, "would have to perform feats of casuistry unseen since the days when Ignatius Loyola strode the earth to do so." Calling Scalia a cheap-shot artist, *Washington Post* columnist Richard Cohen maintains that the justice's mind is rigid on constitutional issues between church and state: "Anyone who thinks Scalia will give First Amendment issues a fair and reasoned hearing is, it seems, proceeding in a way Scalia would appreciate: solely on faith."

These knee-jerk liberal denunciations are appalling in a way, but while some of these comments might set off alarms for William Donohue and his Catholic League cohorts, they do not represent a revival of pure, nineteenth-century anti-Catholicism.

No respectable attack was ever leveled at the Catholicism of Scalia's nemesis, Justice William Brennan. Generally thought by legal scholars (including Scalia) to have been the twentieth century's most influential justice, Brennan may well have also been the most loved. He was a brilliant, strategic, persuasive conciliator who more often than not won the day. He once said, "With five votes you can do anything around here." His "living Constitution" is both the dominant liberal constitutional concept and the polar opposite of Scalia's textualism.

Scalia, in contrast, goes out of his way to give speeches like his provocative 1996 "Fools for Christ's Sake" address at the Mississippi College of Law, a Baptist school. Most (perhaps all) of his critics missed the reference to Saint Paul and therefore misinterpreted the speech, but then Scalia pretty much knew they would. Baiting the opposition—whether outside or inside the Court—is basic to his temperament.

As a Catholic who grew up in working-class neighborhoods (even though his father was an academic), Scalia often reveals a different sensibility from his Brahmin peers. In a 1979 law review article he denounced "the Wisdoms and the Powells and the Whites," whose ancestors participated in the oppression of African Americans, and who as justice sought to correct the effects of that ancestral oppression at the expense of newer immigrants. In a 1987 dissent he defended the "unknown, unaffluent, and unorganized" workers ignored by proponents of affirmative action.

And, then, of course, there's abortion, by far the most divisive social issue of our time, and one that Scalia argues should be settled legislatively rather than judicially. Yet the conservative Rehnquist Court has signaled more than once that it's not going to reverse *Roe v. Wade*. It doesn't really matter to a majority of the Court that Scalia was probably correct when he said, "I do not believe—and for two hundred years, no one believed—that the Constitution contains a right to abortion." In *A Matter of Interpretation* (Princeton), his Tanner Lectures at Princeton, he cautions that creating new constitutional rights may trigger a majoritarian reaction. "At the end of the day," he notes, "an evolving Constitution will evolve the way the majority wishes." One has to wonder whether the 2002 elections giving the House, Senate, and (by extension, the Supreme Court) to the Republicans reflect, in part, this prediction come true.

Scalia's third sin is his shockingly bad temper, in print, toward his intellectual opponents. Some of his harshest language concerning his colleagues came in his criticism of *Roe*: "The emptiness of the 'reasoned judgment' that produced *Roe* is displayed in plain view by the fact . . . that the best the Court can do to explain how it is that the word 'liberty' must include the right to destroy human fetuses is to rattle off a collection of adjectives that simply decorate a value judgment and conceal a political choice."

That temper has regularly been directed at centrist Justice Sandra Day O'Connor, who often must be wooed as the crucial fifth vote in a conservative coalition. In dissenting from *Planned Parenthood v. Casey* (1992), Scalia questioned O'Connor's intelligence. "Reason finds no refuge in this jurisprudence of confusion," he wrote.

Such outbursts have been costly. For many years, O'Connor avoided signing majority opinions authored by Scalia, which meant that Chief Justice Rehnquist—who needed her vote—avoided assigning controversial opinions to Scalia.

Perhaps Scalia's most troubling sin is that he does not always hold himself to his own principles. He explains his judicial rigidity by saying that when "I adopt a general rule, and say 'This is the basis of our decision,' I not only constrain lower courts, I constrain myself as well. If the next case should have such different facts that my political or policy preferences regarding the outcome are quite opposite, I will be unable to indulge those preferences; I have committed myself to the governing principle." Such rules can embolden judges to be courageous when having to issue an unpopular ruling, such as one protecting a criminal defendant's rights. All around, an admirable position.

How then to explain *Bush v. Gore*, the 5-4 ruling that effectively handed the presidency to George W. Bush in 2000? Bush may well have won the election fair and square, but we'll never know for sure. This was the first time in American history that the Court decided a presidential election, and it did so by improbably concluding that Florida's diverse standards for counting votes constituted an equal protection violation under the Fourteenth Amendment. Scalia's respect for established precedents and his disdain for catchall uses of the equal protection clause suddenly didn't seem to apply here—nor did his reverence for the separation of powers. As if the decision weren't mischievous enough, the Court also pronounced—amazingly—that "our consideration is limited to the present circumstances, for the problem of equal protection in election processes generally presents many complexities." Since when does the Supreme Court limit its rulings to present circumstances?

Ironically, Scalia's tightly argued dissent in *Casey* eerily foreshadows his own lead role in the scandal of *Bush v. Gore*: "The Imperial Judiciary lives," Scalia wrote. "It is instructive to compare this Nietzschean vision of us unelected, life-tenured judges—leading a Volk who will be 'tested by following,' and whose very 'belief in themselves' is mystically bound up in their 'understanding' of a Court that 'speak[s] before all others for their constitutional ideals'—with the somewhat more modest role envisioned for these lawyers by the Founders."

How can Scalia reconcile his principled views with his vote in *Bush v. Gore*? There aren't many convincing answers. His opponents claim Scalia acted as a ruthless, self-serving politician who put his own boy in power when it looked like the other side might win. Another possible explanation is that Scalia believes deeply something else he said in his *Casey* dissent, which is that *Roe* "fanned into life an issue that has inflamed our national politics in general, and has obscured with its smoke the selection of justices to this Court, in particular, ever since." In other words, the Court has embroiled itself in political issues that should be left to the people and their representatives—and that only a Republican administration would set the Court back on its right course. (It is not at all clear that this will happen.) Thus Scalia saw nothing wrong with the

language he used in concurring with the Court's stay (by definition an emergency measure) halting the Florida vote recount. Continuing the manual count, wrote Scalia, would "threaten irreparable harm" to Bush "and to the country, by casting a cloud upon what he claims to be the legitimacy of his election." He may never have written a less convincing justification of one of his positions, but it makes some sense if understood in light of how far wrong he thinks the Court has gone.

Scalia has spent most of his career captivating others, who often let their affection for him overcome their distaste for some of his ideas. He is a social animal, and it is possible that his fury about being correct yet alone over several momentous issues has warped his judgment on others—on which he is probably not right. His wrath is born of his self-confidence in the face of universal opposition. Take two 1988 dissents, *Morrison* and *Mistretta*, which, in the words of Northwestern University Law Professor Thomas Merrill, showed Scalia to be "completely isolated" on the Court. Isolated he may have been, but he was also completely right.

Morrison v. Olson was the decision upholding the Independent Counsel Act. Scalia's colleagues thought he had pretty much lost it when he ferociously wrote, "The institutional design of the Independent Counsel is designed to heighten, not to check, all of the institutional hazards of the dedicated prosecutor; the danger of too narrow a focus, of the loss of perspective, of preoccupation with the pursuit of one alleged suspect to the exclusion of other interests." With unchecked discretionary powers and unlimited funds, the independent counsel would be accountable to no one and would be entirely focused on a single target. The office would encourage the worst tendencies in American democracy. "The context of this statute is acrid with the smell of threatened impeachment," wrote Scalia. Indeed.

The history of the Independent Counsel Act is replete with examples of prosecutorial abuse that would have made the Founders recoil. Scalia accurately predicted, "If the prosecutor is obliged to choose his case, it follows that he can choose his defendants. Therein is the most dangerous power of the prosecutor: that he will pick people that he thinks he should get, rather than cases that need to be prosecuted. . . . It is not a question of discovering the commission of a crime and then looking for the man who has committed it, it is a question of picking the man and then searching the law books, or putting investigators to work, to pin some offense on him."

Mistretta v. U.S., the other dissent that isolated Scalia, concerned a revolution in criminal sentencing that has gone almost unnoticed by most Americans. In 1984, Congress established the U.S. Sentencing Commission as an independent rule-making body to promulgate mandatory guidelines for every federal criminal offense. The act specifically rejected rehabilitation as a goal of imprisonment, and mandated instead "that punishment should serve retributive, educational, deterrent, and incapacitative goals." All sentences would become determinate (fixed), with no parole other than a small credit that could be earned by good behavior.

Indeed, the country has grappled with the gross injustices of federal sentencing. In the past, judges were able to use their discretion to minimize inequities in the law. No longer. Now judges are governed by this new branch of government, by what Scalia mockingly calls "a sort of junior-varsity Congress."

Scalia lost on *Mistretta*, but he eventually won on another crucial sentencing issue—victim impact statements. In the mid-1970s, the Supreme Court had begun requiring that defendants in capital cases be allowed to present "mitigating circumstances" during the sentencing phase of capital trials. Yet while defendants in particularly heinous crimes could present evidence about an abusive childhood, victims and their families had no standing to speak. The Supreme Court repeatedly said victim-impact statements created a constitutionally unacceptable risk of arbitrary and capricious decisions by juries. Worse, they would focus attention not on the moral guilt of the defendant's alleged harms to society but on the emotions and opinions of persons who were not parties to the crime. Scalia dissented, attacking the "recently invented" requirement of mitigating circumstances, asking why the jury could not also take into account "the specific harm visited upon society by a murderer." In 1991, in *Payne v. Tennessee*, the Court finally agreed and overturned the ban on victim-impact statements. Justice Marshall announced his retirement the same day—some said because his heart was broken.

This term the Court has ruled 5 to 4 on another sentencing issue—California's three-strikes law. Like victim-impact statements, added punishment for multiple offenses has a long tradition in the common law. Adopted by referendum in 1994, California's harsh law permits judges to treat crimes that would ordinarily be considered misdemeanors as third felonies. (Most states with three-strikes laws require the third strike to actually be a felony, usually a violent one.) The particular cases before the Court involved life sentences for two men whose third crimes were shoplifting—$1,200 worth of golf clubs in one case, and $154 worth of children's videotapes in the other.

Here was a case with Scalia's favorite elements: the direct voice of the majority expressed via referendum, state sovereignty via its law, and centuries of Anglo-Saxon tradition. All of these considerations were to be weighed in determining the punishment of two career criminals who had led astonishingly unproductive lives. What should society do with such people? It is a testament to the revolution Scalia has wrought that this case even came before the Court, much less that the Court upheld three strikes. No longer do courts cavalierly assume that the Constitution prevents Americans from protecting themselves against known repeat predators. We are reminded, again, that in most matters of criminal justice, Scalia is the people champion— even if this decision was written by his protagonist, Justice O'Connor, leaving him to concur. This, in turn, reminds us of the conundrum of his role in *Bush v. Gore*. There he seemed to place the "irreparable harm" that a Florida recount would do to petitioner George W. Bush above the irreparable harm to citizens whose votes would not even be counted. Is Antonin Scalia an opportunist or an originalist? Perhaps he is both.

JULIA VITULLO-MARTIN writes frequently for *Commonweal,* the *Wall Street Journal,* and other publications. She is working on a book on the American Jury and Criminal Law.

UNIT 5

Juvenile Justice

Unit Selections

Key Points to Consider

- What reform efforts are currently under way in the juvenile justice system?

- What are some recent trends in juvenile delinquency? In what ways will the juvenile justice system be affected by these trends?

- Is the departure of the juvenile justice system from its original purpose warranted? Why or why not?

Student Web Site
www.mhcls.com/online

Internet References
Further information regarding these Web sites may be found in this book's preface or online.

Gang Land: The Jerry Capeci Page
   http://www.ganglandnews.com
Institute for Intergovernmental Research (IIR)
   http://www.iir.com
National Criminal Justice Reference Service (NCJRS)
   http://virlib.ncjrs.org/JuvenileJustice.asp
Partnership Against Violence Network
   http://www.pavnet.org

The McGraw-Hill Companies, Inc./Gary He, photographer

Although there were variations within specific offense categories, the overall arrest rate for juvenile violent crime remained relatively constant for several decades. Then, in the late 1980s something changed, bringing more and more juveniles charged with a violent offense into the justice system. The juvenile justice system is a twentieth-century response to the problems of dealing with children in trouble with the law, or children who need society's protection.

Juvenile court procedure differs from the procedure in adult courts because juvenile courts are based on the philosophy that their function is to treat and to help, not to punish and abandon the offender. Recently, operations of the juvenile court have received criticism, and a number of significant Supreme Court decisions have changed the way that the courts must approach the rights of children. Despite these changes, however, the major thrust of the juvenile justice system remains one of diversion and treatment, rather than adjudication and incarceration, although there is a trend toward dealing more punitively with serious juvenile offenders.

This unit's opening article, "Reforming Juvenile Justice" reminds us that a century ago reformers proved that prisons didn't help wayward children. Now America is learning that lesson all over again. In spite of numerous studies casting doubt on DARE's effectiveness, "DARE Program: Sacred Cow or Fatted Calf?" points out that these programs continue through the country.

In the next article in this unit, "The 21st Century Juvenile Justice Work Force," the authors examine the difficulty corrections departments face in recruitment for positions in juvenile corrections. "Teens Caught in the Middle: Juvenile Justice System and Treatment," shows the frustrations and inadequacies of the justice system in dealing with teen crime. In "Jailed for Life After Crimes as Teenagers," Adam Liptak, after noting that this country is one of only a handful that puts young people behind bars for the rest of their lives, writes about some of the young people who are serving such sentences.

Concluding this section, the authors of "Co-Offending and Patterns of Juvenile Crime" show how co-offending is related to the age of offenders, recidivism, and violence.

Reforming Juvenile Justice

A century ago, reformers proved that prisons don't help wayward children. Now America is learning that lesson all over again.

Barry Krisberg

In 1899, Illinois and Colorado established a new "Children's Court." The idea was to substitute treatment and care for punishment of delinquent youths. These changes were promoted by child advocates such as the famous social activist Jane Addams and crusading judges like Denver's Ben Lindsey, as well as influential women's organizations and bar associations. Over the next 20 years, the concept of a separate court system for minors spread to most states. Although the new children's court movement lacked adequate resources to fulfill its lofty mission, the intellectual promise was virtually unchallenged for two-thirds of the 20th century.

Several key assumptions lay behind the juvenile-court idea. First, children were not just "small adults," and they needed to be handled differently. Second, there was a need for specially trained legal and correctional professionals to work with minors. Third, placing children in adult prisons and jails made them more antisocial and criminal. And finally, the emerging science of rehabilitation could rescue many of these troubled young people from lives of crime. In the intervening years, a wealth of research has validated each of these premises.

Despite broad support within the academic, legal, and social-work professions, the ideal often failed to live up to its promise. Over time, the juvenile-justice system in many states reverted to the punitive approach it was designed to replace. Though they were often called "training schools," the institutions were juvenile prisons. And the premise that the court, by definition, was acting "in the best interest of the child" left young offenders without the rights guaranteed to adult criminal defendants. There were repeated accounts of abusive practices. The duration of confinement was often unrelated to the severity of the offense. Juvenile hearings were usually secret, with no written transcripts and no right to appeal. Minors were not provided legal counsel, there were no safeguards against self-incrimination, and offenders were denied liberty without the due process of law guaranteed by the U.S. Constitution.

A series of legal challenges culminated in the landmark 1967 Supreme Court decision *In Re Gault*. Writing for the Court, Justice Abe Fortes proclaimed, "Under our Constitution, the condition of being a boy does not justify a kangaroo court." Reviewing the case of 15-year-old Gerald Gault, who was sentenced to six years in an Arizona youth correctional facility for making an obscene phone call, the Court decreed that minors be afforded most of the due-process rights required in adult criminal courts.

Gault signaled a new era of reforms. One was a movement to divert as many youths as possible from the formal court system and to decriminalize "juvenile status offenses" such as truancy, running away, curfew violations, and incorrigibility. The 1970s witnessed widespread efforts to deinstitutionalize or "decarcerate" youngsters, moving them from secure detention centers and training schools to community-based programs that emphasized education and rehabilitation.

The most dramatic example came in 1972 in Massachusetts, where a respected reformer closed all of the state juvenile facilities and started over. Jerome Miller had been recruited to the state Department of Youth Services (DYS) to clean up a range of scandals and abuses. He encountered an intransigent bureaucracy. Corrections officers opposed even such modest reforms as letting youngsters wear street clothing instead of prison uniforms, or not requiring that their heads be completely shaven. Undeterred, Miller decided to close down the state's network of jail-like training schools. As the young inmates of the notorious Lyman School were loaded onto a bus that would take them to dorms at the University of Massachusetts, to be housed temporarily until being reassigned to community programs, one top Miller deputy proclaimed to the shocked guards, "You can have the institutions; we are taking the kids."

The training schools were replaced with a diverse network of small residential programs, typically with 25 children or fewer, located closer to the youths' home communities. A range of nonresidential programs included day reporting centers and intensive home-based supervision. The DYS continued to operate about half of the most secure facilities. Private nonprofits were recruited to run the rest, as well as all of the community-based programs.

Although Miller left Massachusetts soon after becoming the department's youth-services commissioner, the Bay State continued to expand and refine the alternatives to the old prison-like training schools and never reopened the large juvenile institutions. Research by Harvard Law School and my organization, the National Council on Crime and Delinquency, showed that the Miller reforms successfully reduced the frequency and severity of new offenses of youth in the new programs compared with the training-school graduates.

As the Massachusetts model spread to many other states, Congress in 1974 created the federal Juvenile Justice and Delinquency Prevention Act, with bipartisan backing. The act established a federal Office of Juvenile Justice and Delinquency Prevention (OJJDP) to conduct research, provide training, and make grants to states and jurisdictions that voluntarily complied with the act's mandates. The new law required participating states to remove status offenders and dependency cases from secure confinement, and to separate juveniles from adults by "sight and sound" in correctional facilities. In 1980, the act was amended to require that participating states remove minors from jails. Forty-eight states participated.

Miller went on to implement variations of his Massachusetts reforms in Pennsylvania and Illinois. Other states that broadly followed Miller's model included jurisdictions as politically diverse as Utah, Missouri, and Vermont. Often, publicity about abusive conditions in state facilities and lawsuits in federal courts catalyzed these reforms. From 1980 into the 1990s, Colorado, Indiana, Oklahoma, Maryland, Louisiana, Florida, Georgia, Rhode Island, and New Jersey were among states that began closing large, prison-like youth facilities. For a time, it appeared that the Miller reforms would become the "gold standard" for juvenile corrections, as the federal OJJDP provided training and support to jurisdictions seeking to replicate the Massachusetts approach.

The much-advertised generation of super-predators never materialized. After 1993, serious juvenile crime began a decade-long decline to historically low levels.

The Invention of the "Super-Predator"

The rejection in some quarters of a reform model reflects both ideological preconceptions and misinformation about juvenile crime. Rates of serious violent juvenile crime as measured by the National Crime Survey were relatively constant between 1973 and 1989, then briefly rose by more than one-third and peaked in 1993. Some cited demographics, as the children of the baby boomers reached their teenage years. Others pointed to an epidemic of crack cocaine that fueled urban violence, as well as high unemployment and declining economic prospects

for low-skilled workers, especially among minority groups. No one really knows for sure. But fear of a violent juvenile crime wave led some to predict a new cohort of "super-predators." Conservative academics such as James Q. Wilson and John DiIulio and a small band of mainstream criminologists such as Alfred Blumstein and James Fox forecast societal disaster. Wilson predicted "30,000 more young muggers, killers, and thieves"; DiIulio in 1990 foresaw another 270,000 violent juveniles by 2010. He warned of a "crime bomb" created by a generation of "fatherless, godless, and jobless [juvenile] super-predators."

The media hyped the story, and many elected officials exploited it. The citizenry was told about a generation of babies, born to "crack-addicted" mothers, who would possess permanent neurological damage, including the inability to feel empathy. The scientific evidence supporting this claim was nonexistent. More than 40 states made it easier to transfer children to adult criminal courts. Educators enacted "zero-tolerance" policies to make it easier to expel youngsters from school, and numerous communities adopted youth curfews. Many jurisdictions turned to metal detectors in public schools, random locker searches, drug tests for athletes, and mandatory school uniforms.

The panic was bipartisan. Every crime bill debated by Congress during the Clinton administration included new federal laws against juvenile crime. Paradoxically, as Attorney General Janet Reno advocated for wider and stronger social safety nets for vulnerable families, President Bill Clinton joined congressional leaders demanding tougher treatment of juvenile felons, including more incarceration in both the adult and youth correctional systems.

However, the much-advertised generation of super-predators never materialized. After 1993, rates of serious juvenile crime began a decade-long decline to historically low levels. And this juvenile crime drop happened before the tougher juvenile penalties were even implemented. The fear-mongering social scientists had based their dire predictions on grossly inaccurate data and faulty reasoning, but the creators of the super-predator myth prevailed in the public-policy arena throughout most of the '90s. As we approached the centennial of the American juvenile court, it looked like the juvenile-justice ideal was dying.

The Ideal of Juvenile Justice Survives

Despite adverse political currents, the juvenile-justice ideal has received a new lease on life thanks to pioneering efforts by states and by foundations, as well as the continuing programmatic influence of the federal approach begun in the 1970s and expanded during the Clinton-Reno era.

One key initiative of the federal OJJDP is known as Balanced and Restorative Justice. This approach, now embraced by many jurisdictions, places a major value on involving victims in the rehabilitative process. By coming to terms with harm done to victims, the youthful offender is also offered a way to restore his or her role in the community.

The second significant federal program is the Justice Department's Comprehensive Strategy for Serious, Violent, and Chronic Juvenile Offenders, first adopted in 1993. The research showed that a very small number of offenders committed most serious juvenile crimes, and that identification and control of these "dangerous few" was key. However, unlike the response to the supposed super-predators, this strategy does not call for an across-the-board crackdown on at-risk youth. A comprehensive body of research assembled by two senior Justice Department juvenile-justice officials, John J. Wilson and James C. Howell, showed that prevention was the most cost-effective response to youth crime, and that strengthening the family and other core institutions was the most important goal for a youth-crime-control strategy.

The proposed comprehensive strategy was adopted by Reno as the official policy position of the Justice Department in all matters relating to juvenile crime, and the program was successfully implemented in more than 50 communities nationwide. The basic idea was to help local leaders build their youth-service systems to provide "the right service, for the right youth, at the right time." This collaborative planning process helped policymakers and professionals to debunk the myths about juvenile crime and to learn about interventions that were proven, as well as to foster more cooperative activities among multiple agencies. Most important, the effort showed community participants how to effectively respond to juvenile lawbreaking without resorting to mass-incarceration policies.

A third major national reform movement was launched by the Annie E. Casey Foundation in 1992. The goal: to reduce the overuse of juvenile-detention facilities and to redirect funding toward more effective services for at-risk youngsters. The foundation also sought to improve the conditions of confinement for detained youth and to reduce the overrepresentation of minority youths in detention.

The Casey Foundation approach required a multiagency planning process and included the development of improved risk screening, expansion of options for most detained youths, and efforts to expedite the processing of cases. After initial demonstration projects, the foundation has expanded the program to scores of communities. It also offers technical assistance and convenes an annual meeting. At the last such convening, in San Francisco, more than 700 people from across the nation gathered to discuss ways to further reduce unnecessary juvenile detention. The original demonstration project has led to a vibrant national movement, which includes high-quality replication manuals and a documentary, plus academic and professional publications.

These approaches all require collaborations among many sectors of the community. They all employ data and evidence-based practices to guide the reform agenda. Diversity is recognized as vital because one-size-fits-all programs usually fail. Instead, they seek to create a comprehensive continuum of appropriate services. Preventive strategies and early interventions are viewed as far more cost-effective than punitive approaches. All these programs place a great emphasis on involving youth, plus their families and neighbors, in shaping solutions. The core values of the juvenile-justice ideal continue to live. Like the reform impulse of a century ago, the goal is to commit the juvenile-justice system to pursuing the best interests of the child, to strengthening family and community solutions to youth misconduct, and to emphasizing humane and fair treatment of the young.

In spite of the promise embodied in approaches like these, unlawful and brutal practices continue to plague youth correctional facilities in many states. Some jurisdictions are being investigated by the federal government for statutory and constitutional violations of the rights of institutionalized minors. In other locales, advocates for young people are successfully litigating against youth detention and corrections facilities. At the same time, the political hysteria surrounding the super-predator myth appears to be in remission. The chorus is growing to reject approaches such as youth correctional boot camps or "scared straight" programs that use prison visits to try to frighten youngsters away from criminal lives. While some of these dangerous programs continue to exist, many jurisdictions have shut them down. There is growing awareness about the prevalence of mental illness among institutionalized youngsters and the emergence of several initiatives to better meet their health-care needs.

This year's most positive development was the Supreme Court's decision to end the death penalty for those younger than 18 at the time of their offense. But this progress does not minimize the severe problems of the juvenile-justice system. Funding for services for troubled young people in the juvenile-justice and child-welfare systems remains woefully inadequate. Young people still do not have anything resembling adequate legal representation. Too many continue to be banished to the criminal-court system and languish in adult prisons. And racism, sexism, and class biases continue to tarnish the promise of equal justice for all.

The Way Forward

This *American Prospect* special supplement includes reports from places as diverse as California, Texas, New Mexico, Missouri, and Louisiana. All suggest that reform coalitions, often with strange bedfellows, can acknowledge the superiority of the reform approach and change practices that dehumanize young people and fail to reduce juvenile crime. By now the evidence is clear: Small, community-based approaches that stress prevention, education, and restitution rather than prison-like punishment are simply better policy. At the same time, as Ellis Cose recounts, racial disparities remain immense. And as Sam Rosenfeld reports, far too many children who need mental-health services are being dumped into the juvenile-justice system.

Given the overwhelming evidence that reform works, why is there continuing resistance? The answer to this question is complex. First and foremost, since the mid-'60s, crime policy in the United States has been heavily politicized. Democrats and Republicans have competed to position themselves as tough on crime. Being perceived as soft on juvenile offenders is considered a political liability. Second, the media continue to exaggerate the amount of violent crime committed by minors. Isolated stories about vicious crimes that are committed by very young adolescents are widely disseminated and become the grist for talk radio and other media commentary. The simplistic solution has been that tough responses to juvenile crime will deter youthful offenders.

Resistance to proven juvenile-justice models often comes from public-employee unions that fear the loss of jobs as traditional youth correctional facilities are downsized and some funding goes to community-based organizations. Also, severe state and local budget problems have led to a retrenchment in needed services, even as more innovative juvenile-justice models could actually save money. In some locales, organizations purporting to represent families of crime victims have lobbied for tougher penalties for juvenile offenders.

Progressive reforms are often undercut by entrenched biases about the predominantly poor and minority families caught up in the juvenile-justice system. These racial, ethnic, and class prejudices are too often reinforced by media reports that breed fear among the electorate about the "barbarians at the gates." As long as economic and fiscal pressures fuel anxiety over immigrants, the increased competition for jobs, and the deteriorating public-school system, it will be hard to generate compassionate and rational responses for youthful lawbreakers.

Jerome Miller once observed that the history of juvenile justice reflects a pattern of abuse and scandal followed by humanistic changes, but then a return to the previous conditions and bad practices. In a new millennium, one can only hope that proponents of the juvenile-justice ideal can figure out how to end this tragic cycle.

BARRY KRISBERG is president of the National Council on Crime and Delinquency, which is based in Oakland, California.

DARE Program: Sacred Cow or Fatted Calf?

Julia C. Mead

"Are you ready to rock?" Police Officer Theresa Tedesco shouted into the microphone. In thunderous unison, 300 sixth graders at Hampton Bays Elementary School shouted back, "Yes!"

Parents and some grandparents packed the bleachers and lined up along the walls for the Jan. 23 ceremony put on for graduates of DARE, the Drug Abuse Resistance Education program. The students turned cartwheels, performed a rap song and took turns reciting lines in skits they wrote themselves. The first-place finishers in an essay contest each read their winning submissions.

The essays, like the hand-drawn posters hung on the gym walls, offered variations on a single theme: that tobacco, illegal drugs and violence are dangerous. It's the central message that thousands of students across Suffolk are taught each year in the DARE program.

Suffolk is not alone. The DARE America curriculum, developed two decades ago by members of the Los Angeles Police Department, has been adopted by 80 percent of all schools nationwide. It puts uniformed officers in elementary and middle-school classrooms to teach about the dangers of tobacco, alcohol, controlled or illegal drugs and violence. The officers also propose ways to help students resist the temptation to experiment or to act out aggressions, and they provide warnings about the consequences if they don't.

But there's a catch: numerous studies across the country, including one in Suffolk two years ago, cast doubt on DARE's effectiveness. Its graduates are no less likely to use drugs than other children, the studies have concluded.

Nevertheless, the program remains enormously popular. So popular, in fact, that any suggestion that it be replaced with a more effective or less expensive program tends to raise howls of protest from parents, school officials and the police.

As a result, Suffolk lawmakers girding to do battle with a projected $250 million budget shortfall in 2005 are reluctant to take any overt jab at DARE, even though it costs the police department nearly $3 million a year.

"We suspect that there are gaping holes in the program and that it may not be cost-effective, but legislators are politicians," said one Suffolk legislator, who spoke on the condition that his name

not be used. "No one's going to risk their political future by doing anything other than standing up with the parents. Parents vote."

Other legislators said that asking school districts to help bear the cost of DARE has never been more than talk. "The schools are up against a rock and a hard place already," said Joseph Caracappa, the Legislature's presiding officer. "And it would just shift the tax burden from one district to another."

Steve Levy, the new county executive, was elected on a reform platform that called for a soup-to-nuts evaluation of all county spending and promised aggressive change wherever he found waste and inefficiency. Although the police department's budget is squarely in his crosshairs, Mr. Levy declined last week to say that DARE was.

What Mr. Levy would say was that within a month his staff would begin looking at ways to use DARE officers for other police work during school vacations.

He also said that the new police commissioner, Richard Dormer, would help evaluate DARE itself for possible improvements and that civilian teachers might be used in parts of the program. "We're believers in the concept, but we have to find the best implementation," Mr. Levy said. "It will likely stay in place through the rest of this school year as it is. If there are changes, they'll take place in September."

In an echo of a recommendation made two years ago by a countywide study, he said those changes could include moving some DARE officers out of elementary schools and into high schools. The program might also be extended to both the lower and higher grades. "We may have to experiment to find the best age bracket," he said.

Most Suffolk schools customize DARE America's curriculums and pick and choose which grades to use them in. Some, like Hampton Bays, use the program only in one grade, typically the fifth or sixth.

Dr. Lee Koppelman, the executive director of the Long Island Regional Planning Board, said the board's 2001 study looked at schools across Suffolk and at the incidence of drug abuse among DARE graduates. It concluded, as studies elsewhere have, that the program was ineffective in the long term.

"You can't have a 10-week session in sixth grade and expect it to have enduring, lifelong qualities," Dr. Koppelman said.

"We found it was generally effective while the students were in the program, but in terms of lasting impact, it didn't measure up. If I had my druthers, it would be taught from fifth through 12th grade. That would be a real opportunity to address addictive behavior."

Asked what became of his study, he replied, "Nothing."

Mr. Dormer, the new police commissioner, was noncommittal about DARE, saying only that he planned to evaluate the program with one eye on the 2005 budget.

DARE America has countered criticisms by revamping its curriculum for middle-school students, compacting what was a 17-week course into 10 weeks and trying to make it more realistic, said Sgt. Enrico Annichiarico, the head of the Suffolk Police Department's DARE office. He supervises 28 officers, 6 of them with teaching degrees, who work in about 180 schools.

Sergeant Annichiarico said the new curriculum placed emphasis on the seventh and ninth grades, which he called a sign that DARE America was "keeping up with the times" and was responding to criticism about not addressing the needs of older students who are more at risk.

Bemoaning the lack of any frank public discussion of DARE's shortcomings, Dr. Koppelman said its widespread popularity was "part of the problem."

School administrators like DARE because it allows them to send out an anti-drug message at no cost to their districts. Police departments pay most of the costs, and the local P.T.A. typically covers the incidentals, like the DARE T-shirts given to every graduate and for pizza for the graduation party.

"It really is a good deal for the district," said Marc Meyer, the acting principal of Hampton Bays Elementary School. Mr. Meyer, like officials in other districts, said he had heard about but had not read studies critical of DARE. "I have to admit that my view is skewed because I love the program," he said.

Other school officials said they had never studied its effectiveness and had no intention to do so. "We've never discussed that," said George Leeman, the Hampton Bays school board president. "We've always supported its continuation."

Parents say they like DARE because they believe their children's enthusiasm is a sign that they are getting the "Just Say No and Mean It" message.

Dorothy and John Capuano, whose daughter Amanda, 11, graduated from the Hampton Bays DARE program on Jan. 23, said that the program helped students resist peer pressure, encouraging them to think about the possible consequences of drug and alcohol use and to choose positive alternatives, like sports.

"It puts in the kids' faces what can happen if they make bad choices," Mrs. Capuano said. "Some parents don't know how to do that."

Her husband said: "We both quit smoking 10 years ago, and we talk to our kids about the mistakes we made. But I also tell them that, because we didn't have DARE when I was a kid, we didn't know that we had choices."

They conceded their daughter was probably too young to experience real temptation. "But it's a good influence," Mr. Capuano said. "It's another opportunity for her to make a good decision."

Besides, his wife added, "The kids think it's cool to be in DARE."

Police officials are equally enthusiastic about DARE. "Putting a uniformed officer into the school helps build relationships with the kids, with the community," said David Hegermiller, the chief of the Riverhead Town Police Department. "Police departments certainly do get a lot of public relations mileage out of that."

Although he was aware of the criticism of DARE, he and other police officials called the program the one "proactive thing" that departments can do to fight violence and drug and alcohol use. Everything else, they said, amounts to reactive mopping up after the damage has been done.

"The parents go crazy if anyone talks about stopping it," Chief Hegermiller said. "They like the contact between the officer and the kids, too, but when I talk about putting officers in the schools in some other capacity, they start screaming. It doesn't make sense to me because I see them as the same thing."

But Dr. Koppelman said he found that DARE's message and its widespread popularity provide little more than a false sense of security and an unearned opportunity for parents, the police and educators to be self-congratulatory.

"The kids like it because they get recognition and having a police officer in the classroom is a novel thing," he said. "And parents whose kids don't have drug problems to begin with think that DARE is responsible. But the real serious problem is that behind all the fun and recognition and hoopla is a valid concept that hasn't been allowed to work because it isn't pounded into these children throughout the educational process. Like anything else, it wears off."

The 21st Century Juvenile Justice Work Force

MEGHAN HOWE, ELYSE CLAWSON AND JOHN LARIVEE

Corrections is facing a work force crisis, as are many other fields in the public sector. Changing demographics are leading to a dwindling number of motivated, qualified workers entering and remaining in the corrections field. This reduction of potential employees is coupled with the challenges that agencies face in a dynamic field, where the number of clients is increasing and policy and practice are continuously evolving. The field is facing a serious question of how to keep up.

The American Correctional Association is meeting this challenge with its Building a Correctional Workforce for the 21st Century project. This includes both adult and juvenile corrections, and has begun to identify the work force needs and concerns regarding front-line workers in both arenas. This begs the question: Is it appropriate to consider juvenile and adult correctional workers as one work force? While both groups fulfill a critical public safety role, juvenile justice is additionally charged with a child welfare role. The potential of the work force to nurture the positive growth and development of children, or conversely to place children in harm's way, adds another dimension to the consequences of a work force crisis in juvenile justice. Thus, it is worthwhile to consider this work force as a separate entity.

Juvenile Jusitice Workers

There is little specific information available on the juvenile justice work force. Aggregate data on the number of workers in the field, their education and experience levels, average salary, and demographic information are generally best-guess estimates. This is the case for several reasons. Juvenile justice often is not considered a field on its own, which discourages the collection and tracking of data on the work force. The Bureau of Labor Statistics[1] does not maintain a job classification for juvenile detention workers or juvenile probation officers, so no specific trend or forecasting data are available at the national level. In many cases, individual agencies maintain work force data for their own population, but no comprehensive efforts have been undertaken to compile and analyze this Information.

However, three initiatives have shed some light on the state of the juvenile justice work force. The first is ACA's 21st century work force effort, which is aimed at developing a strategic plan for the correctional work force and draws predominantly from data on the adult correctional work force. The second is the Human Services Workforce Initiative, funded by the Annie E. Casey Foundation (of which the authors are grantees) and administered through Cornerstones for Kids. This initiative is attempting to improve outcomes for children and families by improving the quality of the human services work force, including juvenile justice. The third initiative relies on data compiled by the National Center on Juvenile Justice, such as state profiles that include some training, caseload and salary information for probation officers. In addition, some of these data are confounded with information from adult correctional departments.

Together, these initiatives describe several characteristics of the work force, as well as several areas for further research:

- According to the Annie E. Casey Foundation, the juvenile justice work force comprises approximately 300,000 workers earning an average of $30,000 per year.[2]
- Several studies[3] indicate that workers remain in the field because they enjoy working with children and families, and they want to help children achieve meaningful outcomes.
- Workers leave the field because of long hours, insufficient support from supervisors, low pay, lack of a career ladder and high stress.[4]
- Workers perceive that they are managing more high-need children than in the past, such as those with substance abuse or mental health disorders, and that they are not trained to manage this population.[5]
- Working conditions vary widely between agencies, but many workers feel that they work in unsafe conditions.[6]

Though this information is not representative, it paints a picture of many employees who are dedicated to the needs of children but often frustrated with stressful working conditions and a lack of recognition and opportunities for advancement.

The Human Services Workforce Initiative also sought to identify the competencies (i.e., the knowledge, skills and attributes) that make an effective juvenile justice worker. Both front-line staff and managers listed similar competencies, including good communication skills, patience, creativity, respect, motivation, compassion and commitment to youths. However, many workers also agreed that these attributes were not necessarily reflected in job descriptions and that agencies do not always know how to hire for those competencies.

Role Duality in Juvenile Justice

Juvenile justice workers fulfill a dual role: a public safety and accountability role, which involves the management of youths' behavior, and a rehabilitation and youth development role, which involves mentoring and coaching youths in pro-social skill development. This duality is a source of frustration as well as opportunity among the juvenile justice workers.

A source of frustration is that the field is not well defined for potential and current employees. This results in confusion for workers who are not well prepared for their role[7] and difficulty in recruiting workers who are appropriately educated and trained. Many juvenile justice positions now require a bachelor's degree. However, degrees in the social sciences or social work do not prepare candidates for the public safety aspect of the job, and programs in criminal justice do not address the youth development role of the juvenile justice worker. In both cases, it is possible to complete a degree without ever taking a course specifically related to juvenile justice; such courses may not even be offered for interested students. As a result, students may leave college without considering juvenile justice as an option, without an understanding of what the work entails or with the idea that juvenile justice is simply a stepping stone to a career in adult corrections.

For entry-level employees, role duality can be especially frustrating because the job is not what they expected, because they see inconsistency within the organization or because they do not see their colleagues as supportive. For example, corrections-minded individuals may not perceive their treatment-minded colleagues as supportive in maintaining safety and holding youths accountable for their behavior, while treatment-minded workers may feel that corrections-minded workers treat children too much like adult offenders. These are generalities, of course, and most employees fall on a continuum rather than at the extremes of these perceptions. However, the attempt to blend these two mindsets is a source of frustration for juvenile justice workers.

The opportunity of this duality lies in the fact that juvenile justice falls into the realm of corrections and human services work. Juvenile justice can take advantage of work force development efforts in both arenas. In addition, potential juvenile justice workers can be drawn from the applicant pool for both sectors, thereby increasing the likelihood of recruiting candidates with required competencies. If social work and criminal justice students are given opportunities for informational sessions, coursework and internships in juvenile justice, they may find that the mix of competencies required in juvenile justice is an excellent match to their skills.

Unique Concerns

Several issues in juvenile justice differ from adult corrections and human services, and require attention. The results of a 2003 ACA work force study[8] emphasize the need to market juvenile justice as a viable career option and to work with educational institutions to ensure that new workers are prepared for the challenges of the job.

According to the survey, 24 percent of respondents from juvenile correctional facilities reported that recruitment was "extremely difficult," compared with only 10 percent of those from adult institutions.

In addition, juvenile facilities were more likely to cite a "shortage of applicants" (42 percent juvenile vs. 33 percent adult), "too few applicants that meet job requirements" (24 percent vs. 13 percent) and "young people lack knowledge of profession" (21 percent vs. 12 percent).

Data from a Brookings Institution survey[9] of students pursuing Bachelor of Arts and social work degrees at top colleges support ACA's findings:

- When asked whether they had considered working in juvenile justice, 86 percent answered "not too seriously" or "not seriously at all."
- When asked how informed they were about career opportunities in juvenile justice, 73 percent were "not too informed" or "not informed at all."

These data point to a marketing crisis in juvenile justice. To increase the potential applicant pool, the field must engage in a public relations campaign to improve understanding of what juvenile justice work entails. This lack of public awareness could intensify the work force crisis if other fields start to vigorously recruit available workers. Many juvenile justice employees report that they came to juvenile justice as a stepping stone to other jobs and discovered that they loved the work. If in-demand workers no longer need the juvenile justice stepping stone, juvenile justice may be bypassed as a career option.

Where to Go from Here

As the demand for correctional and human service workers grows, juvenile justice agencies will face competition from both fronts in hiring and retaining a qualified work force. Juvenile justice agencies, in partnership with their human services and adult corrections counterparts, can take several steps to ameliorate a juvenile justice work force crisis.

Collect more data on the work force. A dearth of information is available on work force demographics, working conditions and, most notably, the pathways by which individuals enter and leave the field. Without more primary research, the unique needs of the juvenile justice work force cannot be completely understood.

Tailor promising practices to the needs of the juvenile justice work force. Juvenile justice work is unique among both corrections and human services professions, combining elements of youth development, child welfare, education and public safety. Many work-force-related promising practices put forth in corrections and human services are relevant to juvenile justice but must be tailored to attract the right people for the job. This should include raising the profile of juvenile justice as a career option.

Address adult and juvenile justice work force in tandem. Unless jurisdictions' work force issues are addressed simultaneously in the adult and juvenile systems, an improvement in one will likely be at the expense of the other. If both adult and juvenile corrections increase their desirability as employers, then employees can self-select the workplace that best suits them, and agencies can more carefully match employees to their population.

Increase public perception of juvenile justice as a desirable career choice. Qualified individuals are not going to enter juvenile justice without an awareness of what the work entails and the opportunity to access appropriate education and training. Unless the field increases the visibility of the unique aspects of juvenile justice work and facilitates opportunities for education and training, other more visible fields will lure away qualified applicants.

Increase the diversity of the work force. Though juvenile justice is increasingly employing more women, individuals of color and bilingual/bicultural staff, much more must be done to align staff demographics with client demographics. Targeted recruitment of a more diverse work force serves the dual purpose of increasing the available applicant pool while reflecting the diversity of the community and the client population.

Engage in a comprehensive work force planning process. Work force planning is a systematic approach to assessing the condition of the current work force, as well as an agency's future needs, and then creating a plan to address gaps. Many government agencies require a work force planning approach, and private and nonprofit agencies are beginning to follow suit. Many resources are available to assist agencies with this process.[10] Unless the "big picture" of current and future work force needs is considered, agencies will be continually playing catch-up with their work force and likely falling short of meeting the needs of youths and the community.

A reduction in the number of working-age Americans is inevitable, but this reduction does not need to translate into a work force crisis. Agencies must plan ahead in order to identify their staffing needs and to create a plan for recruiting and retaining employees with the desired competencies. Juvenile justice settings require employees with a unique blend of correctional and human services mindsets; therefore, identifying these workers may require a specialized approach. Juvenile justice agencies must get on board with the work force planning efforts under way in human services and corrections. Otherwise, the field will have its potential work force lured away. However, juvenile justice also must differentiate itself, so that its opportunities and needs are not subsumed under those of other organizations.

Notes

1. Bureau of Labor Statistics. 2006. *Occupational outlook handbook 2006-2007.* Available at www.bls.gov/oco.

2. Annie E. Casey Foundation. 2003. *The unsolved challenge of system reform: The condition of the frontline human services work force.* Annie E. Casey Foundation: Baltimore.

3. Annie E. Casey Foundation. 2003.

   Light, P.C. 2003. *The health of the human services work force.* Washington, D.C.: The Brookings Institution.

   Howe, M., C. Champnoise, E. Clawson, I. Cutler and S. Edwards. 2006. *The Juvenile Justice work force—Status and the challenge of reform.* Houston: Cornerstones for Kids.

   National Council on Crime and Delinquency. 2005a. *Exploring the effect of juvenile justice system functioning and employee turnover on recidivism rates.* Houston: Cornerstones for Kids.

4. National Council on Crime and Delinquency. 2005b. *Job turnover in child welfare and Juvenile Justice: The voices of former frontline workers.* Houston: Cornerstones for Kids.

   National Council on Crime and Delinquency. 2005a.

5. Howe, M. et al. 2006.

   National Council on Crime and Delinquency. 2005a.

6. National Council on Crime and Delinquency. 2005b.

   Light, P.C. 2003.

7. Liou, K.T. 1995. Role stress and job stress among detention care workers. *Criminal Justice and Behavior,* 22(4):425–436.

8. Workforce Associates. 2004. *A 21st century work force for America's correctional profession.* Indianapolis: Workforce Associates.

9. Light, P.C. 2003.

10. Barlow, E.D. and J.G. Fogg. 2004. Building a strategic work force plan for the correctional organization. *Corrections Today,* 66(5):110–115.

    International Personnel Management Association. 2002. *Workforce planning resource guide for public sector human resources professionals.* Alexandria, Va: International Personnel Management Association.

MEGHAN HOWE is senior project manager at the Crime and Justice Institute. **EIYSE CLAWSON** is executive director of the Crime and Justice Institute. **JOHN LARIVEE** is chief executive officer of Community Resources for Justice.

Teens Caught in the Middle

Juvenile justice system and treatment.

Substance abuse treatment for adults in the criminal justice system is seriously inadequate, causing recidivism and other problems. But the situation is even worse in the juvenile system, according to a new report from Drug Strategies, a research institute based in Boston, Mass. The report, "Bridging the Gap: A Guide to Drug Treatment in the Juvenile Justice System," was released December 6, and focuses on the conflicts between treatment, on the one hand, and criminal justice, on the other. Nobody likes to use the word "punitive" to describe the criminal justice system, but compared to treatment, that's what it is, sources agree.

"The primary goal of drug treatment for adolescents is rehabilitation," Mathea Falco, president of Drug Strategies, told CABL. "But for the juvenile justice system, control is often the dominant concern."

However, the fact that juvenile justice is connected to substance abuse treatment also works in favor of these adolescents. If it were not for juvenile justice referrals, and treatment programs like those profiled in the Drug Strategies report, many of these teens would not be able to access treatment at all.

Best Interests?

In most states, according to the report, the goals of the 51 different juvenile court systems are threefold: to protect public safety, reduce recidivism, and act in the "best interests" of the child. How a child's best interests are defined is up to interpretation, the report notes. But it adds that the juvenile justice goals and the goals of treatment are "not necessarily mutually exclusive" because teens who are not abusing substances are less likely to be rearrested.

In some areas, getting involved in the criminal justice system can be almost a guarantee of substance abuse treatment—for adults. In California, for example, Proposition 36 mandates treatment instead of incarceration for adults. "If we had that for adolescents, we'd have much better services," says Elizabeth Stanley-Salazar, director of public policy for Phoenix Houses of California, whose Phoenix Academy of Los Angeles is profiled in the Drug Strategies report.

"Kids who are at high risk—such as in foster care—simply don't have access to treatment," Stanley-Salazar told CABL. "We know we should be using evidence based practices, but there's only a veneer of funding for substance abuse services." Because of the lack of funding, even teens in the juvenile justice system

---

Eleven Elements of Effective Drug Treatment in Juvenile Justice System

1. Systems integration
2. Assessment and treatment matching
3. Comprehensive, integrated treatment approach
4. Staff who are trained to recognize psychiatric problems
5. Developmentally appropriate program
6. Family involvement in treatment
7. A way to engage and retain teens in treatment
8. Qualified staff who have experience in diverse areas, such as delinquency, adolescent development, depression, or attention deficit disorder
9. Staff with gender and cultural competence
10. Process of continuing care that includes relapse prevention training
11. A way to measure treatment outcomes

Source: Drug Strategies

---

who need treatment have a hard time getting it in California, she says, but she adds that the courts provide one of the few "on-ramps" for treatment. "Most of the kids who come to us come through the court system—a kid almost has to get tied up in the criminal justice system before they can access treatment."

Are there differences between adolescents in treatment because of juvenile justice referrals, and other adolescents in treatment? "The ones in the juvenile justice system are more severe, because their drug use has reached a higher threshold," says Stanley-Salazar. "So at Phoenix House we're receiving kids who have very serious substance abuse problems." However, she says that "many of the kids who are not on probation look similar to kids who have been picked up by probation."

Some of the teens at Phoenix House are on "home probation" or "informal probation." According to Stanley-Salazar, what they have in common with those on formal probation are "very disordered lives." And for those on probation, those lives are more likely to have histories of violence and abuse and neglect.

Programs Profiled in Drug Strategies Report

Travis County Juvenile Justice Integrated Network (Austin, Tex.)
Tampa Juvenile Assessment Center (Tampa, Fla.)
King County Juvenile Treatment Court (Seattle, Wash.)
Adolescent Portable Therapy (New York, N.Y.)
Thunder Road Adolescent Treatment Center (Oakland, Calif.)
Chestnut Health Systems (Bloomington, Ill.)
Multidimensional Family Therapy (Miami, Fla.)
Multisystemic Therapy (Mount Pleasant, S.C.)
Phoenix Academy of Los Angeles
La Bodega de la Familia (New York, N.Y.)

Multiple Agencies

The report builds on an earlier one from Drug Strategies called Treating Teens: A Guide to Adolescent Drug Programs, published in 2003. This report identified 9 key elements of treatment programs for adolescents (see box); this new report adds two elements that are specific to people coming through the juvenile justice system: (1) juvenile offenders are more likely to have co-occurring disorders, and (2) it's important to integrate functions of agencies.

Integrating agency functions is essential but often not done. One of the biggest challenges for a family in the juvenile justice system anywhere is navigating the bureaucracy. And this bureaucracy is particularly daunting in New York City. But this is the focus of Adolescent Portable Therapy (APT), a program of the Vera Institute, which acts as "a liaison" for people in the juvenile justice system, according to Evan Elkin, APT director. "You need to have a cultural understanding of the multiple agencies, of their fiscal, operational, and philosophical constraints, to make treatment work," Elkin told CABL. "You can't just ask for access, and come in and do treatment."

The New York City Department of Juvenile Justice does assessment and pretrial detention but does not house adolescents when they are "placed" or sentenced, as it is called in the adult system—the state does, says Elkin. "Given how briefly a kid can be in the city's custody, it's impressive that the city agency has wanted to be involved in funding drug treatment for a kid who may quickly leave and enter the state system for placement." The city Department of Juvenile Justice, among others, funds APT.

Clinic Without Walls

APT remains involved with an adolescent who is arrested, goes to court, and is sent to placement, as well as with the one who the judge allows to go home. The screening and assessment is integrated into the city's booking process, says Elkin. Then, during the first days of detention, APT assigns a therapist to him. "The kid may go to a residential placement facility for a year, but APT stays with the kid," says Elkin. "Then, they get four months of intensive home services when they get home." If the child is not placed, but returns home with services—which is happening more and more as New York State sends the message that it wants to rely less on institutional placement and more on home-based services—APT will treat that child as well. The key is portability. "We're a clinic without walls," says Elkin.

However, there's one down side to portability: payment. "The agencies who establish the standards of practice for alcohol and drug treatment do not yet recognize the reimbursability of portable home-based services," Elkin told CABL. "We would not get Medicaid reimbursement." APT is, however, licensed by the state Office of Alcoholism and Substance Abuse Services to provide this kind of treatment. "We are the only body that holds a license for this from OASAS," Elkin said proudly. "They created a special category for us 5 years ago."

Thanks to a grant from the Substance Abuse and Mental Health Administration (SAMHSA) for community-based adolescent drug treatment providers, APT was able to expand its services by over 50 percent for a four-year period. Under the SAMHSA grant, APT sees 90 additional teens a year returning home from state custody with the Office of Children and Family Services (OCFS). And under the Department of Juvenile Justice funding, they see 150 a year. That's about 250 families a year treated by APT. "We could triple in size and still not meet the need," says Elkin. The good news is that in recognition of the successful collaboration between APT and OCFS, the program is in the State's 2006 proposed budget for further expansion. "We hope also to remain in the City's budget in 2006."

The Role of the Family

LaBodega de la Familia, a spinoff from the Vera Institute's pre-APT days, is another program profiled in the Drug Strategies report. This New York City-based program focuses on the family as a unit. "Some families come in and say, 'My kid is smoking pot, what should I do," says Carol Shapiro, founder and director of Family Justice, of which LaBodega is a direct service. "In other cases, the teen was arrested, but it's a family member with a drug problem." It's important to engage the whole family, Shapiro, who started LaBodega 10 years ago, told CABL.

By working with the government and families in tandem, LaBodega promotes the notion of family case management. This is an example of the juvenile justice system helping the treatment process, says Shapiro. "The escalation and the hammers of the justice system are an advantage," she says.

Unlike the "clinic without walls" concept of APT, LaBodega is "place-based," says Shapiro. "We have a storefront and a satellite in public housing in a neighborhood that is affected by drugs. We'll do home visits too." And LaBodega's services integrate into the community. "We engage in a lot of things that have nothing to do with drug treatment," says Shapiro. "We help with gardening, poetry, photography, we work with the housing police and the people who are the natural leaders, the social fabric of the neighborhood."

Getting judges to understand that the community, home, and home-based treatment might be in the child's "best interests" is an uphill battle. "We have a problem with getting the justice system to understand that if you match these kids to treatment, using the American Society of Addiction Medicine (ASAM) criteria, you'd be putting them in variable lengths of stay," says Stanley-Salazar, noting that the average stay at Phoenix House is 9 to 12 months. "But corrections doesn't always look through the lens of treatment. They place them because of their offense, but there's not enough capacity to provide the services."

Ideally, she adds, these patients should be treated earlier, before their problems get so severe. "But if they weren't in the justice system, who would pay for their treatment?"

Jailed for Life After Crimes as Teenagers

ADAM LIPTAK

About 9,700 American prisoners are serving life sentences for crimes they committed before they could vote, serve on a jury or gamble in a casino—in short, before they turned 18. More than a fifth have no chance for parole.

Juvenile criminals are serving life terms in at least 48 states, according to a survey by *The New York Times,* and their numbers have increased sharply over the past decade.

Rebecca Falcon is one of them.

Ms. Falcon, now 23, is living out her days at the Lowell Correctional Institution here. But eight years ago, she was a reckless teenager and running with a thuggish crowd when one night she got drunk on bourbon and ruined her life.

Ms. Falcon faults her choice of friends. "I tried cheerleaders, heavy metal people, a little bit of country and, you know, it never felt right," Ms. Falcon said. "I started listening to rap music and wearing my pants baggy. I was like a magnet for the wrong crowd."

In November 1997 she hailed a cab with an 18-year-old friend named Clifton Gilchrist. He had a gun, and within minutes, the cab driver was shot in the head. The driver, Richard Todd Phillips, 25, took several days to die. Each of the teenagers later said the other had done the shooting.

Ms. Falcon's jury found her guilty of murder, though it never did sort out precisely what happened that night, its foreman said. It was enough that she was there.

"It broke my heart," said Steven Sharp, the foreman. "As tough as it is, based on the crime, I think it's appropriate. It's terrible to put a 15-year-old behind bars forever."

The United States is one of only a handful of countries that does that. Life without parole, the most severe form of life sentence, is theoretically available for juvenile criminals in about a dozen countries. But a report to be issued on Oct. 12 by Human Rights Watch and Amnesty International found juveniles serving such sentences in only three others. Israel has seven, South Africa has four and Tanzania has one.

By contrast, the report counted some 2,200 people in the United States serving life without parole for crimes they committed before turning 18. More than 350 of them were 15 or younger, according to the report.

The Supreme Court's decision earlier this year to ban the juvenile death penalty, which took into account international attitudes about crime and punishment, has convinced prosecutors and activists that the next legal battleground in the United States will be over life in prison for juveniles.

Society has long maintained age distinctions for things like drinking alcohol and signing contracts, and the highest court has ruled that youths under 18 who commit terrible crimes are less blameworthy than adults. Defense lawyers and human rights advocates say that logic should extend to sentences of life without parole.

Prosecutors and representatives of crime victims say that a sentence of natural life is the minimum fit punishment for a heinous crime, adding that some people are too dangerous ever to walk the streets.

In the Supreme Court's decision, Justice Anthony M. Kennedy said teenagers were different, at least for purposes of the ultimate punishment. They are immature and irresponsible. They are more susceptible to negative influences, including peer pressure. And teenagers' personalities are unformed. "Even a heinous crime committed by a juvenile," Justice Kennedy concluded, is not "evidence of irretrievably depraved character."

Most of those qualities were evident in Ms. Falcon, who had trouble fitting in at her Kansas high school and had been sent by her mother to live with her grandmother in Florida, where she received little supervision. She liked to smoke marijuana, and ran with a series of cliques. "I was looking for identity," she said.

Like many other lifers, Ms. Falcon is in prison for felony murder, meaning she participated in a serious crime that led to a killing but was not proved to have killed anyone.

In their report, the human rights groups estimate that 26 percent of juvenile offenders sentenced to life without parole for murder were found guilty of felony murder. A separate Human Rights Watch report on Colorado found that a third of juveniles serving sentences of life without parole there had been convicted of felony murder.

The larger question, advocates for juveniles say, is whether any youths should be locked away forever.

At the argument in the juvenile death penalty case, Justice Antonin Scalia said the reasons offered against execution apply just as forcefully to life without parole. Justice Scalia voted, in dissent, to retain the juvenile death penalty.

"I don't see where there's a logical line," he said at the argument last October.

When it comes to Ms. Falcon, the prosecutor in her case said she does not ever deserve to be free. Indeed, she is lucky to be alive.

The prosecutor, Jim Appleman, is convinced that she shot Mr. Phillips. "If she were a 29-year-old or a 22-year-old," he said, "I have no doubt she would have gotten the death penalty."

Ms. Falcon dressed up, as best one can in prison, to meet two journalists not long ago. There was nothing to be done about the plain blue prison dress, with buttons down the front. But she wore gold earrings, a crucifix on a gold chain and red lipstick. Her dark hair was shoulder length, and her eyes were big and brown.

She said her eight years in prison had changed her.

"A certain amount of time being incarcerated was what I needed," she said. "But the law I fell under is for people who have no hope of being rehabilitated, that are just career criminals and habitually break the law, and there's just no hope for them in society. I'm a completely different case."

"My sentence is unfair," she added. "They put you in, and they forget."

Tagging along on a Horrific Night

The case of another Florida teenager, Timothy Kane, demonstrates how youths can be sent away for life, even when the evidence shows they were not central figures in a crime.

Then 14, Timothy was at a friend's house, playing video games on Jan. 26, 1992, Super Bowl Sunday, when some older youths hatched a plan to burglarize a neighbor's home. He did not want to stay behind alone, he said, so he tagged along.

There were five of them, and they rode their bikes over, stashing them in the bushes. On the way, they stopped to feed some ducks.

Two of the boys took off at the last moment, but Timothy followed Alvin Morton, 19, and Bobby Garner, 17, into the house. He did not want to be called a scaredy-cat, he said.

"This is," he said in a prison interview, "the decision that shaped my life since."

The youths had expected the house to be empty, but they were wrong. Madeline Weisser, 75, and her son, John Bowers, 55, were home.

While Timothy hid behind a dining room table, according to court records, the other two youths went berserk.

Mr. Morton, whom prosecutors described as a sociopath, shot Mr. Bowers in the back of the neck while he pleaded for his life, killing him. Mr. Morton then tried to shoot Ms. Weisser, but his gun jammed. Using a blunt knife, Mr. Morton stabbed her in the neck, and Mr. Garner stepped on the knife to push it in, almost decapitating her.

"I firmly believe what they were trying to do was take the head as a kind of souvenir," said Robert W. Attridge, who prosecuted the case.

Mr. Morton and Mr. Garner did succeed in cutting off Mr. Bowers's pinkie. They later showed it to friends.

Mr. Morton was sentenced to death. Mr. Garner, a juvenile offender like Mr. Kane, was given a life sentence with no possibility of parole for 50 years.

Mr. Kane was also sentenced to life, but he will become eligible for parole after 25 years, when he will be 39. However, he is not optimistic that the parole board will ever let him out. Had he committed his crime after 1995, when Florida changed its law to eliminate the possibility of parole for people sentenced to life, he would not have even that hope.

Florida is now one of the states with the most juveniles serving life. It has 600 juvenile offenders serving life sentences; about 270 of them, including Ms. Falcon, who committed her crime in 1997, are serving life without parole.

Data supplied by the states on juveniles serving life is incomplete. But a detailed analysis of data from another state with a particularly large number of juvenile lifers, Michigan, shows that the mix of the life sentences—those with the possibility of parole and those without—is changing fast.

In Michigan, the percentage of all lifers who are serving sentences without parole rose to 64 percent from 51 percent in the 24 years ended in 2004. But the percentage of juvenile lifers serving such sentences rose to 68 percent from 41 percent in the period. Now two out of three juvenile lifers there have no shot at parole.

The Times's survey and analysis considered juvenile lifers generally, while the human rights report examined juveniles serving life sentences without parole. Both studies defined a juvenile as anyone younger than 18 at the time of the offense or arrest. For some states that could not provide a count based on such ages, the studies counted as a juvenile anyone under the age of 20 at sentencing or admission to prison.

Juvenile lifers are overwhelmingly male and mostly black. Ninety-five percent of those admitted in 2001 were male and 55 percent were black.

Forty-two states and the federal government allow offenders under 18 to be put away forever. Ten states set no minimum age, and 13 set a minimum of 10 to 13. Seven states, including Florida and Michigan, have more than 100 juvenile offenders serving such sentences, the report found. Those sending the largest percentages of their youths to prison for life without parole are Virginia and Louisiana.

Some Dismay over Sentences

Juvenile lifers are much more likely to be in for murder than are their adult counterparts, suggesting that prosecutors and juries embrace the punishment only for the most serious crime.

While 40 percent of adults sent away for life between 1988 and 2001 committed crimes other than murder, like drug offenses, rape and armed robbery, the Times analysis found, only 16 percent of juvenile lifers were sentenced for anything other than murder.

In those same years, the number of juveniles sentenced to life peaked in 1994, at about 790, or 15 percent of all adults and youths admitted as lifers that year. The number dropped to about 390, or 9 percent, in 2001, the most recent year for which national data is available.

Similarly, the number of juveniles sentenced to life without parole peaked in 1996, at 152. It has dropped sharply since then, to 54 last year. That may reflect a growing discomfort with the punishment and the drop in the crime rate.

It is unclear how many juveniles or adults are serving life sentences under three-strikes and similar habitual-offender laws.

Human rights advocates say that the use of juvenile life without parole, or LWOP, is by one measure rising. "Even with murder rates going down," said Alison Parker, the author of the new report, "the proportion of juvenile murder offenders entering prison with LWOP sentences is going up."

The courts that consider the cases of juvenile offenders look at individuals, not trends. But sometimes, as in Mr. Kane's case, they express dismay over the sentences that are required.

"Tim Kane was 14 years and 3 months old, a junior high student with an I.Q. of 137 and no prior association with the criminal justice system," Judge John R. Blue wrote for the three-judge panel that upheld Mr. Kane's sentence. "Tim did not participate in the killing of the two victims."

These days, Mr. Kane, 27, looks and talks like a marine. He is fit, serious and polite. He held a questioner's gaze and called him sir, and he grew emotional when he talked about what he saw that January night.

"I witnessed two people die," he said. "I regret that every day of my life, being any part of that and seeing that."

He does not dispute that he deserved punishment.

"Did I know right from wrong?" he asked. "I can say, yes, I did know right from wrong."

Still, his sentence is harsh, Mr. Kane said, spent in the prison print shop making 55 cents an hour and playing sports in the evenings.

"You have no hope of getting out," he said. "You have no family. You have no moral support here. This can be hard."

Mr. Attridge, the prosecutor, who is now in private practice, said he felt sorry for Mr. Kane. "But he had options," Mr. Attridge said. "He had a way out. The other boys decided to leave."

In the end, the prosecutor said, "I do think he was more curious than an evil perpetrator."

"Could Tim Kane be your kid, being in the wrong place at the wrong time?" he asked. "I think he could. It takes one night of bad judgment and, man, your life can be ruined."

Different Accounts of a Crime

Visitors to the women's prison here are issued a little transmitter with an alarm button on it when they enter, in case of emergency. But Ms. Falcon is small and slim and not particularly threatening.

She sat and talked, in a flat Midwest tone married to an urban rhythm, on a concrete bench in an outdoor visiting area. It was pleasant in the shade.

Her mother, Karen Kaneer, said in a telephone interview that her daughter's troubles began in Kansas when she started to hang around with black youths.

"It wasn't the good black boys," Ms. Kaneer said. "It was the ones who get in trouble. She started trying marijuana."

Not pleased with where things were heading, Ms. Kaneer agreed to send Rebecca away, to Panama City, Fla., to Rebecca's grandmother. "It was my husband's idea," Ms. Kaneer said ruefully, referring to Ms. Falcon's stepfather. "Her and my husband didn't have the best of relations."

Ms. Falcon received a piece of unwelcome news about an old boyfriend on the evening of Nov. 18, 1997, and she hit her grandparents' liquor cabinet, hard, drinking a big tumbler of whiskey. Later on, when she joined up with her 18-year-old friend, Mr. Gilchrist, she said, she did not suspect that anything unusual was going to happen. She thought they were taking the cab to a party.

"I didn't know there was going to be a robbery at that time," she said. "I mean, Cliff said things like he was going to try out his gun eventually, but as far as right then that night in that situation I didn't know."

Asked if she played any role in the killing, Ms. Falcon said, "No, sir, I did not."

In a letter from prison, where he is serving a life term, Mr. Gilchrist declined to comment. At his trial, both his lawyer and the prosecutor told the jury that Ms. Falcon was the killer.

The medical evidence suggested that the passenger who sat behind Mr. Phillips killed him. But eyewitnesses differed about whether that was Ms. Falcon or Mr. Gilchrist.

Several witnesses did say that Ms. Falcon had talked about violence before the shooting and bragged about it afterward.

"On numerous occasions she said she wanted to see someone die," Mr. Appleman, the prosecutor, said. Ms. Falcon said the evidence against her was "basically, that I was always talking crazy."

The testimony grew so confused that at one point Mr. Appleman asked for a mistrial, though he later withdrew the request.

Though their verdict form suggested that they concluded that Mr. Gilchrist was the gunman, the jurors remain split about what was proved. "There was no evidence presented to confirm who was the actual shooter," said Mr. Sharp, the jury's foreman.

But Barney Jones, another juror, said he believed Ms. Falcon shot the gun. "She was confused," he said. "She was probably a typical teenager. She was trying to fit in by being a violent person. The people she hung out with listened to gangster rap, and this was a sort of initiation."

Whoever was to blame, Mr. Phillips's death left a terrible void. "Each day we see a cab, the memories of our son and the tragic way he died surfaces," his father and stepmother, Roger and Karen Phillips, wrote at the time of the trial in a letter to Mr. Gilchrist, according to an article in The News-Herald, a newspaper in Panama City.

At the prison here, as Ms. Falcon talked, a photographer started shooting, and she seemed to enjoy the attention, flashing a big smile at odds with the grim surroundings.

It was a break, she explained, from the grinding monotony that is the only life she may ever know. She reads to kill time and to prepare herself in case a Florida governor one day decides to pardon her.

She had just finished a book on parenting.

"If God lets me go and have a kid," she said, "I want to know these things so I can be a good mother."

JANET ROBERTS contributed reporting for this series. She was assisted by Linda Amster, Jack Styczynski, Donna Anderson, Jack Begg, Alain Delaquérière, Sandra Jamison, Toby Lyles and Carolyn Wilder.

Co-Offending and Patterns of Juvenile Crime

JOAN MCCORD AND KEVIN P. CONWAY

Juveniles who commit crimes typically commit them in the company of their peers. This basic fact has been regularly reported in the literature since the late 1920s.[1] Nevertheless, with rare exceptions, contemporary research focuses almost exclusively on juvenile delinquents as individual actors.[2] Indeed, police records tend to undercount co-offending, and published crime rates rarely take co-offending into account.

Most crime rates are computed from individuals, with an assumption that each criminal event reported by or about an individual represents a crime event (see "Measuring Juvenile Crime"). Yet co-offenders provide a basis for multiple reports of single crime events. Not only are those who first offended before age 13 most likely to be co-offenders, but also the sizes of their offending groups (from 2 to 30 in the current study) tend to further exaggerate the contributions of youthful offenders to crimes. This exaggeration seems to contribute to a fear of youths that may be counterproductive.

Analyses that consider both co-offending and age at first arrest show that youthful offenders are most at risk for subsequent crimes if they commit their crimes with accomplices. Although very young offenders are responsible for a high proportion of juvenile crimes, their annual crime rate is not particularly high unless they are co-offenders.

Violence appears to be learned in the company of others. Those who commit crimes with violent offenders, even if the group does not commit violent crimes, are likely to subsequently commit violent crimes. This suggests that young offenders pick up attitudes and values from their companions.

To address issues raised by co-offending, including whether co-offending increases violence, the National Institute of Justice sponsored a study in Philadelphia that examined the criminal histories of a random sample of juvenile offenders. This Research in Brief discusses the study's findings and implications, considering four questions:

- Why consider co-offending?
- How is co-offending related to the age of offenders?
- How is co-offending related to recidivism?
- How is co-offending related to violence?

Why Consider Co-Offending?

Co-offending distorts reported crime rates by equating number of offenders with number of incidents and may increase a juvenile's risk for committing violent crimes through association with violent peers. Statistics on crimes typically are based on the number of criminals accused or convicted of crimes. Even when self reports are used, they indicate only which individuals within a stipulated population have committed crimes. Such statistics create a distorted picture of crime because many crimes are committed by more than one criminal and the proportion differs among different groups.

The distortion can be seen in the rare instances when crimes by lone offenders have been separated from those committed by multiple offenders. For example, the *Sourcebook of Criminal Justice Statistics*, 2001, reports that 64 percent of the violent crimes attributed to lone offenders were committed by white offenders, but only 51 percent of the violent crimes attributed to multiple offenders were committed by offenders in "all white" groups.[3] These figures suggest that nonwhites are more likely to offend in groups. Therefore, crime rates based on arrests may exaggerate the contributions of nonwhites to crime in the United States.

The distortion has a particularly strong effect for juvenile crimes. In 1997, for example, the Supplemental Homicide Reports indicated that 44 percent of murders known to involve juveniles involved more than one perpetrator.[4] According to the Bureau of Justice Statistics, 23 percent of violent crimes in 1999 attributed to lone offenders were committed by juveniles under the age of 18, whereas over 40 percent of violent crimes attributed to multiple offenders were committed by juveniles.[5]

The fact that particular crimes are committed by more than one criminal not only distorts the connection between criminals and crimes, but also distorts estimates of effects from various crime prevention policies. For example, researchers questioning the focus on incapacitation of high-rate offenders

Measuring Juvenile Crime

Data about juvenile crime typically come from three sources: arrest data, reports from victims, and self-reports about crimes committed. These sources have limitations and important intrinsic inaccuracies—one of which is that they ignore co-offending.

Arrest data. Typically derived from the FBI's Uniform Crime Reports, arrest data count each arrest of each individual as a crime, thus relying on such factors as policies of particular police agencies, cooperation of victims, and the skill of crime perpetrators. If more than one person is arrested for a single crime, information from arrests inflates the crime rate. Multiple arrests of a single person also inflate the crime rate when rates are presented as a proportion of the population who are arrested.

Victims' reports. Victims' reports have been systematically collected since 1973 in the National Crime Victimization Survey. Using a nationally representative sample of households, victims over the age of 12 report their experiences with specific crimes (rape, sexual assault, personal robbery, aggravated and simple assault, household burglary, theft, and motor vehicle theft). Data are not available from this source for homicides, victims under the age of 13, or victims who are not parts of households. Information about perpetrators is available from these records only for crimes involving contact between victim and criminal. Estimates of juvenile crimes depend on the victims' estimates of age. Crimes with more than one victim may have multiple reports in these records.

Self-reports. Self-reports about crimes committed are collected in a variety of settings. Many surveys take advantage of the fact that schools provide a convenient location for data collection, but they typically miss the most likely perpetrators of crimes—those absent from school because of illness, dropping out, or truancy. Many self-reporting questionnaires record delinquencies that would not be considered serious enough to call police, and few obtain information about the more serious types of crimes included on the FBI Indexes. Self-reports of crimes tend to reflect social responses to criminality, with accuracy of reporting varying by gender, ethnicity, and recidivism.

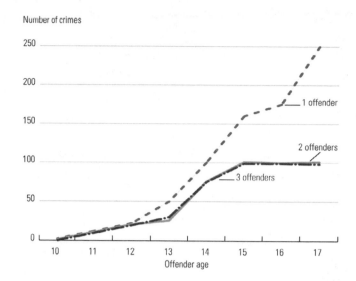

Figure 1 Number of crimes by number of offenders and age.

How Co-Offending Is Related to the Age of Offenders

Because prior evidence[8] suggests that youths who start offending early commit more crimes than those who start late, effects of the age of first criminality should be considered along with co-offending. Most offenders in the Philadelphia study committed their first offense between the ages of 13 and 15. Researchers identified youths who committed a crime before the age of 13 as "young starters" and those who committed a first crime after age 15 as "late starters." They noted a relative decline in co-offending in relation to age, but this reflects a sharp increase in the number of crimes committed by single offenders rather than a decline in the number of co-offenses (see figure 1).

From ages 10 to 17, crimes committed alone, in pairs, and in groups increased. The number of crimes committed alone increased more rapidly than the number of crimes committed with accomplices. Rates for pairs and for groups were almost identical after age 14.

When researchers differentiated property crimes from violent crimes,[9] they found a decline in co-offending after the age of 15 for property offenses (see figure 2). This decline, however, was paralleled by a rise in solo property offending. Co-offending violence increased throughout adolescence, while solo violent offending leveled off around age 15. Among 16- and 17-year-old

---

The fact that particular crimes are committed by more than one criminal not only distorts the connection between criminals and crimes, but also distorts estimates of effects from various crime prevention policies.

---

noted that offenders' crime rates would be exaggerated if they had committed a large proportion of their crimes in groups. To more accurately measure the effect of incapacitation on crime rates, attention also must be given to the continued criminal involvement of the co-offenders who remain in the community.[6]

In addition to distorting crime rates based on individuals and distorting the effects of intervention policies, co-offending may actually increase participation in crimes.[7] Furthermore, the present study provides evidence that co-offending may increase violence (see "How co-offending is related to violence").

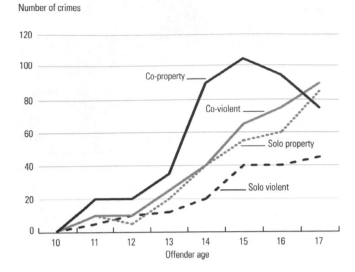

Number of crimes

Figure 2   Crimes, age, and co-offending.

offenders, violent crimes were almost twice as likely to be co-offenses as solo offenses.

The youngest offenders at first arrest were the most likely to mix co-offending and solo offending, but least likely to commit all their crimes alone. Those first arrested at ages 16 or 17, on the other hand, were most likely to commit crimes alone. About 40 percent of offenders committed most of their crimes with accomplices, regardless of their age at first arrest (see figure 3).

How Co-offending Is Related to Recidivism

The Philadelphia delinquents first arrested when they were under 13 years of age had higher rates of recidivism than those first arrested when they were older. Co-offending, however, distorts the picture of recidivism because there are actually fewer crime incidents than individual crime rates indicate (see table 1).

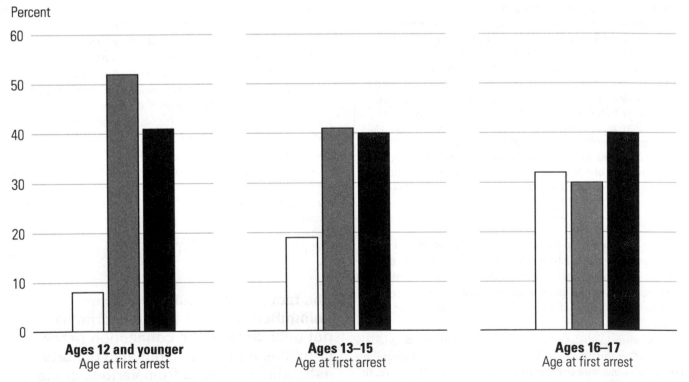

Percent of crimes committed with co-offenders

☐ Mostly solo (0–24%)

■ 25–74% co-offending

■ Mostly co-offending (75–100%)

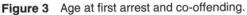

Figure 3   Age at first arrest and co-offending.

Table 1 Crime Incidents and Co-Offenders

Age at first crime	Mean number of		Crime-incident ratio
	Reported crimes	Actual incidents*	
< 13 years	7	3	2.3
13–15 years	4	2	2.0
16–17 years	2	1	2.0

*When co-offending is factored in.

Table 3 Individual Crime Rates and Co-Offending

Age at first arrest	Individual annual crime rates		Ratio of co-offending to solo offending
	Solo crimes	Co-offenses	
< 13 years	0.3	0.6	1.9
13–15 years	0.4	0.6	1.5
16–17 years	0.6	0.7	1.2

Specifically, crime rates are inflated if co-offending is not taken into account. In contrast, crime rates that account for co-offenders count each crime incident once even if multiple offenders have been arrested for the crime. The crime-incident ratio, which accounts for co-offending, is greatest for the young starters—indicating that crime rates for young delinquents are most likely to be inflated when co-offending is not taken into account.

Study findings on recidivism provide a good example of the increased information that comes from recognizing co-offending. The number of Index crimes was consistently higher for delinquents who co-offended at least 25 percent of the time. This pattern was particularly evident for the young starters. The young starters who co-offended at least 25 percent of the time were arrested for almost twice as many Index crimes as the young starters who typically committed solo offenses.[10] Thus, the number of arrests for Index crimes reflected both the age at first arrest and the proportion of crimes that were co-offenses (see table 2), revealing that young-starter delinquents who mostly co-offend committed the most crimes.

An examination of annual crime rates further demonstrates how crime rates can be inflated by inattention to co-offending. In each category of age for first arrest, individual co-offending rates were higher than solo rates (see table 3). The offenders first arrested at ages 16 and 17 had the highest rates for both solo and co-offenses. However, these high recidivism rates are due to both the compressed duration of their measured criminal activities and the fact that such a high proportion of their crimes are co-offenses.

Despite committing crimes at lower rates, the offenders who had first been arrested under the age of 13 had the highest ratio of co-offending to solo offending. But young starters are not high recidivists if one considers the length of time they are exposed to the juvenile justice system.[11]

These analyses show not only that crime rates based on individuals are most inflated for young-starting delinquents, but also that targeting youthful co-offenders could be the most productive approach to reducing future crime.

Table 2 Age at First Crime, Co-Offending, and Index Crimes

Age at first crime and rate of co-offending	Mean number of Index crimes
< 13 years	
Co-offend < 25% of crimes	3
Co-offend 25–74% of crimes	6
Co-offend > 74% of crimes	6
13–15 years	
Co-offend < 25% of crimes	2
Co-offend 25–74% of crimes	4
Co-offend > 74% of crimes	3
16–17 years	
Co-offend < 25% of crimes	1
Co-offend 25–74% of crimes	2
Co-offend > 74% of crimes	1

Note. Figures have been rounded.

How Co-Offending Is Related to Violence

Those who generally committed crimes with others were more likely to commit violent crimes than were solo offenders. The association between co-offending and violence was strongest for young starters.

Young starters. On average, offenders who had accomplices for at least 25 percent of their crimes and had been arrested before the age of 13 committed more than two violent crimes (see table 4).

Young starters who committed most of their crimes alone, however, were not particularly prone to committing violent crimes. On the other hand, co-offending young starters were

Table 4 Young Co-Offenders—At Risk for Violence

Age at first crime and rate of co-offending	Mean number of violent crimes
< 13 years	
Co-offend < 25% of crimes	1.0
Co-offend 25–74% of crimes	2.4
Co-offend > 74% of crimes	2.0
13–15 years	
Co-offend < 25% of crimes	0.9
Co-offend 25–74% of crimes	1.1
Co-offend > 74% of crimes	1.7
16–17 years	
Co-offend < 25% of crimes	0.3
Co-offend 25–74% of crimes	0.8
Co-offend > 74% of crimes	0.8

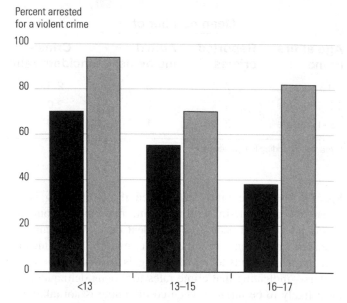

Figure 4 Violent crimes after first co-offense (percent of category).

considerably more likely to commit violent crimes than were late starters, especially late starters who mostly worked solo.

Thus, because the vast majority of young starters commit many of their crimes with others, the effects of age and co-offending on violence tend to be confounded.

Is violence learned? The association between co-offending and violence raises the question of whether kids who tend to be violent hang out together and therefore commit violent crimes or whether learning accounts for some of the high level of violence. To test the latter, researchers identified 236 offenders in the random sample of 400 who had not committed violent crimes before committing a crime with others.

These offenders committed their first co-offenses with 514 accomplices. Groups ranged from 2 to 15 offenders. Pairs committed 42 percent of these crimes. Co-offenders typically matched their accomplices in ethnic identity.[12] Age comparisons revealed that most of the offenders identified in their first co-offense were younger than their accomplices.[13]

Among the 236 offenders who had not been violent before their first co-offense, 90 participated in a violent first co-offense; among these, 62 percent committed at least one additional violent offense after this first one. Another 61 juveniles participated in a nonviolent co-offense with co-offenders who had previously been violent. These juveniles were even more likely to subsequently commit a violent crime than those who had actually participated in a violent crime for their first of offense.[14]

To check whether peer contagion[15] may have influenced the learning of violence, researchers divided the previously nonviolent offenders who committed a first co-offense that was not violent into two groups according to whether their accomplices had been violent before the target co-offense.

Those who committed a nonviolent offense with violent people were considerably more likely to commit a subsequent violent crime—80 percent of those with violent accomplices, compared with 56 percent of those with only nonviolent accomplices, committed at least one violent crime after the co-offense.[16]

The data showed no systematic relationship between age at first offense and whether or not nonviolent offenders co-offended with violent offenders for a first co-offense. Nevertheless, both whether a violent offender participated in the first co-offense and age at first arrest predicted whether a previously nonviolent offender would commit a violent crime (see figure 4).

Committing a first co-offense with violent accomplices contributed to the likelihood that violent crimes would be committed, regardless of age at first arrest. That is, violent peers increase the likelihood that nonviolent offenders will commit violent offenses.

How may violence be learned? Peer delinquency seems to be more than a training process for learning how to be delinquent. Interaction among delinquent peers apparently encourages and escalates their proclivity to commit crimes. Co-offenders may learn through the influence of violent accomplices that violence can be an effective means for getting money or satisfying other desires. They also may learn that insults or fear provide adequate grounds for violence.[17]

An adequate theory of crime should take into account both how others influence individual behavior and how individuals selectively seek companions who are likely to promote criminal

Construct Theory

Several theories have been introduced to explain how people learn from their environments. Many of these involve an assumption that learning takes place in response to receiving rewards or avoiding punishments for specific types of actions. Other learning theories refer to the frequency of encountering particular types of behavior. McCord's learning theory—Construct Theory—explains an individual's intentional actions as the natural result of how that individual constructs his or her environment, based on perceptions and experiences.[a]

According to Construct Theory, delinquents learn to classify criminal actions as appropriate partially through finding that others think it normal to commit crimes. It follows that juveniles would be more likely to consider violent behavior to be appropriate when committing crimes if their companions consider violence appropriate.

Construct Theory differs from other theories purporting to explain criminal behavior in that it does not rest on implied or stated feelings or emotions. Rather, it relies on an empirical judgment that *potentiating reasons* provide the impetus for action. For example, in the case of co-offending, Construct Theory holds that an 11-year-old delinquent often accepts a (usually older) companion's belief that violence is justifiable when committing crimes. This belief becomes a potentiating reason for the youth's own actions.

Some interventions may enhance the effects of co-offending by placing youths in groups that unintentionally provide negative peer learning. Peer values that encourage deviant behavior among misbehaving youths can provide potentiating reasons for continued misbehavior.[b]

The Philadelphia study validates Construct Theory, at least in part, by demonstrating that juvenile offenders are influenced by accomplices who had been violent in prior crimes, even though the present crime was not violent.

a. See McCord, J., "He Did It Because He Wanted To . . .," in *Motivation and Delinquency*, ed. W. Osgood, Nebraska Symposium on Motivation, Lincoln, NE: University of Nebraska Press, 44 (1997): 1–43

b. See McCord, J., "Crime Prevention: A Cautionary Tale," presentation at the Third International Inter-Disciplinary Evidence-Based Policies and Indicator Systems conference, July 2001, published in *Evidence-Based Policies and Indicator Systems, Conference Proceedings*, University of Durham, England, 2002: 186–192.

Study Methodology[a]

A random number generator identified 400 offenders from police tapes listing 60,821 juvenile arrests in Philadelphia during 1987. Half the sample was drawn from a list of offenses the police had recorded as solo offenses and the other half from a list of co-offenses. If an offender's court record could not be found for the listed offense or if the offender had been previously selected, another crime was drawn, again using a random number generator, and that offender became part of the sample. The complete juvenile criminal records were gathered for all 400 offenders in the sample. Adult records were traced through 1994. Accomplices were traced for the 335 randomly selected offenders who had committed at least one co-offense.

Analyses rely on data from court folders, which contained witness, complainant, police, and co-offender reports. A comparison between the court records and police tapes indicated that police records systematically undercounted co-offending.

Some information about the number of offenders was available in more than 95 percent of the incidents. When a range was given, researchers estimated conservatively, taking the lower number. When "group" was mentioned with an unspecified number of offenders, the number was coded as 3.

A crime was considered to be violent if the offenders were accused of murder, attempted murder, rape, robbery, aggravated assault, simple assault, terroristic threatening, intimidating a witness, prowling, or cruelty to animals, or if the complainant, a witness, or the victim reported violence. By these criteria, 38 percent of the crimes were violent. Crimes committed by groups were more likely to be violent.[b]

a. For a complete description of methodology, see McCord, J., and K.P. Conway, "Patterns of Juvenile Delinquency and Co-offending," in *Crime and Social Organization*, vol. 10 of *Advances in Criminological Theory*, ed. E. Waring and D. Weisburd, New Brunswick, NJ: Transaction Publishers, 2002: 15–30.

b. Forty-three percent of crimes committed by groups and 32 percent committed by pairs were violent.

behavior. Construct Theory postulates that co-offending provides a young offender justification for continued delinquency, encouraging him or her to seek out accomplices and commit additional crimes (see "Construct Theory"). This implies that interventions need not be directed at deep-seated emotions. Rather, behavioral change can be expected as a consequence of changing beliefs in relation to grounds for action.

Implications for Policy and Practice

Because many juvenile crimes are committed in the company of others, crime rates cannot be accurately portrayed unless co-offending is accurately recorded. Yet inspection of official records indicates that attention has not focused on this feature of crime events. Too often, a crime is considered to be solved when a single arrest has been made.

Co-offenders may learn through the influence of violent accomplices that violence can be an effective means for getting money or satisfying other desires.

The Philadelphia study demonstrates that crime records should contain accurate information about co-offending. Such accuracy is necessary if the effects of policy shifts are to be measured or if differences in crime rates are to be used as a basis for such preventive actions as deploying police and implementing target-hardening measures.

Perhaps the greatest challenge for intervention is to target youthful co-offenders in a way that reduces the likelihood that they will develop attitudes that promote crime. The study's findings imply that lessons of violence are learned "on the street," where knowledge is passed along through impromptu social contexts, including those in which offenders commit crimes together.[18] Interaction among delinquent peers apparently serves to instigate crimes and to escalate their severity.

More research on this issue is warranted, especially studies that measure peer influence on intentional action, track the selection of accomplices across multiple crimes, examine the learning processes involved in the transfer of violence across offenders, and identify individual offenders who may be particularly susceptible to (or unaffected by) the influence of violent accomplices.

When developing and evaluating strategies designed to prevent or reduce violence, practitioners and evaluators may want to consider co-offending patterns, individuals' choices of accomplices, and factors that increase the risk of co-offending, especially among very young offenders.

Notes

1. A 1928 study found that 82 percent of juveniles brought to court in Cook County, Illinois, committed their offenses as members of groups. See Shaw, C.R., and H.D. McKay, *Juvenile Delinquency and Urban Areas*, revised edition, Chicago: University of Chicago Press, 1969 (first published 1942). For studies that focused on group processes to try to understand juvenile delinquency, see Cohen, A.K., Delinquent Boys, Glencoe: Free Press, 1955; Cloward, R.A., and L. Ohlin, *Delinquency and Opportunity*, New York: Free Press, 1960; and Short, J., and F.L. Strodtbeck, *Group Process and Gang Delinquency*, Chicago: University of Chicago Press, 1965.

2. See Carrington, P.J., "Group Crime in Canada," *Canadian Journal of Criminology* (July 2002): 277–315; Hockstetler, A., "Opportunities and Decision: Interactional Dynamics in Robbery and Burglary Groups," *Criminology* 39 (3) (2001): 737–763; McCarthy, B., J. Hagan, and L.E. Cohen,

"Uncertainty, Cooperation and Crime: Understanding the Decision to Co-offend," *Social Forces* 77 (1) (1998): 155–184; Weerman, F.M., "Co-offending as Social Exchange: Explaining Characteristics of Co-offending," *The British Journal of Criminology* 43 (2) (2003): 398–416.

3. Maguire, K., and Pastore, A.L., *Sourcebook of Criminal Justice Statistics*, 2001, Washington, DC: U.S. Department of Justice, Bureau of Justice Statistics, 2003, NCJ 196438. Calculations have omitted "mixed" and "not known."

4. Supplemental Homicide Reports are part of the FBI's Uniform Crime Reporting system. See also Snyder, H.N., and M. Sickmund, *Juvenile Offenders and Victims: 1999 National Report*, Washington, DC: U.S. Department of Justice, Office of Juvenile Justice and Delinquency Prevention, 1999.

5. Bureau of Justice Statistics, *Sourcebook of Criminal Justice Statistics*, 1998, Washington, DC: U.S. Department of Justice, 1999, NCJ 176356.

6. See Reiss, A.J., Jr., "Co-offending and Criminal Careers," in *Crime and Justice*, vol. 10, ed. N. Morris and M. Tonry, Chicago: University of Chicago Press, 1988: 117–170.

7. See Hindelang, M.J., "With a Little Help From Their Friends: Group Participation in Reported Delinquency," *British Journal of Criminology* 16 (1976): 109–125; and Reiss, A.J., Jr., and D.P. Farrington, "Advancing Knowledge About Co-offending: Results From [a] Prospective Longitudinal Survey of London Males," *Journal of Criminal Law and Criminology* 82 (1991): 360–395. Also, delinquents in co-offending groups studied in Japan reported that they committed more crimes together than alone. See Suzuke, S., Y. Inokuchi, K. Watanabe, J. Kobayashi, S. Okela, and Y. Takahashi, "Study of Juvenile Co-offending," *Reports of the National Research Institute of Police Science* 36 (1995): 2, 64.

8. Before attention was drawn to co-offending, high recidivism rates had been linked with offenders who were particularly young when they began to commit crimes. See McCord, J., and K.P. Conway, "Patterns of Juvenile Delinquency and Co-offending," in *Crime and Social Organization*, vol. 10 of *Advances in Criminological Theory,* ed. E. Waring and D. Weisburd, New Brunswick, NJ: Transaction Publishers, 2002:16.

9. Property crimes were burglary, vehicle theft, theft other than vehicle, arson, vandalism, criminal trespass, forgery or counterfeiting, embezzlement, fraud, and risking or causing a catastrophe. Violent crimes were murder, attempted murder, rape, robbery, aggravated assault, simple assault, terroristic threatening, intimidating a witness, prowling, and cruelty to animals.

10. Index crimes are eight categories of serious crime collected by the FBI's Uniform Crime Reporting Program. Violent Index crimes are homicide, criminal sexual assault, robbery, and aggravated assault/ battery. Property Index crimes are burglary, theft, motor vehicle theft, and arson.

11. If all young criminals spend about 5 years actively committing crimes, only those arrested before their 13th birthdays would spend all their criminal years as juveniles. To compensate for

this potential bias, individual crime rates were computed for both solo offenses and co-offenses, on the assumption that once a juvenile committed a crime, he or she would remain a delinquent until the age of 18. Whatever bias this computation introduced affected solo and co-offending rates alike.

12. The ethnic identity of co-offenders and accomplices matched for 96 percent of black offenders, 83 percent of white offenders, and 83 percent of Hispanic or other offenders. Researchers traced the criminal histories of 396 of the accomplices, a success rate of 77 percent.

13. Sixty-three percent were younger, 19 percent were older, and 18 percent were the same age or very close.

14. $X^2_{(1)} = 5.626$, $p < .02$.

15. For discussion of this issue, see Dishion, T.J., J. McCord, and F. Poulin, "When Interventions Harm: Peer Groups and Problem Behavior," *American Psychologist* 54 (9) (1999): 1–10.

16. $X^2_{(1)} = 9.065$, $p < .003$.

17. Case studies and self-report data converge to suggest that delinquent groups socialize their members in ways that encourage and value violence.

18. See "Construct Theory" sidebar; also see McCord, J., "Understanding Childhood and Subsequent Crime," *Aggressive Behavior* 25 (1999): 241–253.

The late **JOAN MCCORD**, PhD, Professor of Criminal Justice at Temple University, was a groundbreaking criminal justice researcher and an eloquent teacher, speaker, and writer in the field, often focusing on juvenile crime, violence, and the efficacy of intervention programs. **KEVIN P. CONWAY**, PhD, is Deputy Branch Chief of the Epidemiology Research Branch at the National Institute on Drug Abuse. His research interests center on drug abuse etiology and juvenile delinquency, with emphasis on links between antisocial behavior and drug abuse.

From *National Institute of Justice Journal*, NCJ 210360, December 2005, pp. ii, 1–15. Published by Office of Justice/U.S. Department of Justice.

UNIT 6

Punishment and Corrections

Unit Selections

Key Points to Consider

- How does probation differ from parole? Are there similarities?

- Discuss reasons for favoring and for opposing the death penalty.

- Should college-level education be available to inmates?

Student Web Site

www.mhcls.com/online

Internet References

Further information regarding these Web sites may be found in this book's preface or online.

American Probation and Parole Association (APPA)
http://www.appa-net.org
The Corrections Connection
http://www.corrections.com
Critical Criminology Division of the ASC
http://www.critcrim.org/
David Willshire's Forensic Psychology & Psychiatry Links
http://members.optushome.com.au/dwillsh/index.html
Oregon Department of Corrections
http://egov.oregon.gov/DOC/TRANS/CC/cc_welcome.shtml

In the American system of criminal justice, the term 'corrections' has a special meaning. It designates programs and agencies that have legal authority over the custody or supervision of people who have been convicted of a criminal act by the courts. The correctional process begins with the sentencing of the convicted offender. The predominant sentencing pattern in the United States encourages maximum judicial discretion and offers a range of alternatives, from probation (supervised, conditional freedom within the community) through imprisonment, to the death penalty.

Selections in this unit focus on the current condition of the U.S. penal system and the effects that sentencing, probation, imprisonment and parole have on the rehabilitation of criminals.

In "Changing Directions," James V. Peguese writes in favor of a new program under consideration in Maryland to address inmate rehabilitation and re-entry. According to Alan Greenblatt's "Felon Fallout," the problems of overcrowded prisons and soaring costs are causing some states to take another look at the concept of rehabilitating our nation's convicts, rather than simply warehousing them.

Any answer to the question: What do we get from imprisonment? has to recognize that U.S. imprisonment operates differently than in any other democratic state in the world. This point is made in Todd R. Clear's essay, "The Results of American Incarceration." A prison warden says that crime is a social disease that we cannot ignore in the hope it will go away. In "Experiment Will Test the Effectiveness of Post-Prison Employment Programs," Erik Eckholm reports on a new program that tests the effectiveness of giving temporary jobs to ex-convicts in order to help them learn how to hold permanent jobs.

Differing perspectives on the utility of the death penalty are found in the essay entitled "Do We Need the Death Penalty?" Which view do you hold? In "Private Prisons Expect a Boom," Meredith Kolodner reports that by the fall of 2007 the Bush administration expects to spend almost a billion dollars annually on locking up illegal immigrants, and much of that money is expected to go to private companies. "Jail Time Is Learning Time" discusses the efforts of New York state's Onondaga County Justice Center in rehabilitating its inmates by offering

Brand X Pictures

them valuable classroom instruction. In the next article, "The Professor Was a Prison Guard," Jeffrey J. Williams writes about how the time he spent working in a prison compares with his present position as a college professor.

The following article, "Supermax Prisons," by Jeffrey Ian Ross is a warning about the possible constitutional and human rights violations occurring in these institutions. Next, why Texas leads the nation in executions is examined by Joseph Rosenbloom in "The Unique Brutality of Texas." In "Help for the Hardest Part of Prison: Staying Out," Erik Eckholm reports that in response to the problem of prisoners with little chance of getting a job being sent home without help, some states are changing the way the criminal justice system deals with repeat offenders. Finally, Changing the Lives of Prisoners: A New Agenda," argues that the much-touted outcomes of faith-based prisons are, at least in part, a product of counting the winners and discounting the losers.

Changing Directions

JAMES V. PEGUESE

For many years now, we have watched the pendulum of corrections in our country swing from one extreme to the other. At times, we only focus on the premise of locking offenders up and throwing away the key. While at other times, we find ourselves focused on treatment and rehabilitation. Neither idea is new, perhaps only the way we go about applying them. Many factors, right or wrong, impact on the philosophy of the day. Social issues such as crime rates, funding and political power play key roles in how corrections does business.

During the times when we are only thinking about the "lock 'em up" theory, emphasis is placed on longer sentences, fewer paroles, higher security levels and virtually no focus on rehabilitative programs. Most of the funds allocated to correctional departments during this time are devoted to security personnel (i.e., officers), and more of them are needed to handle the continuously growing inmate populations. But the soaring costs do not stop there. More funds are needed for inmates' needs such as food, clothing and health care. Some of these costs will have long-term effects. For example, under the "lock 'em up" theory, inmates will be spending longer terms in prison. That means that more inmates will grow old in prison. The older they get, the greater the need for extensive medical attention and medication. We all know the costs associated with medical coverage these days. Pointing out these rising costs is not by any means an endorsement for shorter sentences or more liberal paroles, but is merely intended to illuminate the problems that executive-level administrators, legislators, governors and citizens will have to face at some time in the near future.

Also, the "lock 'em up" theory does not adequately, or fails altogether to, address the issue of where we are going to put these people who we lock up. The costs associated with building new prisons are staggering. As offenders and the crimes they commit become more high-tech, so must the prisons we build to house them in. Many jurisdictions have entertained, where practicable, retrofitting their existing prisons with high-tech equipment. However, they are finding that in many cases those costs are equal to or greater than the cost of new prisons. In other cases, older prisons are being required to handle those high-tech inmates without benefit of any renovations.

The demands of society and the response by our politicians and legislators have been heard. Law enforcement officers are making more arrests, prosecutors are trying more cases and judges are handing out stiffer sentences. Lawmakers are wrestling more discretionary powers from the judges and enacting mandatory sentencing guidelines. To determine whether this is good or bad is not the scope of this article. Rather, the intent is to invoke thought and perhaps increase dialogue so that we might be better prepared for the future.

An important part of the equation—increased costs and arrests, and long sentences—is often overlooked, perhaps accidentally, perhaps not. Where do we house these people? What do we offer them while incarcerated? What do we, as a society, hope to gain other than temporarily removing them from the streets? Are they likely to return to society? Will they be prepared to become productive members of society or more likely to reoffend?

The reality is that most inmates will eventually return to society; only a fraction of them are serving life sentences. What are the odds of a person serving a 10-year prison sentence not to re-offend when he or she is placed in a prison with an inmate serving a life sentence? Quite often, these pairings happen due to limited bed space. That situation coupled with the fact that the "lock 'em up" theory offers very little by way of programs is a formula for failure. By the time the inmate is ready to return to society, he likely has learned most of the things that will surely return him to prison. He probably has become bitter toward a system that treated him as if he had committed the same crime as the person in the adjacent cell. He had to learn to be hard just to survive, and now that represents most of what he knows. No one offered him any help for his substance abuse problems or illiteracy. No one offered any help with life skills or realistic job skills. He was only 18 when he was sentenced and his cell partner was 35 years old with 10 years already in. Who do we expect to have had the most influence on his life?

As much as we would like to brush it away or hide it in the closet, crime is a social disease. We cannot ignore it and hope it will go away. So, too, is corrections a social responsibility. Society cannot wish this away nor is it likely that we will see much positive change under the philosophy of lock them up and throw away the key. Correctional employees will not agree that this is the school of thought they subscribe to, but if you look at the substance of their operations, it may prove differently.

The change corrections is looking for and sorely needs is much more difficult and probably a little more costly on the front end. However, if we are willing to stay the course, we should see some very positive results. What corrections is in need of and what the state of Maryland is trying to embark on is a philosophy that deals with just that.

During the times when we are only thinking about the "lock 'em up" theory . . . virtually no focus [is] on rehabilitative programs.

Re-entry, Enforcement Services Targeting Addictions, Rehabilitation and Treatment (RESTART) is a bold initiative that strikes at the very soul of recidivism. Maryland's correctional department seeks to address not just the growing housing problem, but the far more delicate issue of rehabilitation and treatment. It takes much more courage to pursue this type of philosophy. The public cries out for change and a less financially burdensome system, but few are willing or even understand what will be required of them to see this through. An initiative such as RESTART requires the commitment of those in charge of the prison system, political leaders and most important, the citizens. Appropriate funds must be allocated and the correctional leaders given the latitude to implement the process. And political leaders must be willing to stay the course as the process experiences the inevitable growing pains.

A philosophy such as this represents a dynamic change from how corrections used to do business. Therefore, we cannot expect to see the desired results right away. It is important for us to remember that corrections and society did not get this way overnight, and therefore, we cannot solve this overnight. Partial commitment from either party will destine the philosophy for failure. In corrections, you can never successfully ride the fence. You will quickly be identified as weak and indecisive.

We must not let the philosophy of rehabilitation and reentry die in the chambers. Yes, there are concerns as with any new endeavor. But, if we already know that the old system is broken, someone must take the lead and risk trying something new. RESTART is only new to Maryland. The philosophy has a positive, proven track record in other states. As I see it, the only possibility for failure in Maryland will come from lack of support from those resistant or afraid of change. We as corrections professionals and citizens must not allow this to fail.

As much as we would like to brush it away or hide it in the closet, crime is a social disease. We cannot ignore it and hope it will go away.

RESTART offers a viable solution. And, yes, it will require resources. However, it should be viewed as an investment into our future and our children's future. Times are calling on us to be proactive in tackling one of the biggest woes of modern society: recidivism. How do we keep offenders from re-offending? It is not a problem that can be resolved single handedly but rather collectively as a people, as a society. Recidivism is like a disease, a cancer, that if left untreated will have devastating effects on our communities. We witness every day the negative effects of doing nothing. We see the damage. We witness the pain. We must join forces in support of such a courageous undertaking. We must do our part to ensure the success of RESTART, for the cost of failure is much too high.

JAMES V. PEGUESE, CCE, is warden at the Maryland House of Correction-Annex in Jessup.

From *Corrections Today,* July 2005, pp. 15, 101, 110. Copyright © 2005 by American Correctional Association, Alexandria, VA. Reprinted by permission.

Felon Fallout

Overcrowding and soaring corrections costs are pushing prison reform to the top of states' policy agendas.

ALAN GREENBLATT

A couple of years ago, the state of California did something surprising. It changed the name of its Department of Corrections, tacking on the words "and Rehabilitation" to the agency's title. It was a small step—the modification wasn't accompanied by any sudden surge in funding for rehabilitation programs. But it was symbolically important nonetheless. Thirty years ago, the state officially recast the department's mission from rehabilitation to incarceration and punishment. Since then, the idea of rehabilitating prisoners has been a much lower priority than locking up more of them. Now, with the state's prisons bursting at the bars, that may be about to change.

California's prison system houses more than 170,000 inmates, roughly double the number it was designed to hold. Overcrowding has precipitated riots and viral outbreaks, as well as straining basic services such as water and sewer. A federal judge has given state lawmakers until June to come up with a feasible solution for handling the heavy volume or risk a court takeover of the entire system. Two other courts are also entertaining motions to put a cap on the prison population. And, in response to yet another case, a federal court has already taken control of the prison health care system, ordering changes that could cost the state as much as $1 billion. The California prison system was undeniably facing a crisis anyway, but pressure from the courts has made prison management and reform one of the most pressing issues in Sacramento this year.

"We are at the point where if we don't clean up the mess, the federal court is going to do the job for us," said Governor Arnold Schwarzenegger. He has asked lawmakers to approve an $11 billion package in response. Most of the money would go toward building more prison and jail capacity. But Schwarzenegger also aims to make good on the promise of rehabilitation suggested by the corrections agency's name change. He wants nearly double the present funding for vocational, educational and drug treatment programs.

In looking to change its approach on corrections, California is just starting to play catch-up with the rest of the country. While no one wants to be accused of being "soft" on crime, fiscal concerns in many states have helped to revive liberal notions that had been abandoned for decades. In the aggregate, state governments are now spending more than $40 billion per year on prisons—five times as much as during the mid-1980s. Corrections departments have become the largest public employers in many states. A few are even spending more on corrections than on higher education. As a result, the ground underlying the corrections debate has clearly shifted. Nearly every state has stepped up its efforts to prepare prisoners for release, hoping that at least some of them will gain the skills and attitude necessary to avoid coming back.

Granted, the word "rehabilitation" is still too charged to return to broad use. The new buzzword is "reentry," a term that tacitly acknowledges that the vast majority of inmates will return to their communities at some point. The problem is that most of them will end up behind bars again, if not for new crimes then for parole violations. In California, seven out of 10 released prisoners are re-incarcerated within three years. That's one of the worst rates in the nation. But most states recognize that if they can cut their recidivism rates by just a small fraction, they will save enormous amounts of money.

Since 2004, for example, Connecticut has been putting more money into reentry programs such as parole, housing and drug treatment. Apparently as a result, the state has seen its prison population decline after a worrisome spike upwards. Connecticut was able to avoid building more prison space, and less crowding meant the cancellation of its multimillion-dollar contract with Virginia to house 500 prisoners it previously had no room for. "Around the country, it's becoming politically safe to do this stuff," says Michael Lawlor, chair of the Connecticut House Judiciary Committee, "because there's something in it for everybody, social progressives and fiscal conservatives."

More policy makers are becoming convinced of the need for offering prisoners some choices other than staring at the wall, but rehabilitation still doesn't sit well with the public.

Of course, not everyone has come around to this way of thinking. The idea that has dominated state corrections policy for more than a decade—that it is better to lock up offenders than waste energy worrying about how they're treated while they're in prison—still has enormous political resonance. And although more policy makers are becoming convinced of the need for offering prisoners some choices other than staring at a wall, the notion of investing in felons for the purposes of rehabilitation still doesn't sit well with the public at large.

In California, voters have strongly indicated their continued desire for a get-tough approach. Last November, they approved one of the harshest sex-offender laws in the country—which, among other things, will put thousands more behind bars. That came on the heels of voter rejection of an attempt to soften the state's "Three Strikes" law, which puts habitual offenders away for decades or for life. "Republicans generally feel we should build more prisons," says Dick Ackerman, the party's leader in the state Senate. "The California taxpayer wants to put these people away."

The Roots of Overcrowding

Like most of the rest of the country, California has spent the past quarter-century on a prison-building spree. The state's prison population has increased eightfold during those years, so that despite nearly tripling the number of its prisons since 1980, the corrections department has just about run out of room. It predicts the system will reach its absolute capacity in June or July, which is just about the time a federal judge might take over the system.

The roots of overcrowding are clear. Beginning in 1976, California's legislature and voters began approving a slew of tougher sentencing laws—some 1,000 altogether, culminating with the 1994 passage of Three Strikes. Although virtually all the laws lengthened sentences, the penal code as a whole has become a hodgepodge. It's easy to sketch out scenarios under which a criminal may face any one of four or five different mandatory sentences—each carrying a different penalty—for the exact same crime.

"The accusations that we became just a warehouse are true."

—James Tilton
California Corrections Secretary

The one thing that has become certain for virtually all prisoners, however, is the date of release. Determinant sentencing has stripped the corrections department of its former authority to make judgments about when and whether a prisoner is ready to be released. Rather than getting time off for good behavior, or shortening their sentences by completing drug treatment programs, prisoners know they will be released on a fixed day, even if they have been dangerous enough to be kept in solitary until the day of their release. "We have more stringent requirements for young people graduating high schools than we do for people being released from prison," says state Senator Mike Machado.

If prisoners have no incentive for participating in rehab programs, there aren't adequate programs available to them anyway. For instance, more than half the state's prisoners are in "high need" of drug treatment, but only about 9 percent of them are likely to be enrolled at any given time, according to the UC Irvine study. Such programs are traditionally understaffed and poorly financed, but overcrowding has meant there's literally no place for them. The state prisons have classrooms and gymnasiums, but many are filled with some of the 19,000 inmates who are sleeping not in cells but in double or triple bunks lined up in every available space. "The accusations that we became just a warehouse are true," says James Tilton, Schwarzenegger's corrections secretary.

Release and Return

Under Schwarzenegger's plan, counties would house more short-term prisoners and help them get access to community-based programs. His proposal includes $5.5 billion for local jails, but counties remain nervous that the state will pass too many costs and responsibilities onto them. According to the sheriff's association in the state, more than 200,000 prisoners at the county level failed in 2005 to serve any or all of their sentences because 20 county jails are under court-ordered population caps, with 12 more maintaining voluntary caps under court pressure. Tilton, undaunted, has been working to convince counties and local law enforcement officials that local programs provide an alternative to the unworkable revolving-door recidivism system currently in place. "My presentation is that, if you want the status quo, if you want an inmate who is not prepared to be in your community, then to be honest you can have that if you like."

With so many of the state's prisoners either functionally illiterate or addicted to drugs (or having a combination of both problems), it's hardly surprising that so many of them return to prison after a brief stint on the outside. In Kansas, says state Representative Pat Colloton, two-thirds of prison admissions are related to parole and probation violations, and 80 percent of these are due to substance abuse or mental illness. In many cases, people are going to prison for violating probation, even though they weren't sentenced to jail time for their original crime.

If their crimes weren't severe enough to warrant a prison sentence in the first place, the state doesn't want them occupying expensive beds or distracting parole officers from more dangerous offenders. Toward that end, Kansas ran a pilot program in Shawnee County that sought to coordinate housing, substance abuse, job training and other programs for parolees. It cut the usual parole-revocation rate from 80 percent to 30 percent. Colloton has introduced twin bills that aim to build on this success by offering grants to more counties. "By giving this support, we can substantially reduce the number of people coming back to jail," she says. "We think that reforming people is the way to go, rather than building more prison beds."

Colloton, a Republican, is not some '60s liberal. Her proposal, like so many among the new generation of rehab programs, would be funded with strings attached. Accountability, after all, has become another universal buzzword. In order to continue to receive funding under Colloton's legislation, a county in Kansas will have to show that it has cut its revocation rate by at least 20 percent. In Oregon, the legislature has imposed a statutory requirement on the corrections department to monitor the success rate of reentry programs. In Washington State, a legislative study found that spending $1,000 per inmate for academic and vocational training programs was a good deal, crediting such programs with savings of more than $10,000 per prisoner in the form of lower crime rates and drops in recidivism of up to 9 percent.

Because the early results look good—and there's suddenly grant money and research available from sources such as the U.S. Department of Justice and the Council of State Governments' new Justice Center—more states are willing to look hard at funding reentry programs as an alternative to spending far more on prison beds. Even in tough-on-crime Texas, which leads the nation not only in executions but also its per capita rate of incarceration, lawmakers are talking seriously about the need to increase programming in prisons and in communities to address illiteracy, drug addiction and other stumbling blocks common to prisoners and parolees. "We're trying to do the smart thing," says Jerry Madden, chairman of the House Committee on Corrections. "The answer is not just building more prisons."

Lack of Political Will

Governor Schwarzenegger has talked seriously about making major changes to California's corrections system throughout the course of his administration. But, according to his critics, whenever push has come to shove, he's stopped pushing. Not long after taking office, Schwarzenegger appointed a prison study commission, headed by former Governor George Deukmejian, and called for an overhaul of the state's overtaxed parole system. So confident was his administration of success with its parole changes—it promised savings of $75 million per year—that it suspended operations at the correctional officer training academy, anticipating the need for fewer officers. But neither the implementation of parole changes nor the savings ever came off.

The lack of new trained officers is just one reason why the corrections department is understaffed by about 4,000 employees. California had one of the nation's lowest guard-to-inmate ratios anyway, but the closure of the training academy has meant hefty overtime payments to those on duty; 6,000 department employees, mostly rank-and-file guards, earned six figures during the past fiscal year. Indeed, the average base salary for prison guards there is 50 percent above the national average.

The guards' main union, the California Correctional Peace Officers Association, has become one of the most powerful forces in Sacramento. It was the leading donor to Schwarzenegger's two immediate predecessors. Schwarzenegger has openly derided the union as a "special interest," sought to cut its power by changing its means of collecting political dues from members, and attempted to shut the union out from prison policy discussions for the first time in years.

The CCPOA also didn't like the fact that he suspended its members' promised pay raises during a tough budget year, or that he tried to revoke some of the managerial control over its members that the union had won from his predecessor, which allows CCPOA to determine which officers will get which jobs 70 percent of the time. After Schwarzenegger unveiled his parole plan, the union helped a victims' rights group air TV ads claiming that the plan would let murderers, rapists and child molesters roam the streets.

Last year, two corrections secretaries quit in the space of a couple of months, later testifying in court that the governor's top political aides had decided to cave in to union demands. The courts grew publicly concerned about the administration's "retreat" from prison reform, with a special master complaining about CCPOA's "disturbing" amount of clout.

But if the union is sometimes cast in the role of villain in California's ongoing prison policy drama, there is plenty of blame left for others. Schwarzenegger called a special session last summer to address the overcrowding issue, asking the legislature to approve $6 billion for prison construction. The Senate passed a heavily revised version of the governor's plan, but the Assembly balked. Legislators claimed they needed more time to address such a complex issue, but the fact that the special session was a failure—coupled with the fact that the Democrats who control the legislature have shown more interest in Schwarzenegger's proposed sentencing commission than his latest construction money request—has led Republicans to level the familiar charge that they are soft on crime and criminals.

Schwarzenegger was seeking changes to the state's sentencing structure even before the U.S. Supreme Court ruled in January that major portions of it are unconstitutional. His fellow Republicans in the legislature claim that a sentencing commission, which would aim to straighten out some of the many inconsistencies in California's penal code, is "code for early release." Sentencing commissions, which have been tried in about 20 states, have not all been successful, but neither have they universally called for shorter sentences.

In North Carolina and Virginia, commonly cited as models in California, sentences for violent crimes were significantly lengthened, although both commissions diverted funds to community-based rehab and reentry programs. But Republican legislators in California are convinced that Democrats mean to use any new sentencing commission as cover for cutting jail time. "My biggest fear is that the liberals are going to drive an agenda where they will give the governor sentencing reform," says Assembly Republican Todd Spitzer, "and will not give any additional resources for prison beds, claiming that sentencing reform is enough to solve the problem."

Chance of a Lifetime

The stop-and-start nature of California's prison debate over the past couple of years has bred plenty of cynicism. But most observers think that the threat of a court takeover will succeed in prodding the political players into finally addressing the problem. Schwarzenegger has gotten nowhere with his earlier prison reform efforts because the political stakes were too high. Now, the dynamic has changed and the penalty for inaction may have become greater than for agreement. No one wants to be blamed when a court orders the release of thousands of convicts or watch the same court freely spend billions of additional dollars from state coffers. The Department of Corrections and Rehabilitation's budget has soared 52 percent over the past five years and is set to exceed $10 billion this year. Those numbers are scary enough without risking the prospect of a court receiver backing up a truck to the state treasury. "We don't need the federal government coming in here and writing blank checks out of our general fund," says Mike Villines, leader of the Assembly Republicans.

Villines, Spitzer and other Republicans clearly mean to keep banging the "tough on crime" gong in order to pressure Schwarzenegger and Democratic legislative leaders. They may or may not succeed in their goals of keeping a sentencing commission's authority limited and prison construction spending high. But even they talk about the need for the state to do a better job with rehabilitation programs in order to cut costly recidivism. The guards' union, for its part, also has embraced the need for rehabilitation programs and publicly stated that sentencing reform is going to happen in California, whether through the legislative process or via court edict.

The debate in California is just beginning, but it's clear that reconciling all the complex and politically touchy issues surrounding sentencing, parole, rehabilitation and, in all likelihood, new prison construction will be tremendously difficult. (To make things even more complicated, the guards' contract is up for renegotiation.) Yet it's quite possible that the state, having let its prison problems grow literally out of its control, will finally take a comprehensive look at solving them.

"Sometimes a crisis will drive decisions, and we are certainly in a crisis situation," says Tilton, the corrections secretary. "This really presents an opportunity that hasn't been around for the 30 years I've been in state government to work through the issues about who should be in prison versus who should be somewhere else."

ALAN GREENBLATT can be reached at agreenblatt@governing.com

The Results of American Incarceration

**Any answer to the question "What do we get from imprisonment?"
has to recognize that U.S. imprisonment operates differently
than it does in any other democratic state in the world.**

TODD R. CLEAR

L et's begin with a little thought experiment. Today, there
are 1.3 million federal prisoners; over 2 million citizens
are incarcerated in state prisons and local jails. Imagine
that those numbers grow methodically for the next generation.
By the time people born today reach their thirtieth birthday, there
will be over 7 million prisoners and, if local jails are counted,
more than 10 million locked up on any given day. How are we
to react to such daunting numbers?

First, let's agree that the experiment seems unrealistic. This
kind of growth would result in about 2 percent of the population
incarcerated on any given day. Taken as a percentage of males
aged 20–40 (most of those behind bars are from this group), the
proportion locked up would be stupefying.

A rational person might say, "State and local governments
have trouble affording today's prisons and jails, so how could
they pay for such a mind-boggling expansion? What kind of
society could justify locking up so many of our young men?"

After a bit more thought, that person might also say, "Well,
if we are going to do it, then at least we will eliminate a lot of
crime."

This is perhaps a disturbing thought experiment, but it is not
a far-fetched one.

The 'War' on Crime

To illustrate, go back a full generation, to the beginning of the
1970s. Richard Nixon is president, and we are having a bit of a
"war" on crime (puny, by today's standards). Crime rates seem
disturbingly high, and the nightly news seems dominated by
stories about disorder in the streets.

Imagine, for a moment, attending a futurist seminar, and the
speaker has turned his attention to the topic of social control.
He has said a few words about the coming days of electronic
surveillance through bracelets on people's ankles and wrists,
pictures and home addresses of convicted criminals displayed
for all to see at the touch of a keyboard, detention in an offender's home enforced by threat of prison, chemical testing of a
person's cells—detectable from saliva left at the scene of a

crime—instead of fingerprints to prove guilt at trial, and so
on. The audience would rightfully have been a bit awed by the
prospect.

Then he makes the most stunning prediction of all. He says,
"In the next 30 years, the prison population is going to grow by
600 percent. Instead of today's 200,000 prisoners, we will have
more than 1.3 million."

Anyone who heard such predictions in the early 1970s would
have been more than a bit skeptical. But they have all come true.

Any answer to the question, "What do we get from imprisonment?" has to begin with a frank recognition that incarceration
in the United States today operates differently than in any other
modernized or democratic state in the world, and that this phenomenon has resulted from very recent changes in U.S. penal
policy. Today, we lock up our fellow citizens at a rate (700 per
100,000) that is between 5 and 10 times higher than in comparable industrial democracies.

A Washington, D.C., prison reform group, the Sentencing
Project, has offered these comparisons: European states such
as Germany, Sweden, France, the Netherlands, and Switzerland
have incarceration rates of less than 100 per 100,000, one-seventh
of ours. The big lock-up states—England, Spain, Canada, and
Australia—have prison/jail rates of between 100 and 200, or
one-fourth of ours. Our only competitors are Russia and South
Africa, with prison-use levels that are 90 and 60 percent of ours,
respectively.

That is not the whole story. Our world leadership in the use
of prison is a fairly recent accomplishment. U.S. prison population statistics go back to 1925, when there were about 100,000
prisoners. Between 1925 and 1940, a period of fairly substantial
immigration and U.S. population growth, the number of prisoners doubled. During the years of World War II, the prison
population dropped by about a third. (Most observers think this
drop was due to the large number of young men in the armed
forces and unavailable for imprisonment). Between 1945 and
1961, the number of prisoners grew by 68 percent, to a high of
about 210,000 in the early 1960s, staying more or less stable
into the 1970s.

U.S. Leads World in Incarceration

- Today, the United States locks up its citizens at a rate (700 per 100,000) that is between 5 and 10 times higher than in comparable industrial democracies.
- In European states such as Germany, Sweden, France, the Netherlands, and Switzerland, incarceration rates are under 100 per 100,000.
- The big lockup states—England, Spain, Canada, and Australia—have prison/jail rates of between 100 and 200, or one-quarter of ours.
- The only competitors for prison and jail use are Russia and South Africa, with levels that are 90 and 60 percent of ours, respectively.
- Since the 1990s, almost all the growth in the prison population has been due to longer sentences, not more crime or prisoners.
- In effect, the U.S. anomaly in prison use results mostly from the policies we enact to deal with crime, much less than from crime itself.

Social scientists looked at these numbers and saw a pattern of profound stability. In 1975, two researchers from Carnegie-Mellon University, Alfred Blumstein and Jacqueline Cohen, argued that after accounting for such factors as war, immigration, and changes in youth population, there had been a "homoeostatic" level of stability in punishment for the first three-quarters of the twentieth century. That theory no longer applies. Between 1971 and 2002, the number of prisoners grew by an astounding 600 percent. Why did everything change?

Why the Growth in Crime?

It is easy to say that prison populations grew because crime—or at least violent crime—grew. But this view turns out to be simplistic. In their recent book, *Crime Is Not the Problem*, UCLA criminologists Franklin Zimring and Gordon Hawkins point out that several countries have violent crime rates that rival ours, yet use prison less readily than we do. Moreover, those European countries with low rates of incarceration seem to have property crime rates that are not so different from ours.

Besides, the growth of the U.S. prison population has been so consistent for a generation that nothing seems to affect it much. Since 1980, for example, prison populations grew during economic boom times and recessions alike; while the baby boomers were entering their crime-prone years and as they exited those years; and as crime dropped and while it soared.

Today's nationally dropping crime rates—a trend in some big cities that is almost a decade long—suggest that prison growth has helped make the streets safer. But when we take the long view, aside from burglary (which has dropped systematically for 20 years), today's crime rates are not very different than at the start of the big prison boom in the 1970s. Since then, crime rates went up for a while, down for a while, back up again, and are now (thankfully) trending downward. Prison populations, by contrast, went only one way during this entire period: up.

Blumstein and Department of Justice statistician Allen Beck have studied trends in criminal justice since the 1980s to better understand what accounts for the recent growth in the prison population. They argue that you can divide the growth into three distinct periods. In the late 1970s and early 1980s, prisons grew because crime was growing and more criminals were being sentenced to prison. In the 1980s into the beginning of the 1990s, prison growth was partly due to crime rates, but it was much more a product of greater numbers of criminals being sentenced to prison and of longer terms for those sentenced there.

By the 1990s and into the early 2000s, the story has changed, and almost all of the growth in the prison population is due to longer sentences, not more crime or more prisoners. In effect, the U.S. anomaly in the use of prison is a result mostly of the policies we enact to deal with crime, and much less of crime itself.

A Street's-Eye View

But all of this exploration looks for broad patterns. What about the view from the streets? John DiIulio of the University of Pennsylvania, former codirector of the White House Office on Faith-Based Initiatives, once observed, "A thug in jail can't shoot my sister?" Isn't it apparent on its face that a person behind bars is someone from whom the rest of us are pretty safe?

Yes, but that may not be the most effective way to deter crime. The irony is that while people who are behind bars are less likely to commit crimes, that may not mean those crimes are prevented from occurring.

Drug crime is the obvious example. Almost one-third of those sent to prison are punished for drug-related crimes, and one prisoner in four is serving time for a drug crime. In most of these cases, the criminal activity continued without noticeable interruption, carried out by a replacement. One of the recurrent frustrations of police work is to carry out a drug sweep one day, only to see the drug market return in a matter of hours. Locking up drug offenders is not an efficient strategy for preventing drug crime.

This line of analysis can be misleading, though, because most drug offenders are not specialists in drug crime. Analyses of criminal records show that people in prison who are serving time for drug-related activity typically have arrests and/or convictions for other types of offenses. Doesn't locking them up for drugs prevent the other crimes from happening? At least some other crime is prevented, but not as much as might be thought.

A few years ago, Yale sociologist Albert Reiss reported that about half of all criminal acts are perpetrated by young offenders acting in groups of two or more. Rarely are all of the members of the group prosecuted for the crime. This discovery led to a string of studies of what has been referred to as "co-offending," the commission of crimes by multiple offenders acting in concert. When one person out of a group is arrested and imprisoned, what impact does the arrest have on the crimes the group had been committing? A lot rides on the nature and behavior of criminal groups.

Much research is now under way to better understand how crimes are committed by offenders acting alone and in a group. It would be convenient if criminal groups had stable leaders and were systematic in the way they planned criminal activity. If so, arresting the leaders might break up the groups, and strategies of deterrence might reduce the likelihood of criminal actions. Neither characteristic applies.

Criminologist Mark Warr of the University of Texas has studied the way young males form co-offending groups and engage in criminal acts. He reports that leadership is sporadic and often interchangeable, that criminal actions are spontaneous, and that co-offending groups are loosely formed and vary over time. His findings suggest that well-respected strategies of targeted prosecution and focus on leaders of criminal activity are likely to have diminishing returns in crime prevention. As Rutgers University's Marcus Felson has argued, this analysis of dynamic, spontaneous, loosely organized criminal activity applies not simply to some youth but to most gang behavior. Arresting one person in the network and sending him to prison is far from a guarantee that the crime that person was involved in will stop.

Are Crime and Punishment Connected?

None of this is to argue that imprisonment prevents no crime. Professor David W. Garland of New York University School of Law, one of the most widely respected social critics of imprisonment, puts it well when he says that only the naive would claim that prisons and crime are unrelated. But even if it is recognized that crime and prisons are connected, under close scrutiny, we can find various reasons why wildly growing rates of imprisonment might not lead willy-nilly to wildly reducing rates of crime. Said another way, we can find explanations for the fact that the period in which incarceration has grown so much has not been matched by a corresponding drop in crime.

A new literature is emerging about the unintended consequences of incarceration. Prison populations, for example, are drawn predominantly from the ranks of poor people from minority groups. Today, one in eight black males aged 25–29 is locked up; this rate is almost eight times higher than for white males. Estimates reported by the Department of Justice indicate that of black males born today, 29 percent will go to prison for a felony offense, while currently 17 percent of all African-American males have spent time in prison. These rates are about six times higher than for white males.

Patterns of racial segregation mean that imprisonment also concentrates residentially. James Lynch and William Sabol, researchers from the Urban Institute, have estimated that in some very poor neighborhoods in Washington, D.C., and Cleveland, Ohio, upwards of 18–20 percent of adult males are locked up on any given day. New York City's Center for Alternative Sentencing and Employment Services reported that in 1998, in two of Brooklyn's poorest Council Districts, one person went to prison or jail for every eight resident males aged 20–40.

These high rates of incarceration, concentrated among poor minority males living in disadvantaged locations, are a new phenomenon that results from a generation of prison population growth in the United States. Social scientists are beginning to investigate whether this socially concentrated use of prison sentences has long-term effects on such factors as neighborhood order, family structure, and child development.

One can imagine, for example, that a neighborhood where a large proportion of parent-age men are missing is a neighborhood that would grapple with a number of problems, from family stability to child supervision. My own research with my colleagues Dina Rose and Elin Waring seems to suggest that high incarceration rates produce socially destabilizing results that may be a factor in sustaining high rates of crime.

The prison is a blunt social instrument, while crime is a much more nuanced social problem. Given what we know about crime, it should not surprise us that so much prison has provided so little in the way of broad public safety.

When trying to weigh the benefits of prison, perhaps we are used to asking the wrong question. We tend to ask about whether prison is a good idea compared to alternative sentencing. In today's America, this may be a fascinating question but it is not a very meaningful one. The more appropriate question would be, "Given our experience with incarceration over the last century, what might we expect from further increases in its use; what might happen if we began to cut back in its use?" This question, which we might perhaps save for another day, would recognize the political reality that U.S. prison rates are going to be internationally out-of-scale for a long time. The only question we face is, how much?

TODD R. CLEAR is Distinguished Professor in Community Justice and Corrections at John Jay College of Criminal Justice in New York City.

Experiment Will Test the Effectiveness of Post-Prison Employment Programs

ERIK ECKHOLM

Chicago—As raw garbage streamed by on a conveyer belt, newly released convicts pulled out paper, plastics and other recyclables on a recent morning, throwing aside the occasional brick or mattress.

Noisy, dusty and smelly, paying $6.50 an hour, the jobs yield neither the swagger nor the swag that these men and women chased as drug dealers, thieves or worse. But many of them see the temporary work as a fresh start.

The jobs are arranged by a Chicago charity, the Safer Foundation, which works with current and former prisoners. Offering transitional jobs like these—immediate, closely supervised work and help finding permanent employment—is a growing tactic in the effort to usher felons back to society and curb recidivism. Now the effectiveness of this approach is about to be tested scientifically for the first time.

Starting in January, the employment and recidivism rates of 2,000 newly released male prisoners, all with similar histories of little work and poor schooling, will be studied in Detroit, Milwaukee, St. Paul and Chicago.

Half of the men will receive more limited aid: instruction in work behavior, résumé preparation and other employment skills and help looking for a job. The other half will get those services and also a few months of temporary work in places like the recycling plant here—a chance for them to get into the unfamiliar rhythms of a regular job.

The experiment, which will track the two groups over three years, is being sponsored by the Joyce Foundation in Chicago and directed by the Manpower Demonstration Research Corporation in New York, which specializes in scientific studies of poverty programs.

Separately, the research group is conducting a controlled study of the transitional jobs program at the Center for Employment Opportunities in New York, which provides maintenance crews for public facilities and has been a national model.

"If you ask inmates what they want most, they want a job," said Mindy Tarlow, executive director of the center in New York. "But they don't know what that means."

She added, "What we're competing with is making some money at night on a street corner instead of having to show up somewhere at 8 A.M. every day."

Despite the apparent promise of transitional jobs, questions remain about their long-term effectiveness that the study hopes to address.

Are those who last through these programs such a select group—so motivated to change—that they would succeed anyway, or can well-timed help turn others around, too?

Can work-site counseling, sobriety meetings and a strong dose of mainstream work overcome the criminal pull of old haunts and friends?

And more fundamentally: will people with low skills, even if they adapt to steady work, ever make wages high enough to support a family and stifle the temptation to return to crime?

Roberto Reyes, a 36-year-old high school dropout in Chicago who has served seven years on burglary, gun and drug charges, works the conveyer belt at a recycling plant that is run for the city by Allied Waste Services.

Mr. Reyes has labored at the plant for four months, the longest he has held a job. "The money here is not that much, but it's better than nothing," he said. "Sometimes you wake up and don't want to come to work, but I'm not going to leave this until I find another job. I knew I couldn't just keep going on with that lifestyle and see life pass me by."

Mr. Reyes's determination is evident, but the numbers and records of people in his situation are daunting.

In Chicago, more than 20,000 prisoners come home from state facilities each year. Fifty-four percent are re-incarcerated within three years for new crimes or parole violations—a tale of wasted lives and victimized communities that is repeated nationwide among more than 600,000 prisoners that are released annually.

While common sense, and prisoners themselves, say that employment is vital to an honest new life, the obstacles are huge. A majority of those leaving prison did not finish high school and have little legitimate work experience. Many have serious drug or psychological problems that must be treated before they can hold a regular job. And while transitional programs may acclimatize them to the time-clock world of the workplace, many are likely to remain stuck in low-end jobs anyway.

Those who work with prisoners say that enticing onetime thugs to give work a try is not always as hard as it sounds. "They tell us that what comes with the street life is looking over your shoulder all the time," said Diane Williams, president of the Safer Foundation. One key, she said, seems to be getting released prisoners into work quickly, when the desire to normalize their lives is strongest.

Jimmy Parker, 24, was in and out of prison and hustling until six months ago when he decided, as he put it, "enough is enough."

"This job is rough, but I'm trying to change my life around," he said during a break at another recycling site run by Allied. "I've accomplished one thing—I got my own studio apartment—and someday I want to get custody of my daughter."

The Safer Foundation has eight employees who search for companies willing to hire former prisoners. Allied Waste's experience with such workers has been positive, said Robert Kalebich, general manager for the company in Chicago. Safer keeps a full-time "job coach" at each work site to advise workers and deal with disputes.

"If anything we see an advantage in this arrangement," Mr. Kalebich said. "If we hire off the street we have to wonder are they trained, are they here legally, are they properly drug tested."

Raphael Carter served drug time when he was 18, stayed out for nearly a decade, then found himself in prison again. "I woke up and said, I can't do this anymore, it's a dead end road," he recalled, adding that he now has two children, 13 and 6, who depend on him.

"You have to weigh the options, would you rather go back to jail or get a little increment of money and see your kids," said Mr. Carter, 30, who lives with his girlfriend and her four children. "Being older, I made the right choice."

He worked for six months at the recycling job, then found a chance in a nearby city driving a forklift for the attractive wage of $11.60 an hour. But his car broke down once too often during the hour and a half drive to work, he said, and he was let go.

Now he works for a company that erects large party tents, a seasonal job at $8.50 an hour, and he is consulting the Safer listings for a permanent job.

"By myself I wouldn't have had any of these opportunities," he said.

Do We Need the Death Penalty?

It Is Just and Right

DUDLEY SHARP AND STEVEN W. HAWKINS

There is nothing quite like hanging out with your best friend. Jenny Ertman, 14, and Elizabeth Peña, 16, shared their hopes and dreams with each other. Like millions of other teenagers, they liked to have fun, to laugh and smile. One summer evening in Houston, Texas, they shared their last moments on earth together—their own murders.

They were late returning home and took a shortcut through the woods, next to some railroad tracks. They ran into a gang initiation. They were both raped: orally, anally, and vaginally. The gang members laughed about the virgin blood they spilled. When they had finished, they beat and strangled the girls. But Jenny and Elizabeth wouldn't die. With all their strength, with their souls still holding on to the beautiful lives before them, they fought for life.

The gang worked harder. The girls were strangled with belts and shoelaces, stomped on and beaten. Their dreams disappeared as life seeped away from their broken bodies.

Their parents are left to visit empty rooms, to cry upon the beds of their daughters and think what could have been. How beautiful Elizabeth would have been in her prom dress. Her corsage was replaced by the flowers on her grave.

And Jenny's future children, would their grandparents have spoiled them? You know the answer. The immutable joy of grandchildren's laughter was silenced by the cruel selfishness of murder.

Why the Death Penalty

Sometimes, the death penalty is simply the most appropriate punishment for the vile crime committed. In such cases, jurors are given the choice between a death sentence and a variety of life sentences, depending upon the jurisdiction. It is never easy for juries to give a death sentence. Neither hatred nor revenge is part of their deliberations. The search for justice determines the punishment.

The murder of the innocent is undeserved. The punishment of murderers has been earned by the pain and suffering they have imposed on their victims. Execution cannot truly represent justice, because there is no recompense to balance the weight of murder. For some crimes, it represents the only just punishment available on earth.

Today, much more than justice is part of the death penalty discussion. Opponents are relentlessly attacking the penalty process itself. They insist that it is so fraught with error and caprice that it should be abandoned. At the very least, they say, America should impose a national moratorium so the system can be reviewed.

The leading salvo in those claims is that 101 innocent people have been released from death row with evidence of their innocence. The number is a fraud. Unfortunately, both the international media and, most predictably, the U.S. media have swallowed such claims and passed them along to the public.

Even many of our elected officials in Washington have blindly accepted those numbers. Sen. Patrick Leahy, chairman of the Senate Judiciary Committee, has said: "What we know is that nearly 100 innocent people have been released from death row since 1973."

The source for these claims is the Death Penalty Information Center (DPIC), the leading source of antideath penalty material in the United States. Richard Dieter, head of the DPIC, has admitted, in the June 6, 2000, *ABA Journal*, that his group makes no distinction between the legally innocent ("I got off death row because of legal error") and the actually innocent ("I had no connection to the murder") cases. Although the DPIC has attempted to revise its standards for establishing innocence, none of the various contortions even suggests actual innocence.

As everyone knows, the debate is about the actually innocent. To strengthen their case, death penalty opponents have broadened their "innocent" count by cases that don't merit that description. On June 20, for example, the Florida Commission on Capital Cases released its review of 23 death sentence cases that the DPIC had called into question. Its conclusion was that in only 4 of those cases were there doubts as to guilt.

Though the DPIC claims that 101 cases were released from death row with evidence of innocence, the actual number is closer to 30. That is 30 cases out of 7,000 sentenced to death since 1973. It appears that the death penalty may well be this country's most accurate criminal sanction, when taking into account the percentage of actual innocent convicted (0.4 percent) and the thoroughness of preventing those allegedly innocent from being executed (100 percent).

Of all the world's social and governmental institutions that put innocents at risk, I can find only one, the U.S. death penalty, that has no proof of an innocent killed since 1900. Can you think of another?

Saving Innocent Lives

Two other factors weigh into the innocence consideration. First, the death penalty remains the most secure form of incapacitation, meaning that executed murderers do not harm and murder again. Living murderers do, quite often. This is unchallenged. Second, although the deterrent effect of capital punishment has been unjustifiably maligned, the evidence is overwhelming that the potential for negative consequences deters or alters behavior. History and the social sciences fully support that finding.

Three major studies were released in 2001, all finding for the deterrent effect of the death penalty. One, out of Emory University, finds that "each execution results, on average, in 18 fewer murders—with a margin of error of plus or minus 10."

Another, out of the University of Houston, found that a temporary halt to executions in Texas resulted in an additional 90–150 murders, because of the reduction in deterrence. One author, Professor C. Robert Cloninger, states: "[Our] recent study is but another of a growing list of empirical work that finds evidence consistent with the deterrent hypothesis. It is the cumulative effect of these studies that causes any neutral observer to pause."

Death penalty opponents want us to believe that the most severe criminal sanction—execution—deters no one. However, if reason is your guide and you remain unsure of deterrence, you are left with the following consideration. If the death penalty does deter, halting executions will cause more innocents to be slaughtered by giving murderers an additional opportunity to harm and murder again. If the death penalty does not deter, executions will punish murderers as the jury deems appropriate, preventing them from harming any more victims. Clearly, ending or reducing executions will put many more innocents at risk.

Another major factor in the debate was introduced in a study headed by James Liebman, a professor at Columbia University Law School. *A Broken System: Error Rates in Capital Cases* revealed that there was a 68 percent reversal rate in death penalty cases from 1973 to 1995. The error rate within that study has not been publicly discussed.

Professors Barry Latzer and James Cauthen of John Jay College of Criminal Justice found a 25 percent error within the study's calculations, bringing the reversal rate down to 52 percent. Unfortunately, they had to accept the accuracy of Liebman's assessments, because he refused to release his database. Case reviews in Florida, New Jersey, Utah, and Nevada have provided specific cause to challenge his data. Florida challenges any assessment of error in 33 percent of the cases identified by Liebman, suggesting that the national "error" rate may be closer to 35 percent.

But even that number is suspect. The Supreme Court has stated that the death penalty system receives super due process.

Not an Easy Decision

- Sometimes, the death penalty is simply the most appropriate punishment for a violent crime committed.
- In such cases, jurors are given the choice between a death sentence and a variety of life sentences, depending upon jurisdiction.
- It is never easy for juries to give a death sentence. Neither hatred nor revenge is supposed to be part of their deliberations.
- The search for justice determines the punishment.

This means that the courts are extraordinarily generous in granting reversals in death penalty cases. In fact, the appellate courts are twice as likely to reverse the sentence in death penalty cases as they are the conviction.

Traditionally, death penalty opponents have stated that racism and poverty determine who receives the death penalty. Those arguments persist. What they fail to reveal is that white murderers are twice as likely to be executed as black murderers and are executed 12 months faster.

Some claim that the race of the victim determines the sentence. While those who murder whites dominate death row, it is also true that, overwhelmingly, whites are the victims in robberies, rapes, burglaries, and car-jackings, which make up the majority of death penalty crimes.

No one disputes that the wealthy have an advantage in avoiding a death sentence. The United States executes about 0.1 percent of its murderers. Is there any evidence that it is less likely to execute the wealthier ones, based on the ratio of wealthier to poorer capital murderers? Surprisingly, no.

The Justice Factor

This brings me back to where I started: justice. Some say that executions show a contempt for human life, but the opposite is true. We would hope that a brutal rape may result in a life sentence. Why? We value freedom so highly that we take freedom away as punishment. If freedom were not valued, taking it away would be no sanction.

Life is considered even more precious. Therefore, the death penalty is considered the severest sanction for the most horrible of crimes. Even murderers tell us that they value life (their own) more than freedom. That is why over 99 percent of convicted capital murderers seek a life sentence, not a death sentence, during the punishment phase of their trials.

Even some of those traditionally against capital punishment have decided that some crimes are justly punished with death. Timothy McVeigh's 2001 execution was thought a just punishment by 81 percent of the American people, reflecting an all-time high of support. When 168 innocents were murdered, including 19 children whom McVeigh described as "collateral damage," the collective conscience of the American people reached an overwhelming consensus. A Gallup poll, released on May 20, shows that 72 percent supported the death penalty, with nearly half those polled saying the sanction is not imposed enough.

Why didn't I invoke the murder of 3,100 innocents on September 11? Because the murder of one Jenny Ertman is enough—much too much. Which one of the murdered innocents was more valuable than another? Was one child blown apart in Oklahoma City not enough? Was a father forever lost on September 11 not enough? A son? A granddaughter?

Is it the numbers, at all? No, it is the realization that those innocent lives, so willfully ripped from us, represent individuals who contributed to someone's life and happiness. The sheer numbers of murders committed each year may numb us beyond what an individual murder can. But that is only because we must shield ourselves from the absolute horror represented by one innocent murdered. It is a matter of emotional self-preservation.

Often, in the most horrible of times, we find that the goodness in people stands out. At one point during the attack, Jenny was able to escape and run away. Elizabeth's cries brought Jenny back in a fruitless attempt to aid her friend. Love, friendship, and devotion overcame fear.

Of the six attackers who brutalized these girls for over an hour, five received the death penalty. The sixth was too young to prosecute for death. And why did five separate juries give death? Justice.

DUDLEY SHARP is vice president of Justice for All, a criminal justice reform organization in Houston, Texas. Web sites include www.jfa.net, www.prodeathpenalty.com, and www.murdervictims.com.

It Is Immoral and Ineffective

STEVEN W. HAWKINS

When the Supreme Court struck down death penalty laws in 1972, former Justice Potter Stewart compared the arbitrariness of the death penalty to the freakishness of being struck by lightning.

Thirty years later, were he still alive, Justice Stewart would probably appreciate his choice of words. In the past five years, an average of 78 people a year have been executed in the United States; in 1995, according to the National Center for Health Statistics, 76 Americans were struck by lightning.

Americans who support the death penalty think it should be reserved for the worst of the worst. The reality of capital punishment, however, shows that it is reserved for racial minorities, people who are retarded or mentally ill, and those who cannot afford to hire a good attorney. It is also all too often reserved for people who are factually innocent of the crime for which they were convicted and sentenced to be executed.

Doubt that the death penalty is racist? Consider this: 55 percent of the inmates who make up America's death row population are people of color (43 percent of death row inmates are black). Two of every three juvenile offenders on death row are people of color, as are a majority of retarded inmates.

Furthermore, the race of the victim plays a role in who ends up on death row. Nationwide, just half of murder victims are white, yet four out of every five people executed in the United States have died for killing white people.

Signs of Racism

Of course, the numbers do not paint a complete picture. Racial minorities have been the victims of particularly cruel and vindictive wrongful prosecutions, particularly in the South. Consider the case of Clarence Brandley, who spent 10 years on death row in Texas for a crime he did not commit.

Brandley was the head janitor at a high school where a young white female student was found strangled. When police arrived at the crime scene and saw Brandley, a black man, and another janitor, who was white, one officer reportedly declared, "One of you is gonna hang for this. Since you're the nigger, you're elected." Brandley was freed from prison when all charges against him were dropped after a Department of Justice and FBI investigation uncovered trial misconduct.

Doubt that the death penalty is reserved for people who are retarded or mentally ill? Since executions were allowed to resume in 1976, we've executed 44 mentally retarded inmates. (And that is a conservative number. Many inmates are not evaluated for mental retardation before they are executed.)

These 44 inmates include Morris Mason of Virginia who, on his way to the death chamber, turned to a prison worker and I said. "You tell Roger [another death row inmate] when I get back, I'm going to show him I can play basketball as good as he can." Ricky Rector of Arkansas separated his pecan pie from his last meal and left it on the windowsill of his prison cell. He wanted to eat it after the execution.

Doubt that the death penalty discriminates against those who cannot afford a good attorney? Consider the case of Ronald Keith Williamson, who was convicted in Oklahoma and sentenced to death for murder and rape in 1988.

Williamson's conviction was tossed out because of ineffectiveness of counsel; a federal appellate court wryly noted that his attorney failed to investigate and present to the jury the fact that another man had confessed to the rape and murder. It was a case of you get what you pay for—the attorney had received

---

A Racist Judgment

- Capital punishment is reserved for racial minorities, people who are retarded or mentally ill, and those who cannot afford a good attorney.
- All too often, it is reserved for people who are factually innocent of the crime.
- Fifty-five percent of the inmates who make up America's death row population are people of color.
- Two of every three juvenile offenders on death row are people of color, as are a majority of retarded inmates.
- Furthermore, the victim's race plays a role in who ends up on death row. Just half of murder victims are white, yet four out of every five of those executed have died for killing white people.

---

only $3,200 for his defense. Later, DNA evidence would exonerate Williamson.

Of course, that is just the tip of the iceberg. We've seen capital murder suspects represented by drunken lawyers, sleeping lawyers, biased lawyers, inexperienced lawyers, lawyers who were later disbarred, and lawyers who would be institutionalized due to mental illness.

Aden Harrison Jr., a black man, had as his court-appointed counsel 83-year-old James Venable, who had been an imperial wizard of the Ku Klux Klan for more than 15 years. Judy Haney's court-appointed lawyer was so drunk during the trial in 1989 that he was held in contempt and sent to jail. The next day, both client and attorney came out of the cellblock and the trial resumed. George McFarland's attorney slept through much of the trial. He objected to hardly anything the prosecution did, and every time he opened his eyes, a different witness was on the stand.

The Importance of the Trial Attorney

As Supreme Court Justice Ruth Ginsburg put it, "People who are well represented at trial do not get the death penalty. I have yet to see a death penalty case among the dozens coming to the Supreme Court on eve-of-execution stay applications in which the defendant was well represented at trial."

Doubt that the death penalty ensnares innocent Americans in its complicated legal web? More than 100 people have been freed from death row due to actual innocence, while close to 800 people have been executed. This means that for every eight people we are executing, one person is completely exonerated.

Think of it this way. What if a prescription drug cured eight of every nine people who took it but killed the ninth? What if an airline carrier successfully completed eight of every nine flights it launched, but the ninth resulted in mechanical failure?

What if you are able to successfully reboot your computer eight of every nine tries, but the rest of the time, it crashes and destroys your document? As a society that depends upon

a functioning criminal justice system, should we have confidence when that same justice system sends innocent people to death row?

As Supreme Court Justice Sandra Day O'Connor put it, "If statistics are any indication, the system may well be allowing some innocent defendants to be executed. More often than we want to recognize, some innocent defendants have been convicted and sentenced to death."

Kirk Bloodsworth of Maryland and Clyde Charles of Louisiana should know. Bloodsworth spent nine years in prison—two on death row—before DNA testing of old evidence proved him innocent of the only crime for which he had ever been arrested, the brutal rape and murder of a nine-year-old girl. While he was in prison, his mother passed away, and Bloodsworth was forced to view the body while wearing shackles. The real child predator and killer remains unidentified.

Charles spent 19 years at Angola in Louisiana, one of the country's most notorious prisons. He fought for 9 years to get DNA testing done. The results proved that Charles could not have committed the crime, and he was released.

His children grew into adults while he was in prison, and both his parents died; he also caught tuberculosis and developed diabetes. The same DNA test that exonerated Charles identified the real criminal—who had since been tested for committing other crimes against innocent victims while the wrong man was in jail.

Some death penalty proponents quibble over the number of people who have been found to have been factually innocent. The exact number isn't really what's important. What's important is that not one of us—death penalty opponents or proponents—would conclude that executing even one innocent person constitutes acceptable criminal justice policy in the United States.

Who Is Listening?

Arguments against the death penalty are easy to make, but is anyone listening? The bad news is that most Americans continue to support capital punishment in theory. The good news is when you start to probe, there is a growing sense of unease and ambivalence.

For example, 80 percent of voters want to abolish or significantly reform the death penalty system. Sixty-nine percent of voters are more worried about executing an innocent person than executing the guilty. And 64 percent of voters—including 50 percent of Republican voters—want to suspend executions until issues of fairness can be resolved.

The fact is that people are beginning to respond to concerns about the system. Across the United States, a healthy and vibrant moratorium movement is gathering steam. Elected bodies in 73 municipalities have passed resolutions in favor of a moratorium.

Two governors, Republican George Ryan in Illinois and Democrat Parris Glendening in Maryland, have each declared a moratorium. Some 14 states have debated moratorium legislation; in New Hampshire, the legislature passed a bill abolishing the death penalty, only to see it vetoed by the governor.

In Nevada and Maryland, bills imposing a moratorium passed one chamber, only to be defeated in the other. In New Mexico, a bill to abolish the death penalty failed in the Senate by one vote. Next year, as legislatures across the nation convene for their 2003 session, we can expect many more moratorium bills to be debated—as well as bills calling for outright abolition.

Let's face it. The death penalty experiment in America has been tried and found wanting. It is time for the lethal injection gurney to go the way of the stake, the guillotine, and the gallows. It is time to relegate this gruesome practice to the dustbin of history. Our common decency demands no less.

STEVEN W. HAWKINS is executive director of the National Coalition to Abolish the Death Penalty, located in Washington, D.C. NCADP was founded in 1976 and is the only fully staffed national organization devoted specifically to abolishing the death penalty. For more information, please visit www.ncadp.org.

Private Prisons Expect a Boom

Immigration Enforcement to Benefit Detention Companies

MEREDITH KOLODNER

As the Bush administration gets tougher on illegal immigration and increases its spending on enforcement, some of the biggest beneficiaries may be the companies that have been building and running private prisons around the country.

By the fall of 2007, the administration expects that about 27,500 immigrants will be in detention each night, an increase of 6,700 over the current number in custody. At the average cost these days of $95 a night, that adds up to an estimated total annual cost of nearly $1 billion.

The Corrections Corporation of America and the Geo Group (formerly the Wackenhut Corrections Corporation)—the two biggest prison operators—now house a total of fewer than 20 percent of the immigrants in detention. But along with several smaller companies, they are jockeying for a bigger piece of the growing business.

Corrections Corp. and Geo are already running 8 of the 16 federal detention centers.

With all the federal centers now filled and the federal government not planning to build more, most of the new money is expected to go to private companies or to county governments. Even some of the money paid to counties, which currently hold 57 percent of the immigrants in detention, will end up in the pockets of the private companies, since they manage a number of the county jails.

"Private companies are positioning themselves as suppliers, and are positioned to take the majority of new beds available," said Anton High, an analyst with Jefferies & Company, the brokerage firm. He has recommended that his clients buy Corrections stock.

Louise Gilchrist, vice president for marketing and communication at Corrections Corp., said her company would have no trouble meeting the federal government's needs. "We believe as their demand increases, they will need to rely on providers who have bed space available," she said. "The company feels it is well positioned."

Wall Street has taken notice of the potential growth in the industry. The stock of Corrections Corp. has climbed to $53.77 from $42.50, an increase of about 27 percent, since February when President Bush proposed adding to spending on immigrant detention.

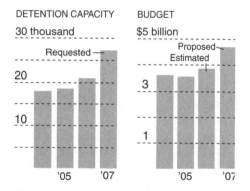

Figure 1 An increasing population. Private prison companies are poised to benefit from an expected increase in the number of illegal immigrants detained. Bureau of Immigration and Customs Enforcement.

Geo's stock rose about 68 percent in the period, to $39.24 a share from $23.36.

The increasing privatization of immigrant detention has its critics. Immigrant advocates say health care at some centers has fallen short. They contend that some centers have treated immigrants as if they are criminals—restricting their movements unnecessarily, for instance—even though many are still awaiting a ruling on their legal status.

Because those who cross the border illegally are not considered criminals, they are not automatically assigned a lawyer. But, the advocates say, there have been repeated instances when immigrants have not had access to working phones to call for legal assistance.

"Private prisons have unleashed an entrepreneurial spirit in this country that is unhealthy," said Judith Greene, director of the nonprofit research group Justice Strategies. "Standards are violated on a regular basis in order to cut costs."

Holding cells are more profitable than regular incarceration.

The companies counter that they are living up to their contractual obligations. "If you develop a reputation as a company that cuts corners, you will lose your contracts," said Steve Owen, director of marketing at Corrections. The allegations, he added, "are completely false."

Immigration experts say the need for more prison space is not a result of an increase in the number of people entering the United States illegally. According to the Pew Hispanic Center in Washington, the number of unauthorized immigrants arriving in this country is down by about 50,000 a year from the late 1990's.

Instead, the increase in spending on detention is part of a crackdown on illegal residents living in the United States as well as an expected increase in the number of immigrants captured as they try to cross the border.

The government also plans to detain more immigrants, especially those from countries other than Mexico, while they await their hearings, instead of releasing them on their own recognizance. This effort to end what is known as "catch and release" means more capacity is needed immediately.

"The issue is not how many immigrants," said Joe Onek, a senior policy analyst at the Open Society Institute. "There's incredible pressure on the administration from members of its own party and from some sectors of the population to crack down."

Revenues for the prison management companies will grow not only because of the rising number of detainees, but also because profit margins are higher at detention centers than prisons, analysts say.

Last year, the Correction Corp.'s revenue from holding immigrants jumped 21 percent, to $95 million from $70 million in 2004. Geo, the second largest prison operator, received $30.6 million last year, about the same as the year before.

While the companies would not comment on profit margins from their immigration business, Wall Street analysts said that detention centers produce profit margins of more than 20 percent.

That compares with margins in the mid-teens for traditional prison management, they said, because prisoners are provided with more costly services like high school degree programs and recreational activities.

Even with the expected growth in the number of immigrant detainees, the main source of income for the private prison companies will continue to be revenue from state and federal governments for housing regular inmates.

The state and local prison population totaled more than 1.5 million last year, with about 100,000 of those held in privately managed prisons. But the number of state and federal inmates rose by just 1.4 percent from June 2004 to June 2005, slower growth than the average 4.3 percent annual increases from 1995 to 2000.

By contrast, the number of immigrants in detention is expected to increase by about 20 percent over the next three months alone.

Federal immigration contracts generated about $95.2 million, or 8 percent, of Correction Corp.'s $1.19 billion in revenue last year, and about $30.6 million, or 5 percent, of Geo's $612 million total income.

In the first quarter of 2006, Corrections Corp.'s detention revenue rose to $25.5 million. The federal immigration agency is now the company's third-largest customer, after the federal Bureau of Prisons and the United States Marshals Service.

The detention market is projected to increase by $200 million to $250 million over the next 12 to 18 months, according to Patrick Swindle, a managing director at Avondale L.L.C., an investment banking firm that has done business with both Geo and Corrections Corp. He said that a company's capacity would play an important role in how much of the market it would be able to capture.

The company "currently has 4,000 empty beds in their system," Mr. Swindle said. "They are bringing on an additional 1,500 beds within the border region."

"Reasonably, about 3,000 to 4,000 beds could be made available" for immigrant detention, he said.

Having empty cell space that can be made available quickly is considered an advantage in the industry since the government's need for prison space is often immediate and unpredictable. Decisions about where to detain an immigrant are based on what is nearby and available. Immigration officials consider the logistics and cost of transportation to the detention center and out of the country.

"We can use the beds whenever and wherever we like," said Jamie Zuieback, a spokeswoman for United States Immigration and Customs Enforcement. "We are funded for a certain number of beds but there are many beds around the country that are available and it depends where and when we need them if we use them."

While companies do not release how much space they currently have available, analysts estimate that Geo has about 1,500 empty places. To increase capacity, the company announced in June that it was building a 576-inmate expansion of the 875-inmate Val Verde Correctional Facility it owns in Del Rio, Tex.

George C. Oley, Geo's chief executive, said in a statement at the time of the Val Verde announcement: "We are moving forward with the expansion of this important facility in anticipation of the expected increased demand for detention bed space by the Federal Government."

Despite the two companies' dominance, they face competition from smaller players in the corrections business. A new federal detention center set to open in Texas at the end of July will be run by the Management and Training Corporation, a privately owned company based in Utah.

The Cornell Companies, based in Texas, currently operates two centers that hold detainees. It is the third-biggest private corrections company, though significantly smaller than Corrections Corp. and Geo, controlling just 7 or 8 percent of the market, according to Mr. Swindle.

"What's great about the detention business," Mr. High of Jefferies said, "is not that it's a brand-new channel of demand, but that it is growing and significant."

Jail Time Is Learning Time

Signe Nelson and Lynn Olcott

There is excitement in the large, well-lit classroom. Student work, including history posters and artwork, adorn the walls. A polite shuffling of feet can be heard, as names are called and certificates presented. It is the graduation ceremony at the Onondaga County Justice Center in Syracuse, N.Y. The ceremony is held several times a year, recognizing inmates in the Incarcerated Education Program who have passed the GED exam or completed a 108-hour vocational program. The courses in the Incarcerated Education Program are geared to prepare inmates to transition successfully to several different settings.

The Incarcerated Education Program is a joint effort by the Syracuse City School District and the Onondaga County Sheriff's Office, and is housed inside the nine-story Onondaga County Justice Center in downtown Syracuse. The Justice Center is a 250,000 square-foot maximum-security, nonsentenced facility, completed and opened in 1995. The facility was built to contain 616 beds, but currently houses 745 inmates. Between 13,000 and 14,000 inmates passed through booking during 2004. About 2,500 of them were minors.

The Justice Center

The Justice Center is a state-of-the-art facility, designed for and operating on the direct supervision model. Direct supervision is a method of inmate management developed by the federal government in 1974 for presentenced inmates in the Federal Bureau of Prisons. There are about 140 such facilities operating throughout the United States and a few hundred currently under construction. Direct supervision places a single deputy directly in a "housing pod" with between 32 and 64 inmates. Maximum pod capacity in the Onondaga County Justice Center is 56 inmates. Inmates are given either relative freedom of movement within the pod or confined to their cells based on their behavior.

The program has been providing courses and classes at the Justice Center for 10 years, but this partnership between the school district and the sheriff's office began almost 30 years ago with the provision of GED instruction. The Incarcerated Education Program was originally conceived to ensure education for inmates who are minors. The program has grown tremendously and now has more than 20 offerings in academic, vocational and life management areas.

The Syracuse City School District professional staff includes six full-time and 18 part-time teachers and staff members. The program is unique in that there are three Onondaga County Sheriff's sergeants who hold New York State Adult Education certification and who teach classes in the vocational component. An average of 250 inmates, or about one-third of the Justice Center's incarcerated population, are enrolled in day and/or evening classes. There are about 250 hours of class time in the facility per week.

Varied Educational and Training Opportunities

As in the public education sector, vocational programs have evolved with the times. The Basic Office Skills class now offers two sections, and includes computer repair and office production skills. A course in building maintenance can be complemented by a course in pre-application to pre-apprenticeship plumbing, or in painting and surface preparation, a class that includes furniture refinishing. A baking class and nail technology have been added in the past few years. All vocational courses, before implementation, are approved by the New York State Education Department and are designed to be consistent with New York State Department of Labor employment projections for Onondaga County. No vocational programming is implemented without first identifying whether the occupation is an area of growth in the community.

Additionally, a broadly inclusive advisory board, made up of community representatives who are stakeholders in the local economy and in the quality of life in the Syracuse metropolitan area has been established. The Incarcerated Education Advisory Board meets approximately three times a year to discuss the perceived needs of the community and to address strategies for transitioning students into employment. Ongoing topics of study are issues surrounding employment, continuing education and housing.

Incarcerated Education Program planners are very aware that job skills are ineffective without proper work attitudes. Job Readiness Training addresses work ethic, proper work behavior, communication and critical behavior skills. Vocational classes are voluntary for the nonsentenced population. However, because of their popularity, a waiting list is maintained for several courses. Among these popular courses are Basic Office Skills and Small Engine Repair. An additional section of Small Engine Repair has been added for female inmates in the class to ensure gender equity in this training opportunity.

New York State law requires that incarcerated minors continue their education while incarcerated. The Incarcerated Education Program enrolls inmates, ages 16 to 21, in Adult Basic Education/GED classes and addresses students with special needs. Other adult inmates attend on a voluntary basis. Inmates are given an initial placement test to determine math and reading skill levels. Because inmates work at a wide range of ability levels, instruction is individualized and materials are geared to independent work. English as a second Language and English Literacy/Civics are complementary offerings for inmates who are in need of assistance in English language proficiency and knowledge of American culture and history.

The GED exam is given at the Justice Center every 60 days or more often as needed. In the past three years, 225 students have taken the exam. Passing rates fluctuate between 63 percent and 72 percent. The average passing rate for correctional institutions in New York is about 51 percent. The state average passing rate for the general public in community-based courses is fairly stable at 50 percent.[1]

Of course, not everyone will take the GED. Student turnover is high, as inmates are released, bailed out, sent to treatment centers, or sentenced to county, state and federal correctional facilities. Judy Fiorini is a GED teacher who has been with the program for more than 10 years. "Many go back out into our community. We try to teach them something useful for their lives," Fiorini explains.

Transition services form an integral part of the program. The focus is on minors, but help is available for everyone. Two fulltime staff members assist people upon release, with such important tasks as acquiring a driver's license, seeking housing, reenrolling in high school or preparing for job interviews. A very important part of transition services is helping people acquire birth certificates, social security cards and other documents crucial for identification.

Tackling Cognitive Issues

Corrections professionals and educators are aware that it is not enough to improve the skill base of an inmate. There must be cognitive changes as well. The justice center is not a treatment facility, but it has been evolving into a therapeutic community. As the Incarcerated Education Program has grown, there has been the flexibility to add several important courses dealing with life issues, attitude and decision-making. According to data provided by the justice center, about 80 percent of inmates have substance abuse-related issues at the time of their arrest. To support desired cognitive changes, the justice center began establishing "clean and sober" pods in 2002. Currently, there

are several clean and sober pods, including pods for adult men, women and youths. There are waiting lists for placement in the clean and sober pods.

The Incarcerated Education Program has been offering anger management groups for several years. Anger management helps group members deal with compulsive behavior and focus on long-term goals. Other life management offerings include family education, action for personal choice and a course called Parent and Child Together. Most courses of study are developed inhouse by experienced professional faculty. Additionally, the program established gender-specific courses, Men's Issues and Women's Issues, to help inmates become more directly aware of their own responsibilities, separate from the role of a partner or significant other in their lives. The Men's Issues class is led by certified professionals and focuses on actions and their consequences. As in most jails, male inmates significantly outnumber female inmates. Courses and groups continue to be added, though it is sometimes difficult to find space for the abundance of activity in the program.

The program is financially supported, using state and federal funds, via nine carefully coordinated grants. Also significant for the success of the program has been ongoing encouragement and technical assistance from the New York State Education Department, the New York State Association of Incarcerated Education Programs and support from the New York State Sheriffs' Association.[2]

The Incarcerated Education Program continues to encounter challenges. It takes energy and dedication to keep the varied curricula substantial and cohesive, despite high student turnover and complex student needs. With a large civilian staff, the program requires close coordination between security and civilian concerns to help civilian staff work most effectively within the safety and security priorities of the facility. Biweekly meetings facilitate ongoing communication.

Making the Most of Time

Every available square inch of classroom space is in constant use. Classes have exceeded available space and some classes meet in core areas of the justice center as well. Several classes are held in the residence pods, where heavy, white tables are pulled together and portable white-boards are erected to create nomadic classrooms. Overall, the program is succeeding in several ways. Incarcerated minors are directly and meaningfully involved in high school equivalency classes, and inmates older than 21 receive academic and vocational services on a voluntary basis. All inmates are offered the opportunity for life-skills classes and for transitional services upon release. Time served at the Onondaga County Justice Center can also be time used for valuable academic, vocational and life management achievements.

Notes

1. New York State Department of Education maintains statistics for educational activities at correctional facilities in New York state. Patricia Mooney directs the GED Program for the state

through the GED Testing Office in the State Department of Education. Greg Bayduss is the State Department of Education coordinator in charge of Incarcerated Education Programs throughout New York state.

2. State Professional Organizations: The New York State Association of Incarcerated Education Programs Inc. is a professional organization for teachers, administrators and security personnel (www.nysaiep.org). Its mission is to promote excellence in incarcerated education programs in the state, support research in this field and advocate for incarcerated education initiatives through collaboration with other professional organizations. The authors must mention the valuable assistance of the New York State Sheriffs' Association, supporting each county sheriff, as the chief law enforcement officer in his or her county (www.nyssheriffs.org). The association provides valuable information and technical assistance to county sheriffs to help implement programs in their jails.

SIGNE NELSON is the coordinator of the Incarcerated Education Program, and **LYNN OLCOTT** is a teacher at Auburn Correctional Facility in New York, formerly with the Incarcerated Education Program. The program could not have attained its present strength without the vision and support of law enforcement officials Sheriff Kevin Walsh, Chief Anthony Callisto, and Syracuse City School District administrator Al Wolf. Special thanks to Capt. John Woloszyn, commander of Support Services; Sgt. Joseph Powlina, administrative compliance supervisor; and Deputy Joseph Caruso, photographer. Their assistance in the production of this article was crucial and much appreciated.

The Professor Was a Prison Guard

JEFFREY J. WILLIAMS

When I was 20, I left college and took a job in a prison. I went from reading the great books as a Columbia University undergraduate to locking doors and counting inmates as a New York State correction officer. Since I'm an English professor now, people never entirely believe me when the issue comes up, probably because of the horn-rimmed glasses and felicitous implementation of Latinate words. I fancied I'd be like George Orwell, who took a job as an Imperial Police officer in Burma and wrote about it in "Shooting an Elephant." I thought I'd go "up the river" to the "big house" and write "Shooting an Inmate" or some such thing. It didn't quite happen that way, although as a professor, I've worked 14 of 16 years in state institutions.

For the most part, I worked at Downstate Correctional Facility, in Fishkill, N.Y. (You can see it in a hollow along the north side of Interstate 84, just east of the Newburgh-Beacon Bridge.) Newly opened and still under construction when I started, in 1979, the place was billed as the prison of the future. It adopted a "campus" style, with clusters of 36 cells arranged in a split-level horseshoe shape, rather than the traditional warehouse style of long rows of 40 or so cells stacked three or four stories high. The new style presumably granted a more pleasant environment, or simply less chaos. Downstate was also threaded with electronic sensors that would supposedly indicate if a cell door was open, or if someone was walking between the rows of razor wire encircling the facility. The electronics were bruited as a wonder solution to security, as well as being more economical, since the old design of a maximum-security prison required a small island of cement, with walls 30 feet high and 20 feet into the ground. The sensors, however, were moody, a sticky door registering locked and unlocked like a temperamental Christmas-tree light, and a raccoon, a bit of rain, or a poltergeist setting off the ones between the fences. Though annoying, they kept you awake if you drew a shift on the berm overlooking the grounds.

Downstate was designed to replace Sing Sing Correctional Facility, in Ossining, as the "classification and reception center" for New York's state prison system. If you were convicted of a felony and sentenced to a sizable term, you were shipped from a county jail to Downstate. County jails are essentially holding tanks, mixing innocent and guilty awaiting trial, 18-year-old shoplifters and 40-year-old murderers awaiting the next stop. State correction officers looked down on the jails as poorly run zoos, the nursery schools of the prison taxonomy; state officers had substantial training, and state prisons were the higher rehabilitation. Every male inmate in the state system spent his first six weeks at Downstate (women, who at the time numbered less than 5 percent of the prison population, went to Bedford Hills Correctional Facility), taking tests and getting interviewed so counselors could decide where he'd do his time. If he was young, maybe Elmira or Coxsackie; if on a short stretch, a minimum like Taconic; if on a long sentence, behind the high walls of maximums like Great Meadow, Green Haven, Attica, and Clinton. Since most of those convicted came from New York City and environs, Sing Sing had earned the sobriquet "up the river" because it was a 30-mile barge ride up the Hudson. Downstate continued the tradition another 30 miles up, although the present-day conduit is I-84 and the mode of transport a bus.

When you work in prison, just as when you work in academe, you experience a world that has its own language, its own training, its own hierarchy, its own forms of recognition.

Before getting a badge, correction officers did 12 weeks in the training academy in Albany. It was a cross between a military and a technical college, with calisthenics in the morning and classes all day. Wake-up was 6 A.M., with a couple of miles around the track; like in the military, your bed had to be made with crisp corners, belongings neatly stowed in your locker, hair short and face cleanshaven. There were periodic spot inspections, and you got demerits if you missed a step. The academy held hourly classes, punctuated by a bell (lateness was one demerit). One class gave background on the taxonomy and geography of New York's correctional system, from minimum to maximum, prisons dotting the state like community colleges. Another was on relevant law, defining necessary as opposed to excessive use of physical force (one should restrain an inmate from doing harm to himself or others, but not beat him once restrained), and enumerating rights (if an inmate complained of a physical ailment, you had to notify the hospital, even if you thought he was lying). One course covered procedures, detailing how to do a count, how to keep a notebook (in part for legal protection but mostly to pass on information to the next shift), and how to do searches (never ignore an inconvenient corner, even if you don't want to reach, but be careful of hidden pieces of glass or razor blades). One course taught rudimentary psychology, or "interpersonal communication," in which the instructors taught you how to deal with, say, an enraged inmate by responding with something to the effect of, "So you are telling me you're pissed off because. . . . " Although it seemed mindlessly redundant, it was not a bad lesson in how to stop and listen. Prisons, like any social institution, run best when they respond appropriately to needs as well as misdeeds. Contrary to the popular image of sadistic prison guards, the motto the academy drummed into you was "firm, fair, and consistent."

Everyone asks if I carried a gun, but inside the walls you were always outnumbered, and a gun would more likely be used for a takeover or escape. Instead, the most severe weapon was a nightstick. The only place you were issued a gun was on a perimeter post, at one of the gates or on the berm. At the academy, there were classes in weapons—at the time, in the trusty Smith & Wesson .38 revolver, which everyone had to qualify to use; the Remington pump-action shotgun, which you just had to shoot without falling over; and a long-distance .30-30, basically a deer rifle, which granted a special qualification to work in a tower at one of the walled prisons. After you were on the job, you had to qualify with the .38 every year, and, like a field trip, we looked forward to the day we went out to the shooting range. The one part we didn't look forward to was getting tear-gassed, deemed necessary so you knew what it felt like to have the rabid sting of CS or CN gas on your skin and wouldn't panic.

The lessons were usually reinforced with black humor, anecdotes, and morality tales. For example, you can use lethal physical force to prevent an imminent escape but not if an inmate is still on prison grounds. One quip was that if you shot an inmate scaling the fence, you had better make sure he landed on the outside—otherwise you'd end up inside. One story to remind us not to slack off on searches was about an escape from the Fishkill Correctional Facility (actually in Beacon, across the highway from Downstate). The inmate, so the story went, had gotten a gun smuggled in the bottom of a bucket of Kentucky Fried Chicken because the correction officer searching packages had supposedly eaten a piece off the top and passed the bucket through. Another story, to reinforce the rule that you should not eat state food or accept favors, however slight, from inmates, went something like this: An inmate, who worked in the mess hall and prepared the trays that got sent to the blocks for ill or keep-locked inmates, regularly brought BLT's to the correction officer on his block. One day the kitchen officer happened upon the inmate using a bodily fluid as a condiment on the bread. I never knew whether the story was true, but I always brought my lunch.

The first thing you learn when you get behind the walls or concertina wire is that prison has its own language. We received a glossary of terms at the training academy, but, just as with learning a foreign language, the words didn't mean much until you got inside. A prison guard is not a "screw," as in a James Cagney movie, but a "correction officer," or usually just a "CO." A prisoner is not a "convict" but an "inmate." A sentence is a "bid." A cell is a "crib." To calm down is to "chill." A homemade knife is a "shiv."

The university represents the hope, prison the failing, of the meritocracy.

Life in prison is punctuated by counts, three or four for every eight-hour shift. When I was in training at Elmira, which was an old prison with what seemed like mile-long rows of cells three stories high, I remember walking down the narrow runway to take the evening count. There were whispered goads—"CO, you look gooood," "Who you eyeballing?," "Hey motherfucker"—or simply hissing, which was the worst. I didn't turn around to look, since you rarely knew where the voices came from, amidst the echoes of reinforced concrete. Besides, turning would show that they were getting under your skin, which would just fuel the hiss.

What makes time go by in prison is the talk. Talk among the guards was a constant buzz—about life, yesterday's mail, what happened in the visiting room, the food in the mess hall this morning, the lieutenant who was a hard-ass and snuck around at night to catch you sleeping, if you were going fishing on your days off, if you were getting any. With the inmates, though, as in a game of poker, you never let too much show. The one time you worried was when the buzz stopped. You didn't have to know the literary definition of foreshadowing to know that something was aching to happen.

I got good at finding things, as much to stave off boredom as from a sense of duty. Once I found a 10-inch shiv hung in a crevice of cement behind a fuse-box door. It was fashioned from a soup-ladle handle purloined from the kitchen, filed laboriously on cement to a knife edge, its handle wrapped with white athletic tape. I would periodically find jugs of homemade booze, made from fruit and fermented in floor-wax containers, wedged behind a clothes dryer to cook or stowed beneath the bag in a utility vacuum. Once I found a few joints taped under a toilet tank. The joints bothered me more than the rest, not because they were harmful—in fact, one way to still a prison population would be to hand out joints, whereas booze, especially homebrews, tends to prime people for a fight—but because they came from outside. They could have come in through visits, swallowed in a condom, or they could mean a CO or other worker had a business they weren't declaring on their 1040. It violated the boundaries of the place, boundaries that you did not want to get fuzzy.

Prison carries its own set of lessons. One was about how life works, albeit life in a crockpot: mostly by repetition and habit, punctuated by sudden, sometimes scary, but strangely exhilarating moments that shattered the routine. Once when I was at Elmira, whiling away a shift after the inmates were locked in, except for the porters, who did the cleaning, I heard a clomping on the stairs. I looked over to see a porter, head dripping blood, running down the stairs, with another following a few steps back, carrying a piece of jagged glass in his hand. I followed to find two officers on the first tier pinning both inmates to the floor. Danger raises your blood pressure, which isn't good for you over the long term, but acts as a drug in the short.

Another lesson was "Do your job," which was a kind of mantra, repeated by CO's and inmates alike. It meant take your responsibility, don't slough off, don't dump your job on someone else, or you'd be not very tactfully reminded on the cellblock, in the parking lot, or at the next union meeting. The ecological balance of prisons is probably not much more fragile than those of other institutions, or there wouldn't be many prisons still standing, but its imbalances take on a particular intensity. If an inmate had a visitor, you made sure that inmate was escorted to the visiting room right away; otherwise he would have a legitimate beef, which would make life harder for everyone. Especially in the summer, when cement holds heat like barbecue bricks and you didn't want any sparks.

Another lesson was "Don't back down." If an inmate didn't go into his cell at count, you had to confront him and write it up or be ready to hit the beeper you wore on your belt; otherwise, the next day, three people would be lingering at the TV. It was a different kind of lesson than I had learned at Columbia. One might find it in the Iliad but not, in my experience, in most academic venues, where aggression is usually served with the sugary coating of passive circumlocution. I miss the clarity of it and, as with single malt, prefer my aggression straight.

Something else to remember was to the effect of "There but for the grace of God go I." There wasn't much room for moral superiority inside the razor wire, and you quickly lost it if you had it. I worked for a time in draft processing, which is where inmates first arrive after coming through the gates. They got a speech, a shower and delousing, a crew cut, and a khaki uniform cut like hospital scrubs, and then were assigned to a block. To avoid bias, officers generally didn't have access to rap sheets, except in draft and transport, when the sheets were like passports that traveled with the inmates. There was a young kid, maybe 18 or 19, who had been returned from Florida after escaping from a minimum. He had gotten three to five for stealing—taking a joy ride in—a dump truck in upstate New York, and the escape would probably double his sentence. On his sheet, there was an entry that read "act attributed to: drinking a case of beer." I'm not exaggerating.

Prison gave me a kind of adult education that, as a scholarship boy, I had not gotten in the humanities sequence at Columbia. It gave me an education about people, how they get by and how they don't. One of the ways they get by is loyalty. The people I worked with, even some of the inmates, "had my back": If a lieutenant gave you a hard time, the union rep would be in his face. If you were out too late and took a nap in the bathroom, another CO would cover for you. If an inmate saw the superintendent coming while you were watching TV and he thought you did your job, he would warn you. The better species of loyalty is, in fact, not blind: If you screw up, someone you work with should tell you. The corruption of loyalty is when no one says anything.

It's always curious to see how colleagues react when they find out about my time—as I like to put it—in prison. Some are fascinated and quote Cool Hand Luke, but clearly it's just a fantasy to them. Some take on a more serious cast and ask what I think of Foucault's Discipline and Punish, but then prison has become a disembodied abstraction, something they know as much about as dairy farms (as with most prisons, set a long way from any roads they've been on). Some look away, as if I had a swastika tattooed on my forearm. What they don't seem to realize is that correction officers are of the unionized working classes, like cops, whom my colleagues wouldn't hesitate to call if they had an accident or their house was broken into. It is often said that literature expands your world, but it can also close it off.

It is also often said that the university is not the real world, but in my experience each institutional parcel of life has its own world. When you work in prison, just as when you work in academe, you experience a world that has its own language, its own training, its own hierarchy, its own forms of recognition, its own forms of disrepute, and its own wall from the outside. In some ways, prison is the flip side of meritocracy. Both prisons and universities originated in religious institutions and are based on the model of the cloister; both are transitional institutions; both house and grade people; and both marshal primarily the young. The difference, of course, is that the university represents the hope, prison the failing, of the meritocracy. It's an unseemly sign that we invest more in the underside than in the hope.

JEFFREY J. WILLIAMS is a professor of English and literary and cultural studies at Carnegie Mellon University, and editor of the minnesota review. His most recent book is the collection *Critics at Work: Interviews, 1993–2003* (New York University Press, 2004).

Supermax Prisons

Jeffrey Ian Ross

Each time a crime occurs, an arrest is made, the trial ends, and a person is sentenced to prison, the public has a recurring curiosity about where the convict is sent. Over the past two decades, a phenomenal number of individuals have been sentenced to jails and to state or federal prisons.

But this is just the beginning of the journey. Prisoners are classified into a whole host of various kinds of facilities. They typically vary based on the level of security, from minimum to high. But since the mid-1980s, a dramatic change has underscored corrections in the United States and elsewhere. Correctional systems at all levels have introduced or expanded the use of Supermax prisons.

Supermax prisons, also known as Administrative Control Units, Special (or Security) Handling Units (SHU), or Control Handling Units (CHU) (Here, "CHUs" is pronounced "shoes.") are stand-alone correctional facilities, wings or annexes inside an already existing prison. They are a result of the recent growth in incarceration that has occurred throughout many of the world's advanced industrialized countries.

There is, however, a well-documented turning point in the history of Supermax prisons. In October 1983, after the brutal and fatal stabbings of two correctional officers by inmates at the federal maximum-security prison in Marion, Illinois, the facility implemented a 23-hour-a-day lockdown of all convicts. The institution slowly changed its policies and practices and was retrofitted to become what is now considered a Supermax prison. Then, in 1994, the federal government opened its first Supermax prison in Florence, Colorado, specifically designed to house Supermax prisoners. The facility was dubbed the "Alcatraz of the Rockies."

Research on Supermax Prisons

Although much has been written on jails, prisons, and corrections, the mass media and academic community have been relatively silent with respect to Supermax prisons—and with good reason. It is difficult for journalists and scholars to gain access to prisoners, correctional officers, and administrators inside this type of facility. Reporting on correctional institutions has never been easy, and many editors and reporters shy away from this subject matter. Correctional professionals are also reluctant to talk with outsiders for fear that they may be unnecessarily subjected to public scrutiny.

Numerous books on corrections, jails, and prisons have been published for trade, classroom, and professional audiences; only a few monographs offer an in-depth look at Supermax prisons. In December 2002, the American Correctional Association (the largest professional association for correctional practitioners in the United States) published *Supermax Prisons: Beyond the Rock*. This edited monograph, consisting of seven chapters written by prison officials, is more of a technical guide for prison administrators who run one of these types of facilities. Unfortunately, it suffers from the biases of its sponsor and limited targeted audience. *The Big House: Life Inside a Supermax Security Prison* (June 2004) is a memoir written by Jim Bruton, former warden of the Minnesota Correctional Facility-Oak Park Heights facility. Although pitched as a memoir of a Supermax administrator, Oak Park is without question primarily a maximum-security facility with only one of the nine complexes used as an Administrative Control Unit (or Supermax). Largely because of the numerous entertaining anecdotes, in many respects the book's treatment is superficial. Moreover, Bruton is overly self-congratulatory about his ability to solve problems on his watch and thus serious scholars have easily dismissed the book.

There has also been a handful of publicly available government reports published on the topic of Supermax prisons. These have consisted primarily of statistical compilations outlining the numerous Supermax facilities throughout the United States and the composition of the inmates housed within.

The academic treatments (journal articles or chapters in scholarly books) fall into three groups: general overviews, those that focus on the individuals that are sent to solitary confinement or Supermax prisons, and those that focus on the effects of Supermax prisons. The research centers disproportionately on American Super-max prisons and, while this is a start, this literature treats Supermax prisons in isolation of other countries' experiences. Rigorous comparative examinations of foreign-based Supermax prisons have yet to be performed.

There are many unanswered questions about Super-max prisons. Why are Supermax prisons necessary? What particular circumstances led to the creation of Supermax prisons in different states and countries? Is the construction and increased reliance on Supermax institutions due to the fact that today's prisoners are more incorrigible and dangerous, and thus more difficult to handle? Or is it a reflection of the correctional system's failure or mismanagement, or pressures by the general public for a get-tough stance against dangerous criminals? Who are the typical persons sent to Supermax prisons? Why have the Supermax prisons and similar institutions in other countries engendered intense public outcry? What are the similarities and differences among American supermaxes and comparable facilities elsewhere?

The academic treatments (journal articles or chapters in scholarly books) fall into three groups: general overviews, those that focus on the individuals that are sent to solitary confinement or Supermax prisons, and those that focus on the effects of Supermax prisons.

Why Supermaxes Have Proliferated

Since the mid-1980s, many state departments of corrections have built their own Supermax prisons. Several reasons can account for their proliferation. First, many states had similar experiences to the blood that spilled at Marion. In Minnesota, for example, the escape of a prisoner, kidnapping of correctional officers, fatal stabbing of a warden, and a series of prison disturbances in the early 1970s created an environment that was ripe for the construction of a new facility that would house the "worst of the worst." Another explanation for the growth of Supermax prisons lies in the development of a conservative political ideology that began during the Reagan administration (1981–1989). As a response to an increased public fear of crime and to the demise of the "rehabilitative ideal," a punitive agenda took hold of criminal justice and led to a much larger number of people being incarcerated.

Reagan's Republican successor, George H.W. Bush, continued this approach from 1989 to1993. Since then several factors prompted a dramatic increase in the number of people entering jails and prisons: the construction of new correctional facilities; new and harsher sentencing guidelines (particularly "truth in sentencing" legislation, mandatory minimums, and determinant sentencing); the passage of "three strikes you're out" laws and the war on drugs.

In short, many of the gains that were part of the so-called "community corrections era" of the 1960s were scaled back. Congress and state legislatures passed draconian laws that reversed such time-honored practices as indeterminate sentencing and invoked a host of laws that lengthened prison sentences for convicted criminals.

Another factor that contributed to the growth of Supermaxes is the careerism of correctional administrators. Some have argued that without the leadership of particular wardens, government rainmakers, and commissioners and/or secretaries of respective state Departments of Corrections, Supermax facilities would not ever have been built in the first place. Finally, it should be understood that, in many respects, Supermaxes symbolize the failure of rehabilitation and the inability of policymakers and legislators to think and act creatively regarding incarceration. Supermax prisons are excellent examples of the way that America, compared to other countries, has dealt with lawbreakers.

Originally designed to house the most violent, hardened, and escape-prone criminals, Supermaxes are increasingly used for persistent rule-breakers, convicted leaders of criminal organizations (e.g., the mafia) and gangs, serial killers, and political criminals (e.g., spies and terrorists). In some states, the criteria for admission into a Supermax facility and the review of prisoners' time inside (i.e., classification) are very loose or even nonexistent. These facilities are known for their strict lockdown policies, lack of amenities, and prisoner isolation techniques. Escapes from Supermaxes are so rare that they are statistically inconsequential.

In the United States alone, 6.47 million people are under the control of the criminal justice system. Approximately 2.3 million are behind bars in jails or prisons, while 3.8 million are on probation and 725,527 are on parole. The Supermaxes, maintained by the Federal Bureau of Prisons (FBOP) in Marion and Florence, for example, incarcerate 1,710 people—including such notable political criminals as "Unabomber" Ted Kaczynski and Oklahoma City bombing co-conspirator Terry Nichols.

Nevertheless, only a fraction of those incarcerated in state and federal prisons are sent to a Supermax facility. In 1998, approximately 20,000 inmates were locked up in this type of prison, representing less than 2 percent of all the men and women currently incarcerated across the country. Most of the U.S. Supermaxes, such as the federal facility in Florence, are either brand new or nearly so; others, however, are simply free-standing prisons that have been retrofitted. Meanwhile, the number of convicts being sent to Supermax prisons is steadily growing.

Many prisons have earned their individual reputations largely through well-known events that have taken place within their walls and have subsequently been covered by the media. Places like Attica, Folsom, San Quentin, Sing Sing, and Stateville are etched in the consciousness of many Americans. The Supermaxes, on the other hand, are known for their conditions and effects on prisoners within their walls.

Conditions of Confinement

Although cells vary in size and construction, they are generally built to the dimensions of 12 by 7 feet. A cell light usually remains on all night long, and furnishings consist of a bed, a desk, and a stool made out of poured concrete, as well as a stainless steel sink and toilet.

One of the more notable features of all Supermax prisons is the fact that prisoners are usually locked down 23 out of 24 hours a day. The hour outside of the prison is typically used for recreation or bathing/showering. Other than their interaction with the supervising correctional officers (COs), prisoners have virtually no contact with other people (either fellow convicts or visitors). Access to phones and mail is strictly and closely supervised, or even restricted. Reading materials are often prohibited. Supermax prisoners have very limited access to privileges such as watching television or listening to the radio.

Supermax prisons also generally do not allow inmates either to work or congregate during the day. In addition, there is absolutely no personal privacy; everything the convicts do is monitored, usually through a video camera that is on all day and night. Any communication with the correctional officers most often takes place through a narrow window on the steel door of the cell, and/or via an intercom system.

In Supermaxes, inmates rarely have access to educational or religious materials and services. Almost all toiletries (e.g., toothpaste, shaving cream, and razors) are strictly controlled. When an inmate is removed from his cell, he typically has to kneel down with his back to the door. Then he is required to place his hands through the food slot in the door to be handcuffed.

In spite of these simple facilities and the fact that prisoners' rehabilitation is not encouraged (and is next to impossible under these conditions), Supermax prisons are more expensive to build and to run than traditional prisons.

Prisoners are sentenced or transferred to Supermaxes for a variety of reasons that often boil down to a judge's sentence, classification processes, and inmates' behavior while they are incarcerated.

Officially, prison systems design classification categories as a means to designate prisoners to different security levels. Typically, the hard-core, violent convicts serving long sentences are assigned to maximum-security facilities; the incorrigible prisoners serving medium-length sentences are sentenced to medium-security prisons; and the relatively lightweight men serving short sentences are sentenced to minimum-security camps, farms, or community facilities.

For some convicts, the decision of where they will be sent is made long before they hop on their very first prison van. In the sentencing phase of a trial, the judge may specify where the convict will spend his or her time. For example, Ramzi Yousef, the convicted bomber in the 1993 attack on the World Trade Center, was sent directly to the federal Supermax in Florence, Colorado. Depending on sentencing guidelines and an individual's criminal history, officials must determine which security level is most appropriate for each convict. Alternatively, prisoners who are new to the system will be transferred to a receiving and departure setting, where they are classified into the appropriate receiving facility.

The classification of inmates serves many functions for the Department of Corrections (DOC) and the individual correctional institutions. In general, this process determines which facility and security level is best suited to each prisoner. This decision may ultimately facilitate a prisoner's rehabilitation and/or protect correctional officers from being hurt (as officials clearly do not want, for example, a violence-prone convict in a minimum-security prison). Classification also saves taxpayers money (since sending too many prisoners to higher-security prisons, which are more costly to operate, results in a greater expense) and saves the Department of Corrections resources.

Where a convict is sent depends on a number of factors. The division of probation and parole usually prepares a Pre-Sentence Investigation, which is another attempt by the criminal justice system to collect a prisoner's personal information. The probation or parole officer reviews a number of factors relevant to the convict's circumstances, including criminal history. They prepare a report, which makes a recommendation as to which facility would best suit the particular criminal. This report is then shared with the judge, defense attorney, and prosecutor—and the judge retains the ability to accept or dismiss the recommendation. By the same token, some well-heeled and high-profile defendants (e.g., Martha Stewart) or their loved ones may employ the services of sentencing consultants like Herb Hoelter of the National Center for Institutions and Alternatives. For a hefty fee, these hired individuals can prepare a report that recommends where a client should be sentenced. The defendant's attorney then passes the report on to the prosecutor (and judge) in hopes that it may ultimately influence the presiding judge.

In most lock-ups and prisons, the majority of the inmates do not get into trouble because they follow the rules. The problem population comprises approximately 1 percent of the prisoners in an institution. When there is an incident, such as a stabbing on a tier, correctional officers cannot place all of the suspects on administrative segregation (i.e., "in the hole"). But when this type of extreme punishment becomes the norm for a particular prisoner, the administration is usually prompted to transfer the inmate to a higher-security prison. Over time, a prisoner who repeatedly finds himself in this type of situation becomes more and more likely to end up at a Supermax facility.

Typically, the hard-core, violent convicts serving long sentences are assigned to maximum-security facilities; the incorrigible prisoners serving medium-length sentences are sentenced to medium-security prisons; and the relatively lightweight men serving short sentences are sentenced to minimum-security camps, farms, or community facilities.

Effects of Incarceration

All told, the isolation, lack of meaningful activity, and shortage of human contact take their toll on prisoners. Supermax residents often develop severe psychological disorders, though, unfortunately, we do not have specific psychological data, per se, on individuals kept in these facilities. However, numerous reports based on anecdotal information have documented the detrimental effects of these facilities.

The conditions inside Super-max prisons have led several corrections and human rights experts and organizations (like Amnesty International and the American Civil Liberties Union) to question whether these prisons are a violation of (1) the Eighth Amendment of the U.S. Constitution, which prohibits the state from engaging in cruel and unusual punishment, and/or (2) the European Convention on Human Rights and the United Nations'

Universal Declaration of Human Rights, which were established to protect the rights of all individuals, whether living free or incarcerated. According to Roy D. King, in an article published in the 1999 volume of *Punishment and Society,* "Although the effective reach of international human rights standards governing the treatment of prisoners remains uncertain, there seems little doubt that what goes on in a number of Supermax facilities would breach the protections enshrined in these instruments . . . . The International Covenant on Civil and Political Rights, which the United States has ratified, for example, has a more extensive ban on 'torture, cruel, inhuman or degrading treatment or punishment' than the Eighth, Amendment prohibition of 'cruel and unusual' punishment, and requires no demonstration of intent or indifference to the risk of harm, on the part of officials" (164).

Supermax prisons have plenty of downsides, and not just as far as the inmates are concerned. Some individuals have suggested that Supermax prisons are all part of the correctional industrial complex (i.e., an informal network of correctional workers, professional organizations, and corporations that keep the jails and prisons system growing). Most of the Supermaxes in the United States are brand new or nearly so. Others are simply freestanding prisons that were retrofitted. According to a study by the Urban Institute, the annual per-cell cost of a Supermax is about $75,000, compared to $25,000 for each cell in an ordinary state prison.

Future Prospects

The United States has plenty of super-expensive Supermax facilities—two-thirds of the states now have them. But these facilities were designed when crime was considered a growing problem; the current lower violent-crime rate shows no real sign of a turn for the worse. However, as good as these prisons are at keeping our worst offenders in check, the purpose of the Supermax is in flux.

No self-respecting state director of corrections or correctional planner will admit that the Supermax concept was a mistake. And you would be wrong to think that these prisons can be replaced by something drastically less costly. But prison experts are beginning to realize that, just like a shrinking city that finds itself with too many schools or fire departments, the Supermax model must be made more flexible in order to justify its size and budget.

One solution is for these facilities to house different types of prisoners. In May 2006, Wisconsin Department of Corrections

officials announced that, over the past sixteen years, the state's Supermax facility in Boscobel—which cost $47.5 million (in 1990) and holds 500 inmates—has always stood at 100 cells below its capacity. It is now scheduled to house maximum-security prisoners—serious offenders, but a step down from the worst of the worst.

The Maryland Correctional Adjustment Center, a.k.a. the Baltimore Supermax prison, opened in 1989 at a cost of $21 million with room for 288 inmates. Like its cousin in Wisconsin, the structure has never been at capacity. Not only does it hold the state's most dangerous prisoners, it also houses 100 or so inmates who are working their way through the federal courts and serves as the home for Maryland's ten death row convicts.

Converting cells is one approach, but not the only one. Other ideas include building more regional Supermaxes and filling them by shifting populations from other states. This would allow administrators to completely empty out a given Supermax, and then close it down or convert it to another use.

There is also the possibility that some elements of the Supermax model could be combined with the approaches of more traditional prisons, creating a hybrid that serves a wider population. But different types of prisoners would have to be kept well away from each other—a logistical problem of no small concern.

The invention and adoption of Supermax prisons is perhaps the most significant indictment of the way we run correctional facilities and/or what we accomplish in correctional facilities. Most relatively intelligent people know that the United States incarcerates more people per capita than any other advanced industrialized country. And the average American rarely questions this fact. Then again, many people believe that individuals doing time are probably guilty anyway. Thus reforming or changing prisons is and will remain a constant struggle.

JEFFREY IAN ROSS, PhD is an Associate Professor in the Division of Criminology, Criminal Justice and Social Policy, and a Fellow of the Center for International and Comparative Law at the University of Baltimore. He has researched, written, and lectured on national security, political violence, political crime, violent crime, corrections, and policing for over two decades. Ross' work has appeared in many academic journals and books, as well as popular outlets. He is the author, co-author, editor and co-editor of twelve books including most recently *Special Problems in Corrections* (Prentice Hall, 2008). He has also appeared as an expert commentator on crime and policing issues in many media outlets such as newspapers, magazines, and nationally televised shows. His website is www.jeffreyianross.com

From *Society,* Vol. 44, no. 3, March/April 2007, pp. 60–64. Copyright © 2007 by Jeffrey Ian Ross. Reprinted by permission of the author.

The Unique Brutality of Texas
Why the Lone Star State Leads the Nation in Executions

JOSEPH ROSENBLOOM

Gathering dust in texas governor rick Perry's inbox is a clemency petition from Joe Lee Guy, a death-row inmate. The petition declares that "the integrity of Guy's capital trial was severely compromised." Considering how horrendously the wheels of Texas justice turned for Guy, the petition's claim seems, if anything, understated.

In 1994, Guy was sentenced to death for his role, the year before, in the robbery of a grocery store and the murder of its proprietor, Larry Howell. Guy was the unarmed lookout for two other men, Ronald Springer and Thomas Howard. Springer supplied the .22 caliber pistol that Howard used to shoot Howell. Springer and Howard received life sentences.

Guy's involvement in the crime was never in question, but something went terribly wrong in his legal defense. Frank SoRelle, the investigator hired by the defense, developed a "relationship" with Howell's elderly mother, who was seeking Guy's execution, and SoRelle eventually inherited her $750,000 estate. The work performed by SoRelle and Guy's lawyer was woefully inadequate: The sentencing jury never heard important mitigating evidence, such as the fact that Guy grew up poor and neglected by a gambling-addicted mother, and that he was hampered by extremely limited intelligence.

When the circumstances of Guy's case came to light years after his conviction, it was more than even the Texas Board of Pardons and Paroles could stomach. The board reviews clemency appeals in death-penalty cases and recommends "yes" or "no" to the governor (who may grant clemency only if the board recommends it). The board almost never votes "yes" in a case where a death row inmate seeks clemency; it's done so just four times since 1990. But in January, the board unanimously urged Perry to commute Guy's sentence to life.

Despite that extraordinary vote, however, Perry is withholding a decision until all federal appeals are exhausted. That Perry is ducking the question speaks volumes about the political climate around the issue of capital punishment in Texas. At a time when many other states have been questioning their death-penalty systems, the Texas political establishment has expressed no such doubts.

Is it any surprise, then, that the state's death penalty machinery has been steaming right along?

A Democrat turned Republican, Perry was lieutenant governor during the gubernatorial tenure of George W. Bush, and he became governor in January 2001, when Bush took office as president. During Bush's six years in Austin, Texas executed 152 people—a modern-day record for a governor. Since then, 82 more have been put to death—a rate that approaches Bush's. The numbers on Perry's watch would almost certainly have been higher if a Supreme Court ruling two years ago had not prevented the execution of 38 death-row inmates in Texas because of mental-retardation claims.

Why Texas continues to execute people at much the same clip seems rooted not so much in public opinion (polls show that the proportion of Texans favoring capital punishment approximates the national average) as in the state's peculiar political and judicial circumstances. Conservative Republicans have consolidated their power over all the state's main political institutions, including the judiciary. Judges, who are elected in Texas, know that any decision appearing to offer leniency in a capital case could cost them dearly in the next Republican primary.

If capital-defense lawyers are at a disadvantage in many states because of a lack of resources available to them next to what prosecutors have at their disposal, the imbalance is particularly striking in Texas, experts say. Robert O. Dawson, a professor of criminal law at the University of Texas School of Law, decries the "disparity of resources" in capital cases Texas-style. "Why is that? Because it's hard to sell [criminal defense] politically. I think that's a wrongheaded political judgment," Dawson says.

Among the 38 states that have capital punishment, Texas is far and away the modern-day leader in implementing it. Although it has 7.6 percent of the nation's total population, Texas carried out 35 percent of the nation's executions between 1976 and last month—putting to death 321 of 909 condemned prisoners, according to the Death Penalty Information Center in Washington. Virginia was a distant second with 91 executions. And since 2002, the record is still more lopsided, with Texas responsible for 42 percent of the nation's total. As executions have emptied death-row prison cells, moreover, Texas juries have quickly filled them back up. The state's death-row population has held steady (in the 450 range) since the late 1990s.

As an executioner of juvenile offenders, Texas also stands out not just in this country but around the globe. Since 1998, the state has put to death eight offenders who were under 18 at the time of their crime—nearly half the worldwide total of 17, according to Amnesty International.

How Texas handles death penalty cases has attracted international scrutiny of another kind. In March, the International Court of Justice (World Court) held that the United States had violated the rights of Mexican nationals on death row in nine states, including Texas. Of the 52 inmates now covered by the opinion, 15 are in Texas prisons. At the time of the Mexicans' arrests, they were not notified of their right to meet with their government's consular representatives, as the Vienna Convention on Consular Relations requires, the court said. It ordered the United States to remedy the violations of the treaty, which this country signed in 1963, by undertaking an "effective review" of the Mexicans' convictions and sentences.

The ruling brought this retort from Governor Perry's spokesman: "Obviously the governor respects the World Court's right to have an opinion, but the fact remains [that the court has] no standing and no jurisdiction in the state of Texas."

There is some logic, however tortured, to Perry's position. Treaties signed by the United States are binding on the states under the federal Constitution, but it is also true that the World Court lacks enforcement power. The United States ignored the court's order in a consular-notification case and allowed Arizona to execute two German brothers in 1999.

By openly defying the court's authority, however, Perry is burnishing his tough-on-crime credentials. That may pay political dividends in Texas, but it leaves him little room to maneuver on consular notification. Perry's chest-thumping contrasts with how Oklahoma Governor Brad Henry, another death-penalty supporter, dealt with one of the Mexicans covered by the court's order. In May, Henry commuted the death sentence of Osbaldo Torres to life without parole.

Perry's death penalty posture is not at odds with the Republican-dominated Texas Legislature. Strengthened by legislative redistricting, the GOP gained a majority of seats in the House (where Republicans outnumber Democrats 88 to 62) in 2002 for the first time since Reconstruction and tightened its grip on the Senate (where the margin favors Republicans 19 to 12). Now, the Republicans have a lock on the legislature and occupy every statewide office.

In 2003, the last time the legislature met in a regular biennial session, it rejected a bill to establish a consular notification procedure. Proposals to authorize the governor to impose a moratorium on executions and create a death-penalty study commission were bottled up in committee.

One death-penalty proponent who has gained influence due to the rightward tilt is state Representative Terry Keel. A Republican, ex-sheriff, and former county prosecutor, Keel became chairman of the Criminal Jurisprudence Committee in the Texas House of Representatives last year.

A bill that Keel helped quash would have allowed Texas juries in capital cases to impose, as an alternative to a death sentence, a penalty of life imprisonment without the possibility of parole. Only two of the 38 death-penalty states, Texas and New Mexico, do not offer juries that choice. Keel opposed the measure on the grounds that "incarcerating the most violent of criminals for life, with no hope of parole, places corrections employees in inexcusable danger," as he wrote in a newspaper column, although the point is widely disputed by corrections experts. "The system of justice [in Texas] is sound. I believe we have a high level of integrity," Keel told a newspaper reporter last summer.

Where keel sees soundness and integrity, other observers see deep flaws. One who has an upclose view is Charlie Baird, a former judge on the Texas Court of Criminal Appeals who now sits as a visiting judge in criminal trials and appeals. According to Baird, a critical weakness of the Texas judiciary is the lack of meaningful appellate review. The deliberations of the state appeals court in capital cases are typically "exceedingly poor" and "devoid of any kind of critical legal reasoning," Baird says.

All judges in Texas are elected. Baird was one of the last two Democrats to serve on the criminal appellate court. After eight years on the court, which hears all death-penalty appeals in Texas, he lost his bid for re-election in 1998. The other Democrat retired the same year.

When judges run for re-election, the death penalty is rarely an issue—unless there is a contest about who is most for it. All nine members of the Texas Court of Criminal Appeals are conservative Republicans, and eight of them are former prosecutors with little or no experience as capital defenders, sources say. The court's rate of affirming death sentences is "probably the highest" of any appellate court in the nation, Baird says. "When I was there, [the court] had such a results oriented ideology that no matter what issue was raised on appeal, [the judges] were going to affirm the conviction and sentence."

To illustrate what's wrong with the appellate judiciary in Texas, critics point especially to two well-publicized cases that eventually reached the U.S. Supreme Court, *Banks v. Dretzke* and *Miller-El v. Cockrell*. In the first, Delma Banks Jr. was convicted of fatally shooting a 16-year-old boy and stealing his car near the northeast Texas town of Nash. But it turned out that prosecutors had withheld evidence that would have allowed Banks to discredit two key witnesses against him, including the fact that one of them was a paid police informant. The Texas Court of Criminal Appeals found that Banks' appeal had come too late. But in February, the Supreme Court found otherwise—and unanimously granted Banks the right to appeal.

In the second case, a jury sentenced Thomas Miller-El to death for the robbery and murder of a Holiday Inn employee. The trial of Miller-El, an African American, was held in a Dallas County court in 1986. Miller-El's lawyer objected that the prosecutors had used racially discriminatory tactics to select the jury, which the lawyer said resulted in 10 of the 11 African Americans eligible to serve on the jury being excluded. The Texas appellate court rebuffed Miller-El's claim. Last year, by an 8-to-1 vote, the Supreme Court sided with the Texas defendant, finding that Miller-El had been denied the right to a fair trial.

Another weakness of Texas justice is the quality of capital-defense representation. "I think at the heart of the problem in Texas is that [capital-defense representation] is underfunded," says Andrea Keilen, deputy director of the Texas Defender Service, a death-penalty research and consulting organization that brings appeals on behalf of some of the state's death-row inmates.

A critical weakness of the Texas judiciary is the lack of meaningful appellate review in death-penalty cases.

In Texas, judges appoint lawyers on a case-by-case basis from a list of "qualified" counsel. Lawyers' fees vary widely from county to county. The amount provided to defend indigents in capital cases is typically much lower in rural areas. In Fort Bend County, for example, the fees lawyers are paid to try such cases are as low as $200 a day. Investigators earn a maximum of $600 per case, and the total sum for experts is $750.

The maximum available for a habeas-corpus appeal to the Texas Court of Criminal Appeals is $25,000, which must pay lawyers, investigators, and experts. A habeas appeal is time-consuming. It requires the defense team to go beyond the trial record and seek out any possible factor—such as new evidence of a convicted offender's innocence or prosecutorial misconduct during the trial—that might justify further appellate review.

"The competent attorneys are not drawn to the cases because they know they're going to lose money, or they're going to lose the case because they don't have the money to do a proper investigation or something else that's necessary to win the case," says Keilen.

Unlike California and Florida, two other states where capital trials are common (but executions are not), Texas has no state-wide public defender system. There are public-defender offices in Dallas, El Paso, and Wichita Falls, but they handle only a fraction of the death-penalty cases even in their own cities. The lack of a significant public-defender system puts capital defenders—many of whom are solo practitioners—at a disadvantage against the organized corps of death-penalty specialists that are common in prosecutors' offices.

Many lawyers appointed to represent death-row inmates in habeas petitions to the Texas Court of Criminal Appeals are "unqualified, irresponsible or overburdened and do little if any meaningful work for the client," a study by the Texas Defender Service concluded two years ago. One lawyer approved by the court as "qualified," for example, had been disciplined for dereliction of duty to his client. Five qualified lawyers proved ineligible because they already held jobs that created potential conflicts of interest. One lawyer named as qualified was dead.

Although the Joe Lee Guy case was not singled out in the report, its particulars echo these findings. Besides having an ill-trained and self-serving investigator, Guy had the misfortune of being assigned a lawyer, Richard Wardroup, whose record at the State Bar of Texas would show numerous reprimands and suspensions between 1985 and 2000, including sanctions for misrepresenting to a client that he had filed a suit, missing deadlines to seek a new trial and to appeal, failing to act competently as a lawyer, and otherwise neglecting his clients.

What's more, Wardroup's drug and alcohol use was "pervasive" during the period that he was Guy's lawyer, and he "did approximately three to four lines of cocaine" while driving to Guy's trial one morning, says a sworn affidavit of the lawyer's former secretary, Regina Young.

Wardroup was appointed as Guy's appellate lawyer but was suspended from practice while the appeal was pending. The appellate brief filed by a substitute lawyer also "did not address [investigator] SoRelle's actions or his relationship with Mrs. Howell," according to Guy's clemency petition.

SoRelle's bizarre role as Guy's investigator did not come to light until pro bono lawyers from Minneapolis tackled the case in early 2000 and appealed to a federal court. Guy's execution, which Texas had scheduled for June 28 of that year, was stayed by a federal judge just 15 days earlier. The possibility remains that the federal courts, if not Governor Perry, will rectify the injustices in Guy's case. Whether Texas will do the same in the case of its death-penalty system is another question altogether.

JOSEPH ROSENBLOOM is a *Prospect* senior correspondent.

Help for the Hardest Part of Prison: Staying Out

Erik Eckholm

In April, Debra Harris took her 15-year-old son along for what she thought was a final visit to her parole officer. Instead, because of a "dirty urine" test two weeks before, proof of her relapse to crack use, state troopers led her straight back to prison for three more months.

Troopers then drove Ms. Harris's son to the rented home on the south side of Providence where her boyfriend was suddenly left to tend to three of her children. Ms. Harris had forgotten to pay the gas bill, so service was cut and they lived through her sentence without a stove, surviving on fast food and microwave items.

Such jolting events are part of the fabric of life in South Providence, as some women and many more men cycle repeatedly through the state's prisons. As the country confronts record and recurring incarcerations, the search for solutions is focusing increasingly on neighborhoods like it, fragile places in nearly every city where the churning of people through prison is intensely concentrated.

Rhode Island is among the states beginning to make progress in easing offenders' re-entry to society with the goal of bringing the revolving door to a halt, or at least slowing it. But sometimes it can be hard to see much of a difference.

The 1980's and 90's were an era of get-tough, no-frills punishment; inmate populations climbed to record levels while education and training withered. Prisoners with little chance of getting a job and histories of substance abuse were sent home without help.

Now a countertrend is gathering force, part of an unfolding transformation in the way the criminal justice system deals with repeat offenders. After punishment has been meted out and time has been served, political leaders, police officers, corrections officials, churches and community groups are working together to offer so-called re-entry programs, many modest in scope but remarkable nonetheless.

Inmates now meet with planners before their release to explore housing, drug treatment and job possibilities.

Once the inmates are back outside, churches and community groups have been enlisted to take them by the hand and walk them through the transition home.

"What we're witnessing is a great turning of the wheel in corrections policy," said Ashbel T. Wall II, the Rhode Island corrections director.

The flood of more than 600,000 inmates emerging from the nation's prisons each year, and the dismal fact that more than half of those will return, plays out relentlessly here, as elsewhere, keeping already troubled families in emotional and financial turmoil. Even with the new programs, the odds against staying straight are formidable.

"There's a lot starting to happen," said Sol Rodriguez, director of the Family Life Center, established in South Providence in 2003 to help returning prisoners and their families. "But this is still a very poor community, and people are coming back into already overburdened neighborhoods."

In South Providence, where many families share aging two-story wood houses on deceptively quiet streets, nearly one in four male residents, and half of all black men, are under the supervision of the State Corrections Department—in prison, on parole or, by far the most common, on probation, Mr. Wall said.

Eight miles away, the state prison complex is an almost palpable presence. Of some 3,500 inmates released each year, one-fourth return to a core zone of South Providence of just 3.3 square miles with 39,000 residents, most of whom are Hispanic or black.

"One day somebody is just missing in action," said Rev. Jeffery A. Williams, pastor of the 800-member Cathedral of Life Christian Assembly in South Providence. "The father gets a three- or five-year sentence, and the family structure disintegrates. Mothers try to survive on state aid or work multiple jobs, and you see kids practically raising themselves, which perpetuates the problem."

The strains on families take many forms. Not far from the Harris household, Alberto Reyes, 27, a forklift operator, was put on probation last winter for burglary. But in March, Mr. Reyes failed to meet his parole officer and was sent to prison for three and a half months. Without his help, his girlfriend, who makes just $280 a week as a nurse's aide, was left in desperate straits, he acknowledged, and had to rely on charity to get summer clothes for their baby.

Erick Betancourt, 26, spent 2 years in prison for dealing crack and will be on probation for the next 10 years, leaving him vulnerable to confinement for any mistake. "Everybody you bump into is on probation or parole," said Mr. Betancourt, who has landed a job counseling youths in the streets.

"You're not supposed to hang out with others on probation," he said. "So you want to go back with your old friends, but that can be dangerous, because if the police stop you, that could be a violation."

For Cerue Williams, 61, the repeated jailing of her 34-year-old son on drug and probation violations is causing financial burdens and social isolation. Laid off from her job engraving school rings, Ms. Williams is scraping by as she cares for her son's teenage daughter.

Ms. Williams lives in a neat, rent-subsidized house, but she never talks with her neighbors. "I keep this inside, it's embarrassing," she said. "Nobody visits me, and I don't visit nobody."

South Providence is cut off from the city's downtown and prosperous east side by an Interstate highway. Young men drive with their seats folded far back, their faces concealed behind the doorjamb—a fashion and a mock protective measure.

Parts of the area are gentrifying, and a Hispanic influx has brought small shops to the avenues. In abandoned jewelry factories, vacant lots and a few low-rise housing projects, roaming teenagers stir trouble with drugs, but the community's woes are mostly hidden inside wooden multifamily homes.

Tyrone McKinney, 45, has been in prison 9 or 10 times since 1979—he is not sure at this point—on charges ranging from shoplifting to attempted murder.

The last time Mr. McKinney was released, in January, he said, "they gave me a bus token, and I went out into the belly of the beast with no job, nowhere to go."

Drifting through homes of South Providence, he resumed using drugs and stealing and was back in prison by April, for six months. He spoke in the prison gym, where he has bulked up over the years.

As a condition of his discharge this fall he must go into a residential drug treatment program, where he will also get help applying for benefits like food stamps and finding work and a longer-term home.

"The goal now is to see if you can rehabilitate lives instead of just locking them up," said Gov. Donald L. Carcieri,

a Republican, using words that once may have seemed politically risky. Mr. Carcieri has directed state agencies involved with education, drugs, mental health, housing and other issues to work with current and former prisoners.

Following an example set by Connecticut, Rhode Island has pledged to reinvest any savings from reduced prison populations in new aid for departing inmates.

Mayor David N. Cicilline of Providence has assembled a re-entry council, bringing together the police chief, religious leaders, businessmen and other community leaders. The council seeks to offer aid to every offender returning to the most affected neighborhoods, like South Providence.

In Washington, in another sign of the shifting national mood, the Second Chance Act, a bill to increase federal financing for re-entry programs, is moving through Congress with strong bipartisan support and the endorsement of the White House.

With its joining of public agencies and community groups, Rhode Island is part of a movement that is taking hold in dozens of states, said Debbie A. Mukamal, director of the Prisoner Reentry Institute at the John Jay College of Criminal Justice in New York.

Yet in Rhode Island, as elsewhere, money and facilities, especially to support people once they return to the community, have not caught up with the new goals.

Inside the prison, offenders have more access to education, skills training and counseling. But many who are approved for parole must still spend extra months behind bars, waiting for drug treatment beds to open up. Those with no homes to return to face a severe shortage of transitional housing.

"Discharge planning doesn't always mean a lot because there are still so few services out here," said Ms. Rodriguez, of the Family Life Center.

Most days, recently freed inmates drop into the center to check job notices, join counseling sessions or enroll in G.E.D. classes. The center is also, with the aid of the Corporation for Supportive Housing, a national nonprofit group, developing 25 units of permanent housing for troubled former offenders, and it successfully lobbied the state to stop barring former drug offenders from receiving food stamps.

Two weeks after his release, Mr. Reyes, the convicted burglar, was scouring job listings at the Family Life Center. "I have to get a job soon or I might have to go back to jail," he said, noting that employment was a condition of his release. Like many other former prisoners, he cannot live with his girlfriend and son because she is in public housing that bans felons, so he is staying with his mother.

Social services are vital, but nothing can substitute for personal will, said Ms. Harris, 47, the mother who returned to prison after a parole violation. Before that, she had been imprisoned three times over the years for shoplifting.

She was released on parole again on July 26 with an ankle bracelet to ensure that she stayed inside her home except when explicitly permitted to leave.

"I lost too much over the years," she said the day after her release, in the two-story home with a small backyard she cherishes but cannot sit in now without permission. She held a grandson as teenagers raced in and out, and she awaited the return of two younger children, who had moved in with their father during her months away.

"I knew this time that I didn't want to lose all this," she said, referring to her house, her children and her boyfriend, Victor, who stuck with her.

In prison, she started a 12-step program. Now, as a condition of her freedom, she must attend a three-hour recovery meeting at least three times a week. She has also been given a job, as an assistant to a church leader.

Ms. Harris fingered the black plastic bracelet with a transmitter on her ankle and said, "In some ways I feel like I'm back in the same old spot."

But the bracelet also offered a strange comfort. "It kind of keeps my life structured for now," she said, noting that she saw a drug transaction through her front window her first evening home.

"It's crazy out there," she said.

Changing the Lives of Prisoners: A New Agenda

LAWRENCE T. JABLECKI

Today more than two million people are incarcerated in state and federal prisons, 600,000 are released every year, and within three to five years 50 to 60 percent return to prison for committing new crimes or for violating their conditional releases. This deplorable rate of recidivism results in many thousands of new crime victims, the public response to which could lead to another era of billions spent on new prisons.

In an ostensible effort to turn this situation around—to promote rehabilitation of inmates and reduction in recidivism—special faith-based prisons have sprung up over the past few years in California, Florida, Georgia, Iowa, Kansas, Maryland, Minnesota, Ohio, Tennessee, Texas, and other states. And the Corrections Corporation of America, which privately runs prisons for governments, has also jumped on the religious bandwagon. Funding for these programs, however, comes from state revenues distributed directly or indirectly to sectarian religious organizations. Because of this, such efforts engender obvious church-state entanglements. But there are problems with program effectiveness as well.

For example, despite reported rehabilitation successes, not all prisoners are eligible to participate. In effect, only those most likely to change need apply, such as medium- to low-risk drug offenders. Thus we see millions of U.S. tax dollars being routed through religious organizations to salvage the lives of only a select few while doing little to change the lives of the vast majority of inmates, most of whom will eventually be released with or without some form of supervision.

Beyond this, the much-touted positive outcomes are, at least in part, a product of counting the winners and ignoring the losers. "Graduating" from a faith-based program is often defined not only as sticking with a demanding course over a number of months but also getting a job after release. Since getting a job is itself among the most reliable predictors of a former inmate staying out of trouble, then the "proven" success of graduates has been demonstrated largely with circular logic. Participants who drop out, are kicked out, or who get early parole and don't finish usually aren't counted in program statistics at all.

Because of all this, existing faith-based prisons offer insufficient evidence that "a Christ-centered biblically-based program" designed to root out sin is more effective than secular programs that use a therapeutic model of creating and restoring human relationships. Indeed, a number of secular approaches have well-documented success rates. So, if society wants to dramatically reduce the amount of serious crimes and social havoc perpetrated by former state and federal inmates, a new and more inclusive agenda is needed for changing lives and reducing recidivism.

Opinion polls of the last several years on crime and punishment in the United States demonstrate the consensus that two major consequences should occur in the lives of convicted criminals who are sentenced to prison. First, that the duration of their loss of freedom in society is for most of the sentence in real calendar time; and second, upon release they are "better" people. Increased prison capacity and the implementation of truth in sentencing are approximating the first demand. Presumably, a better person is understood to mean one whose thinking has been redirected or transformed during incarceration and who, following release, will be equipped to resist any temptation to return to a life of crime. There are no fairies to distribute magic wands to prison administrators to wave over the heads of inmates immediately prior to their release that will sprinkle virtue dust on them and transform them into better people.

The research data of the same opinion polls inform us that the "vast majority" of Americans believe that most prison inmates are capable of changing into law-abiding members of society and should during their incarceration be given a significant variety of opportunities for change. Therefore, a massive infusion of new funding into the annual budgets of the prison and parole components of all state and federal agencies is needed. Such prison program expenditures should be restricted to the following:

The creation and expansion of general educational programs culminating in General Education Diplomas and high school diplomas and the creation and expansion of college and university programs in which inmates can earn undergraduate and graduate degrees. Though many, if not most, Americans have mixed feelings or are opposed to helping finance college or university degrees for prison inmates, the benefits of higher education for those who are capable is grounded in the research data of numerous evaluations, all of which verify that the recidivism rate of those who complete these programs is significantly less than for inmates who are released with lesser or no educational accomplishments. Of course, inmate opportunities shouldn't take anything away from any ordinary person who meets the eligibility criteria for educational grants and loans. In this connection, Congress should introduce legislation enabling prison inmates to receive Pell grants, which were previously discontinued when many in Congress were duped into believing that multitudes of needy and law-abiding citizens were being denied these grants because of awards to prison inmates.

The creation and expansion of vocational programs, the completion of which would qualify inmates for good-paying employment in numerous blue-collar professions.

The creation and expansion of counseling programs, staffed by well-qualified people, designed to meet the needs of those inmates with any substance abuse problem or psychological or psychiatric issue.

The creation and expansion of visitation opportunities for families of inmates in order to strengthen and reestablish bonds of affection and support, which are of vital importance for successful reentry into communities.

Just doing these things will go a long way toward more effectively promoting the rehabilitation of inmates and a reduction in recidivism.

Then it's time to "think outside the box." With the aim of increasing the number of opportunities for all inmates eligible for release to participate in education programs capable of igniting the desire and strength of will to become a better person, a commitment should be made to Project Habilitation or Changing Lives through Literature.

Project Habilitation entails the abandonment of the "myth of rehabilitation" in favor of a much more accurate account of the thinking and behavioral habits of the majority of prison inmates. The universally accepted definition of rehabilitation is to restore a person to a former state of good health or a useful and constructive purpose. But most of the people in our prisons have never developed habits of thinking and conduct conducive to living a law-abiding life. Instead, they think and act as if they and their immediate desires are the center of the universe around which all human life revolves. It would therefore be a serious mistake to rehabilitate them. Habilitation, by contrast, is the civilizing, educational, and life-transforming experience caused by the power of knowledge to grab a human mind and redirect the course of a person's life. More specifically, habilitation is a "spiritual conversion" to thinking and acting in compliance with the cardinal requirement of an ethical life: namely, that our civil society is a moral community in which all members are entitled to certain human rights and are bound by the obligation to respect the rights of others.

Changing Lives through Literature is a bold experiment that can be used as a paradigm for creating similar programs in both state and federal prisons. It was designed in 1991 by Robert Waxler, a professor of English literature at the University of Massachusetts at Dartmouth, and Robert Kane, a district court judge in New Bedford, Massachusetts, to serve as a sentencing option for recalcitrant male probationers facing the prospect of a prison sentence. Waxler made the highly unconventional request that the court "send a group of eight to ten of those bad guys to me at the university and I will introduce them to the transformative power of some of the great works of literature." Kane embraced the challenge and "go to school and read books or go to jail" became a new choice for some probationers in New Bedford. In 1992, following a meeting with Waxler and Kane, Jean Trounstine, a professor of humanities at Middlesex Community College in Lowell, Massachusetts, with the enthusiastic support of District Court Judge Joseph Dever, instituted a similar program for female probationers.

The probationers selected for these programs aren't creamed from the group most likely to succeed but must demonstrate an eighth-grade reading level. The texts for the men's classes include *The Old Man and the Sea* by Ernest Hemingway, *Of Mice and Men* by John Steinbeck, and *Animal Farm* by George Orwell. The texts for the women's classes include *The Bluest Eye* by Toni Morrison, *The House on Mango Street* by Sandra Cisneros, and *Their Eyes Were Watching God* by Zora Neale Hurston.

During its fourteen-year history this genuine revolution in criminal justice has spread to a significant number of other states, as well as to Canada and the United Kingdom. This is due largely to the indisputable findings of independent evaluations that numerous lives have been redirected in a crime-free path as a direct result of reading and discussing powerful presentations of the issues and questions endemic to the human condition. Qualified scholars in the humanities can assemble a long list of significant readings accessible to the mental abilities of most of the people incarcerated in our state and federal prisons.

The successful implementation of these new initiatives, however, will require major changes in how we use some of our existing prison facilities, the criteria for the employment and retention of correctional officers, and the creation of new policies designed to reward inmates for good conduct and the completion of educational and vocational programs.

First, most prisons are extremely noisy places. Some of them, and large sections of others, should be transformed into education units in which inmates are housed and can work, learn, and study in a quiet environment. Second, we must follow the lead of those who are working to transform the culture of correctional staff into a real profession, requiring some post high school education and entitlement to higher annual salaries. Third, it is totally unrealistic to expect masses of inmates to decide to become better people in the absence of a substantial incentive. This is where we have another opportunity to "think outside the box" by initiating a bold plan to satisfy legitimate grievances of parole-eligible inmates and maintain protection of the public interest.

Inmates are more likely to embrace educational and vocational programs and behave with civility if the following information is given to them in written form and fully explained during their orientation and evaluation as incoming prisoners:

Every inmate, upon reaching eligibility for parole, is entitled to a public hearing administered by a three-member panel of parole commissioners. This panel will allow oral and written testimony from all parties in favor of or against the granting of parole. This means that victims and prosecutors will appear in some cases to protest the release of a violent and dangerous person. It also means that witnesses for the inmate—for example, spouses, children, parents, clergy, and teachers—will be given time to state why they are urging the panel to grant parole. Inmates shall have the right to address the panel from the witness stand in order to explain their accomplishments and how they have changed subsequent to incarceration. Inmates shall have the right to retain counsel to prepare their case and to guide them through their testimony.

Any decision by the panel of parole commissioners would require two votes. Immediately following the admission of all testimony in a case, the members may vote and explain their judgment in the open hearing, or they may decide to take the matter under advisement for a period not to exceed thirty days. The hearing would then be reconvened, at which time each panel member would explain her or his vote to the inmate. This procedure is nearly equivalent to the inmate's trial at which evidence was presented, guilt was confessed or determined, and a sentence was imposed. In short, the critically important function of this procedure is that it steers clear of a nondiscretionary, mandatory release of inmates judged to be a continuing threat to society and encourages the decision makers to grant release to numerous inmates who, in the panel's judgment, have reached or are on their way to habilitation.

In this connection, state governors will need to resist the temptation to appoint their own cronies to these important positions in the administration of criminal justice. Parole commissioners should be assigned a caseload with a minimum-maximum range and this become the benchmark for determining the number of such positions in every state. The minimum qualifications for appointment should be a four year degree from an accredited college or university, a documented knowledge of criminal justice, and a reputation for possessing the courage to express one's beliefs in a public forum. Appointments should be for a term of five years and eligibility restricted to two successive terms. These positions would be full time and earn an annual salary commensurate with responsibilities.

The goal is simply to protect the lives and property of law-abiding citizens.

With these recommendations, however, the fact remains that some of the 600,000 people released annually from prisons are going to commit more crimes and spit defiantly in the face of any new policies and programs. There are no silver bullets armed with a guarantee to habilitate all of them. But we must not allow this grim and inevitable reality to derail our determination to stay the course. The inmates who complete counseling and vocational and education programs, and are nearing release, must be the focus of attention of the agencies charged with preparing them for reentry and with supervision following their release.

Of interest in this regard is the fact that Texas is the birthplace of a paradigm that should be replicated and funded in every state and federal jurisdiction that supervises ex-offenders. It was in 1985 that a two-city experiment called Project RIO, the reintegration of offenders, was launched. The mission of this ambitious and optimistic state program was and is to provide job preparation services to prison inmates in order to give them a head start in the post-release search for employment. The project has been funded entirely by the state's general revenues and "represents an unusual collaboration between two state agencies . . . the Texas Workforce Commission (the state's employment agency) and the Texas Department of Criminal Justice (Institutional and Parole Divisions)." And from its small beginning to the present, Project RIO has established a track record of assisting and finding employment for thousands of ex-offenders, documented a significantly lower recidivism rate than comparable groups of non-participants, and saved the state millions of real tax dollars.

Given the publicly verified accomplishments of Project RIO and the potential for nationwide replication, there should be a national commitment to fund and a sufficient number of professional and support staff to:

- provide a comprehensive job readiness orientation for all prison inmates within three to six months of their release
- recruit and train a legion of non-paid volunteers to serve as mentors to inmates prior to and after their release
- contact and recruit corporations, companies, and small business operations willing to hire ex-offenders
- support changes in federal and state legislation to increase tax credits for those who hire ex-offenders.

The lure of federal dollars, many tied to matching grants, should be used to entice the majority of states to set in motion the guts of this new agenda.

Beyond the reintegration of the newly released comes the reintegration of the previously released. Toward this latter end, a governmental commission needs to be created—composed of some of the nations most influential scholars in constitutional law, jurisprudence, criminal justice, and the humanities—with marching orders to make some realistic recommendations for eliminating most of the numerous barriers or collateral consequences preventing millions of former prison inmates from being eligible to receive assistance from a variety of state and federal programs. And they would also make recommendations regarding the timely restoration of the civil and political rights of the former prison inmates.

The goal of everything discussed here is simply to protect the lives and property of law-abiding citizens. This new agenda isn't based on the false belief that the majority of criminal offenders are victims of a sick society or some psychological illness and therefore actually *deserve* all the programs and services advocated. There is nothing here to throb a bleeding heart. There is no assumption that everyone, deep down inside, is basically a good person. Rather the motivation, plain and simple, is the public interest. This new agenda is purely practical. Thus it holds the promise of bipartisan support.

Compare this with the idealistic, unrealistic, impractical, and ideologically driven notion that sectarian faith is the answer.

And understand that this new agenda requires no violation of or amendment to the U.S. Constitution. Moreover, it is consistent with the proud tradition of "American knowhow," "Yankee ingenuity," and that "can-do" spirit of rolling up one's sleeves to "get the job done."

LAWRENCE THOMAS JABLECKI holds a PhD in political philosophy from Manchester University in Manchester, England. He is a part-time lecturer in the Sociology Dept. at Rice University in Houston, where he teaches classes in Criminology and The Criminal Justice System. He also teaches the Changing Lives Through Literature class for the adult probation department in Brazoria County, Texas. Since 1989, as an Adjunct Faculty member at the University of Houston at Clear Lake, he has taught a wide range of philosophy classes (graduate and undergraduate) to prison inmates who earn degrees from the university. Previously he was Director of the adult probation department in Brazoria County, Texas for eighteen years. His writings have appeared previously in *The Humanist*.

Test-Your-Knowledge Form

We encourage you to photocopy and use this page as a tool to assess how the articles in *Annual Editions* expand on the information in your textbook. By reflecting on the articles you will gain enhanced text information. You can also access this useful form on a product's book support Web site at *http://www.mhcls.com/online/*.

NAME: DATE:

TITLE AND NUMBER OF ARTICLE:

BRIEFLY STATE THE MAIN IDEA OF THIS ARTICLE:

LIST THREE IMPORTANT FACTS THAT THE AUTHOR USES TO SUPPORT THE MAIN IDEA:

WHAT INFORMATION OR IDEAS DISCUSSED IN THIS ARTICLE ARE ALSO DISCUSSED IN YOUR TEXTBOOK OR OTHER READINGS THAT YOU HAVE DONE? LIST THE TEXTBOOK CHAPTERS AND PAGE NUMBERS:

LIST ANY EXAMPLES OF BIAS OR FAULTY REASONING THAT YOU FOUND IN THE ARTICLE:

LIST ANY NEW TERMS/CONCEPTS THAT WERE DISCUSSED IN THE ARTICLE, AND WRITE A SHORT DEFINITION:

We Want Your Advice

ANNUAL EDITIONS revisions depend on two major opinion sources: one is our Advisory Board, listed in the front of this volume, which works with us in scanning the thousands of articles published in the public press each year; the other is you—the person actually using the book. Please help us and the users of the next edition by completing the prepaid article rating form on this page and returning it to us. Thank you for your help!

ANNUAL EDITIONS: Criminal Justice 08/09

ARTICLE RATING FORM

Here is an opportunity for you to have direct input into the next revision of this volume.
We would like you to rate each of the articles listed below, using the following scale:

1. **Excellent: should definitely be retained**
2. **Above average: should probably be retained**
3. **Below average: should probably be deleted**
4. **Poor: should definitely be deleted**

Your ratings will play a vital part in the next revision.
Please mail this prepaid form to us as soon as possible.
Thanks for your help!

RATING	ARTICLE	RATING	ARTICLE
	1. What Is the Sequence of Events in the Criminal Justice System?		22. Looking Askance at Eyewitness Testimony
	2. Preparing for the Future		23. Why Do Hung Juries Hang?
	3. Arraigning Terror		24. Exiling Sex Offenders from Town
	4. Of Crime and Punishment		25. Judges Turn Therapist in Problem-Solving Court
	5. Global Co-op Feeds FBI's Botnet Fight		26. When the Poor Go to Court
	6. Toward a Transvaluation of Criminal 'Justice': On Vengeance, Peacemaking, and Punishment		27. Justice & Antonin Scalia
	7. Trust and Confidence in Criminal Justice		28. Reforming Juvenile Justice
	8. Do Batterer Intervention Programs Work?		29. DARE Program: Sacred Cow or Fatted Calf?
	9. Telling the Truth About Damned Lies and Statistics		30. The 21st Century Juvenile Justice Work Force
	10. Violence and the Remaking of a Self		31. Teens Caught in the Middle
	11. Understanding Stockholm Syndrome		32. Jailed for Life After Crimes as Teenagers
	12. Sexual Assault on Campus: What Colleges and Universities Are Doing About It		33. Co-Offending and Patterns of Juvenile Crime
	13. Ordering Restitution to the Crime Victim		34. Changing Directions
	14. The NYPD's War On Terror		35. Felon Fallout
	15. Racial Profiling and Its Apologists		36. The Results of American Incarceration
	16. Ethics and Criminal Justice: Some Observations on Police Misconduct		37. Experiment Will Test the Effectiveness of Post-Prison Employment Programs
	17. Stress Management . . . and the Stress-proof Vest		38. Do We Need the Death Penalty?
	18. Dealing with Employee Stress		39. Private Prisons Expect a Boom
	19. Settling Disputes across a Table When Officer and Citizen Clash		40. Jail Time Is Learning Time
	20. Jury Consulting on Trial		41. The Professor Was a Prison Guard
	21. Jury Duty: When History and Life Coincide		42. Supermax Prisons
			43. The Unique Brutality of Texas
			44. Help for the Hardest Part of Prison: Staying Out
			45. Changing the Lives of Prisoners: A New Agenda

BUSINESS REPLY MAIL
FIRST CLASS MAIL PERMIT NO. 551 DUBUQUE IA

POSTAGE WILL BE PAID BY ADDRESSEE

McGraw-Hill Contemporary Learning Series
501 BELL STREET
DUBUQUE, IA 52001

ABOUT YOU

Name   Date

Are you a teacher? ☐ A student? ☐
Your school's name

Department

Address   City   State   Zip

School telephone #

YOUR COMMENTS ARE IMPORTANT TO US!

Please fill in the following information:
For which course did you use this book?

Did you use a text with this ANNUAL EDITION? ☐ yes ☐ no
What was the title of the text?

What are your general reactions to the Annual Editions concept?

Have you read any pertinent articles recently that you think should be included in the next edition? Explain.

Are there any articles that you feel should be replaced in the next edition? Why?

Are there any World Wide Web sites that you feel should be included in the next edition? Please annotate.

May we contact you for editorial input? ☐ yes ☐ no
May we quote your comments? ☐ yes ☐ no